MW00489587

# Starting and Operating a Business in Tennessee

## A Step-by-Step Guide

**By Michael D. Jenkins and the
Entrepreneurial Services Group of Ernst & Young**

OASIS
PRESS

The Oasis Press® / PSI Research
Grants Pass, Oregon

91 AA

Published by The Oasis Press
© 1987, 1991 by Michael D. Jenkins and Ernst & Young

All rights reserved. No part of this publication may be reproduced or used in
any form or by any means, graphic, electronic or mechanical, including
photocopying, recording, taping, or information storage and retrieval systems
without written permission of the publishers.

This publication is designed to provide accurate and authoritative information
in regard to the subject matter covered. It is sold with the understanding that the
publisher is not engaged in rendering legal, accounting, or other professional
service. If legal advice or other expert assistance is required, the services of a
competent professional person should be sought.

> *—from a declaration of principles jointly adopted by a committee of*
> *the American Bar Association and a committee of publishers.*

The principal author and technical editor of the entire *Starting and Operating a
Business* series is Michael D. Jenkins. The co-author of the state chapter of
*Starting and Operating a Business in Tennessee* is E. Bishop Leatherbury of
Ernst & Young.

Administrative Editor: Rosanno Alejandro

Series Editor: Scott Crawford

Assistant Editor: Vickie Reierson

Page Design & Typography: Constance C. Dickinson

Please direct any comments, questions, or suggestions regarding this book to
The Oasis Press, Editorial Department at the address below.

The Oasis Press offers PSI Successful Business Software for sale.
For information, contact:

PSI Research
300 North Valley Drive
Grants Pass, OR 97526
(503) 479-9464

The Oasis Press is a Registered Trademark of Publishing Services, Inc.,
an Oregon corporation doing business as PSI Research.

Library of Congress Catalog Card Number: 80-83053

ISBN 1-55571-147-2 (paperback)
ISBN 0-916378-68-3 (binder)

Printed in the United States of America
Second edition  10 9 8 7 6 5 4 3 2 1 0   Revision Code:  AA

 Printed on recycled paper when available.

# Table of Contents

## Forms and Worksheets in this Book

# What's New

This new update of chapters 1–10 features a number of major additions, including new sections on emerging trends and issues, environmental laws, and the Americans with Disabilities Act. You will also find changes in current federal tax rates, legislation, and credits. To help you identify the most significant changes and additions to the text, review the list below. This list gives you the chapter–section number where you will find the specific discussions.

- New section on the requirements imposed by the Americans with Disabilities Act – 5.11
- A review of sexual harassment and its definition – 5.8
- A new section and review of environmental laws that affect your business including information on the Comprehensive Environmental Response Compensation and Recovery Act (CERCLA) and the Resource Conservation and Recovery Act (RCRA) – 9.9, 9.14
- A change in how home office expenses are reported – 8.14
- A simplification of the FUTA tax return for small employers – 5.3
- Several types of proposed legislation that will affect many businesses – 9.14
- A new legal form of business organization: the limited liability company – 2.1
- A new exemption from federal wage-hour laws for some small businesses – 5.7
- A new deduction for S corporations regarding medical insurance – 2.4
- A change in requirements for paying estimated corporate taxes – 4.6
- New exemption requirements for outside salespersons – 5.7
- Several fringe benefit plans, including 401(k) plans gain popularity – 8.3
- New information on equal credit opportunity laws – 9.10
- How to avoid having independent contractors treated as employees for tax purposes – 9.11
- More background on the Foreign Direct Investment and International Financial Data Improvements Act of 1990 – 9.13
- A new section on emerging trends and issues that may affect and influence your business – 9.14
- New toll-free hotlines for information and help from federal agencies – 10.3
- Changes in corporate income tax rates limiting some of the tax reasons for incorporating – 2.4

**About the Author**

The author of chapters 1–10 of the entire *Starting and Operating a Business* series, is Michael D. Jenkins. Mr. Jenkins, an attorney at law and a certified public accountant, is a graduate of Harvard Law School. He has worked in Los Angeles and San Francisco as an accountant and as an attorney with a prominent San Francisco firm well-known in the venture capital arena. He is a member of the State Bar of California, the American Bar Association, the American Institute of Certified Public Accountants, and the California Society of Certified Public Accountants.

# How to Use this Book

## 0.1 Getting the Most Out of this Book

To most effectively use this book, become acquainted with the many helpful features it provides. Remember that each edition is updated annually to provide you with the most current information available. To find the most recent changes made to federal laws in chapters 1–10, refer to the What's New page. For similar state information, refer to the Notes page, which immediately precedes Chapter 11.

## 0.2 Numbered Section Heads Correspond to Table of Contents and Index

**Text**

Discussions range from explaining how to start and operate your business to examining such practical issues as insurance, marketing, cash-flow management, internal financial controls, and much more. This book also explains federal and state government requirements and tax laws, as well as a number of emerging trends and issues your business may face.

**Topics Noted in Margins**

To make the information in this workbook easily accessible to busy people, the primary topics discussed within each numbered section are identified by "sideheads" in the margin beside the text.

**Smaller Heads for Subtopics**

When subsections of primary topics are discussed, the sideheads are slightly smaller.

**Lists**

- This small bullet helps you easily locate lists of requirements, things to do, and aspects of a particular subject or law.

**Checklists**

☐ Small boxes encourage you to enter a check, so that you can clearly see those items you've considered and dealt with — and those left to do.

**Worksheets**

**Where the Action Begins**

A number of worksheets are provided for you to answer questions and fill in numbers that form the basis for action plans, self-evaluation, budgeting, personnel policies, marketing feasibility studies, and the like.

The worksheets are set apart by boxes to clearly show where your interaction is required, to focus your thoughts, to record information, and to create the plans and reports that will help you establish and guide your business.

**Resources**

**Sources and Data**       Resources are set in tabular form       **Contacts**
to highlight the many agencies       Addresses
and companies listed to assist       Phone Numbers
you.       (listed in directory style)

**Table of Contents**

The detailed Table of Contents will help you quickly find any specific section of the book you wish to refer to. The first digit of the chapter–section number indicates the chapter, followed by a period and the section number.

**Footnotes**

The footnotes follow each chapter and are provided to assist you in accessing specific statutes, cases, regulations, and publications and to use this book as a starting place for legal research.

**Index**

The subject-matter index, organized alphabetically with cross-referenced entries, provides an exhaustive list of the topics, indexed not only by the terms actually used in the entries but also by various other terms you might think of instead. The Index is referenced by the chapter–section number, not by page number, to help you find the corresponding discussion in the text.

**Related Resources**

At the back of this book, you'll find a compendium of additional resources that will save you valuable research time and money.

**Appendix**

The Appendix features a checklist of tax and various other major requirements for most businesses and a checklist of official government posters and notices required to be displayed by a business.

**Forms**

Since many business requirements depend on submitting specific forms to various government agencies, some samples of these forms are included for your reference and listed in the Table of Contents.

**Post Cards**

At the back of this book, you will also find post cards preaddressed to government agencies and other sources so you can request additional information, posters, and forms.

# Preface

When I wrote the first edition of *Starting and Operating a Business in California* more than a decade ago, little did I know that its success would spawn a nationwide series. Back then, there was talk of small business declining and big business rising and only a few, if any, small business assistance centers were operating in the United States. There were even fewer "how-to" books available.

Today, however, there are Small Business Development Centers (SBDCs) and "one-stop" business permit offices in almost every state and, while state governments are cutting services left and right, states are expected to maintain or increase services in economic development and assistance to small businesses. Why the turnaround? States recognize how new and existing small businesses can strengthen their economies and provide jobs to their residents, and they are doing as much as possible to encourage business growth, expansion, and relocation.

According to *Time* magazine, an estimated 1.3 million businesses were started in 1991, up nearly 9% from 1980, despite the current recession. Researchers say this increase is mainly due to the fact that most people prefer working for themselves; both white and blue collar workers are being automated out of their jobs with larger companies; and the explosive growth of the "information society" is creating a favorable economic environment for the small, technically oriented firm.

By advising small and large businesses over the years — first as an economic and management consultant, then later as an attorney and more recently as a certified public accountant — I had always been keenly aware of the need for a single authoritative and practical guide that would serve people starting and operating a business in a particular state and their professional advisers.

While most bookstores featured many books that purported to advise the entrepreneur on how to become successful and rich by starting a business, conspicuously absent was a nuts-and-bolts guide that would help an entrepreneur through the maze of red tape at both the federal and state levels of government, as well as provide the basic steps and advice needed to get a business off the ground.

Thus, in 1980, when my friend and publisher, Emmett Ramey, approached me with the idea of writing a starting and operating a business book for the state of California, I was particularly receptive. His idea was to create an operating manual that would draw together — in a readable, usable, and nontechnical format — the practical facts of life a person needed to know when establishing a business in California. Once written, *Starting and Operating a Business in California* accomplished these goals by explaining in layperson's language many of the key financial, tax, and legal pitfalls, as well as planning options, an entrepreneur needed to know before and after embarking on a business venture. The California book's format consisted of chapters 1–10, which focused on general start-up information and federal laws and regulations, and Chapter 11, which focused on the state's laws and regulations.

The success of *Starting and Operating a Business in California* resulted in other state editions, and as of 1991, all 50 state editions, plus the District of Columbia, have been published. Each state chapter is updated annually, and chapters 1–10 are updated every January. These editions make up the 51-volume *Starting and Operating a Business* series.

So, if you want an up-to-date guide to the basic financial, legal, and tax ground rules that apply to most businesses operating in your state, the *Starting and Operating a Business* series has been designed with you in mind as a self-help tool. It is also intended to be a useful reference source to the attorney who has only a limited knowledge of business taxation and the basic regulatory requirements of a large number of federal, state, and local government agencies. Accountants will also find this series a useful resource for understanding the broad scope of government regulations that affect his or her small business clients.

While the *Starting and Operating a Business* books provide an authoritative discussion of many legal and tax matters regarding small business, they are not intended to be a substitute for professional legal or tax advice. On the contrary, they are designed to help you focus on key points to explore in greater depth with your attorney or accountant. By being better informed, you can use your professional advisers' time more efficiently.

Chapter 1 is designed to sharpen the focus of the decision process you typically go through while your new business is still in the idea stage.

Chapter 2 describes the various legal forms in which your business may be operated under — sole proprietorships, partnerships, corporations, and limited liability companies — and outlines the most significant advantages and disadvantages of each. Chapter 3 will prove helpful if you are considering buying an existing business or opening a franchise operation.

Chapters 4–7 describe the various tax authorities and other governmental agencies that most or all businesses must deal with. Chapter 8 describes in nontechnical terms a number of the major income tax benefits that you may be able to enjoy, while chapters 9 and 10 describe miscellaneous business pointers and sources of information that are made available to small businesses by government agencies and private institutions.

Chapter 11 addresses the areas covered in chapters 1–10 by focusing on how the state's laws and regulations deal with those areas. Each Chapter 11 of the series is designed to provide as much state-specific information as possible.

The publisher and I welcome your suggestions or constructive criticisms that may assist us in refining or expanding future editions.

Michael D. Jenkins

January 1992

**Dedication**

To America's entrepreneurs — tenacious, courageous men and women — whose contribution to the variety, richness, and quality of our lives is immeasurable.

# Preliminary Considerations

**Part I**

Chapter 1

# Making the Decision to Go into Business

*Being boss doesn't make you right; it only makes you boss.*

— Milton Metz

## 1.1 Introduction

Neither this book nor any other book can tell you whether or not you should take the plunge and go into business for yourself. That is a difficult decision that you alone must make.

Before you make this decision, however, there are a number of very basic questions you should first consider very thoroughly. This introductory chapter is designed to alert you to a number of key points you may not have considered yet, as well as assist you in dealing successfully with some of the initial problems you will face.

To get started in most kinds of new businesses, a major financial risk must be taken. Once you have committed yourself, it will not be a simple or easy thing to change your mind and back out.

In evaluating the risks, you should be aware that there is a high failure rate among new businesses. Nearly two out of every three new businesses fail within five years.[1] Year in and year out, statistics show that a very high percentage of those business failures result from poor management.

Poor or ineffective management is usually a lack of balanced experience and competence in three areas:

- Marketing strategies — This means knowing what kind of product or service to sell, how to target and reach your customers, and how to sell your product or service at a price that maximizes your profits.

- Technical ability — You must be able to get the work done and do it right, so you will have satisfied customers. If you are going into the auto repair business, for example, you better know a lot about how to keep autos running right, or you will not be in business very long.
- Financial knowledge — While you do not necessarily have to be a financial wizard, you do need to know how to plan and control your business' cash flow; raise or borrow the money you will need to start your business; and get through tight periods without being caught short of cash. A certain amount of financial sophistication is becoming more and more important in today's increasingly complex financial world, even for the small business owner.

If you are seriously deficient in one or more of these three critical areas, the odds of your business becoming one of the relatively few that succeeds are greatly reduced.

In addition, many other facts will influence the odds of your succeeding or failing in your own business. For example, the magazine *Canadian Business* reported on a survey conducted by Thorne Riddell, a large Canadian accounting firm, of 2,000 sole proprietorships started in Canada. In a follow-up survey three years later, they found four major factors that seemed to separate the winners from the losers. Besides these four factors, the study also determined an interesting fact about these particular businesses; and that is, only 25% of the surveyed firms with male owners survived, while 47% of the ones started by women were still around.

Keeping in mind that the Canadian economy is somewhat different from that of the United States, examine the four main factors below to help you gain an extra insight into successfully starting up your business.

| Factor | Successful Firms | Failures |
|---|---|---|
| Degree of preparation | Spent 6 to 10 months to research and prepare for their ventures. | Spent less than 4 months to prepare for start up. |
| Use of advisers | 90% utilized professional advisers, such as lawyers and accountants, in starting up. | Only 25% sought professional help at an early stage. |
| Business education, reading | Almost 70% had taken business-related courses before starting business and regularly read business books and magazines. | Only 10% had attended business courses or now took time to read business material. |
| Expectations of income | More than half said they started with modest expectations and were prepared to be patient for signs of success. | 36% said they fully expected to make barrels of money within 3 years. The anticipated level of annual earnings they most often quoted was more than 3 times the income level typically quoted by those in the successful category.[2] |

More recent research, using the much larger U.S. Small Business Data Base, indicates that failure rates are lower than commonly believed and reveals a tie between growing firms — defined as those adding at least one job every two years — and success. In this study of 458,000 firms, of those businesses which did not add at least one job every two years, about 30% failed within two years after start up, and a total of 73% had failed after six years.

Firms that grew by at least one job every 24 months, however, experienced a much greater survival rate; only 8% closed within two years, and only 34% after six years.[3] Although the ability of a firm to generate jobs is not the sole factor in reducing the failure rate, it often increases the firm's flexibility in weathering periods of economic contraction.[4]

This chapter engages you in the process of realistically evaluating your entrepreneurial strengths and weaknesses. It is also intended to cause you to focus on some of the typical start-up problems and choices you are likely to face, as well as assist you in dealing effectively and rationally with those issues.

Where worksheets are provided, feel free to pick up a pencil and write in your responses. Often, the simple process of writing down your thoughts on specific problem areas may provide significant new insights that may suddenly seem terribly obvious to you once you have raised them to the level of conscious thought.

# 1.2　Advantages and Disadvantages of Owning Your Own Business

Have you realistically considered both the advantages and the disadvantages of owning and operating your own business? If not, the time to do so is before, not after, you have committed yourself.

If you are actively considering going into business for yourself, you most likely have already thought about the potential advantages, such as:

**Advantages**

- Being your own boss and not having to report to a superior;
- Having the independence and power to make your own business decisions, for better or for worse;
- Direct contact with customers, employees, suppliers, and others;
- The personal satisfaction and sense of achievement that comes with being a success, plus the recognition that goes with it;
- The opportunity to create substantial wealth and job security for yourself;
- The opportunity to be creative, to develop your own idea, product, or service;

- The chance to make a living doing something you truly enjoy; and
- Doing something that contributes to others, whether it be providing an excellent product or service, providing employment, paying dividends to stockholders, or doing something else that is useful or that creates value.

## Disadvantages

If you are like most people, you may not have thought much about the downside of going into business; however, awareness of the potential disadvantages should not discourage you from your goal of going into business for yourself, if you have a strong commitment to that goal.

Seriously consider whether you and your family are prepared to handle these disadvantages inherent in being an entrepreneur:

- In a lot of ways, you are still not your own boss. Instead of having one boss, you will now have many — your customers, the government agencies to whom you must report, and, in some cases, your key suppliers.
- There is a large financial risk. The failure rate is high in new businesses, and you may lose not only your own money but also that of your friends and relatives who may have bankrolled you.
- The hours are long and hard. When you start your business, you will no longer be working 9 to 5. Count on working 10- to 12- or even 15-hour days, often six or seven days a week.
- You will not have much spare time for family or social life. And you can forget about taking any long vacations for the first few years, since the business is unlikely to run itself without your presence for any great length of time.
- Your income may not be steady like a salary. You may make more or less than you could working for someone else, but in either case, your income may fluctuate up and down from month to month.
- The buck stops with you. If a problem arises, there is no boss you can take it to and say: "What do we do about this?" You are the boss and all the responsibility is yours. If anything goes wrong, the cost comes out of your pocket.
- You may be stuck for years doing work you do not like. Unlike an employee, you cannot simply quit and look for a better job. It may take you years to sell the business or find some other way to get out of it without a major financial loss.
- As a business grows, the amount of activity not associated with the primary business objective will increase. You will spend more time on personnel, administrative, and legal matters and less doing what you may have wanted most to do in your business.
- Increasing legislation and litigation make owning a business very risky. You can work a lifetime to build a business only to have it lost because of a lawsuit or a new law or regulation.

# 1.3 Typical Characteristics of the Successful Entrepreneur

A good deal is known about what it takes to be a successful entrepreneur. For the most part, it seems that the one overriding factor is a tremendous need to achieve. In short, attitude seems to have almost everything to do with success in business, while factors, such as intelligence, education, physical appearance, and a pleasing personality, are much less important. Characteristics of typical successful entrepreneurs include:

- An overpowering need to achieve, as opposed to a need to be liked, or to exercise power; the form in which different individuals measure their achievement varies widely, ranging from amassing wealth to building a larger organization to creating a better mousetrap than anyone else;
- The trait of following through on a commitment, not quitting half-way through when the going gets tough: in short, perseverance;
- A positive mental attitude or the ability to remain optimistic in new and unfamiliar situations, which essentially grows out of being self-confident about one's abilities;
- Objectivity — the ability to accurately weigh and assess risks associated with a particular course of action, as well as being realistic about one's own abilities and limitations;
- A respectful attitude toward money, but a tendency to look upon money as a means for accomplishing things, or a way of keeping score in the game of business, rather than as a thing to be sought as an end in itself;
- The tendency to anticipate developments and to make things happen rather than constantly reacting to problems as they arise;
- Resourcefulness — the ability to solve unique problems in unique ways and to be able to handle things that come up for which the entrepreneur has no previous experience to rely on as a guide;
- Good personal relations skills — the characteristics of being cheerful and cooperative, and usually getting along well with, without necessarily being close to, employees and associates;
- Well-developed communication skills, both in oral and written presentations; and
- Well-rounded technical knowledge with emphasis on the knowledge about the physical process of producing goods and services.

How do your personal characteristics stack up against the foregoing profile of the typical successful entrepreneur? If that profile doesn't sound very much like you, maybe you had better give some long, hard thought as to whether you are cut out for making it as a business owner.

Running a business is not like working for someone else. No one is there to tell you what to do when something goes wrong. You are responsible for everything.

Are you capable of handling that kind of total responsibility? Are you a self-starter, capable of planning, organizing, and carrying out projects on your own? If not, you may find that starting and running a successful business is not for you.

Running a business demands a great deal in the way of initiative, hard work, self-discipline, and resourcefulness. On the other hand, solving the problems that arise from day to day and making it all work out can be a source of immense satisfaction, as well as be financially rewarding.

Before reading further, get a pencil and complete Worksheet 1, which is a useful questionnaire that may help you to get a better idea of your suitability for playing the role of entrepreneur in the real world.

## Worksheet 1
## Self-evaluation Checklist for Going into Business

**Under each question, check the answer that says what you feel or comes closest to it. Be honest with yourself.**

**Are you a self-starter?**

☐ I do things on my own. Nobody has to tell me to get going.

☐ If someone gets me started, I keep going all right.

☐ Easy does it. I don't put myself out until I have to.

**How do you feel about other people?**

☐ I like people. I can get along with just about anybody.

☐ I have plenty of friends; I don't need anyone else.

☐ Most people irritate me.

**Can you lead others?**

☐ I can get most people to go along when I start something.

☐ I can give the orders if someone tells me what we should do.

☐ I let someone else get things moving; then I go along if I feel like it.

**Can you take responsibility?**

☐ I like to take charge of things and see them through.

☐ I'll take over if I have to, but I'd rather let someone else be responsible.

☐ There's always some eager beaver around wanting to show how smart she is. I say let her.

**How good of an organizer are you?**

☐ I like to have a plan before I start. I'm usually the one to get things lined up when the group wants to do something.

☐ I do all right unless things get too confusing; then I quit.

☐ Just when I'm all set, something comes along and presents too many problems, so I just take things as they come.

**How good of a worker are you?**

☐ I can keep going as long as I need to. I don't mind working hard for something I want.

☐ I'll work hard for a while, but when I've had enough, that's it.

☐ I can't see that hard work gets me anywhere.

**Can you make decisions?**

☐ I can make up my mind in a hurry if I have to and it usually turns out okay, too.

☐ I can, if I have plenty of time. If I have to make up my mind fast, I think later I should have decided the other way.

☐ I don't like to be the one who has to decide things.

**Can people trust what you say?**

☐ You bet they can. I don't say things I don't mean.

☐ I try to be on the level most of the time, but sometimes I just say what's easiest.

☐ Why bother if the other fellow doesn't know the difference?

**Can you stick with it?**

☐ If I make up my mind to do something, I don't let anything stop me.

☐ I usually finish what I start if it goes well.

☐ If it doesn't go right away, I quit. Why beat my brains out?

**How good is your health?**

☐ I never run down.

☐ I have enough energy for most things I want to do.

☐ I run out of energy sooner than most of my friends seem to.

**Count the checks you made.**

How many checks are there beside the first answer to each question? _____

How many checks are there beside the second answer to each question? _____

How many checks are there beside the third answer to each question? _____

If most of your checks are beside the first answers, you probably have what it takes to run a business. If not, you're likely to have more trouble than you can handle by yourself. Better find a partner who is strong on the points you're weak on. If many checks are beside the third answer, not even a good partner will be able to shore you up.

Source: U.S. Small Business Administration.

# 1.4 Knowing Your Market

One of the most important questions you should ask yourself is whether you feel that you know and understand the market for the particular kind of products or services you intend to sell. Do you know who your competition is and whether the particular market you intend to appeal to is large enough for both you and the existing competition? Also, how will your products or services measure up against those of your competitors in terms of quality and price?

If your product or service is something new or unusual, you need to have a sense of whether you will be selling an item that is wanted and needed in the marketplace. Or, even if you intend to sell a product or service that you know there is a need for, you should be satisfied in your own mind that you are going to be making it available at the right place at the right time. Few sights are sadder than the boarded-up mom-and-pop store or restaurant — in which the owners have sunk their life savings — that never got off the ground for some obvious reason, such as lack of visibility from the street, lack of substantial foot traffic by its doors, or some other fatal flaw that the inexperienced owners overlooked.

To succeed, you must find the right business opportunity. If you do not have a clear idea of what business you want to go into and where you want to operate it, you will need to do some intelligent investigation of all possible opportunities that might be suitable for you. If you already have a concept of what you want to do, you will still need to do a great deal of investigating to make sure it is as good an opportunity as it appears to be. In either case, a lot of initial research and footwork is going to be advisable, unless you want to close your eyes and indulge in wishful thinking. As the Canadian study mentioned earlier in this chapter indicated, most of the successful new ventures surveyed had gotten started only after 6 to 10 months of careful investigation and planning.

**Determining Market Feasibility**

In other words, to quote a well-known brokerage firm: "Investigate before you invest." This often entails doing your own marketing feasibility study before committing yourself to opening a new business. On the other hand, if you have several thousand dollars to spend and a well-defined idea of what it is you want to do, you can hire a professional economist or marketing consultant to do a feasibility study. In every major city, there are several firms that can do a thorough marketing and demographic study for you. Such a feasibility study can be quite valuable, but it will also be fairly expensive. Most people starting a new business probably choose do their own marketing feasibility study.

When choosing a business to go into, keep these thoughts in mind:

- If you see that a particular business is doing quite well and you want to go in and compete head-to-head with it, don't make the mistake of adopting a me-too approach and going in with the assumption that you can take away a lot of their business by competing on a price basis. Other than price, you better have a lot of good reasons why you think another business' customers will switch over to you. Other good reasons could include a distinctly better product, service, or location.

▪ Keep your eyes open for developing social, economic, and technological trends that will create new markets that you can move into at an early stage. It will help if you are a voracious reader of magazines such as *Time, Newsweek* (social trends); *Forbes, Business Week* (economic trends); or *Omni* or *Discover* (technological innovations).

An example of how observing social trends can translate into profits — in this instance stock market profits — is the case of an investment analyst in the 60s who noticed the trend toward mini-skirts and correctly anticipated that the spread of mini-skirts among women would create a boom market for panty hose. The analyst made a killing by buying stocks of panty hose makers.

So how do you go about analyzing the market for your product or service once you have focused on a particular business you might want to start? Worksheet 2 will help you in pinpointing the kind of information you need to develop to satisfy yourself that a good market exists for whatever it is you are planning to sell. Before you read any further, take out a pencil and spend some time writing down your responses to each of the items in Worksheet 2.

## Worksheet 2
## Marketing Feasibility Study Checklist for Your Product or Service

**Your Product**

Describe briefly the nature of the product or service you will offer: _____

_____

_____

Most products or services have a life cycle, beginning with very rapid growth in the introductory stage, which slows down in the maturity stage, flattens out in the saturation stage, and finally begins shrinking in the declining stage. Which stage of its market cycle do you believe your product or service is in?

   ☐ introductory (high growth)        ☐ saturation (little or no growth)

   ☐ maturity (slower growth)         ☐ declining (negative growth in demand)

If you believe your product is in one of the earlier, faster growing stages of its life cycle, what edge do you believe your product will have over similar products that may be introduced by new competitors who may come into the field? ____

_____

_____

_____

(Continued)

(Continued)

If you are entering at a fairly late stage of the product marketing cycle, why is it you believe that you can succeed in taking away others' market share with your product? _____

_____

_____

How is your product different in terms of quality and price from what is already on the market? _____

_____

_____

Is there good reason to believe that your customers will recognize the difference? _____ If so, why? _____

_____

_____

What is different about your marketing strategy or distribution strategy that will enable your product or service to succeed in a market where there is little, if any, growth? _____

_____

_____

### Your Customers

Not everyone is a potential customer. Certain age groups, income levels, geographic areas, ethnic groups, and educational levels will be more likely than others to be your customers. You need to focus on who will need your product and be most likely to buy it and then where to locate your business or how to structure your marketing approach to reach those segments of the market that you are most interested in reaching. Spell out below, as clearly as you can, who your customers are most likely to be.

The particular area from which I will be able to draw most of my customers is: _____

_____

_____

In addition, I should draw a significant number of customers from the following area or areas: _____

_____

_____

My plan or strategy for reaching potential customers in the above areas can be summarized as follows: _____

_____

_____

The chief market for my product, in terms of age and sex groups, should be among the following persons (describe):

_____

_____

_____

In terms of income groups, my particular product should appeal primarily to people in the following income levels:

☐ Under $25,000 a year household income

☐ $25,000 – $35,000 a year

☐ $35,000 – $50,000 a year

☐ $50,000 – $75,000 a year

☐ $75,000 – $100,000 a year

☐ More than $100,000 a year

My product or service is likely to be more in demand by certain social, cultural, and ethnic groups than others. The groups that are most likely to be customers, if any, are: _____

_____

_____

The groups that are least likely to be customers are: _____

_____

_____

**Your Competition**

Even though you may have done a great job in pinpointing and studying your market segment, the job isn't done until you have considered your competition.

Main competitors in my market area are (list firms by name):

(1) _____

(2) _____

(3) _____

(4) _____

(5) _____

(6) _____

Based on my market research of statistical data, such as *Sales Marketing and Management Magazine*, the amount of buying power per business represented in my area is $_____.

If I can generate that amount of sales, it: will ☐, will not ☐ be sufficient for me to operate successfully.

Five reasons why customers would buy from me rather than my competitors are:

(1) _____

(2) _____

(3) _____

(4) _____

(5) _____

(Continued)

(Continued)

Five weaknesses my business will have, in comparison to my competitors, are:

(1) _____

(2) _____

(3) _____

(4) _____

(5) _____

To overcome these weaknesses, I will: _____

_____

_____

## Market Data Resources

Once you have identified your most likely potential customers, you will need to find out how to locate your business or structure and to direct your advertising and promotional efforts to most efficiently reach them. Fortunately, there is a great deal of published data you can use if you need to do this type of research. One of the best sources is *Sales Marketing and Management Magazine*, which publishes *Survey of Buying Power* each year. This survey provides breakdowns in population, households, retail sales by type of business, and total purchasing dollars for each county in the United States and for cities with a population of more than 10,000. To request information on *Survey of Buying Power*, see Statistical Information in Section 10.4.

Another excellent source is the 1990 U.S. census data, which gives vast amounts of detailed information on the U.S. population and its buying habits by individual census tract. You may want to obtain a couple of useful pamphlets from your nearest U.S. Small Business Administration field office. Ask for the pamphlet entitled *Researching Your Market* for guidance on how to do your own marketing research and the pamphlet entitled *Choosing a Retail Location*.

## Finding the Optimum Site

Even more important in your local community may be studies and future projections as to population and income trends that have been done by local groups, such as your local chamber of commerce or, in some areas, the local planning commission. If finding the optimum site to locate is important to your marketing effort, do the following:

- Talk to a knowledgeable person at your local chamber of commerce about business and other trends in the area where you intend to locate.
- Talk to a staff person at your local planning commission about census tract projections of future population growth, income trends, and

economic development in the area you are considering. Also, they (or some other local agency, such as a traffic or streets department) will usually have done traffic counts showing how many cars pass certain points every day. This information can be very useful if you are opening a retail business. Also, consult any trade association, which serves your business and may have available information tailored exactly to your needs.

For a complete guide to specifying, ranking, and evaluating the factors you must consider when choosing an optimum site for your new or relocating business, obtain a copy of *Company Relocation Handbook*. This handbook features a list of related reference publications and economic development organizations. Get your copy through your local book source, or:

**The Oasis Press**
(800) 228-2275

# 1.5 Knowing the Business

Do you have any experience in the area of business in which you will be engaged? Of course it is possible to learn while doing, but it helps a great deal to know the business before you start. Often the most successful businesses are started by people who have worked in a particular line of business for years and who finally decide that they know the ropes well enough to leave their employer and start their own similar operation.

It helps to have experience in the particular business you propose to enter, but in most cases, your experience working in some other line of business will also have considerable carryover value. If you have neither type of experience, you may find that you have a lot to learn once you commence.

A major management weakness that causes businesses to fail is the inability to get the job done, and do it right, on time, and efficiently enough to charge a competitive price for your product or service and still make a profit. For example, you may have done a lot of market research and decided that, with the tremendous proliferation of personal computers, a great business to go into is repairing small computers. You may be absolutely right, but unless you have the technical capability to do such repairs, or the ability to properly select and hire employees who can do the job, you had better look for some other kind of business to go into.

In many cases, if you know you lack the technical experience you need to open a particular kind of business, your best approach will be to get a job in that industry and work for someone else for a few years until you learn what you need to know. This may require a lot of patience, but it is definitely preferable to getting into a business you do not know well and losing your shirt in the process.

## Worksheet 3
## Estimated Cash Inflow from Sales for Year _____

| Item:                                    Month: | | | | | |
|---|---|---|---|---|---|
| **Gross Sales for Month** | | | | | |
| **Less:** Credit Sales Made | | | | | |
| **Sub-total: Cash Sales** | | | | | |
| **Plus:** Collections on Prior Credit Sales | | | | | |
| **Less:** Bad Debts* | | | | | |
| **Total: Net Cash Flow from Monthly Sales** | | | | | |

\* Consider using some percentage, say 1% or 2% of credit sale collections, to estimate your uncollectible debts.

# 1.6  Money

Can you afford to start a full-time business, if it will mean giving up your current employment and income? Many small businesses never really have a chance to succeed, because the owners run out of money before the business becomes a viable operation. As a result, the owners often wind up having to go back to work for someone else again, disappointed and broke.

You should carefully calculate and schedule out, in as much detail as possible, the income and expenses that you can reasonably expect for at least the first year of operation, as well as your living expenses and a reserve for emergencies.

Be sure that you have enough money to last until the business reaches the point where you expect to make enough profit to live on.

Remember that there are a lot of expenses involved in starting up almost any kind of business and that most businesses start out operating in the red for a time.

Completing worksheets 3 through 5 will help you plan your cash flow for the crucial first year of business. Worksheet 3 will help you to project your monthly sales revenue in terms of actual cash to be received. Worksheet 4 projects your monthly operating expenses for the first year of business, plus one-time, start-up expenses. Worksheet 5 is a schedule of your estimated personal living expenses during the first year.

Once you have completed worksheets 3 through 5, enter the bottom line figures from each on Worksheet 6, which is a summary of your cash needs. This will show you how much cash you will have to put into the business each month — and on a cumulative basis — during the first

| | | | | | | | Annual Totals |
|---|---|---|---|---|---|---|---|
| | | | | | | | |
| | | | | | | | |
| | | | | | | | |
| | | | | | | | |
| | | | | | | | |
| | | | | | | | |

year of business. Once you have completed Worksheet 6, you will have a pretty good handle on how much money it's going to take you to get the business started and approximately when you will need it.

If, under your most realistic projections, you are still running a deficit in cash flow each month at the end of the first year, you may want to do a similar projection out into the second year of operation.

If it appears that you will need to borrow or raise money to keep the business operating until it gets into the black, find out well in advance whether and how much you will be able to raise. If you plan to borrow, do you know how to put together a strong presentation to demonstrate to the prospective lender how you will be able to repay the loan? If not, see Section 9.7 and Chapter 10 for sources of information and help in obtaining financing for a small business.

For help in putting together an impressive loan application package, you may want to obtain a copy of *The Loan Package*, which will help you identify essential financial information for a loan, analyze your cash needs, and focus on the direction of your company. *The Loan Package* is available through your local book source or the toll-free number below.

Affordable and easy-to-use software programs that are helpful for small businesses have been developed by PSI Successful Business Software. Many of the programs, such as *Financial Templates for Small Business* or *Small Business Expert*, complement this *Starting and Operating a Business* book.

**PSI Successful Business Software**
(800) 228-2275

## Worksheet 4
## Estimated Business Cash Outlays for Year _____

| Item:                              Month: | | | | | |
|---|---|---|---|---|---|
| **Monthly Expenses** | | | | | |
| Rent | | | | | |
| Salaries and wages (except owner) | | | | | |
| Payroll taxes | | | | | |
| Advertising and promotion | | | | | |
| Insurance | | | | | |
| Federal estimated income tax | | | | | |
| State estimated income tax | | | | | |
| Owner's FICA or SE tax | | | | | |
| Telephone and utilities | | | | | |
| Inventory replacement purchase | | | | | |
| Interest on loans | | | | | |
| Maintenance | | | | | |
| Legal and accounting fees | | | | | |
| Office supplies | | | | | |
| Delivery expense | | | | | |
| Miscellaneous | | | | | |
| **One-time Expenses** | | | | | |
| Fixtures and equipment | | | | | |
| Decorating and remodeling | | | | | |
| Initial stock of inventory | | | | | |
| Utility and lease deposits | | | | | |
| Licenses and permits | | | | | |
| Other | | | | | |
| **Total Expenses for Month** | | | | | |
| **Plus:** Loan principal payment | | | | | |
| **Less:** Purchases on credit | | | | | |
| **Plus:** Payment on prior credit | | | | | |
| **Net Monthly Cash Outlay** | | | | | |

| | | | | | | | Annual Totals |
|---|---|---|---|---|---|---|---|
| | | | | | | | |
| | | | | | | | |
| | | | | | | | |
| | | | | | | | |
| | | | | | | | |
| | | | | | | | |
| | | | | | | | |
| | | | | | | | |
| | | | | | | | |
| | | | | | | | |
| | | | | | | | |
| | | | | | | | |
| | | | | | | | |
| | | | | | | | |
| | | | | | | | |
| | | | | | | | |
| | | | | | | | |
| | | | | | | | |
| | | | | | | | |
| | | | | | | | |
| | | | | | | | |
| | | | | | | | |
| | | | | | | | |
| | | | | | | | |
| | | | | | | | |
| | | | | | | | |
| | | | | | | | |
| | | | | | | | |
| | | | | | | | |
| | | | | | | | |
| | | | | | | | |

## Worksheet 5
## Estimated Personal and Living Expenses for Year _____

| Item:                               Month: | | | | | |
|---------------------------------------------|--|--|--|--|--|
| **Regular Payments** | | | | | |
| Rent or house payment | | | | | |
| Property taxes | | | | | |
| Condo owner's dues | | | | | |
| Car payments | | | | | |
| Furniture and appliance payments | | | | | |
| Loan payments | | | | | |
| Health insurance | | | | | |
| Other insurance | | | | | |
| | | | | | |
| **Household Expenses** | | | | | |
| Food – restaurants | | | | | |
| Food – at home | | | | | |
| Telephone and utilities | | | | | |
| Water | | | | | |
| | | | | | |
| **Personal Expenses** | | | | | |
| Clothing and laundry | | | | | |
| Medical, dental, and drugs | | | | | |
| Education | | | | | |
| Dues and subscriptions | | | | | |
| Gifts and charity | | | | | |
| Gasoline and auto | | | | | |
| Entertainment and travel | | | | | |
| Miscellaneous spending | | | | | |
| | | | | | |
| | | | | | |
| **Total Personal Expenses (Draw Required)** | | | | | |

| | | | | | | | Annual Totals |
|---|---|---|---|---|---|---|---|
| | | | | | | | |
| | | | | | | | |
| | | | | | | | |
| | | | | | | | |
| | | | | | | | |
| | | | | | | | |
| | | | | | | | |
| | | | | | | | |
| | | | | | | | |
| | | | | | | | |
| | | | | | | | |
| | | | | | | | |
| | | | | | | | |
| | | | | | | | |
| | | | | | | | |
| | | | | | | | |
| | | | | | | | |
| | | | | | | | |
| | | | | | | | |
| | | | | | | | |
| | | | | | | | |
| | | | | | | | |
| | | | | | | | |
| | | | | | | | |
| | | | | | | | |
| | | | | | | | |
| | | | | | | | |
| | | | | | | | |
| | | | | | | | |
| | | | | | | | |
| | | | | | | | |

**Worksheet 6**
**Summary of Estimated Cash Requirements for Year _____**

| Item:                                                                             Month: | | | | | |
|---------------------------------------------------------------------------------|---|---|---|---|---|
| **Net cash for month from sales** – Worksheet 3 | | | | | |
| **Less:** Net monthly cash outlay – Worksheet 4 | | | | | |
| **Subtotal:** Net operating cash flow (or deficit) | | | | | |
| **Less:** Owner's draw for living & personal expenses – Worksheet 5 | | | | | |
| **Add:** Money borrowed | | | | | |
| **Add (or subtract):** Equity capital paid in (or withdrawn) from the business | | | | | |
| **Total: Net cash flow (or deficit) for month** | | | | | |
| **Cumulative\* cash flow (or deficit)** | | | | | |

\* Add this month's net cash flow to the previous month's cumulative total.

# 1.7  Signing a Lease

If you will need to lease space for your business location, have you located a suitable place that is available? If so, there are a number of critical points you need to consider before you sign a lease with a landlord.

Remember that a lease is a binding legal contract, and if you agree to pay rent of $1,000 a month for two years, you are on the hook for $24,000, unless you can sublease or assign the lease to someone else, which could be difficult or impossible to do, depending on the terms of the lease. Key points to consider include:

- What are the terms of the lease? Most businesses tend to start off by either growing rapidly or quickly folding. Thus, except in a retail or service business, you will probably be better off initially leasing on a month-to-month basis or for as short a lease term as you can get, such as three or six months, even if the monthly rent is higher than for a longer lease. You will already have enough financial problems if your business fails, without being saddled with a long-term lease obligation.

- Can you put up the kind of sign you must have on the building? A business like a restaurant can be devastated if the landlord doesn't permit a sign that is sufficiently visible to passersby.

- Will the landlord permit you to make necessary improvements and alterations to the leased premises?

| | | | | | | | Annual Totals |
|---|---|---|---|---|---|---|---|
| | | | | | | | |
| | | | | | | | |
| | | | | | | | |
| | | | | | | | |
| | | | | | | | |
| | | | | | | | |
| | | | | | | | |
| | | | | | | | |

- Will the local health department, fire and police departments, air pollution control authorities, and zoning rules permit operation of your particular type of business at the location you have chosen?
- Is your location in a high-crime area that will require expensive burglary insurance and security precautions?
- Is there enough parking nearby or good public transit access for customers?
- Is the location appropriate to the kind of business you will conduct? There is usually no need to locate a manufacturing operation in a busy, high-traffic area. On the other hand, retail businesses are usually heavily dependent on the number of people passing nearby on foot or by car.

  For example, the Pillsbury Company reportedly selects its sites for Burger King fast food restaurants by looking for locations that have at least 16,000 cars passing by each day at an average speed of about 30 miles per hour.[5]
- Does the lease provide you with an option to renew — and at what rental price — after the initial term expires?
- If the lease is for more than just a few months, do you have the right to sublease or assign the lease? If so, under what conditions or restrictions?

# 1.8 Will You Hire Employees?

In certain kinds of businesses, during the initial start-up phases — and perhaps even afterwards — you may be able to operate without employees by either doing all your work yourself, with the help of family members, or by contracting out certain functions to independent outside contractors. To the extent you can do so, you will probably find your life is much simpler. Once you hire even one employee, you take on a great many responsibilities as an employer, over and above meeting a payroll every week or two.

This section reviews some of the legal restrictions on your hiring practices and provides you with a working outline of what you will need to consider in the way of personnel policies once your business reaches the point where you will have to hire employees. See Section 5.9 regarding U.S. Immigration Law restrictions on hiring.

**Hiring Practices**

Hiring personnel can be complicated because of the broad array of state and federal laws designed to prevent an employer from hiring on the basis of discriminatory factors, such as age, sex, race, or religion. Most of these laws affect all but the smallest employers, so you will have to be alert to most of these rules to avoid even the appearance of discrimination in your hiring practices.

While anti-discrimination rules apply to promotions, job assignments, firing, and other aspects of the employment relationship as well as to hiring, the focus here is mainly on hiring practices. This is the area where most small business owners are likely to stumble into trouble, even when they have no intention to discriminate.

**Things Not to Do**

All questions or information you express should relate to job qualifications only and not to extraneous factors, such as age, race, sex, or physical size or condition.

If there are special occupational requirements — for example, hard physical labor that might preclude hiring certain handicapped individuals — be sure to carefully document such unusual situations or requirements.

**Help Wanted Ads**

Use the list below to guide you when writing a help wanted advertisement.

- Do not mention race or national origin or any attribute of national origin, such as native language.
- Do not refer to sex classifications, such as "girl wanted."
- Avoid any type of reference to age, such as "young boy" or "recent high school graduate."

**Sample Employment Application Form**

---

**Employment Application**
**Personal Data**

Name: _____
            (last)                                    (first)                                    (middle)

Present address: _____
                            (street address)                                    (city)            (state)      (zip)

Telephone numbers: _____   _____
                                    (home)                    (work)

**Education**

High School: _____   Graduated? Yes ☐  No ☐   Location: _____

College or University: _____   Graduated? Yes ☐  No ☐   Degree(s): _____

Other (specify type): _____   Graduated? Yes ☐  No ☐   Certificate(s): _____

                      _____   Graduated? Yes ☐  No ☐   Certificate(s): _____

**Work Experience**

List below all present and previous employment, starting with the most recent.

Company name: _____   From (mo/yr): _____   Type of work: _____

Address: _____   To (mo/yr): _____   Name of Supervisor: _____

                      _____   Reason you left: _____

Company name: _____   From (mo/yr): _____   Type of work: _____

Address: _____   To (mo/yr): _____   Name of Supervisor: _____

                      _____   Reason you left: _____

Company name: _____   From (mo/yr): _____   Type of work: _____

Address: _____   To (mo/yr): _____   Name of Supervisor: _____

                      _____   Reason you left: _____

Company name: _____   From (mo/yr): _____   Type of work: _____

Address: _____   To (mo/yr): _____   Name of Supervisor: _____

                      _____   Reason you left: _____

May we contact the employers above?   Yes ☐  No ☐   If yes, list any employers you do not wish us to contact:

_____

Remarks: _____

_____

_____

Applicant's Signature: _____   Date _____ , 19 __

## Job Application Forms

Your employment application forms should avoid any questions or information on these topics:

- Arrest record;
- Whether the applicant has ever filed for unemployment benefits;
- Place of birth or where parents were born; )
- Physical characteristics, such as height or weight;
- Social Security number;
- Marital status;
- Labor union affiliation;
- Request for photograph;
- Religious affiliation;
- Mode of transportation to work;
- Sex;
- Race or national origin;
- Clubs or organizations, unless you instruct the applicant not to list organizations that indicate race or national origin; and
- Native language or how the applicant learned a foreign language.

A sample employment application form is provided for your review on the previous page. If you wish to add additional questions to it, be careful not to indirectly request anything that would reflect on the applicant's race, religion, sex, age, marital status, national origin, or physical condition. Because state laws differ, check with your legal adviser or state employment department before preparing your employment application.

## Employment Interviews

During interviews with potential employees, refrain from asking questions, such as:

- Are you a U.S. citizen?
- When did you attend grade school, high school, or college?
- Do you have children, and who will care for them while you are working?
- Do you have any physical or mental handicap?
- What does your spouse do for a living, and are you likely to move elsewhere?
- Would your religion prevent you from working on holidays or certain days of the week?

Federal law generally bans the use of any kind of lie detector tests in most private employment situations, except for drug manufacturers and distributors and certain security firms.[6] Many state laws are even more stringent.

In addition, questions on possible felony convictions, previous military service, and drug or alcohol addiction are not necessarily illegal in all cases, but they may entail difficulties and probably should be avoided.

**Checking References**

As a general rule, former employers have no legal obligation to give you any information about a former employee. As a practical matter, however, most former employers will at least verify the former employee's employment and the date of employment. Since a former employer can get into trouble for giving you negative information that they cannot substantiate, don't expect them to volunteer much information or to put anything negative in writing. For that reason, you should generally do reference checks by phone. Acceptable questions would include those on:

- Verifying information given by the applicant;
- Asking about the applicant's principal strong points, weak points, and degree of supervision needed;
- Asking about the applicant's attitude;
- Asking how the applicant's performance compared with others; and
- Asking if the applicant would be rehired.

**Personnel Policies**

Even before you hire your first employee, you will need to outline some basic personnel policies. Better yet, if you write down your policies on matters such as hours, vacation time, and sick leave and can give such a written summary to new employees, it will greatly help to clarify the employment relationship. Perhaps it will even prevent a misunderstanding that could lead to legal action against you by an employee.

Worksheet 7 provides a series of questions that will help you focus on different personnel policies that are typical in a small to medium-sized business. For a more thorough treatment of this area and if you wish to develop a personnel policy manual for your business, you may want to obtain a copy of *A Company Policy and Personnel Workbook* (The Oasis Press, 1991).

**Related Information**

To supplement the information you have just read in this chapter, you may want to read the following sections which discuss more related information:

- Employee or Independent Contractor? — Section 9.11
- Fair Employment Practices — Section 5.8
- Sexual Harassment — Section 5.8
- Immigration Law Restrictions on Hiring — Section 5.9
- Hiring a Spouse as an Employee — Section 8.12
- Employee Wage-Hour and Child Labor Laws — Section 5.7
- New Civil Rights Act — Section 9.14
- The Americans with Disabilities Act — Section 5.11

In addition, to get an overview of other legal obligations that come with the territory when you have employees, scan through Chapter 5.

## Worksheet 7
## Defining Your Company's Personnel Policies

**Working Hours**

Describe briefly the policy you will set for working hours, including:

Starting time? _____

_____

How much time will be allowed for lunch? _____

_____

Quitting time? _____

_____

Which days of the week employees will be expected to work? _____

_____

If, like many companies these days, you want to adopt some kind of "flex-time" system, spell out how that will work.

_____

_____

_____

**Overtime**

Outline your policy on overtime work. Refer to Section 5.7 of this book for legal requirements for paying overtime premiums. See also Section 11.5 regarding state wage laws. Points to consider here include:

Will you pay exempt employees (administrative or professional) overtime if they work extra hours? _____

_____

Will you require employees to obtain permission to work overtime? _____

_____

**Compensation**

Make a list of the job positions in the company other than your own and the compensation level for each. On a separate piece of paper, write out a specific job description for each position, outlining duties and responsibilities. Refer to sections 5.7 and 11.5 of this book for a description of hourly minimum wage requirements.

| Position | Hourly wage | Salary | Total monthly pay |
|----------|-------------|--------|-------------------|
| _____ | _____ | _____ | _____ |
| _____ | _____ | _____ | _____ |
| _____ | _____ | _____ | _____ |
| _____ | _____ | _____ | _____ |
| _____ | _____ | _____ | _____ |
| _____ | _____ | _____ | _____ |
| _____ | _____ | _____ | _____ |

**Vacation Policy**

Describe how much paid vacation employees will have and how this may increase after a certain number of years of service. _____

_____

Will vacation time and sick leave time off be combined into a single category for employees (as some companies now do to reward employees who do not abuse sick leave and to discourage others from using sick leave as additional vacation by playing hooky)? _____

_____

Will you pay employees, who terminate, for unused vacation? (The laws of many states require you to do so.) _____

_____

**Sick Leave Policy**

Outline your policy for both paid sick leave and unpaid sick leave, or whichever you choose to provide, if not both. (Note: Sick pay is no longer exempt from FICA tax, in general.)[7]

Sick leave _____

_____

Unpaid sick leave _____

_____

**Leaves of Absence**

What will your policy be towards employees who request unpaid leaves of absence? _____

_____

**Time Off with Pay**

Will you provide other time off with pay for such eventualities as funerals or emergencies in an employee's immediate family?

Funerals or family emergencies? _____

_____

Jury duty? _____

_____

Birth of a child? _____

_____

**Promotions and Evaluations**

Outline your policy for evaluating employees' performance and determining when promotions will be made. _____

_____

_____

_____

_____

(Continued)

(Continued)

**Fringe Benefits**

Consider which employee fringe benefits you will provide and specify your policy for each.

Medical Insurance: _____
_____

Long-term Disability Insurance: _____
_____

Life Insurance: _____
_____

Dental Insurance: _____
_____

Medical Expense Reimbursement: _____
_____

Child Care Benefits: _____
_____

Maternity Benefits: _____
_____

Pension or Profit-sharing Plans: _____
_____

Paid Holidays: _____
_____

Automobiles or Allowances: _____
_____

Expense Accounts: _____
_____

Employee Discounts on Purchases: _____
_____

Stock Options (if incorporated): _____
_____

Incentive Bonus Plan: _____
_____

**Placement Fees**

If you hire employees through a personnel agency or "headhunting" firm, will you pay the placement fee? _____
_____

# 1.9 Other Questions You Need to Ask

- Will or should you advertise? If you do, you need to decide what kind of advertising will be the most cost-effective for your business, whether it be newspaper ads, direct mail, radio, posters, handbills, or other forms of advertising and promotion.
- Do you understand what will be involved in purchasing, managing, and restocking your inventory of goods?
- How will you go about selling? Will you hire sales clerks or outside salespeople, or will you do most of the selling yourself?
- Will you sell to customers on credit? If so, how will you protect yourself from bad credit risks and outright deadbeats?
- How much of your personal savings are you putting at risk by going into business? Are you willing to risk losing all of it if the business is a failure?
- Can you run the business alone — or with help from family members — or would you do better with one or more partners or business associates to provide additional capital and skills and to divide up some of the responsibilities of running the business?

Again, the questions posed in this chapter are not intended to discourage you from going ahead with starting your business. Chances are you have already considered most of the points raised in this chapter and are reasonably confident that you will be able to do what is necessary to make your business work. If so, many of the questions raised above probably seem rather elementary and obvious to you, as they will to most individuals seriously considering going into business, and you will now want to proceed to the discussions in the remainder of this book.

If you have not previously given serious thought to most of the above points that are relevant to the type of business you are planning to start, now is the time to take a long, hard look at whether you are adequately prepared to embark upon such a venture.

# Footnotes

1. McCarroll, *Entrepreneurs: Starting Over,* TIME MAGAZINE (Jan. 6, 1992).

2. Cook, *Women: The Best Entrepreneurs*, CANADIAN BUSINESS (June, 1982). Reproduced with permission.

3. *The State of Small Business, A Report of the President*, Superintendent of Documents, Wash. D.C. (1989).

4. Phillips and Kirchoff, *Analysis of New Firm Survival and Growth*, J. SMALL BUS. ECON. (Winter 1989).

5. San Francisco *Chronicle*, Aug. 3, 1980.

6. The Employee Polygraph Protection Act, 29 U.S.C. 2001.

7. I.R.C. §3121(a)(4).

Chapter 2

# Choosing the Legal Form of the Business

*The hardest thing in the world to understand is Income Tax.*

— Albert Einstein

## 2.1 General Considerations

There are many ways in which a business venture can be structured; however, the law classifies businesses so that most fall into one of three legal forms — the sole proprietorship, the partnership, or the corporation. There are also certain variations on some of these basic legal forms. For instance, the limited liability company, a relatively new form of business organization, is gaining legal status in a number of states. Limited liability companies are intended to provide the limited liability of corporations and the pass-through taxation of partnerships.

If you are planning to start a business, consider the following questions when deciding your business' legal form:

- Will someone else share in ownership of the business? If so, it will not be a sole proprietorship. Thus, the choice will be between a partnership arrangement and a corporation.

- How important is it to limit personal liability for debts or claims against the business? If this is a major consideration, incorporating the business would generally be the best means of limiting your liability.

- Which form of business organization will result in the least taxes? While there is no universal answer to this question, the rest of this chapter explains when it is and isn't beneficial to incorporate for tax reasons.

## Sole Proprietorships

A sole proprietorship is generally the simplest, least regulated form of business and can usually be initiated without any formalities. If you simply start doing business without a partner, the law will classify your business as a sole proprietorship. You do not need a lawyer or approval of any government agency to create a sole proprietorship.

## Partnerships

A partnership can also be started with a minimum of formalities. A partnership need not be more than a handshake agreement with your business partner, but it is generally advisable to have a written partnership agreement defining your respective rights and responsibilities, and that usually means incurring fairly significant legal fees. A limited partnership, in which the liability of one or more of the partners is limited, is much more involved, as discussed in Section 2.3 of this chapter.

## Corporations

The corporation is the most formalized and regulated business entity; therefore, the costs of establishing and maintaining the legal status of a corporation are generally greater than for a sole proprietorship or partnership.

## Limited Liability Companies

In addition to the three traditional forms of business organization discussed above, several states in recent years have created, by statute, a new type of entity called a limited liability company. This entity, which closely resembles and is taxed as a partnership, also offers limited liability like corporations.

In 1988, the IRS's Revenue Ruling 88-76 concluded that a Wyoming limited liability company could be classified as a partnership for federal income tax purposes — which is favorable, from a taxpayer's standpoint, in many cases — based on the following rationale:

- No member has any personal liability for debts of the company; therefore, the company has limited liability.
- The interests of the members are assignable only upon written consent of all the remaining members. This is similar to a partnership; however, the ruling recognized that mere assignees are entitled to receive profits and other compensation.
- Like a partnership, the company is dissolved in situations which are very similar to the dissolution of a limited partnership.
- The company has centralized management.

Because of the absence of continuity of life and free transferability of interests in the entity, the Wyoming limited liability company was held to be a partnership for tax purposes. Florida has also recently adopted a Limited Liability Company Act, which is virtually identical to that of Wyoming. In 1990, Colorado enacted legal provisions that permit the formation of limited liability companies. Colorado's limited liability companies are not subject to income tax and are to be treated as partnerships for state tax purposes. They also have limited liability. The Colorado companies also appear to meet the IRS tests for taxability as a partnership. In addition to these states, several other states have adopted limited liability companies acts. For more information, contact your secretary of state's office.

**Changing Legal Forms**

How difficult is it to change from one legal form to another? As a broad generalization, it is usually a simpler matter to change from a sole proprietorship to a partnership, or to change from a sole proprietorship or partnership to a corporation, than it is to move in the opposite direction.

For example, converting a business that is operated as a corporation into a sole proprietorship or partnership may result in substantial individual and corporate-level taxes when the corporation is liquidated. This would happen if the value of the business transferred to the owners of the stock of the corporation were greater than their cost or tax basis for such stock or if any corporate assets have values in excess of their tax basis.

While there are almost always some expenses and complications in changing the legal form, such changes are quite routine transactions. Many businesses start off as sole proprietorships, develop into partnerships and later incorporate, if tax and other considerations indicate that it no longer makes good business sense not to be incorporated. Thus, the choice of one legal form when starting a business should not be considered a final choice.

## 2.2 Advantages and Disadvantages of Sole Proprietorships

The great advantage of operating a new business as a sole proprietorship is that it is simple and does not require any formal action to set it up. You can start your business today as a sole proprietorship — there is no need to wait for an attorney to draft and file documents or for the government to approve them.

Of course, you will need a business license, and a few states require you to register to do business. As a sole proprietor, you are the sole owner of your business. If married, however, your spouse will usually have a one-half interest in the business in a state which has community property laws.

**Personal Liability**

As the owner of the sole proprietorship, you will be personally liable for any debts or taxes of the business or other claims, such as legal damages resulting from a lawsuit. This is one reason why many entrepreneurs prefer to use a corporation rather than a sole proprietorship. Unlimited personal liability is perhaps the major disadvantage of operating a business in the form of a sole proprietorship.

All of the profit or loss from your business belongs to you and must be reported on your federal income tax return, *Schedule C, Income (or Loss) from a Business or Profession,* on *Form 1040.* This can either be an advantage or a disadvantage for income tax purposes, depending on the circumstances.

If operating the business results in losses or significant tax credits, you may be able to use the tax losses or tax credits to reduce taxes on income from other sources. Or, if your sole proprietorship generates modest profits — but not more than about $60,000 to $75,000 a year — overall taxes may be less than if incorporated, assuming you need most of the income to live on.

## Income Tax Advantage Similar to Corporations

After the Tax Reform Act of 1986 and the Omnibus Budget Reconciliation Act of 1987 (OBRA), a sole proprietorship is now less likely to become disadvantageous in terms of tax rates as compared to a corporation. For one thing, the highest corporate tax rate for 1992 is 34% — 39% on income between $100,000 and $335,000 — which is higher than the maximum nominal individual tax rate of 31%. Thus, corporate tax rates are no longer lower than individual rates, except that the first $50,000 of corporate income is taxed at only a 15% rate and the next $25,000 at 25%.

## Unemployment Taxes

As a sole proprietor, you are not considered an employee of your business. As a result, you will avoid having to pay unemployment taxes on your earnings from the business.

Both the state and federal governments impose unemployment taxes on wages or salaries but not on self-employment income. For 1992, the federal unemployment tax rate is effectively 0.8%[1] of the first $7,000[2] of wages paid to each employee, with a $56 maximum per employee. Refer to Section 11.2 regarding the state unemployment taxes you must pay for each employee.

As a sole proprietor, your income would not be subject to either of these taxes. Note that a corporation would normally get an income tax deduction for the unemployment tax it paid on your salary, so that the actual after-tax savings from operating as a sole proprietorship would be somewhat less than the unemployment taxes you would avoid paying.

Another advantage of a sole proprietorship is that you can shift funds in and out of your business account or withdraw assets from the business with few tax, legal, or other limitations. In a partnership, you can generally withdraw funds only by agreement and, in the case of a corporation, a withdrawal of funds or property will usually be taxable as a dividend or capital gain and may violate some states' corporation laws.

A major disadvantage of sole proprietorships and partnerships is that they cannot obtain a number of significant tax benefits regarding group-term life insurance benefits, long-term disability insurance coverage, and medical insurance or medical expense reimbursements. To qualify for favorable tax treatment regarding such fringe benefit plans, it is necessary to incorporate. Note, however, that until July 1, 1992, a self-employed individual is allowed to deduct 25% of his or her health insurance in computing adjusted gross income.[3] Congress has extended this 25% deduction in the past, but if they don't, no deduction will be available after July 1, 1992.

**Limited Tax Savings for Fringe Benefits**

The special advantages of corporate pension and profit-sharing plans have largely been eliminated since 1984. As of now, there are virtually no differences in the tax treatment of self-employed (Keogh) plans of sole proprietorships and partnerships, as compared with corporate retirement plans. See Section 8.3.

See Section 2.4 for further discussion on advantages and disadvantages of sole proprietorships as compared to corporations.

Also, see the table at the end of this chapter which summarizes the key characteristics of sole proprietorships, partnerships, and corporations.

# 2.3 Advantages and Disadvantages of Partnerships

A business partnership is much like a sole proprietorship in many respects, except that it has two or more owners. Creating a partnership can be a very simple matter, since the law does not require any formal written documents or other formalities for most partnerships. As a practical matter, however, it is much sounder business practice for partners in a business to have a written partnership agreement that, at a minimum, spells out their agreement on such basic issues as:

**General Partnerships**

- How much and what kind of property each partner will contribute to the venture;
- What value will be placed on the contributed property;
- How profits and losses will be divided among the partners;
- When and how profits will be withdrawn;
- Whether or how certain partners will be compensated for their services to the partnership or for making capital available to the partnership; and
- How changes in ownership of interests in the partnership will be handled.

A written partnership agreement should be prepared by an attorney and, if possible, should be reviewed by a tax accountant before it is put into effect.

Partnerships are a bit like marriages; they usually start out with a great deal of trust but have a high break-up rate. Be advised that partnerships are easy to get into, require a lot of patience and understanding to live with, and are often costly and painful to get out of.

## Liability of Partners

As a partner, you are an agent for the partnership and can do anything necessary to operate the business, such as hire employees, borrow money, or enter into contracts on behalf of the partnership. You and each of your partners (except for a limited partner in a limited partnership) have personal liability for the debts, taxes, and other claims against the partnership.

If the partnership's assets are not sufficient to pay creditors, the creditors can satisfy their claims out of your personal assets. In addition, when any partner fails to pay personal debts, the partnership's business may be disrupted if his or her creditors proceed to satisfy their claims out of his or her interest in the partnership by seeking what is called a charging order against partnership assets.

## State and Federal Tax Requirements

While a partnership must file federal and usually state information returns — *Form 1065* is the federal form — it generally pays no income tax. Instead, it reports each partner's share of income or loss on the information return, and each partner reports the income or loss on *Schedule E* of his or her individual tax return, *Form 1040*.

In 1987, tax legislation was passed allowing partnerships and S corporations to elect to retain their fiscal tax year rather than change to a calendar year, as the 1986 Tax Reform Act generally mandated. This election requires the partnership or S corporation to report and pay a tax directly each year under an extremely complex formula — as long as there is a tax-deferral benefit to their partners or shareholders. This complicated extra accounting is the price for retaining a fiscal tax year.[4]

In addition, since 1985, partnerships have been required to file a special report, *Form 8308*, with the IRS each time a sale or exchange of an interest in the partnership occurs.[5]

Like a sole proprietor, a partner is not generally considered an employee of the partnership for income tax and payroll tax purposes. The income tax advantages and disadvantages of a sole proprietorship are equally applicable to a partnership, since a partner's share of income from a partnership is treated essentially the same as income from a sole proprietorship. For example, your income from a partnership may be subject to federal self-employment tax but not to federal and state unemployment taxes as discussed in Section 2.2.

## Dissolution

Unless a partnership agreement provides otherwise, a partnership usually terminates when any partner dies or withdraws from the partnership. This is in contrast to a corporation which, theoretically, has perpetual existence.

Under the laws of most states, bankruptcy of a partner or the partnership itself will cause the dissolution of the partnership, regardless of any agreement.

**Limited Partnerships**

The law provides for a special kind of partnership in which partners have limited personal liability: the limited partnership. The limited partnership is more regulated than the common general partnership discussed above, but it allows investors who will not be actively involved in the partnership's operations to become partners without being exposed to unlimited liability of the business' debts, if it should go out of business.

A limited partner risks only his or her investment but must allow one or more general partners to exercise control over the business. In fact, if the limited partner becomes involved in the partnership's operations, he or she may lose his or her protected status as a limited partner. The general partners in a limited partnership are fully liable for the partnership's debts. Every limited partnership must have one or more general partners as well as one or more limited partners.

State law requires certain formalities in the case of a limited partnership that are not required for other partnerships. To qualify for their special status, limited partnerships must usually file a *Certificate of Limited Partnership* with the secretary of state or other state and county offices. Establishing a limited partnership also requires a written partnership agreement. See Section 11.2 regarding special filing requirements for partnerships under state law.

# 2.4 Advantages and Disadvantages of Corporations

A corporation is an artificial legal entity that exists separately from the people who own, manage, control, and operate it. It can make contracts, pay taxes, and is liable for debts. Corporations exist only because state statutory laws allow them to be created.

A business corporation issues shares of its stock, as evidence of ownership, to the person or persons who contribute the money or business assets which the corporation will use to conduct its business. Thus, the stockholders or shareholders are the owners of the corporation, and they are entitled to any dividends the corporation pays and to all corporation assets — after all creditors have been paid — if the corporation is liquidated.

**Limited Personal Liability**

The main reason most businesses incorporate is to limit owner liability to the amount invested in the business. Generally, stockholders in a corporation are not personally liable for claims against the corporation and are, therefore, at risk only to the extent of their investment in the corporation.

Likewise, the officers and directors of a corporation are not normally liable for the corporation's debts, although in some cases an officer whose duty it is to withhold federal income tax from employees' wages may be liable to the IRS if the taxes are not withheld and paid over to the IRS as required.

## Potential Loss of Limited Personal Liability

The advantage of limited liability is not always completely available through incorporation. For example, don't start a corporation on a shoestring. If your corporation is capitalized too thinly with equity capital (your money) as compared to debt capital (borrowed money), the courts may determine that your corporation is a thin corporation and hold you and your stockholders directly liable to creditors.

Failure to observe corporate formalities and the separate legal existence of the corporation can have a similar result. This is called "piercing the corporate veil" by the courts, and means if a corporation is not adequately capitalized and properly operated to protect the interests of creditors, the courts can take away the veil of limited liability that normally protects the stockholders.

Piercing the corporate veil is relatively uncommon. A much more frequent problem is that many banks and other lenders will not loan money to a small incorporated business unless someone, usually the stockholders of the corporation, personally guarantees repayment of the loan. Despite this common business practice, the limited liability feature can still be an important protection from personal liability for other debts, such as accounts payable to suppliers and others who sell goods or services to the corporation on credit, typically without requiring any personal guarantee of payment by the owners.

Even this partial protection is a significant advantage of incorporating for most small businesses. Being incorporated can also protect you from personal liability regarding lawsuit damages not covered by your corporation's liability insurance policies; for example, someone slips on a banana peel in your store and sues the corporation for $10 million. To help you avoid personal liability for corporate acts, a partial checklist of do's and dont's is provided at the end of this chapter.

## Continuous Existence

Unlike a sole proprietorship or partnership, a corporation has continuous existence and does not terminate upon the death of a stockholder or a change of ownership of some or all of its stock. Creditors, suppliers, and customers, therefore, often prefer to deal with an incorporated business because of this greater continuity.

Naturally, a corporation can be terminated by mutual consent of the owners or even by one stockholder in some instances.

If you would like to learn more about these and other corporate issues, *The Essential Corporation Handbook,* by Carl R.J. Sniffen, is a new, easy-to-understand introduction into the corporate world. This handbook discusses the initial set up of your corporation and explains all the necessary corporate formalities — such as, shareholders' meetings, consent resolutions, and recordkeeping — involved in maintaining your corporation as a successful corporate entity. For more information on *The Essential Corporation Handbook,* contact your book source or:

**The Oasis Press**
(800) 228-2275

**Cost of Incorporating**

To set up a corporation, you must file articles of incorporation with the state office that grants and approves corporate charters. See Section 11.2 for more information on state incorporating requirements.

Legal fees usually run between $500 and $1,000, even for a simple incorporation, and if it is necessary to obtain a permit from the state to issue stock or securities, legal fees can be much more.

Thus, it should be apparent that one of the disadvantages of incorporating is the cost involved, which will be substantial even for the simplest incorporation. In addition to the costs of establishing a corporation, there will be recurring costs, often including annual franchise or corporate income taxes.

**Federal Corporate Income Taxes**

Corporations filing their income tax returns on *Form 1120-A* or *Form 1120* will be taxed at different rates depending on the amount of their taxable income. The corporate tax rates listed on the following table indicate the current federal tax rates. Note that there is a 5% tax on taxable income over $100,000; thus, the 39% rate. The rate drops back to a flat rate of 34% once the taxable income reaches more than $335,000.

**Corporate Tax Rate Table**

| Taxable Income | Tax Rate |
|---|---|
| Not over $50,000 | 15% |
| $50,000 to $75,000 | 25% |
| $75,000 to $100,000 | 34% |
| $100,000 to $335,000 | 39% |
| More than $335,000 | 34% |

As an owner, you will most likely draw a salary from your corporation, which will be subject to FICA (Social Security) taxes and state and federal unemployment taxes. These unemployment taxes are not imposed on your income from a sole proprietorship or partnership. FICA taxes, in 1990 and subsequent years, are generally the same (in total) on the wages of a corporate employee/owner as would be the self-employment tax on the same amount of business income if you were a sole proprietor or a partner in a partnership.

For certain types of unincorporated businesses, however, such as a firm whose income is from interest or real estate rentals, or both, there is no self-employment tax on the income, which could make not incorporating such a firm advantageous for tax purposes.

**Personal (Professional) Service Corporations**

If you operate a qualified personal (professional) service corporation, you will be taxed at a flat rate of 34%.[6] You cannot use the graduated tax rates listed previously.

According to the *Tax Guide for Small Business, Publication 334,* which is published by the Internal Revenue Service, a qualified personal service corporation is defined by these characteristics:

- At least 95% of the value of its stock is held by employees or their estates or beneficiaries; and
- The employees perform services at least 95% of the time in the following fields: health, law, engineering, architecture, accounting, actuarial science, performing arts, or consulting.

**Double Taxation of Dividends Distributed to Shareholders**

Another potential disadvantage of a corporation is the double taxation of its income that is distributed to its shareholders. If a corporation has taxable income, pays corporate income taxes on it, and the shareholders withdraw money in the form of a dividend, they will also pay tax on the dividend, as a rule. Thus, the use of a corporation can obviously be disadvantageous if it results in this double taxation of the business' income. Most incorporated small businesses, however, with good tax planning, can avoid double taxation and, instead, often can use the corporation to save taxes.

Since double taxation occurs only if a corporation pays out money or property that is taxable as dividend to its shareholders, most small corporations never, or rarely, pay dividends. Instead, they retain the lightly taxed profits in the business. This is ideal for a business that needs funds to invest in expansion of operations. Many highly profitable businesses could be better off unincorporated or as S corporations since the highest corporate tax rate is now higher than the maximum individual rate.

**Accumulated Earnings Tax**

Even where the business does not need to retain the profits, the corporation can still safely accumulate up to $150,000 of after-tax profits over a period of years, which can be invested by it in stocks, bonds, real estate, etc., without fear of incurring an accumulated earnings tax.[7] This exemption is $250,000 for most businesses except that only a $150,000 exemption is allowed for professional and certain personal service corporations. Any accumulation of profits, however, in excess of $150,000 or $250,000 that is not needed for use in the business may be hit by the accumulated earnings tax, which is a penalty tax in addition to the regular corporate income tax.

The penalty tax is 28% on these accumulated earnings, which are specially defined and not necessarily the same as net profits for accounting purposes or taxable income.[8] This penalty tax is designed to keep corporations from accumulating large amounts of profits at low corporate tax rates, unless they need to accumulate the profits to reinvest in their business.

You should consult a tax adviser as to what constitutes a legitimate business purpose for your corporation to accumulate profits beyond the $150,000 or $250,000 exemption, since the law in this area is quite complex. The key point to remember is that under present law your corporation can generally accumulate up to $150,000 or $250,000 in profits without incurring an accumulated earnings tax. This can make it an excellent tax shelter.

## Income-Splitting

By using a corporation, it may be possible to split your overall profit between two or more taxpayers, so that none of the income gets taxed in the highest tax brackets. For example, with an overall economic profit of $100,000, an incorporated business may be able to reduce its taxable income to $50,000 by paying (and deducting) a $50,000 salary to its owner, as an officer/employee of the corporation. The corporation would pay tax only on the remaining $50,000 profit, at a maximum federal tax rate of only 15%, while the owner would pay tax on the $50,000 salary received.

Because of the progressive tax rate structure under the federal income tax laws, the tax on the $100,000 income divided between the owner and his or her corporation would typically be much less than if the whole $100,000 were taxable to the owner. In 1992, for example, a single individual would pay $26,655 in federal income taxes on $100,000 of taxable income, while if the income were split evenly between the owner and his or her corporation, the corporation's tax would be $7,500 and the owner's $11,212, a saving of $7,943 — assuming the corporation is not a personal services corporation subject to a 34% flat rate of tax.

Another way to split the income of a business between multiple taxpayers is for you to make your children part owners of the business. Ideally, the children should be given an interest in the business when it is started, since the value of the gifts to them will often be minimal for gift tax purposes at that time.

It is frequently more feasible to split corporate income with your children by giving them some of the corporation's stock. This approach, however, will work only if your corporation has filed for an S corporation election on *Form 2553* with the IRS. As discussed later in this chapter, the taxable income of a corporation that qualifies as an S corporation (formerly called a Subchapter S corporation) is taxable to its shareholders — in proportion to the stock they own in the corporation — and is generally not taxed to the corporation.

By giving a number of shares of stock in such an S corporation to one or more of your children, part of the taxable income of the business can often be shifted to the children[9] and taxed at their low tax brackets — assuming, as is usually the case, that the children do not have a lot of taxable income from other sources. If, however, the parents attempt to shift too much income to the children by drawing no salary or too little salary from the corporation, the IRS has the power to reallocate the corporation's income to the parents to reflect the value of services rendered to the corporation. Under the Tax Reform Act of 1986, shifting significant income to your children will not work if the children are under 14 years of age.[10]

## Retirement Plans

For many years, corporations — except for S corporations — have had very significant tax advantages over unincorporated businesses with respect to pension and profit-sharing plans; however, this is no longer the case.

Perhaps the most significant remaining difference is that an owner/employee who participates in a Keogh plan, or a shareholder/employee in the retirement plan of an S corporation, cannot borrow money from the plan without incurring a prohibited-transactions excise tax on such a loan.[11] On the other hand, a participant in a regular corporate retirement plan may be able to borrow as much as $50,000 from the plan, if various tax requirements are met. In addition to covering yourself under a corporate or Keogh retirement plan — or even if you are not covered under either type of plan — it is also possible for you to create your own individual retirement account (IRA) whether or not incorporated. Since only a $2,000-a-year deduction[12] — $2,250 if you have a nonworking spouse — can be taken for contributions to an IRA, it will not be possible to build up a very large retirement fund or to shelter much income from tax with an IRA. Although, it is better than having no tax-qualified retirement plan at all and it can be a useful supplement to a corporate or Keogh plan.

Since 1986, federal law no longer allows deductions for contributions to IRA plans if you or your spouse is also an active participant in a corporate or Keogh qualified retirement plan and if adjusted gross income exceeds $35,000 for a single person or $50,000 for a married couple filing jointly.[13] The maximum $2,000 or $2,250 deduction phases out between income levels of $25,000 and $35,000 for single taxpayers and between $40,000 and $50,000 for married couples.[14]

## Tax Advantages

The primary tax advantages of the three types of tax-qualified retirement plans — corporate, self-employed (Keogh), and IRA — are these:

- Amounts contributed, up to certain limits, are deductible from the income of the corporation or individual taxpayer.[15] This deduction can be as much as 25% of the individual's compensation for the year (not counting the plan contribution) or $30,000, whichever is less. Even larger contributions can be made by so-called defined benefit plans.
- Contributed funds can be invested by pension or profit-sharing plans on a tax-free basis.[16] The qualified retirement trust that is usually set up to hold the retirement funds is exempt from state and federal income taxes on its income or capital gains from investments in stocks, bonds, savings accounts, gold, silver, real estate, and other passive investments.

- When trust funds are paid out to you at retirement, you may be in a lower tax bracket than when you made the contributions to the plan. Thus, not only do you get to defer payment of any tax on amounts contributed to the plan until you retire, but the tax you finally pay at retirement is apt to be at a lower rate than you would have paid when you were working.

- Receipt of all your retirement plan funds in a lump sum at retirement, or in certain other circumstances, may often qualify for special low tax rates if the distribution is from a corporate or Keogh plan but not from an IRA.[17]

**Exemptions from Estate Tax**

Except for the unlimited estate tax marital deduction, there are no longer any exemptions from the federal estate tax.

Before 1983, pension plan benefits left to a beneficiary other than the estate of the deceased employee were exempted from the federal estate tax. For 1983 and 1984, this unlimited exemption was scaled down to a $100,000 exemption for such benefits, and that limited exclusion was finally repealed after 1984.

The Tax Reform Act of 1986, however, retroactively amended certain exclusions from estate tax for pension plan benefits. Under these amendments, an individual who separated from service before January 1, 1983 and was receiving benefits on December 31, 1982 is considered as having made an irrevocable election as to the type of benefits to be received and the value of such benefits may be completely exempt from estate tax, if the form of benefits is not changed before his or her death. A similar rule applies to any person who separated from service before January 1, 1985 and was receiving benefits on December 31, 1984, if the form of benefits is not changed. Such individuals will still qualify for the $100,000 estate tax exclusion for pension benefits.

If you are receiving pension benefits and come within either of the above categories, don't change the form in which your benefits are being paid!

See Section 8.10, under the sidehead of Unlimited Estate Tax Marital Deduction, for a further discussion on estate tax.

**Insurance Benefit Plans**

The tax law permits you, as a corporate employer, to provide a number of different fringe benefits to employees on a tax-favored basis. Generally, you can deduct the insurance premiums or other payments you make on behalf of the employee, while the employee is not taxed on the value of the benefit provided. This is much more favorable than payments of salary to an employee, which are fully taxable.

In an unincorporated business, the payments made on behalf of the sole proprietor or partners for such benefits are generally not deductible as expenses of the business, in contrast to fringe benefits paid for by a corporation for its stockholder/employees. So the tax benefits of employee fringe benefits, such as those described below, are another reason for incorporating your business and becoming an employee of the corporation.

Note, however, that if your corporation is an S corporation, it will be treated much like a partnership for fringe benefit purposes.[18] Until 1991, that meant it was not allowed a deduction for any of the fringe benefits described below for any 2% or greater shareholder.

Then, in 1991, the IRS ruled that an S corporation may deduct the cost of medical insurance paid on behalf of more-than-2% shareholders. These shareholders must include such amounts in W-2 income — of which they may be able to deduct 25% in computing adjusted gross income, plus possibly deduct part of the remainder as itemized deductions.[19]

Presumably, similar treatment will also apply to disability and group-term life insurance premiums, except that neither will be deductible by the individual, unlike medical insurance. The major types of fringe benefit plans, other than retirement plans, that allow for tax deductions to the corporation and no taxable income to the employee are described below.

## Medical Insurance Plans

The corporation that maintains a medical insurance plan, such as Blue Cross or a prepaid health care plan, is permitted to deduct the premiums it pays to the insurer. In addition, the employee is not required to include either the cost of the premiums or the benefits provided by the insurer in his or her taxable income,[20] as a general rule.

## Self-Insured Medical Reimbursement Plans

A corporation can set up a plan under which the corporation directly reimburses employees for medical expenses or even for such expenses as dental care, orthodontic work, and prescription eyeglasses or contact lenses.[21] If the plan satisfies tax law requirements prohibiting discrimination in favor of highly paid employees,[22] the reimbursements paid can be deducted by the corporation and are not taxable to the recipients.

Such plans are often set up in addition to medical insurance plans, either to cover deductibles that the insurance does not pay or to cover particular types of medical or dental costs that the insurance plan does not provide for. Note that costs of cosmetic surgery are no longer deductible as medical expenses after 1990.

In the past, it was possible to set up a self-insured medical reimbursement plan so that it covered only the officers of the corporation. As the tax law now stands, such a plan would probably be considered discriminatory in most cases, and the reimbursements paid to the officers would, therefore, be taxable to them. Under present law, it will usually be necessary for a self-insured medical plan to cover most of the corporation's employees to qualify for favorable tax treatment.

Payment by a corporation of disability insurance premiums is deductible by the corporation and is not taxed to the employees covered by the insurance — except in the case of an S corporation.[23] Sole proprietorships and partnerships may not deduct premiums on disability coverage for the sole proprietor or partners.[24]

If an employee becomes disabled and receives disability benefits under a policy that the employer has paid the premiums for, the benefits will be included in the employee's income for tax purposes. Note that if an individual, such as a sole proprietor or partner, has paid his or her own premiums for disability insurance, any disability benefits received are tax-free.[25]

**Disability Insurance**

You may set up a group-term life insurance plan and deduct the insurance premiums you pay on behalf of your employees. To the extent the life insurance coverage on an employee does not exceed $50,000 under the plan during the taxable year, the premiums paid by you are not taxable income to the employee.[26]

Even to the extent an employee's coverage exceeds $50,000, the amount the employee must include in taxable income from the additional insurance premiums paid by you for the excess coverage is sometimes considerably less than the premium actually paid and deducted.

You cannot deduct the premiums for your own coverage under a group life insurance plan, since you are not considered an employee of the business for tax purposes. See Section 8.3 for a discussion of numerous other kinds of fringe benefit plans.

**Group-Term Life Insurance**

Another important tax advantage of a corporation (other than for an S corporation, discussed in the next section of this chapter) is that, in general, it can deduct 70% of the dividends it receives from stock investments from its federal taxable income.[27] Thus, if you use your corporation to accumulate profits at low corporate tax rates, as was suggested previously in this chapter, you may want to consider investing some of those accumulated funds in common stock or preferred stock of publicly traded U.S. corporations, since the dividends received by your corporation will be 70% tax-free, in most cases, or 80% if your corporation owns 20% or more of the stock of the company paying the dividend. For example, if your corporation receives $1,000 in dividends from an investment in General Motors stock, only $300 would be taxable for federal income tax purposes. Even if your corporation were in the 34% corporate tax bracket, the federal tax on those dividends would be 34% of $300, or $102, which is a maximum effective tax rate of only 10.2% on the dividends received.

Note, however, that this deduction will be reduced if your corporation borrows money, on which it pays interest, to purchase dividend-paying stocks.[28]

**Tax Break for Dividends Received by a Corporation**

Many states' corporation tax laws also permit a deduction for dividends received by a corporation.

**Corporate Income Tax Disadvantages**

While this chapter has outlined a number of important tax advantages of incorporating a business, the picture is not all that one-sided. There are also a number of significant potential tax problems that corporations may face. The potential disadvantages include:

- A maximum corporate tax rate that is now generally higher than the individual tax rate;
- Difficulties in withdrawing profits from the business without incurring double taxation;
- The accumulated earnings tax that may apply if profits are not withdrawn from the corporation or plowed back into the business; and
- The personal holding company tax, a 28% tax that may apply to the undistributed income of certain corporations that have too much passive income.[29]

Each of these potential tax disadvantages of corporations is discussed in more detail in Section 8.9. Note that most of the above disadvantages are not applicable if you elect S corporation status. Deciding whether to incorporate in this state or elsewhere is discussed in Section 9.12.

# 2.5  S Corporations

The first thing to understand clearly about S corporations (formerly referred to as Subchapter S corporations) is that they are no different than any other corporation under state law in terms of corporate law requirements, limited liability of shareholders, or any other aspect except tax treatment. In fact, some states do not even recognize S corporation elections for tax purposes. An S corporation is simply a regular corporation that meets certain requirements and which has to be treated somewhat like a partnership for federal tax purposes. See Section 11.2 for a discussion of how S corporations are taxed in this state, if at all.

Once a corporation has made an election with the IRS to be treated as an S corporation, its shareholders will generally report their share of the corporation's taxable income or loss on their individual tax returns. That is, the corporation "passes through" its income, or loss, and tax credits to the shareholders in proportion to their stock holdings in the corporation, much like a partnership.

The S corporation does not usually pay tax on any of its income.[30] Any domestic S corporation, however, must file *Form 1120S, U.S. Income Tax Return for an S Corporation*, regardless of any tax due. *Form 1120S* must be filed by March 15 if filing under a calendar year basis; or, the 15th day of the third month following the close of a fiscal year.

An S corporation must furnish a copy of *Schedule K, Shareholder's Share of Income, Credits, Deductions* to each shareholder. By not providing *Schedule K* before filing *Form 1120S*, the S corporation could incur penalties.

In certain instances, an S corporation may be subject to tax on "built-in gains." Built-in gains are untaxed gains on the assets of a corporation that would have been recognized as taxable if the assets had been sold at fair market value on the day a corporation became an S corporation. Profits are deemed to be distributed to the shareholders on the last day of the corporation's tax year, whether or not the profits are actually distributed.[31] Thus, if profits of an S corporation are distributed as dividends, the distribution itself is ordinarily not taxable, so that there is no double taxation of distributed profits.

The Tax Reform Act of 1986 has made S corporations a much more attractive form of doing business than before, due primarily to the fact that, for the first time within memory, the top corporate tax rate of 34% (or 39%) is higher than the top individual tax rate of 31% — top rates vary, see sections 2.4 and 2.6. Accordingly, an S corporation election is advisable for many more corporations now than in previous years.

To qualify for S corporation treatment, your corporation must meet the following requirements:

**S Corporation Requirements**

- It must be a domestic corporation, that is, incorporated in the United States.[32]
- No shareholder can be a nonresident alien individual.[33]
- All of its shareholders must generally be individuals, although certain trusts, called Qualified Subchapter S Trusts and Grantor Trusts, may hold stock under certain circumstances. No shareholder can be a corporation or a partnership.[34]
- The corporation can have only one class of common stock and no preferred stock.[35]
- There cannot be more than 35 shareholders.[36] For this purpose, a husband and wife who are both stockholders will be counted as only one stockholder, whether or not they hold the stock in joint ownership.[37]
- The corporation cannot be a member of an affiliated group of corporations.[38] If it owns stock in a subsidiary that is considered an affiliate, it may not be able to qualify under the S corporation provisions.
- Less than 25% of the corporation's gross receipts during three successive tax years must be from passive sources, such as interest income, dividends, rent, royalties, or proceeds from the sale of securities.[39] The passive income limit does not apply at all for a brand new corporation or an existing corporation that has no accumulated earnings and profits when it elects S corporation status.[40]

**Electing S Corporation
Status**

To become an S corporation, your company must meet the above requirements and file an election on *Form 2553* with the IRS. The election must be signed by all of the corporation's shareholders,[41] including your spouse, who may have a community property interest in stock that is in your name. The S corporation election must be filed during the first two months and 15 days of the corporation's tax year for which the election is to go into effect or at any time during the preceding tax year.[42]

Since a newly formed corporation that wants to start out as an S corporation does not have a preceding tax year, it has to file an election in the two-month and 15-day period after it is considered to have begun its first tax year. Its first tax year is considered to start when it issues stock to shareholders, acquires assets, or begins to do business, whichever occurs first. Filing of articles of incorporation with the secretary of state usually does not begin the first taxable year.

Care must be taken to file the election at the right time, which can be tricky, since it is sometimes difficult to determine when a corporation first begins to do business. There can be some horrendous tax consequences if you operate the corporation as though it were an S corporation, and the election is later determined to have been filed too early or too late.

Extreme care must also be taken if a regular C corporation elects to change over to S corporation status; this should not be done without consulting a competent tax adviser. A regular corporation that elects to become an S corporation will generally be subject to an eventual corporate-level tax on any built-in gains on its assets — assets with a value greater than their tax basis — if assets are sold for a gain within 10 years.

**Terminating an
S Corporation Election**

If it becomes desirable to revoke or terminate S corporation status after a few years, as is often the case, this can be done if shareholders owning more than half the stock sign and file a revocation form.[43] A revocation is effective for the tax year it is filed, if it is filed during the first two months and 15 days of that tax year.[44] If it is filed later in the year, it does not become effective until the next tax year.[45]

Doing anything, however, that causes the corporation to cease to qualify as an S corporation — such as selling stock to a corporate shareholder — will also terminate the election, effective on the first day after the corporation ceases to qualify as an S corporation. In that case, the company must file two short-period tax returns for the year, the first — up to the date it ceased to qualify — as an S corporation, the second as a regular taxable corporation. Once a corporation terminates an S corporation election, it cannot re-elect S corporation status for five years, unless it obtains the consent of the IRS.[46]

**Reasons for Electing
S Corporation Status**

For a corporation, electing S corporation status can be very advantageous in some instances, and less so, or even disadvantageous in other situations.

An S corporation election should not be made without the advice and assistance of a tax professional, since it is a very complex and technical area of the tax law.

Electing S corporation treatment for a corporation is usually most favorable in these types of situations:

- Where it is expected that the corporation will experience losses for the initial year or years of doing business and where the shareholders will have income from other sources that the "passed through" losses can shelter from tax. Note that if S corporation losses are passive losses — such as losses from real estate investments — they can only be used to offset other passive activity income.

- Where, because of the low tax brackets the shareholders are in, there will be tax savings if the anticipated profits of the corporation are passed through to them, rather than being taxed at higher corporate tax rates.

- Where the nature of the corporation's business is such that the corporation does not need to retain a major portion of profits in the business. In this case, all or most of the profits can be distributed as dividends without the double taxation that would occur if no S corporation election were in effect.

- Where a corporation is in danger of incurring an accumulated earnings penalty tax for failure to pay out its profits as dividends.

It will often be advantageous for your corporation to operate as an S corporation in its early years, when losses can be passed through to shareholders, or when income is not so great as to push the shareholders into higher tax brackets. Also, the nontax advantage of being incorporated and protected from personal liability if the business fails is generally most important during the early years of operation, when the risk of failure is highest.

Thus, many businesses initially start off as S corporations, obtaining the advantage of limited liability while being taxed much like an unincorporated business. Later, when or if the profit from the business becomes very substantial, the S corporation election can be terminated, and the C corporation can be used to split income between the corporation and its stockholder/employees.

## Disadvantages of S Corporation Election

While there are some significant advantages to operating as an S corporation, the S corporation election is frequently not advisable under some circumstances. Some of the possible disadvantages of operating your business in the form of an S corporation are:

- The change to S corporation status may eventually result in a large corporate-level tax on built-in gains or an immediate LIFO recapture tax.

- The tax law regarding S corporations is very complex and you should expect to pay fairly substantial additional legal or accounting fees to your tax adviser, compared to what would be necessary with a regular corporation.

- S corporations are now treated almost exactly like regular corporations with respect to pension and profit-sharing plans. One important difference remains; any employee who owns 5% or more of the stock and participates in the S corporation's pension or profit-sharing plan is prohibited from borrowing from the plan, unlike a participant in a regular corporation's retirement plan.[47]

- Certain built-in gains of an S corporation may be taxed to the corporation and the shareholder for federal tax purposes.[48]

- Fringe benefit payments for medical, disability, and group-term life insurance for 2% shareholders are deductible, to the corporation, but are taxable to the shareholder/employee.[49]

- Unlike many regular corporations, very few newly electing S corporations may now have a fiscal tax year that ends earlier than September.[50]

For your convenience, a sample of *Form 2553, Election by a Small Business Corporation,* and a summary of key characteristics regarding business organization forms are provided on the following pages.

## Recent Tax Changes for S Corporations

In *Publication 589, Tax Information on S Corporations*, the IRS points out two important changes for 1991 that all S corporations should know. These changes include:

- An increase in corporate estimated tax percentage. For tax years beginning in 1992, the annual estimated tax percentage for S corporations increases from 90%, wherever indicated, to 93%.

- An extension of certain credit provisions. Under the Tax Extension Act of 1991, the research credit, jobs credit, energy credit, and low-income housing credit have been extended through June 30, 1992.

For more information on these and other tax law changes, see *Publication 553, Highlights of 1991 Tax Changes.*

## Corporate Do's and Don'ts Checklist

### Do:

☐ Maintain capital reserves sufficient to meet reasonably foreseeable needs of the corporation, including liability insurance coverage.

☐ Maintain an active and independent board of directors.

☐ If asked to serve on a board of directors, be active and use your best independent business judgment even if that requires you to disagree with management.

☐ Use business cards and letterhead which reflect the corporate name.

☐ Make certain that corporate letters and agreements are signed by the corporation.

☐ Distinguish preincorporation activities by a promoter from post-incorporation activities by officers or directors.

☐ Use formal loan documents, including notes and security agreements, for corporate loans, especially to officers and directors and be sure to have a board resolution authorizing the transaction.

☐ Use written leases, purchase and sale agreements, and bills of sale in transactions involving shareholders, officers, and directors and be sure to have a board resolution authorizing the transaction.

☐ Use separate offices for activities of separate businesses.

☐ Use separate telephone lines for each business.

☐ Use separate employees for each business.

☐ Allow each corporation to own its own assets or equipment or lease them pursuant to written lease agreements.

☐ Apply for all required permits, licenses, and identification numbers in the corporate name.

☐ Obtain necessary business insurance in the corporate name.

### Don't:

☐ Commingle personal and corporate assets or assets among related corporations.

☐ Divert corporate assets for personal use.

☐ Engage in any act for an illegal or improper purpose such as to defraud creditors or oppress minority shareholders.

☐ Hold yourself out as the owner of the corporation; you may be a shareholder, officer, or director, but the corporation should be held out as the legal entity for the action.

☐ Engage in transactions between corporations and their shareholders, officers, and directors on any basis other than on an arm's length basis.

☐ If several corporations are involved, don't use the same people as officers and directors of each corporation.

For more information on protecting your personal limited liability, plus maintaining corporate formalities, see *The Essential Corporation Handbook*, by Carl R.J. Sniffen, from The Oasis Press® (800) 288-2275.

# 2.6 Summary of the Key Characteristics of the Various Legal Forms of

| | Proprietorship | General Partnership |
|---|---|---|
| **Simplicity in Operation and Formation** | Simplest to establish and operate. | Relatively simple, informal, but is usually desirable to have formal written agreement between partners. |
| **Liability for Debts, Taxes, and Other Claims** | Owner has unlimited personal liability. | Partners all have unlimited personal liability. |
| **Federal Income Taxation of Business Profits** | Taxed to the owner at individual tax rates of up to 31% or more, depending on exemptions and deductions which may phase out. | Taxed to partners at their individual tax rates. |
| **Double Taxation if Profits Withdrawn from Business** | No. | No. |
| **Deduction of Losses by Owners** | Yes. May be subject to "passive loss" restrictions. | Yes. |
| **Social Security Tax on Earnings of Owner from Business** | 15.3% of owner's self-employment earnings in 1992 on first $55,500 of income, plus 2.9% on earnings between $55,500 and $130,200, half of which is now deductible for income tax purposes. | 15.3% of each partner's share of self-employment earnings from the business in 1992 on up to $55,500 in earnings, plus 2.9% on earnings between $55,500 and $130,200, half of which is now deductible for income tax purposes on the partner's individual income tax return. |
| **Unemployment Taxes on Earnings of Owner from Business** | None. | None. |
| **Retirement Plans** | Keogh plan. Deductions, other features now generally the same as for corporate pension and profit-sharing plans. But proprietor cannot borrow from Keogh Plan. | Keogh plan. Same as for proprietorships. A 10% partner cannot borrow from Keogh Plan. |
| **Tax Treatment of Medical, Disability, and Group-Term Life Insurance on Owners** | Not deductible, except part of medical expenses may be an itemized deduction on owner's tax return, including medical insurance premiums. But 25% of medical insurance on owner now allowed as a deduction from adjusted gross income — at least until June 30, 1992.[51] | Not deductible, except part of medical expenses may be an itemized deduction on owner's tax return, including medical insurance premiums. But 25% of medical insurance on owner now allowed as a deduction from adjusted gross income — at least until June 30, 1992.[52] |
| **Taxation of Dividends Received on Investments** | Dividends received on stock investments are fully taxable to owner. | Dividends taxable to individual partners. See proprietorship. |

# Business Organization

| Limited Partnership | Regular Corporation | S Corporation |
|---|---|---|
| More complex and expensive to establish than other unincorporated forms of business. Requires written agreement and filing of certificate. Managed by general partners only. | Requires most formality in establishment and operation. | Same as a regular corporation but requires close oversight by a tax adviser (an additional cost). |
| General partners are personally liable; limited partners are liable only to the extent of their investment. | Stockholders are not generally liable for corporate debts, but often have to guarantee loans, as a practical matter, if the corporation borrows money. Also, corporate officers may be liable to the IRS for failure to withhold and pay withholding taxes on employees' wages. | Stockholders are not generally liable for corporate debts, but often have to guarantee loans, as a practical matter, if the corporation borrows money. Also, corporate officers may be liable to the IRS for failure to withhold and pay withholding taxes on employees' wages. |
| Taxed to partners at their individual tax rates. | Taxed to the corporation, at rates higher than those of individuals — maximum of 34% or 39% in 1992. | Taxed to individual owners at their individual rates — certain gains are taxable to the corporation as well. |
| No. | Yes, but not on reasonable compensation paid to owners who are employees of the corporation. | No, in general. |
| Yes. Limited partner's deductions generally cannot exceed the amount he or she has invested in a limited partnership interest — except for real estate, in some instances. Losses generally restricted by "passive loss" rules. | No. Corporation must carry over initial losses to offset future profits, if any. | Yes, in general, for federal tax purposes. But not for state tax purposes in all states. Loss for a shareholder limited to investment in stock plus amount loaned to the corporation. Losses may be subject to "passive loss" restrictions. |
| 15.3% of each partner's share of self-employment earnings from the business in 1992 on up to $55,500 in earnings, plus 2.9% on earnings between $55,500 and $130,200, half of which is now deductible for income tax purposes on the partner's individual income tax return. | Owner/employee of corporation pays 7.65% on his or her salary and corporation pays 7.65%. Total Social Security (FICA) tax on employer and employee is 15.3% of employee's first $55,500 of wages (in 1992). Employee and corporation each pay 1.45% on wages above $55,500, up to limit of $130,200. | Owner/employee of corporation pays 7.65% on his or her salary and corporation pays 7.65%. Total Social Security (FICA) tax on employer and employee is 15.3% of employee's first $55,500 of wages (in 1992). Employee and corporation each pay 1.45% on wages above $55,500, up to limit of $130,200. |
| None. | Yes. State and federal unemployment taxes apply to salaries paid to owners. | Yes. State and federal unemployment taxes apply to salaries paid to owners. |
| Keogh plan. Same as for proprietorships. A 10% partner cannot borrow from Keogh Plan. | Corporate retirement plans are no longer significantly better than Keogh plans. Deduction limits are same now as for Keogh, but participants can borrow from plan. | Plans now essentially identical to regular corporate retirement plans, except that shareholder/employee (5% shareholder) of S corporation cannot borrow from plan. |
| Not deductible, except part of medical expenses may be an itemized deduction on owner's tax return, including medical insurance premiums. But 25% of medical insurance on owner now allowed as a deduction from adjusted gross income — at least until June 30, 1992.[53] | Corporations may be allowed to deduct corporation medical insurance premium or reimbursements paid under medical reimbursement plan. Generally not taxable to the employee, even if employee is an owner. Similar treatment for disability and group-term life insurance plans. | Fringe benefits for 2% shareholders are deductible by corporation, but must be included in income of the shareholder who may be allowed to deduct 25% of medical insurance from adjusted gross income. |
| Dividends taxable to individual partners. See proprietorship. | Dividends are taxable to the corporation. However, 70% of the dividends received are generally free of federal income tax (unless stock is purchased with borrowed money), an important tax advantage. | Dividends taxable to individual shareholders of the S corporation, as in the case of a partnership. |

# Footnotes

1. I.R.C. §§ 3301(1) and 3302(b).
2. I.R.C. § 3306(b)(1).
3. I.R.C. § 162(l).
4. I.R.C. §§ 444 and 7519.
5. I.R.C. § 6050K.
6. I.R.C. § 11(b)(2).
7. I.R.C. § 535(c)(2).
8. I.R.C. § 531.
9. I.R.C. § 1366(e).
10. I.R.C. § 1(g).
11. I.R.C. § 4975(d) (last paragraph).
12. I.R.C. § 219.
13. I.R.C. § 219(g).
14. I.R.C. § 219(g)(3).
15. I.R.C. §§ 219 and 404(a).
16. I.R.C. § 501(a).
17. I.R.C. § 402(e).
18. I.R.C. § 1372(a).
19. Rev. Rul. 91-26, 1991-15 I.R.B.
20. I.R.C. §§ 105–106.
21. I.R.C. § 105(b).
22. I.R.C. § 105.
23. I.R.C. § 106.
24. I.R.C. § 105(g).
25. I.R.C. § 104(a)(3).
26. I.R.C. § 79(a).
27. I.R.C. § 243(a).
28. I.R.C. § 246A.
29. I.R.C. § 541.
30. I.R.C. § 1374.
31. I.R.C. § 1366.
32. I.R.C. § 1361(b).
33. I.R.C. § 1361(b)(1)(C).
34. I.R.C. § 1361(b)(1)(B).
35. I.R.C. § 1361(b)(1)(D).
36. I.R.C. § 1361(b)(1)(A).
37. I.R.C. § 1361(c).
38. I.R.C. § 1361(b)(2)(A).
39. I.R.C. § 1362(d)(3).
40. I.R.C. § 1362(d)(3)(B).
41. I.R.C. § 1362(a)(2).
42. I.R.C. § 1362(b).
43. I.R.C. § 1362(d)(1)(B).
44. I.R.C. § 1362(d)(1)(C)(i).
45. I.R.C. § 1362(d)(i)(C)(ii).
46. I.R.C. § 1362(g).
47. I.R.C. § 4975(d).
48. I.R.C. § 1374(a).
49. Rev. Rul. 91-26, 1991-15 I.R.B.
50. I.R.C. § 1378(a).
51. I.R.C. § 162(l).
52. Id.
53. Id.

# Department of the Treasury
## Internal Revenue Service

# Instructions for Form 2553
## (Revised December 1990)

### Election by a Small Business Corporation

*(Section references are to the Internal Revenue Code unless otherwise noted.)*

**Paperwork Reduction Act Notice.**—We ask for the information on this form to carry out the Internal Revenue laws of the United States. You are required to give us the information. We need it to ensure that you are complying with these laws and to allow us to figure and collect the right amount of tax.

The time needed to complete and file this form will vary depending on individual circumstances. The estimated average time is:

**Recordkeeping** . . . .6 hrs., 28 min.
**Learning about the law or the form** . . . .3 hrs., 16 min.
**Preparing, copying, assembling, and sending the form to IRS** . . . .3 hrs., 31 min.

If you have comments concerning the accuracy of these time estimates or suggestions for making this form more simple, we would be happy to hear from you. You can write to both the **Internal Revenue Service,** Washington, DC 20224, Attention: IRS Reports Clearance Officer, T:FP, and the **Office of Management and Budget,** Paperwork Reduction Project (1545-0146), Washington, DC 20503. **DO NOT** send the tax form to either of these offices. Instead, see the instructions below for information on where to file.

## General Instructions

**A. Purpose.**—To elect to be treated as an "S Corporation," a corporation must file Form 2553. The election permits the income of the S corporation to be taxed to the shareholders of the corporation rather than to the corporation itself, except as provided in Subchapter S of the Code. For more information, see **Publication 589,** Tax Information on S Corporations.

**B. Who May Elect.**—Your corporation may make the election to be treated as an S corporation only if it meets **all** of the following tests:

1. It is a domestic corporation.

2. It has no more than 35 shareholders. A husband and wife (and their estates) are treated as one shareholder for this requirement. All other persons are treated as separate shareholders.

3. It has only individuals, estates, or certain trusts as shareholders. See the instructions for Part III regarding qualified subchapter S trusts.

4. It has no nonresident alien shareholders.

5. It has only one class of stock. See sections 1361(c)(4) and (5) for additional details.

6. It is not one of the following ineligible corporations:

(a) a corporation that owns 80% or more of the stock of another corporation, unless the other corporation has not begun business and has no gross income;

(b) a bank or thrift institution;

(c) an insurance company subject to tax under the special rules of Subchapter L of the Code;

(d) a corporation that has elected to be treated as a possessions corporation under section 936; or

(e) a domestic international sales corporation (DISC) or former DISC.

See section 1361(b)(2) for details.

7. It has a permitted tax year as required by section 1378 or makes a section 444 election to have a tax year other than a permitted tax year. Section 1378 defines a permitted tax year as a tax year ending December 31, or any other tax year for which the corporation establishes a business purpose to the satisfaction of the IRS. See Part II for details on requesting a fiscal tax year based on a business purpose or on making a section 444 election.

8. Each shareholder consents as explained in the instructions for Column K.

See sections 1361, 1362, and 1378 for additional information on the above tests.

**C. Where To File.**—File this election with the Internal Revenue Service Center listed below.

| If the corporation's principal business, office, or agency is located in  | Use the following Internal Revenue Service Center address ▼ |
|---|---|
| New Jersey, New York (New York City and counties of Nassau, Rockland, Suffolk, and Westchester) | Holtsville, NY 00501 |
| New York (all other counties), Connecticut, Maine, Massachusetts, New Hampshire, Rhode Island, Vermont | Andover, MA 05501 |
| Florida, Georgia, South Carolina | Atlanta, GA 39901 |
| Indiana, Kentucky, Michigan, Ohio, West Virginia | Cincinnati, OH 45999 |
| Kansas, New Mexico, Oklahoma, Texas | Austin, TX 73301 |
| Alaska, Arizona, California (counties of Alpine, Amador, Butte, Calaveras, Colusa, Contra Costa, Del Norte, El Dorado, Glenn, Humboldt, Lake, Lassen, Marin, Mendocino, Modoc, Napa, Nevada, Placer, Plumas, Sacramento, San Joaquin, Shasta, Sierra, Siskiyou, Solano, Sonoma, Sutter, Tehama, Trinity, Yolo, and Yuba), Colorado, Idaho, Montana, Nebraska, Nevada, North Dakota, Oregon, South Dakota, Utah, Washington, Wyoming | Ogden, UT 84201 |
| California (all other counties), Hawaii | Fresno, CA 93888 |
| Illinois, Iowa, Minnesota, Missouri, Wisconsin | Kansas City, MO 64999 |
| Alabama, Arkansas, Louisiana, Mississippi, North Carolina, Tennessee | Memphis, TN 37501 |
| Delaware, District of Columbia, Maryland, Pennsylvania, Virginia | Philadelphia, PA 19255 |

**D. When To Make the Election.**—Complete Form 2553 and file it either: **(1)** at any time during that portion of the first tax year the election is to take effect which occurs before the 16th day of the third month of that tax year (if the tax year has 2½ months or less, and the election is made not later than 2 months and 15 days after the first day of the tax year, it shall be treated as timely made during such year), or **(2)** in the tax year before the first tax year it is to take effect. An election made by a small business corporation after the 15th day of the third month but before the end of the tax year is treated as made for the next year. For example, if a calendar tax year corporation makes the election in April 1991, it is effective for the corporation's 1992 calendar tax year. See section 1362(b) for more information.

**E. Acceptance or Non-Acceptance of Election.**—The Service Center will notify you if your election is accepted and when it will take effect. You will also be notified if your election is not accepted. You should generally receive a determination on your election within 60 days after you have filed Form 2553. If the Q1 box in Part II is checked on page 2, the corporation will receive a ruling letter from IRS in Washington, DC, which approves or denies the selected tax year. When Item Q1 is checked, it will generally take an additional 90 days for the Form 2553 to be accepted.

Do not file Form 1120S until you are notified that your election is accepted. If you are now required to file **Form 1120,** U.S. Corporation Income Tax Return, or any other applicable tax return, continue filing it until your election takes effect.

Care should be exercised to ensure that the election is received by the Internal Revenue Service. If you are not notified of acceptance or nonacceptance of your election within 3 months of date of filing (date mailed), or within 6 months if Part II, Item Q1, is checked, you should take follow-up action by corresponding with the Service Center where the election was filed. If filing of Form 2553 is questioned by IRS, an acceptable proof of filing is: **(1)** certified receipt (timely filed); **(2)** Form 2553 with accepted stamp; **(3)** Form 2553 with stamped IRS received date; or **(4)** IRS letter stating that Form 2553 had been accepted.

**F. End of Election.**—Once the election is made, it stays in effect for all years until it is terminated. During the 5 years after the election is terminated under section 1362(d), the corporation can make another election on Form 2553 only with IRS consent.

# Specific Instructions

## Part I

Part I must be completed by all corporations.

**Name and Address of Corporation.**—Enter the true corporate name as set forth in the corporate charter or other legal document creating it. If the corporation's mailing address is the same as someone else's, such as a shareholder's, please enter this person's name below the name of the corporation. Include the suite, room, or other unit number after the street address. If the Post Office does not deliver to the street address and the corporation has a P.O. box, show the P.O. box number instead of the street address. If the corporation has changed its name or address since applying for its EIN (filing Form SS-4), be sure to check the box in item F of Part I.

**A. Employer Identification Number.**—If you have applied for an employer identification number (EIN) but have not received it, enter "applied for." If the corporation does not have an EIN, you should apply for one on **Form SS-4**, Application for Employer Identification Number, available from most IRS and Social Security Administration offices.

**C. Effective Date of Election.**—Enter the beginning effective date (month, day, year) of the tax year that you have requested for the S corporation. Generally, this will be the beginning date of the tax year for which the ending effective date is required to be shown in item I, Part I. For a new corporation (first year the corporation exists) it will generally be the date required to be shown in item H, Part I. The tax year of a new corporation starts on the date that it has shareholders, acquires assets, or begins doing business, whichever happens first. If the effective date for item C for a newly formed corporation is later than the date in item H, the corporation should file Form 1120 or Form 1120-A, for the tax period between these dates.

**Column K. Shareholders' Consent Statement.**—Each shareholder who owns (or is deemed to own) stock at the time the election is made must consent to the election. If the election is made during the corporation's first tax year for which it is effective, any person who held stock at any time during the portion of that year which occurs before the time the election is made, must consent to the election although the person may have sold or transferred his or her stock before the election is made. Each shareholder consents by signing and dating in column K or signing and dating a separate consent statement described below. If stock is owned by a trust that is a qualified shareholder, the deemed owner of the trust must consent. See section 1361(c)(2) for details regarding qualified trusts that may be shareholders and rules on determining who is the deemed owner of the trust.

An election made during the first 2½ months of the tax year is considered made for the following tax year if one or more of the persons who held stock in the corporation during such tax year and before the election was made did not consent to the election. See section 1362(b)(2).

If a husband and wife have a community interest in the stock or in the income from it, both must consent. Each tenant in common, joint tenant, and tenant by the entirety also must consent.

A minor's consent is made by the minor or the legal representative of the minor, or by a natural or adoptive parent of the minor if no legal representative has been appointed. The consent of an estate is made by an executor or administrator.

**Continuation sheet or separate consent statement.**—If you need a continuation sheet or use a separate consent statement, attach it to Form 2553. The separate consent statement must contain the name, address, and employer identification number of the corporation and the shareholder information requested in columns J through N of Part I.

If you want, you may combine all the shareholders' consents in one statement.

**Column L.**—Enter the number of shares of stock each shareholder owns and the dates the stock was acquired. If the election is made during the corporation's first tax year for which it is effective, do not list the shares of stock for those shareholders who sold or transferred all of their stock before the election was made. However, these shareholders must still consent to the election for it to be effective for the tax year.

**Column M.**—Enter the social security number of each shareholder who is an individual. Enter the employer identification number of each shareholder that is an estate or a qualified trust.

**Column N.**—Enter the month and day that each shareholder's tax year ends. If a shareholder is changing his or her tax year, enter the tax year the shareholder is changing to, and attach an explanation indicating the present tax year and the basis for the change (e.g., automatic revenue procedure or letter ruling request).

If the election is made during the corporation's first tax year for which it is effective, you do not have to enter the tax year of any shareholder who sold or transferred all of his or her stock before the election was made.

**Signature.**—Form 2553 must be signed by the president, treasurer, assistant treasurer, chief accounting officer, or other corporate officer (such as tax officer) authorized to sign.

## Part II

Complete Part II if you selected a tax year ending on any date other than December 31 (other than a 52-53-week tax year ending with reference to the month of December).

**Box P1.**—Attach a statement showing separately for each month the amount of gross receipts for the most recent 47 months as required by section 4.03(3) of

Revenue Procedure 87-32, 1987-2 C.B. 396. A corporation that does not have a 47-month period of gross receipts cannot establish a natural business year under section 4.01(1).

**Box Q1.**—For examples of an acceptable business purpose for requesting a fiscal tax year, see Revenue Ruling 87-57, 1987-2 C.B. 117.

In addition to a statement showing the business purpose for the requested fiscal year, you must attach the other information necessary to meet the ruling request requirements of Revenue Procedure 90-1, 1990-1 C.B. 356 (updated annually). Also attach a statement that shows separately the amount of gross receipts from sales or services (and inventory costs, if applicable) for each of the 36 months preceding the effective date of the election to be an S corporation. If the corporation has been in existence for fewer than 36 months, submit figures for the period of existence.

If you check box Q1, you must also pay a user fee of $200 (subject to change). Do not pay the fee when filing Form 2553. The Service Center will send Form 2553 to the IRS in Washington, DC, who, in turn, will notify the corporation that the fee is due. See Revenue Procedure 90-17, 1990-1 C.B. 479.

**Box Q2.**—If the corporation makes a back-up section 444 election for which it is qualified, then the election must be exercised in the event the business purpose request is not approved. Under certain circumstances, the tax year requested under the back-up section 444 election may be different than the tax year requested under business purpose. See **Form 8716**, Election To Have a Tax Year Other Than a Required Tax Year, for details on making a back-up section 444 election.

**Boxes Q2 and R2.**—If the corporation is not qualified to make the section 444 election after making the item Q2 back-up section 444 election or indicating its intention to make the election in item R1, and therefore it later files a calendar year return, it should write "Section 444 Election Not Made" in the top left corner of the 1st calendar year Form 1120S it files.

## Part III

Certain Qualified Subchapter S Trusts (QSSTs) may make the QSST election required by section 1361(d)(2) in Part III. Part III may be used to make the QSST election only if corporate stock has been transferred to the trust on or before the date on which the corporation makes its election to be an S corporation. However, a statement can be used in lieu of Part III to make the election.

**Note:** *Part III may be used only in conjunction with making the Part I election (i.e., Form 2553 cannot be filed with only Part III completed).*

The deemed owner of the QSST must also consent to the S corporation election in column K, page 1, of Form 2553. See section 1361(c)(2).

*U.S. GPO:1991-518-941/20363

Form **2553**

(Rev. December 1990)

Department of the Treasury
Internal Revenue Service

# Election by a Small Business Corporation

(Under section 1362 of the Internal Revenue Code)

▶ **For Paperwork Reduction Act Notice, see page 1 of instructions.**
▶ **See separate instructions.**

OMB No. 1545-0146

Expires 11-30-93

**SAMPLE**

**Notes:**  1.  This election, to be treated as an "S corporation," can be accepted only if all the tests in General Instruction B are met; all signatures in Parts I and III are originals (no photocopies); and the exact name and address of the corporation and other required form information are provided.

2.  Do not file Form 1120S until you are notified that your election is accepted. See General Instruction E.

## Part I   Election Information

*Please Type or Print*

| Name of corporation (see instructions) | **A** Employer identification number (see instructions) |
|---|---|
| Number, street, and room or suite no. (If a P.O. box, see instructions.) | **B** Name and telephone number (including area code) of corporate officer or legal representative who may be called for information |
| City or town, state, and ZIP code | **C** Election is to be effective for tax year beginning (month, day, year) |

**D**  Is the corporation the outgrowth or continuation of any form of predecessor? . . ☐ **Yes** ☐ **No**

If "Yes," state name of predecessor, type of organization, and period of its existence ▶ .........................

**E** Date of incorporation

**F**  Check here ▶ ☐ if the corporation has changed its name or address since applying for the employer identification number shown in item A above.

**G** State of incorporation

**H**  If this election takes effect for the first tax year the corporation exists, enter month, day, and year of the **earliest** of the following: (1) date the corporation first had shareholders, (2) date the corporation first had assets, or (3) date the corporation began doing business. ▶

**I**  Selected tax year: Annual return will be filed for tax year ending (month and day) ▶ .............................

If the tax year ends on any date other than December 31, except for an automatic 52-53-week tax year ending with reference to the month of December, you **must** complete Part II on the back. If the date you enter is the ending date of an automatic 52-53-week tax year, write "52-53-week year" to the right of the date. See Temporary Regulations section 1.441-2T(e)(3).

| **J** Name of each shareholder, person having a community property interest in the corporation's stock, and each tenant in common, joint tenant, and tenant by the entirety. (A husband and wife (and their estates) are counted as one shareholder in determining the number of shareholders without regard to the manner in which the stock is owned.) | **K** Shareholders' Consent Statement. We, the undersigned shareholders, consent to the corporation's election to be treated as an "S corporation" under section 1362(a). (Shareholders sign and date below.)* | | **L** Stock owned | | **M** Social security number or employer identification number (see instructions) | **N** Shareholder's tax year ends (month and day) |
|---|---|---|---|---|---|---|
| | Signature | Date | Number of shares | Dates acquired | | |
| | | | | | | |
| | | | | | | |
| | | | | | | |
| | | | | | | |
| | | | | | | |
| | | | | | | |
| | | | | | | |
| | | | | | | |

*For this election to be valid, the consent of each shareholder, person having a community property interest in the corporation's stock, and each tenant in common, joint tenant, and tenant by the entirety must either appear above or be attached to this form. (See instructions for Column K if continuation sheet or a separate consent statement is needed.)

Under penalties of perjury, I declare that I have examined this election, including accompanying schedules and statements, and to the best of my knowledge and belief, it is true, correct, and complete.

**Signature of officer** ▶                     **Title** ▶                     **Date** ▶

**See Parts II and III on back.**

Form **2553** (Rev. 12-90)

**Part II**  Selection of Fiscal Tax Year (All corporations using this Part must complete Item O and one of Items P, Q, or R.)

**O**  Check the applicable box below to indicate whether the corporation is:

1. ☐ A new corporation adopting the tax year entered in item I, Part I.

2. ☐ An existing corporation retaining the tax year entered in item I, Part I.

3. ☐ An existing corporation changing to the tax year entered in item I, Part I.

**P**  Complete item P if the corporation is using the expeditious approval provisions of Revenue Procedure 87-32, 1987-2 C.B. 396, to request: **(1)** a natural business year (as defined in section 4.01(1) of Rev. Proc. 87-32), or **(2)** a year that satisfies the ownership tax year test in section 4.01(2) of Rev. Proc. 87-32. Check the applicable box below to indicate the representation statement the corporation is making as required under section 4 of Rev. Proc. 87-32.

1. Natural Business Year ► ☐ I represent that the corporation is retaining or changing to a tax year that coincides with its natural business year as defined in section 4.01(1) of Rev. Proc. 87-32 and as verified by its satisfaction of the requirements of section 4.02(1) of Rev. Proc. 87-32. In addition, if the corporation is changing to a natural business year as defined in section 4.01(1), I further represent that such tax year results in less deferral of income to the owners than the corporation's present tax year. I also represent that the corporation is not described in section 3.01(2) of Rev. Proc. 87-32. (See instructions for additional information that must be attached.)

2. Ownership Tax Year ► ☐ I represent that shareholders holding more than half of the shares of the stock (as of the first day of the tax year to which the request relates) of the corporation have the same tax year or are concurrently changing to the tax year that the corporation adopts, retains, or changes to per item I, Part I. I also represent that the corporation is not described in section 3.01(2) of Rev. Proc. 87-32.

**Note:** *If you do not use item P and the corporation wants a fiscal tax year, complete either item Q or R below. Item Q is used to request a fiscal tax year based on a business purpose and to make a back-up section 444 election. Item R is used to make a regular section 444 election.*

**Q**  Business Purpose—To request a fiscal tax year based on a business purpose, you must check box Q1 and pay a user fee. See instructions for details. You may also check box Q2 and/or box Q3.

1. Check here ► ☐ if the fiscal year entered in item I, Part I, is requested under the provisions of section 6.03 of Rev. Proc. 87-32. Attach to Form 2553 a statement showing the business purpose for the requested fiscal year. See instructions for additional information that must be attached.

2. Check here ► ☐ to show that the corporation intends to make a back-up section 444 election in the event the corporation's business purpose request is not approved by the IRS. (See instructions for more information.)

3. Check here ► ☐ to show that the corporation agrees to adopt or change to a tax year ending December 31 if necessary for the IRS to accept this election for S corporation status in the event: (1) the corporation's business purpose request is not approved and the corporation makes a back-up section 444 election, but is ultimately not qualified to make a section 444 election, or (2) the corporation's business purpose request is not approved and the corporation did not make a back-up section 444 election.

**R**  Section 444 Election—To make a section 444 election, you must check box R1 and you may also check box R2.

1. Check here ► ☐ to show the corporation will make, if qualified, a section 444 election to have the fiscal tax year shown in item I, Part I. To make the election, you must complete **Form 8716,** Election To Have a Tax Year Other Than a Required Tax Year, and either attach it to Form 2553 or file it separately.

2. Check here ► ☐ to show that the corporation agrees to adopt or change to a tax year ending December 31 if necessary for the IRS to accept this election for S corporation status in the event the corporation is ultimately not qualified to make a section 444 election.

**Part III**  Qualified Subchapter S Trust (QSST) Election Under Section 1361(d)(2)**

| Income beneficiary's name and address | Social security number |
|---|---|
| Trust's name and address | Employer identification number |

Date on which stock of the corporation was transferred to the trust (month, day, year) ►

In order for the trust named above to be a QSST and thus a qualifying shareholder of the S corporation for which this Form 2553 is filed, I hereby make the election under section 1361(d)(2). Under penalties of perjury, I certify that the trust meets the definition requirements of section 1361(d)(3) and that all other information provided in Part III is true, correct, and complete.

_____     _____
Signature of income beneficiary or signature and title of legal representative or other qualified person making the election              Date

**Use of Part III to make the QSST election may be made only if stock of the corporation has been transferred to the trust on or before the date on which the corporation makes its election to be an S corporation. The QSST election must be made and filed separately if stock of the corporation is transferred to the trust after the date on which the corporation makes the S election.

*U.S. GPO:1991-518-943/20365

Chapter 3

# Buying an Existing Business

*Trust in Allah. But always tie your camel.*
— Arab proverb

## 3.1 General Considerations

Obviously, it may not be necessary for you to build your business from the ground up. If you wish to go into a particular type of business, you may find an appropriate existing business that is for sale. Buying an existing business can have considerable advantages over starting one from scratch, and one of the most important of these is the chance to start out with an established customer base. It is also sometimes possible to have the seller stay on as an employee or consultant for a transitional period to help you become familiar with the operation of the business.

Other advantages of purchasing a going business include:

- You may be able to take a regular draw or salary right from the start, if it is a profitable operation. This is usually not the case in a start-up operation, which typically starts off losing money.

- Your risk is frequently less when you buy an established, profitable business. You know that it has a viable market if it is already profitable. Your main risks are that something will change, such as new competition or product obsolescence, that will adversely affect the business after you acquire it. Another risk is that you will mismanage it.

- Getting started is simpler. By buying an established business, you can focus your attention on giving good service and operating profitably. Since most facilities, operating systems, and employees will already be in place, your efforts will not be diluted by remodeling the premises, trying to hire employees, setting up accounting systems, acquiring initial inventory, and the like. With an existing business, in most cases, you should be able to step right into an operation that has already been established by someone else.

While there are some definite advantages to buying an established business, as compared to starting a new business from nothing, it can also be a lot more complicated and involves many potential pitfalls that you must avoid. The watchword in buying any kind of business should be *caveat emptor* — let the buyer beware.

Because the process of buying and selling businesses is very complicated even for experts, do not attempt it without retaining the services of a reliable attorney and, usually, a good accountant. Even skilled professionals, however, can generally only protect you from certain legal, financial, or tax pitfalls that arise in connection with the purchase of a business. Many of the potential problems that would not become obvious until it is too late can only be spotted in advance, if at all, by the exercise of your good judgment and as a result of your doing the necessary homework. Important pitfalls you should look out for in connection with buying an existing business are discussed in Section 3.3.

## 3.2  Finding a Business for Sale

How do you go about finding a business that is for sale? There are a number of ways to approach the problem, none of which are ideal, so you will probably want to use two or more of the approaches discussed below to find and buy an existing business.

**Advertisements**

The business opportunities section of your local newspaper, regional magazine, or trade association journal can be a major source of leads to businesses that are for sale. Such ads often do not tell you very much about the nature of the business, but at least they can be a starting point in your search. In many cases, the ads will have been placed by a business broker rather than the owner. The business broker will often be representing people who are seeking to sell their business.

**Business Brokers and Realtors**

Business brokers and realtors can be excellent sources to contact in your search for a business that is for sale. The main drawback of going through a business broker or realtor is that their fee (paid by the seller) is usually a percentage, often 10%, of the sales price of the business; so they, like the seller, are trying to get the highest possible price for the business. At the same time, the seller will usually want more than he or she would if the sale were made without a broker, since he or she knows that the broker will take a healthy commission out of the negotiated sales price.

Your local chamber of commerce can usually tell you a great deal about the local business community and also provide you with leads to firms that are for sale.

**Local Chambers of Commerce**

Often professionals, such as accountants, attorneys, and bankers, can provide leads regarding good businesses even before they are on the market. Frequently, a business client will tell his or her accountant, attorney, or banker that he or she is planning to sell out or retire, long before making any formal attempt to put the business up for sale. So, if you have friends who are accountants, attorneys, or bankers, take them to lunch and tell them what you have in mind. Typically, they will have a vested interest in finding a friendly buyer for a retiring client's business, since they may loose that account if the firm is sold to buyers who have their own professional advisers.

**Accountants, Attorneys, and Bankers**

Certified public accountants (CPAs) can be excellent sources of leads. Not only will they usually not charge you any kind of finder's fee, but they usually know which of their clients' businesses are little gold mines. In some cases, a CPA who has a very profitable client who wishes to sell out may even want to go into the business with you as a financial partner, leaving the day-to-day operations to you. In those cases, you can generally be sure that if the CPA is putting up his or her money, he or she has studied the client's business carefully and feels that it is a real money-maker. In short, the CPA will have already done much of the prescreening for you.

Often, if you see a small business that you think you might like to buy, the simplest approach will be to talk to the owner and see if he or she is interested in selling. While an owner may have had no serious thoughts about selling the business before, the appearance of an interested potential buyer is not only somewhat flattering, but it may even cause him or her to decide to sell out to you. Many businesses are bought and sold this way.

**The Direct Approach**

## 3.3 What to Look for Before You Leap

One of the first questions you may want to ask is: "Why are you selling your business?" Often the response will be that the owner wants to retire or is in poor health. While such an explanation may be true in many cases, it is also quite likely to be a well-rehearsed cover story. The real reason may be that the business is in a declining neighborhood, and the owner has been robbed several times recently and wants out. Or, the owners of a profitable little corner grocery store may be anxious to sell out while they can because they have learned that a major chain-store

**Why Is the Business for Sale?**

supermarket will be opening in the neighborhood in a few months. Another common reason behind a planned sale is that the business is either losing money or is not sufficiently profitable to make continuing worthwhile.

Whatever the real reason behind the owner's attempt to sell the business, you are unlikely to discover it without rolling up your sleeves and doing some independent and in-depth investigation.

Perhaps the best way to find that needle in the haystack is to talk to a number of other business people in the vicinity of the business you are investigating, particularly competitors in the same business. The firm's suppliers can also be a source of important information.

Even if you are very diligent and thorough, you may not be able to discover the hidden reason — if there is one — underlying the owner's desire to sell out. You may simply have to rely on your intuition in deciding whether the seller's reason for getting out of the business is the real reason. Just remember that in most cases a good and profitable small business is not something that most people walk away from, unless there is a very good reason to do so or the price offered is too good to turn down.

## What Kind of Reputation Does the Firm Have?

One of the great advantages of taking over an existing business can be the opportunity to enjoy the reputation and goodwill that the existing owner has built up with customers and suppliers over the years. On the other hand, you may be much better off starting your own business from scratch than acquiring a business that has a poor reputation because of inferior work or merchandise or inferior service. It could take you years of hard work and reduced profits to overcome a former owner's poor reputation.

Even if the present owner has an excellent business reputation, you will want to know whether or not that goodwill is based on personal relationships built up between the owner and customers. These types of relationships aren't easily transferable. If the business relies heavily on a few key customers with whom the owner has very favorable business arrangements based on personal relationships, you may find that those business arrangements could be lost when you attempt to take the owner's place. In short, satisfy yourself that the goodwill you are buying is not based solely on personal relationships.

## How Profitable Is the Business Now?

Unless you have some very good reasons to believe that you can operate the business more profitably than the current owner, you should not purchase a going business that does not produce a satisfactory profit under its current ownership. Thus, it is extremely important to find out how the business has fared financially for the last few years. This is where the services of a good accountant, who has knowledge of the particular type of business, will be invaluable.

You should insist on having the seller make available the business' financial and business records to your accountant. Be particularly wary of a business that keeps poor records. Often the most reliable sources of financial information can be the owner's income tax and sales tax returns, since it is not very likely that a business owner will report more income than actually earned for tax purposes.

If the owner is not willing to make financial records available, make it clear that you are not willing to negotiate any further. Buying a business is a lot like buying a used car; you want to make sure it runs before you pay for it.

**Assets and Liabilities**

You will need to review both the tangible and intangible assets of the business to see if they are worth the price you will be paying and also to determine just what assets you will be acquiring under the sales agreement. Personally inspect the business premises, and look for things like obsolete or unsalable inventory, out-of-date or rundown equipment, or furniture or fixtures that you may have to repair or replace. Also, determine whether the business is able to expand at its present location or if it is already too cramped. What you determine might require you to buy or lease additional facilities, if you wish to expand.

Review the terms of any leases. Some businesses close because of the imminent expiration of a favorable long-term lease or because the landlord plans to either raise the rent drastically or not renew the lease at all when the current lease expires.

If you will be acquiring the accounts receivable of the business, review them in detail. An aging of the accounts should be performed to determine how long various receivables have been outstanding. As a general rule, the longer a given receivable has been outstanding, the more likely it will prove to be uncollectible.

If a few large accounts of credit customers make up a significant portion of the receivables, you will want to particularly focus on those accounts and perhaps even have credit checks run on those customers. The bankruptcy of a major credit customer can ruin an otherwise successful business.

Part of your job in investigating a business that you want to buy is to find out what makes it tick — and make sure you will be getting whatever it is. For example, a business that has well-developed customer or mailing lists should ordinarily include those lists in the sales agreement. If there is a favorable lease, make sure it can and will be assigned to you. If patents, trademarks, trade names, or certain skilled employees are vital to the business, be sure that you will get them as part of the package. Also, you need to be aware of potential problems with the government that the seller is experiencing or expects to experience in the near future, such as zoning problems or new environmental restrictions that may hamper the business' profitability.

**Hidden Liabilities**

Liabilities of the business may not always show up on its accounting records. There may be any number of hidden claims against the business, such as security agreements encumbering the accounts receivable, inventory, or equipment, unpaid back taxes of various kinds, undisclosed lawsuits or potential lawsuits, or simply unpaid bills. If you are going to assume the liabilities of the business, the written agreement of sale should specify exactly which liabilities are being assumed and the dollar amount of each.

Other examples of hidden liabilities to look out for are:

- Pension liabilities — You may be taking on significant termination liability as a successor employer if the seller maintains or contributes to a pension fund and has unfunded pension fund liabilities.

- Vacation liability — If you are a successor employer, you may be liable for accrued but unpaid vacation leave of employees, which can be a significant hidden liability in some cases.

- Environmental problems — In many instances, current trend in the law is to impose liability for past environmental abuses on current land owners or lessors. Many banks and savings and loans have recently learned about this the hard way, after foreclosing on land which had been contaminated over the years by toxic substances and being held liable for clean-up costs as the contamination problems came to light. Many companies, when buying land or other companies that own land, now require the sellers to make detailed representations and warranties concerning environmental matters and to undertake extensive and costly environmental audits as a condition to buying a business. See Section 9.9 for a more detailed discussion of these issues.

If you intend to buy a corporation, you will be well-advised to buy the business assets from the corporation rather than purchase the stock of the corporation itself. The latter approach will subject the business to all hidden or contingent liabilities of the old corporation, whether or not you have agreed to pay for any liabilities of the corporation that pre-dated the sale.

One exception to this general rule would be a corporation that had substantial tax loss or tax credit carryovers that you might be able to utilize if you bought the stock of the corporation rather than the assets. Be aware, however, that the tax law is a mine field when it comes to taking over someone else's tax loss or credit carryovers, so be certain before you do so that you seek good tax advice from a tax attorney or tax accountant, or you may find that the carryovers you thought you were acquiring have evaporated like a mirage.

Note that under the provisions of the Tax Reform Act of 1986, a change in ownership of more than 50% of the stock of a corporation in a three-year period will generally result in a severe restriction on the amount of its prior net operating losses that can be deducted in any subsequent taxable year.

# 3.4  Should You Consider a Franchise Operation?

Many small businesses, particularly fast food restaurants and print shops, are operated under franchises from a large national company. There can be substantial advantages to operating a franchised business, such as the benefits of national advertising, training programs, and assistance in setting up and running the business. If you are investigating a franchise, determine whether the franchise can be transferred to you, and if so, provide for the transfer as part of the sale in the sales agreement.

Carefully review the franchise agreement with the help of your attorney to determine whether the franchisor must approve the transfer, what the costs of operating are under the franchise and the other terms of the agreement.

If the franchisor is not a well-known and respected company, you should contact your local Better Business Bureau or an appropriate state agency to see if they have any information regarding the history, ethics, and reputation of the franchisor. You do not want to sign on with one of the less-than-reputable franchising operations that charge substantial franchising fees for very little in the way of useful services.

The Federal Trade Commission and a number of states provide franchising laws and regulations that offer you protection. These laws and regulations mandate the timing and content of the various disclosures which the franchisor must make to you, as the potential franchisee. You or your attorney should make sure that you ask for all of these disclosures on a timely basis, and you should be wary of any franchisor who does not provide these disclosures to you unless you ask for them.

A number of excellent publications, including *Franchise Bible: A Comprehensive Guide*, by Erwin J. Keup, can be obtained to help you evaluate various franchise opportunities. *Franchise Bible* explains what the franchise system entails and presents how both the franchisor and the franchisee should approach a franchising venture or opportunity. For more information on *Franchise Bible* and additional franchise publications, refer to Section 10.10.

If you acquire a franchise, either from the franchising company or as a transfer from another franchisee, you may be able to amortize (write off) the cost of acquiring the franchise, under certain circumstances, for federal income tax purposes. Consult your tax adviser as to whether or not this will be possible in your case.

If it is amortizable, you may want to allocate a significant part of the purchase price for the business to the cost of the franchise, which could save you major tax dollars in the long run; however, 1989 tax law changes have somewhat limited these benefits.

Once you've focused on a particular franchise opportunity, you will find the following checklist useful for evaluating the operation.

## Checklist for Evaluating a Franchise

### The Franchise

YES   NO

☐ ☐ After studying it paragraph by paragraph, did your lawyer approve the franchise contract you are considering?

☐ ☐ Does the franchise call upon you to take any steps which are, according to your lawyer, unwise or illegal in your state, county, or city? _____

_____

_____

☐ ☐ Does the franchise give you an exclusive territory for the length of the franchise? or

☐ ☐ Can the franchisor sell a second or third franchise in your territory?

☐ ☐ Is the franchisor connected in any way with another franchise company handling similar merchandise or services?

If the answer to the last question is "yes," what is your protection against this second franchisor organization?

_____

_____

Under what circumstances can you terminate the franchise contract and at what cost to you, if you decide for any reason at all that you wish to cancel it? _____

_____

_____

☐ ☐ If you sell your franchise, will you be compensated for the goodwill you have built into the business?

### The Franchisor

How many years has the firm offering you a franchise been in operation? _____

☐ ☐ Does the firm have a reputation for honesty and fair dealing among the local firms holding its franchise?

☐ ☐ Has the franchisor shown you any certified figures indicating exact net profits of one or more going firms?

☐ ☐ Have you personally checked these certified figures with the franchisor?

Will the firm assist you with:

☐ ☐ A management training program?

☐ ☐ An employee training program?

☐ ☐ A public relations program?

☐ ☐ Capital?

☐ ☐ Credit?

☐ ☐ Merchandising ideas?

☐ ☐ Will the firm help you find a good location for your new business?

☐ ☐ Is the franchising firm adequately financed so it can carry out its stated plan of financial assistance and expansion?

YES  NO

☐ ☐ Is the franchisor a one-person company? or

☐ ☐ Is the franchisor a corporation with an experienced management trained in depth (so that there would always be an experienced person at its head)?

Exactly what can the franchisor do for you which you cannot do for yourself? _____
_____
_____

☐ ☐ Has the franchisor investigated you carefully enough to assure itself that you can successfully operate one of their franchises at a profit both to them and to you?

☐ ☐ Does your state have a law regulating the sale of franchises? and

☐ ☐ Has the franchisor complied with that law?

**You – The Franchisee**

How much equity capital will you have to have to purchase the franchise and operate it until your income equals your expenses? _____

Where are you going to get the capital? _____
_____

☐ ☐ Are you prepared to give up some independence of action to secure the advantages offered by the franchise?

☐ ☐ Do you really believe you have the innate ability, training, and experience to work smoothly and profitably with the franchisor, your employees, and your customers? _____
_____
_____
_____

☐ ☐ Are you ready to spend much or all of the remainder of your business life with this franchisor, offering its product or service to your public?

**Your Market**

☐ ☐ Have you made any study to determine whether the product or service which you propose to sell under franchise has a market in your territory at the prices you will have to charge?

Will the population in the territory given you increase ☐, remain static ☐, or decrease ☐ over the next five years?

Will the product or service you are considering be in greater demand ☐, about the same ☐, or less demand ☐ five years from now than today?

What competition exists in your territory already for the product or service you contemplate selling:
From nonfranchise firms? _____
From franchise firms? _____

Source: *Franchise Opportunities Handbook*, U.S. Department of Commerce, Washington, D.C., 1982.

# 3.5 Negotiating the Purchase

**The Purchase Price**

Neither this book nor any other can tell you how much you should pay for the business you are planning to buy. You are on your own on that one. If, however, you have done your homework thoroughly in investigating the business in question and have talked to bankers and other business people about what the normal purchase price for a business of that type and size should be, you should have a fairly good basis for determining whether the purchase price is a reasonable one. For example, you may find that small businesses of the type you are considering generally sell for about one and one-half times their annual gross sales. That could be very important to know if the seller is asking three times last year's gross sales.

Even if you conclude that the purchase price is a fair one, or even a bargain, you still must decide whether the price is one you can afford. Assuming that you can get the purchase price together, will it so deplete your liquid resources that you will not have enough working capital to make the business go or put you in a bind if income from the business drops off while you are at the learning stage? Or, if you are financing a substantial part of the purchase price, will your operating budget be able to stand the cost of making the payments on the debt and still leave enough for you to live on?

Remember, just because you can get the purchase price or down payment together does not necessarily mean that you can afford to buy a particular business even when the price is right.

**Disclosure of Financial Information**

At an early stage in the negotiations, specify that you want access to tax returns, books of account, and other financial records of the business, and make it clear that you have no interest in continuing the negotiations unless the seller cooperates fully in this respect. Also, be sure that this condition is expressed in any informal "memorandum of understanding" or letter of agreement between you and the seller that is written up prior to the final contract of sale.

**Allocation of Purchase Price**

One very important item that is often omitted in business sales agreements, perhaps because it is not absolutely necessary, is a provision in the agreement that shows how the parties agree to allocate the purchase price between the various assets that are being acquired. For tax purposes, however, it is often very important to both you, as the purchaser, and the seller to have a written allocation agreement.

Since you and the seller usually have opposing interests in making an agreed allocation, the courts and IRS have generally been willing to abide by any allocation agreement between the parties.

**Allocation Formula**

The Tax Reform Act of 1986, however, has clamped down rather severely on sale price allocations for businesses sold after May 6, 1986.[1] The 1986 law requires that both you and the seller abide by an allocation formula that works as follows:

- First, reduce the purchase price by the amount of any cash or cash equivalents.
- Next, allocate part of the purchase price to assets like certificates of deposit, government securities, readily marketable stocks or securities, and foreign currencies, up to the fair market value of each such asset.
- Then, any remaining unallocated portion of the purchase price is then allocated to tangible and intangible assets (land, improvements, equipment, inventories, patents, etc.), but not to exceed the fair market value of such assets.
- Finally, if there is still any portion of the purchase price left to be allocated, it must then be allocated to goodwill and "going concern" value, which you cannot deduct, depreciate, or amortize.

**Allocation Agreements**

Despite the Tax Reform Act of 1986's four-step formula for allocating the purchase price upon sale of a business, there are still some good reasons for having a purchase price allocation agreement when you buy an existing business.

The main advantage for doing so is to create a rationale for allocating at least some part of the purchase price to intangible assets that can be amortized or otherwise written off over some period of time. For example, you may purchase a business for a price well in excess of the value of its specific, easily identifiable assets. This is particularly likely to be the case in some service businesses where the value of the receivables and a few tangible assets, such as office equipment, furniture, and supplies, may be only a small fraction of the price paid for the business. In those cases, it clearly will not be possible to allocate $50,000 of the purchase price to a $5 supply of paper clips.

Instead, consider provisions in your sales agreement that allocate part of the purchase price to some of the following types of assets: customer lists, intangible assets, and a covenant not to compete.

**Customer Lists**

For some types of businesses, it may be appropriate to create a list of customer accounts that you are buying and an agreed value for each. In recent years, the courts have frequently allowed purchasers of businesses to deduct the price paid for customer accounts on some rational basis, such as writing off the amount agreed to be the value of a particular customer account in the year that customer is lost,[2] or on some other basis.

**Other Intangible Assets**

Similar advantageous tax treatment for you as the purchaser may be gained from allocating part of the purchase price to items, such as a very favorable lease with several remaining years, or to items like blueprints or technical knowhow that have a limited useful life.[3]

Note that legislation is pending in Congress that would provide for a uniform, 14-year amortization of the cost of all intangible assets, including goodwill.

**Covenant Not to Compete**

If the agreement includes a covenant by the seller not to compete with you for some period of time, you should seek an allocation in the agreement of a substantial part of the excess purchase price to the covenant, which, if the value assigned is reasonable, you should be able to amortize — deduct in part each year over the term of the covenant. In the past, a seller would have fiercely resisted such an allocation, since the covenant payments would have all been taxable to him or her as ordinary income; this is less of an issue now that capital gains are taxed at ordinary income rates.

Remember that if there is no agreement as to the value of the covenant not to compete, you lose taxwise, since the IRS generally treats the value of such a covenant as zero unless the parties have agreed that it has a particular value.[4]

Please note that tax regulations require both you and the seller to file *Form 8594* with the IRS any time a business is bought or sold. *Form 8594* reports certain information about the purchase price allocation.[5] Penalties for failure to file this form can be extremely large. Needless to say, the information on your *Form 8594* and that of the seller's should be identical, or you will both be inviting IRS audits.

In addition, legislation passed in 1990 now makes any agreement as to the value of an asset binding upon both parties for tax purposes, in most cases. Thus, it is very important from a tax standpoint to negotiate the best possible allocation of the purchase price among the assets you acquire and have that allocation reflected in the contract of sale.[6]

# 3.6  Closing the Deal

**Legal Steps in Buying a Business**

The legal procedures involved in buying an existing business are rather complex. To ensure you are protected as fully as possible from liabilities you have not agreed to assume, have your attorney take the steps described below.

**File Transfer Notice**

In most states, the purchaser of a retail or wholesale establishment or certain other types of businesses must prepare a notice to creditors of bulk transfer and file it in counties where the business operates and publish it in a general circulation newspaper prior to the purchase of the business. If this is not properly done, the seller's unsecured creditors may be able to attach the property that you thought you were buying free and clear. See Section 11.3 for specific state requirements regarding bulk sales law.

**Check Security Interests**

Before closing the purchase, your attorney should check with the secretary of state's office to determine whether anyone has recorded a security interest — a lien or chattel mortgage — against the personal property of the seller's business. Naturally, if the transaction involves a purchase of real property, you will also have a title search performed to see if the seller has good title and if there are any recorded mortgages or other claims against the property that the seller has not disclosed to you.

For a fee, the secretary of state's office will provide a listing of any security interests that have been recorded as a lien against the assets of the business you are buying.

**Get Tax Releases**

As the purchaser of the business, you should require that, as a condition of the sale, the seller obtain the required form or certificate from the state agency that collects payroll taxes, certifying that all employment taxes due the state have been paid by the seller. Otherwise, if you fail to withhold enough of the purchase price to cover any of the seller's unpaid employment taxes, you may be liable to the state for those taxes. See Section 11.3 for specifics on state requirements.

Similarly, you should insist that the seller obtain and provide you with a sales and use tax certification showing that all outstanding sales and use tax payments due have been made by the seller, so that you do not unwittingly subject yourself to exposure for paying the seller's unpaid sales or use taxes.

**File with IRS**

File *Form 8594* with the IRS regarding the purchase price allocation and other information in connection with the transaction. The penalty for intentional disregard of this filing requirement is 10% of the amount that was not correctly reported, which could mean up to 10% of the entire purchase price. Don't forget to file *Form 8594*.

**Retain a Lawyer**

If there is any one thing discussed in this book that you should not attempt to do, it is buying or selling a business without the assistance of an attorney in reviewing and structuring the deal. Preferably, the attorney should be one who specializes in business law practice rather than a litigation specialist or general practitioner. You will also need competent tax advice, either from your attorney or from an accountant, in negotiating and structuring aspects of the deal such as the allocation of the purchase price and the disposition of any employee benefit plans carried on by the seller for the employees of the business.

**Use an Escrow**

In general, both you and the seller will be protected — from the time the sales agreement is signed until the deal closes — if an escrow is used to handle the sale of the business. The escrow holder, which is usually an escrow company or escrow department of a financial institution, will hold the agreement, escrow instructions, funds, and important documents until all conditions for closing the deal or releasing the funds or documents are fulfilled. At that time, it will disburse the funds to the seller and deliver the documents of title to you, if the deal closes; or, if the deal falls through, make such other disposition as is called for by the escrow instructions. Your attorney or the seller's attorney may also act as escrow holder, but you probably will not want the seller's attorney to act in that role in most cases, for obvious reasons.

**Build in Holdbacks**

If the seller has made misrepresentations to you in the contract of sale regarding assets that do not exist, or the like, you may always seek satisfaction by suing for damages. In view of the cost, delay, and uncertainty in bringing a lawsuit, however, you would generally be far better off if there were some simple way you could merely offset any such overstated asset or understated liability against the purchase price, retroactively.

To make this possible, you should seek to structure the deal so that part of the purchase price is held back for some period, say a year, just in case such a contingency arises. Then, if you discover false representations as to assets or liabilities, it will be relatively simple — compared to bringing a lawsuit against a seller who may have skipped town — to have your claim deducted from the amount held back. Discuss with your attorney the possibilities of structuring the transaction so that you either:

- Give the seller a note as part of the purchase price, with a right to reduce the principal amount of the note if certain contingencies occur; or
- Have part of the cash payment price held in escrow for six months or more after the sale occurs.

# 3.7 Summary Checklist for Buying an Existing Business

**Investigation**

☐ Why does the present owner want to sell the business?

☐ Will the reputation of the business be helpful or harmful if you take it over?

☐ Obtain tax returns, bank deposit records, and other financial records.

☐ If the business is not currently very profitable, why do you think you can run it more profitably than the present owner?

☐ Thoroughly investigate the business' financial records and history, its reputation, and any factors that might unfavorably impact on its future. You may need the help of an accountant or other experts.

☐ Review or have reviewed the provisions of key contracts, leases, franchise agreements, or any other legal arrangements which have a significant effect on the business. Be sure you are not assuming an unfavorable lease or contract or losing the benefits of a favorable one.

☐ Make sure that the purchase price is fair. Even if it is, can you afford it? Will you have enough working capital to run the business properly after you pay the purchase price?

☐ Insist on getting accurate financial information and access to the supporting data, early in the negotiations.

☐ Push for an allocation of the purchase price to specific assets in the sales agreement. Seek to maximize the amounts allocable to depreciable assets and any noncompetition covenant. Seek to minimize allocations to goodwill or land purchased.

☐ Look for hidden liabilities, such as pending lawsuits, accrued vacation liabilities, unfunded pension plan liabilities, or potential exposure to environmental clean-up costs.

**Negotiations**

☐ Retain an attorney to participate in drawing up the sales agreement.

☐ Comply with the requirements of the Bulk Transfer Act if it applies to the particular type of business being acquired.

☐ Be sure that acquired property is not subject to any recorded security interests or other liens beyond those disclosed by the seller.

☐ Have the seller obtain and furnish a certification that all employment taxes due have been paid.

☐ Have the seller obtain and furnish a certification that all sales and use taxes due have been paid.

☐ Seek to hold back part of the purchase price as security to reimburse you for any misrepresentations as to assets or liabilities by the seller.

☐ Prepare *Form 8594* and file it with the IRS.

☐ See Section 11.3 for state law considerations.

**Closing the Transaction**

☐ Determine whether the sale of the business will result in a sales tax liability with respect to part or all of the purchase price. If so, is there a way to reshape the transaction to reduce or avoid sales tax? For example, allocate more of the purchase price to assets not subject to sales tax and less to assets that are.

☐ If you are buying a corporation that has not been paying income taxes because it has carryovers of net operating losses or investment tax credits, be aware that you may be able to use only a small portion of those carryovers to shelter the income of the business once you become the owner. After 1985, in general, if there is more than a 50% change in the ownership of the stock of a corporation that has net operating loss carryovers, only a certain amount of those carryovers, equal to the yield on long-term, tax-exempt bonds multiplied by the value of the "loss" corporation, may be used each year to offset taxable income for all tax years ending after the change in ownership.[7]

**Other Tax Considerations**

☐ If the seller has a favorable experience rating for unemployment tax purposes, make sure you act promptly so that you can succeed to that rating as a successor employer.

☐ If you are acquiring a franchise, trademark, or trade name as part of the purchase, be aware that you may be able to amortize the cost of such franchise, etc. over a period of years;[8] despite the 1989 tax legislation limiting such deductions.

# Footnotes

1. I.R.C. § 1060(a).

2. *Holden Fuel Oil Co. v. Commissioner*, 479 F.2d 613 (6th Cir. 1973); Rev. Rul. 74-456, 1974-2 CB 65; Computing and Software, Inc., 64 T.C. 223 (1975).

3. U.S. Mineral Products, 52 T.C. 177 (1969) (Acq.). (Sale of technical know-how eligible for capital gain.)

4. George Bacon, 36 T.C. Memo 1977-52.

5. Temp. Treas. Reg. 1.1060-1T.

6. I.R.C. § 1060(a).

7. I.R.C. § 382.

8. I.R.C. § 1253.

# Starting the Business

**Part II**

Chapter 4

# A Trip through the Red Tape Jungle: Requirements that Apply to Nearly All New Businesses

*The difference between a taxidermist and a tax collector is that the taxidermist leaves the skin.*

— Old American proverb

## 4.1  General Considerations

The purpose of this chapter is to outline the most common governmental requirements and other red tape that virtually everyone starting a new business must attend to. The requirements discussed will also generally apply if you have bought an existing business, unless you have acquired the stock of an incorporated business.

This chapter assumes that your business has no employees. If you expect to have one or more employees, a large number of additional legal requirements will affect your business immediately. Chapter 5 covers the additional requirements that apply to new businesses that have employees. This chapter does not discuss the special licenses that many types of businesses are required to have. If you do not know whether the type of business you are considering going into requires a special license or licenses from federal, state, or local government agencies, refer to Chapter 6.

## 4.2  Choosing a Name for the Business

The name you choose for your business can be important from a business image standpoint and also in communicating to the public what you have to offer. Most small businesses should select a name that, at least in part, clearly describes the product or service provided. If you ignore this basic common-sense rule, you run the risk of losing many potential customers for the simple reason that they will pass right by without realizing what you do. A fanciful or whimsical name is fine from an image standpoint, but it should also give the public a clear idea of what it is your business provides in the way of goods or services. For example, if you call your restaurant "The Comestible Emporium," a lot of hungry people will probably drive right by without realizing that you serve food.

It is advisable, however, from the standpoint of protecting your business' name as a trademark or service mark under federal or state law, to adopt a name that is also partially arbitrary or nondescriptive, in conjunction with a name that is descriptive of the services or goods provided. An example would be the "21 Club Restaurant." The reason for selecting a name that is partially whimsical or arbitrary is that trademarks or service marks that are merely descriptive of the goods or services cannot be legally protected from use by others unless it can be proven that the name has acquired a secondary meaning, which is very difficult to establish for a new small business.[1]

You also need to think of the possible consequences of putting your name out before the public. You may want to consider using some sort of fictitious name (see Section 4.10) for your business, rather than your name. There is nothing illegal or shady about using a fictitious business name. If you put your name on the business and the venture goes belly up, as so many new businesses do, many people in the community will automatically associate your name with the defunct or bankrupt business, which may make it very difficult if you try to start another business or to obtain credit in the same community in the future.

Once you have settled on a name for your business, you or preferably your attorney, should find out whether the same name, or a confusingly similar name, has already been preempted by someone else. This involves making an inquiry with the state's secretary of state's office to find out whether the name is already being used in the state. Inquiry should also be made of the county clerk, in each county where you will do business, to see if another business is already using the same or a confusingly similar name in the county and has filed a fictitious business name statement. If so, you may have to choose a different name. See Section 9.5 for more information on trademark protection.

## 4.3  Local Business Licenses

Almost every business will need city or county business licenses, or both. These licenses can be obtained at the local city hall or county offices. Failure to obtain a license when you start business will usually result in a penalty when the local government eventually catches up with you; therefore, obtaining the necessary licenses should be among the first steps taken when you start a business.

Some cities and counties impose a gross receipts, income, or payroll tax on most businesses. Certain types of businesses, such as restaurants, may also be required to obtain special permits from local health authorities and fire or police departments.

If your business will construct its own building, it will be necessary to consult your local city or county zoning ordinances. A building permit must be obtained for both new construction and remodeling in most areas.

In addition, whether or not you plan to carry on any construction activity or do any remodeling, you will need to make certain that the business activity you intend to carry on does not violate any zoning regulations or any ordinances regarding hazardous activities. You may also be required to obtain a use permit from the city or county planning commission.

# 4.4  State Licenses

Most states impose license fees or taxes on a wide range of businesses, occupations, and professions. The fees often vary widely among the different types of businesses and occupations, ranging from relatively nominal to substantial amounts or rates, depending upon the activity. The many different types of licenses and permits are usually granted based on some combination of requirements such as registration, bonding, education, experience, and passage of licensing examinations. Since you may not legally operate any of these regulated businesses or professions without being licensed, you should find out whether there is a state licensing requirement for the business you plan to start. If so, determine whether and how you will be able to comply with the licensing requirements. See Section 11.6 for a partial listing of businesses, occupations, and professions that must be licensed under the laws of this state.

# 4.5  Federal Licenses

Most new small businesses are unlikely to require any type of federal permit or license to operate, unless they are engaged in rendering investment advice, making alcohol or tobacco products, preparing meat products, or making or dealing in firearms. Federal permits or licenses would also be necessary to commence certain large-scale operations such as a radio or television station or a common carrier and the production of drugs or biological products. If you wish to engage in any of the foregoing activities, all of which are heavily regulated, you should consult an attorney regarding regulatory requirements well in advance.

# 4.6 Estimated Taxes

**Individual**

As a sole proprietor or partner in a partnership, you will have to make advance payments of estimated federal — and possibly state — income taxes and federal self-employment tax once your business begins to turn a taxable profit. Individual estimated tax payments are due in four annual installments on April 15, June 15, September 15, and January 15 of the following year for an individual whose tax year is the calendar year. Any remaining unpaid federal tax is due with your tax return on April 15 of the following year — which is also the date when the first estimated tax installment is due for that year. An individual files *Form 1040-ES* with his or her federal estimated tax payments. Note that you must now pay 90% of your estimated tax during the year rather than the 80% previously required — before 1988.[2]

**Corporate**

If your business is incorporated, the corporation will generally have to make corporate estimated tax payments, if it has taxable income, as early as the fourth month of its first tax year. In 1992, the percentage your corporation must pay as estimated tax, to avoid underpayment penalties, increased from 90% to 93%. From 1993 through 1996, the tax rate will increase to 95%. Federal estimated tax payments should be computed on *Form 1120-W* — which can be obtained, along with other federal tax forms, from any IRS office — and must be deposited in a bank that is authorized to accept federal tax deposits. The corporate estimated tax deposits must be accompanied by federal tax deposit coupons. Your corporation will be issued one coupon book which contains 23 coupons per book, preprinted with your corporate tax identification number. These coupons can be used for deposits of all types of federal taxes.

On each coupon you must indicate, by checking the applicable box, the kind of tax being deposited and the quarter to which payroll tax deposits are to be applied. The boxes on the coupon indicate the form name for the type of tax being paid.

**Federal Tax Deposits**

| Type of Tax | Box to Check on Coupon |
| --- | --- |
| Payroll tax deposits | 941 |
| Federal unemployment tax | 940 (or 940-EZ) |
| Corporate income tax estimates (and year-end payments) | 1120 |

For deposits of corporate estimated income tax you must indicate the quarter which most closely corresponds to your fiscal year end, not the calendar quarter to which the payment relates. Example: If your corporate year end is May 31, you would check the "1120" box and darken the box which indicates 2nd quarter. For each of the four quarterly estimates, 2nd quarter would be indicated on each deposit coupon.

| Fiscal Year Ends | Applicable Quarter | |
|---|---|---|
| January, February, March | 1st quarter | **Tax Periods** |
| April, May, June | 2nd quarter | |
| July, August, September | 3rd quarter | |
| October, November, December | 4th quarter | |

The coupon books will be sent to you automatically when you file *Form SS-4*, requesting a tax identification number for the corporation. When you receive your coupon book, a reorder form, *Form 8109A*, will be provided, so you can request additional coupon books for the current year, if needed.

A penalty may be imposed for failure to make deposits directly to an authorized government depository bank. In the recent past, when tax deposit cards were unavailable, it was common practice to mail payments to the Internal Revenue Service accompanied by a letter indicating the nature of the tax payment and requesting additional tax deposit cards. This method of paying business taxes is no longer acceptable. Thus, it is important to mail the reorder form in time to receive additional coupon books before you run out; however, the IRS will sometimes send you blank coupons for temporary use.

Refer to Section 11.4 regarding state filing requirements for individual and corporate estimated income taxes.

# 4.7 Miscellaneous Tax Information Returns

As a general rule, every person engaged in a trade or business must report to the IRS any payments of $600 or more made to any person during the calendar year, for items such as rent, compensation for services, commissions, interest, and annuities, plus other items of fixed or determinable income.[3] There are a number of additional new tax reporting requirements listed below you need to be aware of because there are stiff new penalties for failure to comply.

**Reporting Payments to Individuals**

Recently enacted laws make it necessary to obtain the name and Social Security number or other tax identification number of any person to whom you make payments of $600 or more. There is a $50 penalty for failure to obtain their tax identification number — unless you have a

**Obtaining Social Security Numbers**

reasonable excuse, such as their refusal to give you the number.[4] If they do refuse to give you the number, you must withhold 20% of whatever amount you owe them and deposit it with the IRS, or you will be subject to a penalty for failure to withhold.[5]

## Reporting Sales to Direct Sellers

You must now report sales of $5,000 or more of consumer products to any individual who is engaged in direct selling — that is, selling in any way other than through a permanent retail establishment.[6] This will mainly apply to sales made to people in direct sales organizations, such as Tupperware, Amway, or Shaklee. It would also apply in many other situations, such as where the person you sell to sells the goods by mail order. Use *Form 1099-MISC* to report these sales.

## 1099 Forms

These types of payments are usually reportable for each payee on *Form 1099-MISC* (information return) or *Form 1099-INT* (for interest); a duplicate must be sent to the payee. In addition, you must prepare and file a *Form 1096* return summarizing all the information on the 1099-MISC forms and on the other forms in the 1099 series. Each of these forms is due by February 28 each year, for the prior calendar year, and a copy must also be sent to the recipient of the payment by January 31.

Be aware that instructions for *Form 1099* say you should use your personal Social Security number rather than your business' employer identification number on the form. Putting down the wrong taxpayer identification number in such a case will subject you to a penalty.

Payments of compensation to nonemployees — independent contractors — are also reportable on *Form 1099-MISC*.

## Penalties

There are stiff IRS penalties for not filing the above 1099 forms. The penalty for not filing or not giving a 1099 to a payee is $50 per failure. Since there is a separate penalty for not giving a copy of the 1099 to the payee as well as for not filing a copy with the IRS, it can cost you $100 for each person for whom you fail to prepare 1099s.[7] Tax law changes in 1989 have reduced the $50 penalty for late-filed 1099s and certain other information returns to $30, if filed more than 30 days late but before August 1 of the year due, or to only $15, if filed within 30 days after the due date.

## Independent Contractors

In addition, if you erroneously, but in good faith, treat a person as an independent contractor, and it is later shown that the person was actually an employee, you will only be liable as an employer for 20% of the employee's Social Security tax that should have been withheld, and for income tax withholding equal to 1.5% of what you paid the individual provided that you properly filed *Form 1099-MISC* with the IRS.[8] If you failed to file *Form 1099-MISC* for that person, the amount of withholding tax you are liable for is doubled.[9]

Fortunately, a number of important exemptions from the 1099 filing requirements will eliminate most of the people or companies to whom you are likely to make payments of $600 or more. You do not have to report:

- Payments to corporations — except certain corporations in the medical field;[10]
- Payments of compensation to employees that are already reported on their W-2s;[11]
- Payments of bills for merchandise, telegrams, telephone, freight, storage, and similar charges;[12]
- Payments of rent made to real estate agents;[13]
- Expense advances or reimbursements to employees that the employees must account to you (the employer) for;[14] and
- Payments to a governmental unit.[15]

Businesses must report royalty payments of $10 or more to any person.

**Reporting Dividends and Interest**

If your business is incorporated, your corporation will have to file a *Form 1099-DIV* for each person to whom it pays dividends of $10 or more each year.[16] You must also file *Form 1099-INT* for each person to whom you pay $10 or more in interest on bonds, debentures, or notes issued by the corporation in registered form.[17] *Form 1099-DIV* or *Form 1099-INT* is also required for any other payment of dividends or interest on which you are required to withhold tax. Payments reported on *Form 1099-DIV* and *Form 1099-INT* must also be reported on the *Form 1096* summary. *Form 1099-S* must be given to recipients of the proceeds from the sales of real estate, in general.

**Reporting Large Cash Transactions**

Any business that receives a payment of more than $10,000 in cash, in cash equivalents — such as cashier's checks or traveler's checks — or in foreign currency in one transaction, or in two or more related transactions, is required to report the details of the transactions within 15 days to the IRS[18] and to furnish a similar statement to the payor by January 31 of the following year.[19] The form for reporting such "suitcase" transactions is *Form 8300*. The penalties for noncompliance are generally the same as for not filing 1099s, except that in cases of intentional failure to file, there is an additional penalty equal to the higher of $25,000 or the amount of the cash or cash equivalent received in the transaction, up to $100,000.[20]

In addition to the requirement that you file 1099s with the IRS, you may have to file similar forms with the state.

**Reporting Mortgage Interest Received**

Federal law requires that you give *Form 1098* to any individual from whom you receive $600 or more in mortgage interest during the year, in the course of your trade or business. *Form 1098* has the same filing requirements as *Form 1099*.[21]

**Reporting on
Magnetic Media**

Note that the IRS permits you to file *Form 1098* and *Form 1099*, as well as certain other information returns, on magnetic media (computer tapes or disks) rather than the actual paper forms, if very specific formats for the computer tape or disk are met. The IRS requires that certain information returns be filed on magnetic media, if your business files 250 or more such returns for a calendar year.[22] These include *Form 1098*, all of the 1099 series and W-2 series of information returns, and various others, such as *Form 5498* and *Form 8027*.

A "hardship waiver" to excuse you from having to file in magnetic media format may be granted under certain circumstances, if you file a request on *Form 8508* at least 90 days in advance of the due date.

Failure of a taxpayer to file an information return on magnetic media — or on a machine-readable form where magnetic media filing is not required — when required to do so is treated as a failure-to-file and can result in the imposition of applicable penalties for failure to file, as noted above.

If your firm finds that it will be required to file information returns on magnetic media, there are many data processing firms and computer programs you can buy that will encode the data for you, at a relatively small cost, in a way that meets the IRS' highly technical specifications.

# 4.8  Sales and Use Tax Permits

With a limited number of exceptions, every business that sells tangible personal property, such as merchandise, to customers must obtain a seller's permit from the state sales tax agency. Usually, a separate permit must be obtained for each place of business where property subject to tax is sold.

See Section 11.4 for a discussion of the state's sales and use tax laws and permit requirements. Some states have a gross income or a gross receipts tax rather than a sales tax.

In general, as a wholesaler or manufacturer, you will not have to collect sales tax on goods you sell to a retailer for resale, if the retailer holds a valid seller's permit and provides you with a resale certificate in connection with the transaction.

Likewise, if your business, as a retailer, buys goods for resale, you need not pay sales tax to the wholesalers if you provide them with resale certificates. You may buy blank resale certificate forms at most stationery stores in states where such certificates are required.

The sales and use tax laws typically require that a business that sells or leases tangible personal property keep complete records of the gross receipts from sales or rentals whether or not the receipts are believed to be taxable. You must also keep adequate and complete records to substantiate all deductions claimed on sales and use tax returns and of the total purchase price of all tangible personal property bought for sale, lease, or consumption in the state.

## 4.9  Real Estate Taxes

**Property Taxes**

As a rule, you do not need to worry about contacting the county tax assessor's office regarding payment of any real property taxes on real property acquired for your business. They will usually contact you by mailing a property tax bill to the owner of record. See Section 11.4 for a general description of how state or local real property and personal property taxes are assessed and collected.

**FIRPTA Withholding Tax on Purchase of Real Property**

In addition to local property taxes, American citizens and other U.S. residents who acquire U.S. real estate from foreign persons — including partnership interests or stock in certain firms owning U.S. real property — must withhold up to 10% of the purchase price and remit it to the IRS under the Foreign Investment in Real Property Tax Act (FIRPTA). If you fail to withhold the tax, you are liable for it. This is a potentially dangerous tax trap for unsuspecting American buyers of real estate, since it is often difficult to determine whether a seller is a foreign person.

While there is an exception for residences costing $300,000 or less — if you will live in it for at least 50% of the time for two years — it is far safer to obtain a certificate of nonforeign status from the seller if there is any possibility that the seller is a nonresident alien or a foreign company.

To protect yourself when purchasing real estate — or your client, if you are in the real estate business — you should require, as a condition of closing the transaction, that the seller provide you with an affidavit certifying whether or not the seller is a nonresident alien or a foreign company.

If the seller refuses to sign the affidavit and provide the required information, you should withhold 10% of the gross purchase price and transmit it to the IRS within 10 days of the sale along with IRS *Form 8288* and *Form 8288-A*. This can be a real problem in a highly leveraged deal where less than 10% of the purchase price is paid in cash at the closing. Note that some states have recently adopted similar withholding provisions with regard to purchases of real estate within such states where the seller is a nonresident of the state.

If the seller is a foreign person, you will owe the IRS 10% of the purchase price if you fail to withhold the tax, unless you received a certificate of nonforeign status from the seller.

## 4.10  Fictitious Business Name Statement

Every state has laws requiring any person who regularly transacts business in the state for profit under a fictitious business name to file and publish a fictitious business name statement. For a sole proprietorship or partnership, a business name is generally considered fictitious unless it contains the surname of the owner or all of the general partners and does not suggest the existence of additional owners. Use of a name which includes words like "company," "associates," "group," "brothers," or "sons" will suggest additional owners and will make it necessary for a business to file and publish a fictitious business name statement. Putting a name that would be considered a fictitious name on your company letterhead, on your business cards, in advertising, or on your products will be considered a use of the name.

Many newspapers will provide the form for filing, publish the notice, and file the required affidavit. See Section 11.4 regarding specific requirements for filing a fictitious business name statement in this state.

## 4.11  Insurance — A Practical Necessity for Businesses

Insurance, like death and taxes, is an inevitable necessity for the owner of any small business. For almost any business, even one that has no employees, insurance coverage for general liability, product liability, fire and similar disasters, robbery, theft, and interruption of business should be considered.

If your business will have employees, workers' compensation insurance is usually mandatory under state law; and employee life, health, and disability insurance have become virtual necessities in many businesses and professions, if you wish to be competitive with other firms in hiring and retaining capable employees.

Fidelity bonding should be considered for employees who will have access to the cash receipts or other funds of the business. If you have an employees' pension or profit-sharing plan subject to the Employee Retirement Income Security Act of 1974 (ERISA), employees involved in administering the plan or handling its funds are required to be covered by a fidelity bond.[23] See Section 5.5 for further information.

**Insurance Agents**

Since it isn't realistic to expect you to become a sophisticated comparison shopper for insurance while you are trying to get a business off the ground, you should put considerable emphasis on seeking out and finding a good insurance agent whom you can trust and rely upon to give you good advice. There is no easy way to find such an agent, just as there is no sure way of finding a good lawyer or accountant. In general, the best approach will be to ask friends, lawyers, accountants, or other business people you know to refer you to a topflight insurance agent.

Agents who have earned the Chartered Life Underwriter (CLU) designation will, as a rule, be more experienced and capable than those without the CLU credential. This can be an additional factor to consider when selecting your insurance agent.

Agents who deal primarily in property and casualty insurance will not usually have CLU on their business cards. Instead, they may have the initials CPCU — Chartered Property/Casualty Underwriter — after their name, which is a similar mark of distinction in the field of property/casualty insurance.

Another good tip in finding an insurance agent is to analyze your own insurance needs. There are several how-to books that can help you analyze your risks and compare insurance prices.

One such book, *Risk Analysis: How to Reduce Insurance Costs,* written by Gary Robinson, provides insider tips on buying insurance, selecting insurance agents, and lowering your premiums and rates. The book also explains how not to buy any more insurance than your company actually needs. The book can be purchased through your book source or through The Oasis Press.

## Insurance Consultants

If you cannot find an agent with whom you feel comfortable, call an insurance consultant. Ask if — and satisfy yourself that — the consultant is a member of the Society of Risk Management Consultants. To belong to the group, the individual or firm cannot be an insurance broker. These consultants are insurance experts and can give you an objective analysis on risk management and insurance.

**Society of Risk Management Consultants**
58 Diablo View Drive
Orinda, CA 94563
(510) 254-9472

The usual hourly fees may seem high, but most new businesses probably will not need more than an hour of their time. Most will bill in quarter-hour increments.

You will probably recoup the consultant's fee several times over in premium savings in just the first year alone. You should, however, be wary of a consultant who wants to increase the number of hours by offering to create specifications and provide additional services.

Once you have met with an independent consultant and know what is needed, shop for the insurance you need from insurance brokers. Don't let them bid up the amount of coverage or add on additional types of insurance. Use the insurance consultant as you would an attorney or physician — follow his or her advice.

# 4.12 Requirements Specific to the Legal Form of the Business

**Sole Proprietorships**

There are no significant government regulatory requirements that apply specifically to sole proprietorships; however, as a sole proprietor of a business, you will need to attach a form *Schedule C* to your individual federal tax return, on which you will report the income or loss from the business.

Also, if your sole proprietorship shows a profit, you will usually have to pay a self-employment tax equal to 15.3% of your net self-employment income from the business or at least on the first $55,500 of such income, plus an additional 2.9% on self-employment income of more than $55,500, up to $130,200, in 1992. The self-employment tax is computed on *Schedule SE*, which must also be attached to your federal income tax return. See sections 11.2 and 11.4 for how to report business profits on your state income tax returns.

**Partnerships**

Like a sole proprietor, as a partner, you will have to pay a self-employment tax on your share of your partnership's net self-employment income. Net self-employment income usually includes all partnership income less all partnership deductions allowed for income tax purposes. Some types of income, such as interest, may or may not be considered self-employment income. The source of your income and your involvement in the activity from which your income is received will determine whether it is self-employment income.

If your earnings from self-employment is $400 or more for the year, you will have to figure self-employment tax on *Schedule SE* of your federal *Form 1040*. The self-employment tax is a Social Security and Medicare tax for those who work for themselves.

*Schedule E* of your federal *Form 1040* deals with your personal income tax and includes all other taxable income, such as royalties, rentals, and interest. You report your share of partnership ordinary income or loss on *Schedule E*.

In addition, your partnership must file a partnership information return, federal *Form 1065*, reporting the partnership's income and each partner's share of income and other items. The partnership must also file *Form SS-4* with the IRS to obtain a federal employer identification number, even if it has no employees. See sections 11.2 and 11.4 for state partnership return filing requirements, and the end of this chapter for a sample *Form SS-4*.

When a partner buys, sells, or exchanges a partnership interest, the partnership must file a special information return if the partnership's assets include unrealized receivables or substantially appreciated inventory that might cause the seller to have ordinary gain, rather than all capital gain, on the sale or exchange.[24] Statements also have to be sent to the partners involved in the transaction.[25]

A limited partnership, to qualify as such, is usually required to file a *Certificate of Limited Partnership* with the secretary of state or other state agency. In most states, a limited partnership should also file certified copies in each county where it does business or owns real estate.

Corporations are subject to the following requirements not applicable to other legal forms of business organization:

- Filing articles of incorporation;
- Adopting a set of bylaws;
- Observing other corporate formalities on a regular basis, such as the election of directors by shareholders and appointment of officers by action of the board of directors;
- Filing federal income tax returns on *Form 1120* — or *Form 1120-S* for an S corporation — and state income or franchise tax returns in most states where they do business. See Section 11.4 for various filings, taxes, and fees required of corporations that are incorporated or doing business in this state;
- Reporting certain information relating to the transfer of tax-free property under the Internal Revenue Code Section 351 on the corporation's income tax return for that year;[26]
- Filing *Form SS-4* with the IRS to obtain an employer identification number, even if there are no employees; and
- Qualifying with the secretary of state to do business, if the corporation was organized under the laws of another state.

**Corporations**

## 4.13  Checklist of Requirements for Nearly All New Businesses

☐ Obtain local business licenses.

☐ Check on local zoning ordinances, regulations, and other land use restrictions.

☐ Determine if your particular business requires a state license to operate.

☐ Determine whether any type of federal permit or license is required.

☐ Be prepared to make estimated income tax payments almost immediately after starting business or incorporating.

☐ Apply for a sales and use tax seller's permit if you will sell tangible personal property.

☐ File sales and use tax returns, if sales or use tax must be collected on your sales.

☐ File with the county clerk and publish a fictitious business name statement if the business operates under a fictitious name, and then file an affidavit of publication with the county clerk (in most states).

☐ Locate a good insurance agent or retain and meet with an insurance consultant regarding fire, accident, liability, theft, and other types of commercial insurance you need. Then obtain the necessary insurance coverage.

☐ If you purchase real estate, you must withhold up to 10% of the purchase price and remit it to the IRS if the seller is a foreign individual or foreign-owned company, under the Foreign Investment in Real Property Tax Act.[27] Otherwise, you should insist upon receiving an affidavit that the seller is not a nonresident alien, with his or her taxpayer identification number, unless you are certain that he or she is a U.S. citizen or resident.

☐ For a sole proprietorship, report any self-employment income on *Schedule SE* of federal *Form 1040*, and report income or loss on *Schedule C* of *Form 1040*.

☐ A partnership files *Form 1065* reporting partnership income. Each partner reports his or her share of self-employment income on *Schedule SE* of *Form 1040* and income or loss from partnership operations on *Schedule E* of *Form 1040*.

☐ For a limited partnership, file a *Certificate of Limited Partnership* with the secretary of state and copies in counties where the partnership has places of business or real estate (in most states).

☐ For a corporation, file articles of incorporation, adopt bylaws, and observe necessary corporate formalities. File federal income tax return *Form 1120*; *Form 1120-S* for an S corporation. If property is transferred to the corporation tax-free under IRC Section 351, report required information relating to the transfer on the corporation's income tax return for that year.

☐ For a corporation or a partnership, apply for a federal employer identification number on *Form SS-4*, even if the business has no employees. See sample at the end of this chapter.

☐ File annual tax information returns, *Form 1096* and the *Form 1099* series, for payments of $600 or more for items such as rent, interest, and compensation for services, and send 1099s to the payees. File *Form 1098* for mortgage interest of $600 or more your business receives in a year from an individual. Also, report any cash payments or cash equivalents of more than $10,000 that you receive to the IRS within 15 days. Such filing may have to be done on computer-readable magnetic media.

☐ If your business is a corporation, be sure to obtain an adequate supply of federal tax deposit coupons in time to make your estimated tax payments.

See Section 11.4 for a checklist of additional state law requirements that apply to nearly all new businesses.

The above requirements apply to any business, whether it has employees or not. There are many additional requirements for businesses that do have employees, and these are covered in the next chapter.

## 4.14 Securities Laws

Inherent in the choice of the legal form of the business is the potential application of federal and state securities laws, if the new business is to have more than one owner or should it become necessary to raise capital for an existing business. Because of the potentially dire consequences of violating federal or state securities laws, it is important to consult with your attorney as early as possible when considering issuing or transferring a security. Corporate stock and limited partnership interests generally are considered securities, and even a general partnership interest can be a security in appropriate circumstances, as can certain types of debt instruments.

**Registration of Securities**

Since the Securities Act of 1933, federal law has required registration as a prior condition to the issuance or transfer of securities. The law exempts various types of securities and certain types of transactions. The most important of these exemptions for small businesses have been the exemption for securities sold to persons residing within a single state and transactions by an issuer not deemed to involve any public offering. The Securities and Exchange Commission (SEC) from time to time has issued regulations exempting small securities issues, attempting to balance the needs of small businesses to raise capital against the public policy of protecting investors. In 1982, the commission adopted Regulation D as its primary method of regulation of securities offerings by small businesses, although not to the exclusion of other exemptions which might apply.

**Rule 504 Exemption**

Rule 504[28] under Regulation D exempts the issuance of securities by an entity if the aggregate offering price of all exempt securities sold by the entity during a 12-month period does not exceed $1 million — not more than $500,000 of securities can be offered and sold without registration under some states' securities laws. The securities cannot be offered or sold by any form of general solicitation or general advertising, and the securities so acquired cannot be resold without registration or an exemption from registration.

This rule does not require any specific information to be given to the purchasers of the securities; however, since the anti-fraud provisions of the securities laws apply even though the transaction is exempt from registration, it is helpful to memorialize in writing the material information regarding the offering.

**Rule 505 Exemption**

Rule 505[29] exempts offers and sales of securities if the offering price for all exempt securities sold over a 12-month period does not exceed $5 million. To obtain this exemption, the issuer must reasonably believe that there are not more than 35 purchasers exclusive of accredited investors.

Examples of accredited investors include banks, insurance companies, a natural person whose net worth at the time of purchase exceeds $1 million, or a person who has individual income in excess of $200,000 — or $300,000 jointly with a spouse — in each of the two most recent years and expects the same in the current year. Exceptions are also made for certain large investors, including corporations, partnerships, or business trusts with total assets in excess of $5 million, unless formed for the specific purpose of acquiring the securities.

For purposes of Rule 505, the issuer must furnish extensive information and certified financial statements to the investors, unless securities were sold only to accredited investors. The prohibition against advertising and solicitation applies to this rule, as do the anti-fraud provisions of the securities laws.

## Rule 506 Exemption

Rule 506[30] is similar to the exemptions provided by Rule 505, except that the $5 million limitation does not apply. The 35 purchaser limitation does apply, with the exception for accredited investors, but a separate limitation requires that the issuer must reasonably believe immediately prior to making any sale to a nonaccredited investor that such investor either alone, or with a representative, has such knowledge and experience in financial and business matters that he or she is capable of evaluating the merits and risks of the prospective investment. The prohibition against advertising and solicitation applies to this rule, as do the anti-fraud provisions of the securities laws.

Issuers utilizing any of the above exemptions must file *Form D* with the Securities and Exchange Commission generally no later than 15 days after the first sale of securities and at other specified times thereafter. New Rule 507 disqualifies any issuer found to have violated the *Form D* filing requirement from future use of the Regulation D exemptions, if the issuer has been enjoined by a court for violating the notice filing requirement — but apparently will not disqualify prior issuances of securities merely due to failure to file *Form D*.[31]

It should be kept in mind that the exemptions available under the federal securities laws are more liberal than those available under the securities laws of many states. In connection with any issuance or transfer of securities, it is necessary to consider the possible application of securities laws in the state where the business entity is established or operates, and, if different, the states where purchasers of the securities live. See Chapter 11 for further information concerning state securities laws.

# Footnotes

1. *Armstrong Paint and Varnish Works v. New and U-Enamel Corp.* 305 U.S. 315 (1938); *Carter-Wallace, Inc. v. Proctor and Gamble Co.* 434 F.2d 794 (9th Cir. 1970). The author wishes to acknowledge Henry C. Bunsow, esq. of the San Francisco patent and trademark law firm of Townsend and Townsend for alerting him to this important point.

2. I.R.C. § 6654.

3. I.R.C. § 6041(a).

4. I.R.C. § 6724(d)(3).

5. I.R.C. § 3406(a).

6. I.R.C. § 6041A(b).

7. I.R.C. §§ 6721–6722.

8. I.R.C. § 3509(a).

9. I.R.C. § 3509(b).

10. Treas. Regs. § 1.6041-3(c).

11. Treas. Regs. § 1.6041-3(a).

12. Treas. Regs. § 1.6041-3(d).

13. Treas. Regs. § 1.6041-3(e).

14. Treas. Regs. § 1.6041-3(i).

15. I.R.C. § 6041(a) requires filing of information returns for payments made to another "person." As defined in IRC § 7701(a)(1), "person" does not include governmental bodies.

16. I.R.C. § 6042(a).

17. I.R.C. § 6049(a).

18. I.R.C. § 6050I.

19. I.R.C. § 6722.

20. I.R.C. § 6721.

21. I.R.C. § 6050H.

22. Rev. Proc. 89-42, 1989-29 I.R.B. 14.

23. 29 U.S.C. § 1112 (§ 412 of ERISA).

24. I.R.C. § 6050K(a).

25. I.R.C. § 6050K(b).

26. Treas. Regs. § 1.351-3.

27. I.R.C. § 1445(a).

28. 17 C.F.R. § 230.504.

29. 17 C.F.R. § 230.505.

30. 17 C.F.R. § 230.506.

31. Rule 507, as interpreted in Securities Act Release No. 6825, March 14, 1989 (17 C.F.R. § 230.507).

Form **SS-4**
(Rev. April 1991)
Department of the Treasury
Internal Revenue Service

# Application for Employer Identification Number

(For use by employers and others. Please read the attached instructions before completing this form.)

EIN

OMB No. 1545-0003
Expires 4-30-94

**Please type or print clearly.**

**1** Name of applicant (True legal name) (See instructions.)

**2** Trade name of business, if different from name in line 1

**3** Executor, trustee, "care of" name

**4a** Mailing address (street address) (room, apt., or suite no.)

**5a** Address of business (See instructions.)

**4b** City, state, and ZIP code

**5b** City, state, and ZIP code

**6** County and state where principal business is located

**7** Name of principal officer, grantor, or general partner (See instructions.) ▶

**8a** Type of entity (Check only one box.) (See instructions.)
☐ Individual SSN ____ : ____ : ____
☐ REMIC
☐ State/local government        ☐ National guard
☐ Other nonprofit organization (specify) _____
☐ Other (specify) ▶ _____
☐ Personal service corp.

☐ Estate
☐ Plan administrator SSN ____ : ____ : ____
☐ Other corporation (specify) _____
☐ Federal government/military        ☐ Church or church controlled organization
If nonprofit organization enter GEN (if applicable) _____

☐ Trust
☐ Partnership
☐ Farmers' cooperative

**8b** If a corporation, give name of foreign country (if applicable) or state in the U.S. where incorporated ▶

Foreign country

State

**9** Reason for applying (Check only one box.)
☐ Started new business
☐ Hired employees
☐ Created a pension plan (specify type) ▶ _____
☐ Banking purpose (specify) ▶

☐ Changed type of organization (specify) ▶ _____
☐ Purchased going business
☐ Created a trust (specify) ▶ _____
☐ Other (specify) ▶

**10** Date business started or acquired (Mo., day, year) (See instructions.)

**11** Enter closing month of accounting year. (See instructions.)

**12** First date wages or annuities were paid or will be paid (Mo., day, year). **Note:** *If applicant is a withholding agent, enter date income will first be paid to nonresident alien. (Mo., day, year)* · · · · · · · · · · · · · · · · ▶

**13** Enter highest number of employees expected in the next 12 months. **Note:** *If the applicant does not expect to have any employees during the period, enter "0."* · · · · · · · ▶

| Nonagricultural | Agricultural | Household |
|---|---|---|
|  |  |  |

**14** Principal activity (See instructions.) ▶

**15** Is the principal business activity manufacturing? · · · · · · · · · · · · · · · · · · · ☐ Yes   ☐ No
If "Yes," principal product and raw material used ▶

**16** To whom are most of the products or services sold? Please check the appropriate box.        ☐ Business (wholesale)
☐ Public (retail)        ☐ Other (specify) ▶                                                                        ☐ N/A

**17a** Has the applicant ever applied for an identification number for this or any other business? · · · · · · · · ☐ Yes   ☐ No
**Note:** *If "Yes," please complete lines 17b and 17c.*

**17b** If you checked the "Yes" box in line 17a, give applicant's true name and trade name, if different than name shown on prior application.

True name ▶                                                                        Trade name ▶

**17c** Enter approximate date, city, and state where the application was filed and the previous employer identification number if known.

| Approximate date when filed (Mo., day, year) | City and state where filed | Previous EIN |
|---|---|---|
|  |  |  |

Under penalties of perjury, I declare that I have examined this application, and to the best of my knowledge and belief, it is true, correct, and complete.

Telephone number (include area code)

Name and title (Please type or print clearly.) ▶

Signature ▶                                                                        Date ▶

**Note:** *Do not write below this line.     For official use only.*

| Please leave blank ▶ | Geo. | Ind. | Class | Size | Reason for applying |
|---|---|---|---|---|---|
|  |  |  |  |  |  |

**For Paperwork Reduction Act Notice, see attached instructions.**        Cat. No. 16055N        Form **SS-4** (Rev. 4-91)

# General Instructions

*(Section references are to the Internal Revenue Code unless otherwise noted.)*

**Paperwork Reduction Act Notice.**—We ask for the information on this form to carry out the Internal Revenue laws of the United States. You are required to give us this information. We need it to ensure that you are complying with these laws and to allow us to figure and collect the right amount of tax.

The time needed to complete and file this form will vary depending on individual circumstances. The estimated average time is:

| | |
|---|---|
| **Recordkeeping** | 7 min. |
| **Learning about the law or the form** | 21 min. |
| **Preparing the form** | 42 min. |
| **Copying, assembling, and sending the form to IRS** | 20 min. |

If you have comments concerning the accuracy of these time estimates or suggestions for making this form more simple, we would be happy to hear from you. You can write to both the **Internal Revenue Service**, Washington, DC 20224, Attention: IRS Reports Clearance Officer, T:FP; and the **Office of Management and Budget,** Paperwork Reduction Project (1545-0003), Washington, DC 20503. **DO NOT** send the tax form to either of these offices. Instead, see **Where To Apply.**

**Purpose.**—Use Form SS-4 to apply for an employer identification number (EIN). The information you provide on this form will establish your filing requirements.

**Who Must File.**—You must file this form if you have not obtained an EIN before and

• You pay wages to one or more employees.

• You are required to have an EIN to use on any return, statement, or other document, even if you are not an employer.

• You are required to withhold taxes on income, other than wages, paid to a nonresident alien (individual, corporation, partnership, etc.). For example, individuals who file **Form 1042**, Annual Withholding Tax Return for U.S. Source Income of Foreign Persons, to report alimony paid to nonresident aliens must have EINs.

Individuals who file **Schedule C**, Profit or Loss From Business, or **Schedule F**, Profit or Loss From Farming, of **Form 1040**, U.S. Individual Income Tax Return, must use EINs if they have a Keogh plan or are required to file excise, employment, or alcohol, tobacco, or firearms returns.

The following must use EINs even if they do not have any employees:

• Trusts, except an IRA trust, unless the IRA trust is required to file **Form 990-T**, Exempt Organization Business Income Tax Return, to report unrelated business taxable income or is filing Form 990-T to obtain a refund of the credit from a regulated investment company.

• Estates

• Partnerships

• REMICS (real estate mortgage investment conduits)

• Corporations

• Nonprofit organizations (churches, clubs, etc.)

• Farmers' cooperatives

• Plan administrators

*New Business.*—If you become the new owner of an existing business, **DO NOT** use the EIN of the former owner. If you already have an EIN, use that number. If you do not have an EIN, apply for one on this form. If

you become the "owner" of a corporation by acquiring its stock, use the corporation's EIN.

If you already have an EIN, you may need to get a new one if either the organization or ownership of your business changes. If you incorporate a sole proprietorship or form a partnership, you must get a new EIN. However, **DO NOT** apply for a new EIN if you change only the name of your business.

**File Only One Form SS-4.**—File only one Form SS-4, regardless of the number of businesses operated or trade names under which a business operates. However, each corporation in an affiliated group must file a separate application.

If you do not have an EIN by the time a return is due, write "Applied for" and the date you applied in the space shown for the number. **DO NOT** show your social security number as an EIN on returns.

If you do not have an EIN by the time a tax deposit is due, send your payment to the Internal Revenue service center for your filing area. (See **Where To Apply** below.) Make your check or money order payable to Internal Revenue Service and show your name (as shown on Form SS-4), address, kind of tax, period covered, and date you applied for an EIN.

For more information about EINs, see **Pub. 583**, Taxpayers Starting a Business.

**How To Apply.**—You can apply for an EIN either by mail or by telephone. You can get an EIN immediately by calling the Tele-TIN phone number for the service center for your state, or you can send the completed Form SS-4 directly to the service center to receive your EIN in the mail.

*Application by Tele-TIN.*—The Tele-TIN program is designed to assign EINs by telephone. Under this program, you can receive your EIN over the telephone and use it immediately to file a return or make a payment.

To receive an EIN by phone, complete Form SS-4, then call the Tele-TIN phone number listed for your state under **Where To Apply.** The person making the call must be authorized to sign the form (see **Signature block** on page 3).

An IRS representative will use the information from the Form SS-4 to establish your account and assign you an EIN. Write the number you are given on the upper right-hand corner of the form, sign and date it, and promptly mail it to the Tele-TIN Unit at the service center address for your state.

*Application by mail.*—Complete Form SS-4 at least 4 to 5 weeks before you will need an EIN. Sign and date the application and mail it to the service center address for your state. You will receive your EIN in the mail in approximately 4 weeks.

**Note:** *The Tele-TIN phone numbers listed below will involve a long-distance charge to callers outside of the local calling area, and should only be used to apply for an EIN. Use 1-800-829-1040 to ask about an application by mail.*

**Where To Apply.**—

| If your principal business, office or agency, or legal residence in the case of an individual, is located in: ▼ | Call the Tele-TIN phone number shown or file with the Internal Revenue service center at: ▼ |
|---|---|
| Florida, Georgia, South Carolina | Atlanta, GA 39901 (404) 455-2360 |
| New Jersey, New York City and counties of Nassau, Rockland, Suffolk, and Westchester | Holtsville, NY 00501 (516) 447-4955 |
| New York (all other counties), Connecticut, Maine, Massachusetts, New Hampshire, Rhode Island, Vermont | Andover, MA 05501 (508) 474-9717 |
| Illinois, Iowa, Minnesota, Missouri, Wisconsin | Kansas City, MO 64999 (816) 926-5999 |
| Delaware, District of Columbia, Maryland, Pennsylvania, Virginia | Philadelphia, PA 19255 (215) 961-3980 |
| Indiana, Kentucky, Michigan, Ohio, West Virginia | Cincinnati, OH 45999 (606) 292-5467 |
| Kansas, New Mexico, Oklahoma, Texas | Austin, TX 73301 (512) 462-7845 |
| Alaska, Arizona, California (counties of Alpine, Amador, Butte, Calaveras, Colusa, Contra Costa, Del Norte, El Dorado, Glenn, Humboldt, Lake, Lassen, Marin, Mendocino, Modoc, Napa, Nevada, Placer, Plumas, Sacramento, San Joaquin, Shasta, Sierra, Siskiyou, Solano, Sonoma, Sutter, Tehama, Trinity, Yolo, and Yuba), Colorado, Idaho, Montana, Nebraska, Nevada, North Dakota, Oregon, South Dakota, Utah, Washington, Wyoming | Ogden, UT 84201 (801) 625-7645 |
| California (all other counties), Hawaii | Fresno, CA 93888 (209) 456-5900 |
| Alabama, Arkansas, Louisiana, Mississippi, North Carolina, Tennessee | Memphis, TN 37501 (901) 365-5970 |

If you have no legal residence, principal place of business, or principal office or agency in any Internal Revenue District, file your form with the Internal Revenue Service Center, Philadelphia, PA 19255 or call (215) 961-3980.

## Specific Instructions

The instructions that follow are for those items that are not self-explanatory. Enter N/A (nonapplicable) on the lines that do not apply.

**Line 1.**—Enter the legal name of the entity applying for the EIN.

*Individuals.*—Enter the first name, middle initial, and last name.

*Trusts.*—Enter the name of the trust.

*Estate of a decedent.*—Enter the name of the estate.

*Partnerships.*—Enter the legal name of the partnership as it appears in the partnership agreement.

*Corporations.*—Enter the corporate name as set forth in the corporation charter or other legal document creating it.

*Plan administrators.*—Enter the name of the plan administrator. A plan administrator who already has an EIN should use that number.

**Line 2.**—Enter the trade name of the business if different from the legal name.

**Note:** *Use the full legal name entered on line 1 on all tax returns to be filed for the entity. However, if a trade name is entered on line 2, use only the name on line 1 or the name on line 2 consistently when filing tax returns.*

**Line 3.**—Trusts enter the name of the trustee. Estates enter the name of the executor, administrator, or other fiduciary. If the entity applying has a designated person to receive tax information, enter that person's name as the "care of" person. Print or type the first name, middle initial, and last name.

**Lines 5a and 5b.**—If the physical location of the business is different from the mailing address (lines 4a and 4b), enter the address of the physical location on lines 5a and 5b.

**Line 7.**—Enter the first name, middle initial, and last name of a principal officer if the business is a corporation; of a general partner if a partnership; and of a grantor if a trust.

**Line 8a.**—Check the box that best describes the type of entity that is applying for the EIN. If not specifically mentioned, check the "other" box and enter the type of entity. Do not enter N/A.

*Individual.*—Check this box if the individual files Schedule C or F (Form 1040) and has a Keogh plan or is required to file excise, employment, or alcohol, tobacco, or firearms returns. If this box is checked, enter the individual's SSN (social security number) in the space provided.

*Plan administrator.*—The term plan administrator means the person or group of persons specified as the administrator by the instrument under which the plan is operated. If the plan administrator is an individual, enter the plan administrator's SSN in the space provided.

*New withholding agent.*—If you are a new withholding agent required to file Form 1042, check the "other" box and enter in the space provided "new withholding agent."

*REMICs.*—Check this box if the entity is a real estate mortgage investment conduit (REMIC). A REMIC is any entity

1. To which an election to be treated as a REMIC applies for the tax year and all prior tax years,

2. In which all of the interests are regular interests or residual interests,

3. Which has one class of residual interests (and all distributions, if any, with respect to such interests are pro rata),

4. In which as of the close of the 3rd month beginning after the startup date and at all times thereafter, substantially all of its assets consist of qualified mortgages and permitted investments,

5. Which has a tax year that is a calendar year, and

6. With respect to which there are reasonable arrangements designed to ensure that: (a) residual interests are not held by disqualified organizations (as defined in section 860E(e)(5)), and (b) information necessary for the application of section 860E(e) will be made available.

For more information about REMICs see the Instructions for **Form 1066,** U. S. Real Estate Mortgage Investment Conduit Income Tax Return.

*Personal service corporations.*—Check this box if the entity is a personal service corporation. An entity is a personal service corporation for a tax year only if

1. The entity is a C corporation for the tax year.

2. The principal activity of the entity during the testing period (as defined in Temporary Regulations section 1.441-4T(f)) for the tax year is the performance of personal service.

3. During the testing period for the tax year, such services are substantially performed by employee-owners.

4. The employee-owners own 10 percent of the fair market value of the outstanding stock in the entity on the last day of the testing period for the tax year.

For more information about personal service corporations, see the instructions to **Form 1120,** U.S. Corporation Income Tax Return, and Temporary Regulations section 1.441-4T.

*Other corporations.*—This box is for any corporation other than a personal service corporation. If you check this box, enter the type of corporation (such as insurance company) in the space provided.

*Other nonprofit organizations.*—Check this box if the nonprofit organization is other than a church or church-controlled organization and specify the type of nonprofit organization (for example, an educational organization.)

*Group exemption number (GEN).*—If the applicant is a nonprofit organization that is a subordinate organization to be included in a group exemption letter under Revenue Procedure 80-27, 1980-1 C.B. 677, enter the GEN in the space provided. If you do not know the GEN, contact the parent organization for it. GEN is a four-digit number. Do not confuse it with the nine-digit EIN.

**Line 9.**—Check only one box. Do not enter N/A.

*Started new business.*—Check this box if you are starting a new business that requires an EIN. If you check this box, enter the type of business being started. **DO NOT** apply if you already have an EIN and are only adding another place of business.

*Changed type of organization.*—Check this box if the business is changing its type of organization, for example, if the business was a sole proprietorship and has been incorporated or has become a partnership. If you check this box, specify in the space provided the type of change made, for example, "from sole proprietorship to partnership."

*Purchased going business.*—Check this box if you acquired a business through purchase. Do not use the former owner's EIN. If you already have an EIN, use that number.

*Hired employees.*—Check this box if the existing business is requesting an EIN because it has hired or is hiring employees and is therefore required to file employment tax return for which an EIN is required. **DO NOT** apply if you already have an EIN and are only hiring employees.

*Created a trust.*—Check this box if you created a trust, and enter the type of trust created.

*Created a pension plan.*—Check this box if you have created a pension plan and need this number for reporting purposes. Also, enter the type of plan created.

*Banking purpose.*—Check this box if you are requesting an EIN for banking purpose only and enter the banking purpose (for example, checking, loan, etc.).

*Other (specify).*—Check this box if you are requesting an EIN for any reason other than those for which there are checkboxes and enter the reason.

**Line 10.**—If you are starting a new business, enter the starting date of the business. If the business you acquired is already operating, enter the date you acquired the business. Trusts should enter the date the trust was legally created. Estates should enter the date of death of the decedent whose name appears on line 1.

**Line 11.**—Enter the last month of your accounting year or tax year. An accounting year or tax year is usually 12 consecutive months. It may be a calendar year or a fiscal year (including a period of 52 or 53 weeks). A calendar year is 12 consecutive months ending on December 31. A fiscal year is either 12 consecutive months ending on the last day of any month other than December or a 52-53 week year. For more information

on accounting periods, see **Pub. 538,** Accounting Periods and Methods.

*Individuals.*—Your tax year generally will be a calendar year.

*Partnerships.*—Partnerships generally should conform to the tax year of either (1) its majority partners; (2) its principal partners; (3) the tax year that results in the least aggregate deferral of income (see Temporary Regulations section 1.706-1T); or (4) some other tax year, if (a) a business purpose is established for the fiscal year, or (b) the fiscal year is a "grandfather" year, or (c) an election is made under section 444 to have a fiscal year. (See the Instructions for **Form 1065,** U.S. Partnership Return of Income, for more information.)

*REMICs.*—Remics must have a calendar year as their tax year.

*Personal service corporations.*—A personal service corporation generally must adopt a calendar year unless:

1. It can establish to the satisfaction of the Commissioner that there is a business purpose for having a different tax year, or

2. It elects under section 444 to have a tax year other than a calendar year.

**Line 12.**—If the business has or will have employees, enter on this line the date on which the business began or will begin to pay wages to the employees. If the business does not have any plans to have employees, enter N/A on this line.

*New withholding agent.*—Enter the date you began or will begin to pay income to a nonresident alien. This also applies to individuals who are required to file Form 1042 to report alimony paid to a nonresident alien.

**Line 14.**—Generally, enter the exact type of business being operated (for example, advertising agency, farm, labor union, real estate agency, steam laundry, rental of coin-operated vending machine, investment club, etc.).

*Governmental.*—Enter the type of organization (state, county, school district, or municipality, etc.)

*Nonprofit organization (other than governmental).*—Enter whether organized for religious, educational, or humane purposes, and the principal activity (for example, religious organization—hospital, charitable).

*Mining and quarrying.*—Specify the process and the principal product (for example, mining bituminous coal, contract drilling for oil, quarrying dimension stone, etc.).

*Contract construction.*—Specify whether general contracting or special trade contracting. Also, show the type of work normally performed (for example, general contractor for residential buildings, electrical subcontractor, etc.).

*Trade.*—Specify the type of sales and the principal line of goods sold (for example, wholesale dairy products, manufacturer's representative for mining machinery, retail hardware, etc.).

*Manufacturing.*—Specify the type of establishment operated (for example, sawmill, vegetable cannery, etc.).

**Signature block.**—The application must be signed by: (1) the individual, if the person is an individual, (2) the president, vice president, or other principal officer, if the person is a corporation, (3) a responsible and duly authorized member or officer having knowledge of its affairs, if the person is a partnership or other unincorporated organization, or (4) the fiduciary, if the person is a trust or estate.

Chapter 5

# The Thicket Thickens: Additional Requirements for Businesses with Employees

*If anything can go wrong it will. Nature always sides with the hidden flaw.*

— Murphy's Law

*Murphy was an optimist.*

— O'Toole's Law

## 5.1 General Considerations

As the previous chapter indicated, there is a considerable amount of governmental red tape involved in starting almost any new business. If your business will have any employees — even if it is incorporated and you are the only employee — the level of government regulation and red tape will multiply several times over in the typical case. This chapter outlines the bases you must cover, in addition to those described in Chapter 4, if you start a business that will have employees.

## 5.2 Social Security and Income Tax Withholding

Once you go into business and begin paying salary or wages to employees, you will find that you have been appointed, as an agent of the government, to collect taxes from your employees. The most significant taxes you will be required to collect are income taxes and Social Security (FICA) tax withheld from employees' wages, which are discussed in this section. You will also find in this and subsequent sections that there are payroll taxes imposed directly on you, as payor of wages.

## Employer Identification Number

The first thing you must do is to apply for a federal employer identification number. This number will be used to identify your business on payroll and income tax returns and for most other federal tax purposes. To apply for a number, you need to file a completed *Form SS-4* at the earliest possible time, especially if you have employees. This will ensure that you will get tax deposit coupons in time for depositing federal payroll taxes or corporate income tax. Corporations and partnerships must file *Form SS-4* even if they have no employees. A sample of this form is located at the end of Chapter 4.

As a new employer, you should obtain a business tax kit from your local IRS office. At the same time, you can obtain *Circular E, Employer's Tax Guide,* an IRS publication that explains federal income tax withholding and Social Security tax requirements for employers. *Circular E* also contains up-to-date withholding tables that you must use to determine how much federal income tax and Social Security tax is to be withheld from each employee's paycheck.

## Employer Social Security Tax

In addition to withholding Social Security tax from an employee's paycheck — at the rate of 7.65% on gross wages up to $55,500, 1.45% on wages more than $55,500, with a $130,200 limit in 1992 — the employer must also pay an equal amount of employer's Social Security tax. The withheld federal income tax, withheld employee Social Security tax, and employer's Social Security tax are lumped together and paid to the IRS at the same time. In some cases, these taxes can simply be mailed in with your payroll tax return (*Form 941* series) at the end of the calendar quarter or year; however, if you have significant amounts of these taxes to pay, you will generally be required to deposit the taxes with a federal tax deposit form, a precoded coupon, at an authorized commercial bank or a federal reserve bank. As a rule, the greater the amount of taxes due, the sooner they must be paid. How and when federal income and Social Security taxes are to be mailed in or deposited are summarized briefly as follows:[1]

| Undeposited Federal Income and FICA Taxes | Deposit with Bank Is Due by: |
| --- | --- |
| Less than $500 at the end of a calendar quarter. | Last day of the following month — or mail payment with *Form 941* return. |
| $500 or more, but less than $3,000 undeposited at end of any eighth-monthly period (a period ending on the 3rd, 7th, 11th, 15th, 19th, 22nd, 25th, or last day of any month). | 15th day of the following month.[2] |
| $3,000 or more undeposited at the end of an eighth-monthly period. | 3rd banking day after the end of the eighth-monthly period in which undeposited taxes reach $3,000.[3] |
| $100,000 or more undeposited at the end of any day. | 1st banking day following.[4] |

Very large employers may have to make payroll tax deposits frequently. For an employer making eighth-monthly deposits, no penalty for under-deposits will be made if at least 95% of the tax due is deposited when required each month. For a more detailed explanation of federal tax deposits, see IRS *Notice 109*.

Deposits of payroll and withholding taxes may be mailed to a depository bank, if postmarked at least two days prior to the tax deposit due date. But tax deposits of $20,000 or more by employers making more than one deposit a month must reach the bank by the due date, regardless of the postmark date.[5]

## New Employees

When a new employee is hired, you must furnish the employee with a federal *Form W-4*, which he or she must complete and return to you. *Form W-4*, when completed, provides the employee's Social Security number and the number of withholding exemptions the employee is claiming, which is used to determine how much income tax you must withhold from his or her wages. You keep *Form W-4*. Neither it nor the information on it is filed with the IRS, except in the case of an employee who claims more than 10 withholding exemptions, or who claims exemption from income tax withholding.

By January 31 of each year, you must furnish each employee with copies of *Form W-2, Annual Wage and Tax Statement*, showing the taxable wages paid to the employee during the preceding calendar year and the taxes withheld, including state income tax. By February 28, the original of each W-2 and a summary form, *Form W-3*, should be filed with the IRS.

## Independent Contractors

Not all individuals who perform services for your business will necessarily be employees. In many cases, it is possible to structure your legal relationships with persons who provide services to you so that they are considered to be independent contractors for tax and other legal purposes. From your standpoint as an employer, it is much preferable to be able to treat someone as an independent contractor rather than an employee of your business.

If a person is considered to be an independent contractor, you do not have to pay Social Security tax or federal or state unemployment taxes with respect to his or her compensation. The independent contractor is considered to be self-employed for tax purposes and pays self-employment tax. In addition, you are relieved from the obligation to withhold income and payroll taxes from payments made to independent contractors or to file payroll tax returns with respect to their compensation. You must, however, file a *Form 1099-MISC* for each independent contractor to whom you make payments of $600 or more during a calendar year (with certain exceptions), or, in the case of a direct seller of consumer goods, for each such direct seller to whom you sell $5,000 of goods during a year.

Because of the obvious advantages to employers of treating their employees as independent contractors, the IRS has been very aggressive in attempting to reclassify so-called independent contractors as employees where they perform functions in a manner that is more typical of an employer/employee relationship. Requiring businesses to file *Form 1099-MISC* is an attempt by the IRS to identify those businesses that may be improperly treating employees as independent contractors.

Before you decide to treat anyone who works for you as an independent contractor, you should consult your tax adviser, since there can be serious consequences if those individuals are reclassified as employees by the IRS. See Section 9.11 for a discussion of the risks involved.

**State Withholding Taxes**

Each state has its own withholding taxes, which vary from state to state. For information on the withholding tax requirements for this state, see Section 11.5.

# 5.3 Unemployment Taxes

With relatively few exceptions, all businesses with employees must pay both federal and state unemployment taxes. These taxes are imposed entirely on you, the employer. The federal unemployment tax on paper is 6.2% of the first $7,000 of annual wages per employee;[6] however, the federal rate is usually only 0.8% because a credit for up to 5.4% is given for state unemployment taxes paid and for a favorable experience rating for state unemployment tax purposes.[7]

The state unemployment tax rate for an employer can be either more or less than the basic rate, depending upon the amount of unemployment claims by former employees. The more unemployment benefits claimed by your former employees, the higher your unemployment tax rate will be, within certain limits.

**Federal Unemployment Tax**

Your business will be required to pay federal unemployment tax (FUTA) for any calendar year in which it pays wages of $1,500 or more[8] or if it has one or more employees for at least a portion of the day during any 20 different calendar weeks during the year.[9] Needless to say, this will cover almost any business that has even one employee, even part-time.

If the FUTA liability during any of the first three calendar quarters is more than $100, you must deposit the tax with a federal tax deposit coupon, *Form 8109*, at an authorized bank during the month following the end of the quarter. If the tax is $100 or less, you are not required to make a deposit, but you must add it to the taxes for the next quarter. For the fourth quarter, if the undeposited FUTA tax for the year is more than

$100, deposit the tax with a tax deposit coupon at an authorized bank by January 31. If the balance due is $100 or less, either deposit it with the coupon or mail it in with your federal unemployment tax return, *Form 940*, by January 31. *Form 940* is not due until February 10 if all of the FUTA tax for the prior year has already been deposited when due.

The IRS introduced *Form 940-EZ*, a greatly simplified FUTA return for small employers, in the 1989 tax year. In general, the small employers who can use the new *Form 940-EZ* are those:

**Simplified Filing for Small Employers**

- Who pay unemployment tax to only one state;
- Who pay state unemployment taxes by the *Form 940-EZ* due date; and
- Whose wages subject to FUTA are also taxable for state unemployment tax purposes.

The state also imposes an unemployment tax which meshes closely with the federal unemployment tax. Refer to Section 11.5 for details on the state unemployment tax, rates, returns, registration as an employer, etc.

**State Unemployment Tax**

# 5.4 Workers' Compensation Insurance

A business is generally required by state law to obtain workers' compensation insurance for its employees. This means that you, as an employer, may have to immediately seek out and obtain a workers' compensation insurance policy covering all your employees, or you will be subject to possible legal sanctions. Workers' compensation insurance coverage provides various benefits to an employee who suffers a job-related injury or illness.

There are many insurance companies that offer workers' compensation coverage. Many such companies, however, may be reluctant to write a policy that covers only one or a few employees, unless it is tied to other types of insurance policies. See Section 11.5 for a description of other formal requirements applicable to employers under the workers' compensation laws.

# 5.5 Compliance with ERISA — Employee Benefit Plans

If you have employees and provide them with fringe benefits, such as group insurance — other than workers' compensation — other types of employee welfare plan benefits, or if you adopt a pension or profit-sharing retirement plan, you will almost certainly have to comply with at least some aspects of the Employee Retirement Income Security Act of 1974 (ERISA). There are criminal penalties for willful failure to comply with two types of ERISA requirements: reporting to government agencies and disclosure to employees.[10] In addition, there are a number of different types of civil penalties which are incredibly numerous and complex, for unintentional failures to comply with ERISA requirements.[11] In short, compliance with ERISA is a nightmare.

This section is an attempt to lay down some relatively simple and straightforward guidelines you, as a layperson, can follow in trying to recognize when you might have an ERISA compliance obligation, so that you will know when to call your attorney, accountant, or benefit consultant for help. ERISA deals with two kinds of employee benefit plans — pension plans and welfare plans.

## Pension Plans

Pension plans[12] under ERISA are pretty much what you might expect — tax qualified retirement plans including both pension and profit-sharing plans (including Keogh plans), plus other types of benefit programs that defer payments until after employment has terminated. The ERISA reporting and disclosure requirements for pension plans are quite extensive, and if your business adopts any such plans, you will most definitely need professional assistance in meeting the ERISA requirements that may apply. These are summarized later in this section.

## Welfare Plans

Welfare plans[13] under ERISA include most other types of employee benefit plans that are not considered pension plans. These include typical fringe benefit plans adopted by small firms, such as health insurance, long-term disability, group-term life insurance, and accidental death insurance plans. ERISA compliance for welfare plans is usually less of a burden than for pension plans, but is required for almost every business that provides any kind of benefits for employees of the type mentioned above.

Note that a number of so-called fringe benefits that are in the nature of payroll practices, such as paid holidays, vacation pay, bonuses, overtime premium pay, and most kinds of severance pay arrangements, are usually not considered to be either pension or welfare plans under ERISA.[14] Thus, these kinds of payroll practices are not subject to ERISA at all.

Compliance requirements for reporting and disclosure under ERISA are briefly discussed below.

## Summary Plan Description

The one ERISA compliance requirement that applies to almost all small businesses is the requirement for you to prepare a summary plan description (SPD) for distribution to all employees covered by any type of welfare plan you sponsor, such as typical health, accident, life, or disability insurance plans.[15] An SPD must contain more than 20 specific items of information listed in the U.S. Department of Labor Regulations,[16] including an ERISA rights statement which must be copied more or less verbatim from the regulations.

An SPD must be prepared for each plan and distributed to covered employees within 120 days after the plan is first adopted.[17] Each new employee must be given a copy of the SPD within 90 days after becoming a participant in the plan.[18] Since an SPD must be prepared for each employee plan subject to ERISA, even a very small business may find that it has to produce three or four of these documents, each of which must meet detailed technical requirements.

One important consideration in taking out insurance coverage for employees should be a firm commitment from the insurance company or brokers that they will prepare the necessary SPDs for the insurance plans they are selling you. Otherwise, you may need to have your attorney or benefit consultant prepare the SPDs, which can result in substantial professional fees.

Other than the need for you to prepare SPDs and distribute them to employees, there are no significant ERISA requirements that apply to most kinds of insured-type welfare plans that cover fewer than 100 employees.[19] You must, however, make available the insurance policies and other plan documents for inspection by your employees and you must furnish copies to them upon request.[20]

If your business should grow to have 100 or more employees who are covered by a plan, or if you adopt any type of uninsured funded welfare plan, you will suddenly become subject to a whole array of additional ERISA requirements, including:

**Additional ERISA Requirements**

- Filing a copy of the SPD with the U.S. Department of Labor;[21]
- Filing an annual return/report or registration (*Form 5500* series) with the IRS each year;[22]
- Preparing and distributing a summary annual report to covered employees each year;[23]
- Preparing a summary of material modifications of the plan, if necessary, and filing it with the U.S. Department of Labor and distributing it to covered employees;[24] and
- Filing a terminal report if the plan is terminated.[25]

The ERISA compliance requirements for a pension or profit-sharing plan of even a very small business are very onerous, complex, and expensive, despite numerous attempts by the IRS and U.S. Department of Labor to simplify the reporting requirements, in response to a barrage of criticism from small businesses.

Because these compliance requirements are so very complex and are constantly in a state of flux, no attempt to spell them out in detail is made here. Instead, the basic ERISA compliance requirements for most pension and profit-sharing plans are summarized on the next page.

## Summary of Basic ERISA Compliance Requirements

| Item | Provided to |
| --- | --- |
| Summary plan description. | U.S. Department of Labor; participants; beneficiaries |
| Annual return/report (*Form 5500, 5500-EZ, 5500-C* or *5500-R*). | IRS (now required even for a simple one-person Keogh plan) |
| *Schedule A, Form 5500* series (insurance information). | IRS |
| *Schedule B, Form 5500* series (actuarial information prepared and signed by an enrolled actuary for "defined benefit" plans only). | IRS |
| *Schedule SSA, Form 5500* series (registration statement). | IRS |
| *Form W-2P* (report of periodic plan benefit payments made during the year). | IRS; recipient of distribution |
| *Form 1099-R* (report of total distribution of benefits during the year). | IRS; recipient of distribution |
| *Form W-3* or *W-3G* (transmittal of *Form W-2P* and *Form 1099-R*). | IRS |
| *Form PBGC-1* (premium payment of required plan termination insurance — for "defined benefit" plans only). | Pension Benefit Guaranty Corporation (a government agency that insures pension plans of corporate employers) |
| Summary annual report. | Participants; beneficiaries |
| Individual deferred vested benefit statement to separated employee. | Former participant in plan |
| Summary of material modifications to a plan. | U.S. Department of Labor; participants; beneficiaries |
| Terminal report (when plan is terminated). | U.S. Department of Labor; participants; beneficiaries |
| Written explanation of joint and survivor annuity and financial effect of not electing to receive it (if plan provides benefits in the form of an annuity). | Participants |
| Written explanation of reasons for denying benefit claim and description of appeal procedures. | Person claiming entitlement to plan benefit |
| Various documents and information to be provided on request. | U.S. Department of Labor; participants |
| Various formal notices upon occurrence of certain events. | IRS; U.S. Department of Labor; Pension Benefit Guaranty Corporation; participants |

If your business maintains a pension or profit-sharing plan, it should be obvious from this summary of basic ERISA compliance requirements that you need some expert help from an attorney, accountant, or pension consulting firm — or all of them — if you are going to be able to properly comply with the requirements of ERISA and avoid potential fines and other civil and criminal penalties.

The cost of maintaining these plans has unfortunately multiplied several times over since the passage of ERISA in 1974, followed by a labyrinth of ERISA regulations issued by several different federal agencies. In short, unless you make substantial contributions to and obtain significant tax savings from an employee retirement plan, it may not be worth having because of the heavy costs of compliance with ERISA.

**Bonding and Withholding Requirements**

Besides the ERISA reporting and disclosure requirements discussed above, there are two other points you should be aware of regarding ERISA — the bonding requirement and withholding requirements on pension or profit-sharing plan distributions. All employees who are deemed to handle assets of a pension or welfare plan that is subject to ERISA must be covered by fidelity bond.[26] Consult your attorney or benefit consultant to see if any required bonding needs to be paid regarding any benefit plans you maintain for your employees. This is particularly important if you have a pension or profit-sharing plan.

Secondly, withholding is now mandatory on distributions of pension and profit-sharing benefits,[27] unless the recipient elects in advance not to have any tax withheld.

In addition to reporting and disclosure requirements under ERISA, there are other federal reporting and recordkeeping requirements for certain types of fringe benefit plans.[28] For example, employers maintaining educational assistance programs, group legal services plans, and so-called cafeteria plans are currently required to file annual reports with the IRS on *Form 5500, Form 5500-C*, or *Form 5500-R* and, if needed, to maintain records to show that those plans qualified for tax purposes for each year after 1984.[29]

# 5.6 Employee Safety and Health Regulations

As has been discussed in Section 5.4, employers are required by state law in many states to carry workers' compensation insurance for the protection of employees who develop job-related illnesses or who are injured on the job. In addition, there are comprehensive and far-reaching federal laws that set safety standards designed to prevent injuries arising from unsafe or unhealthy working conditions. The primary federal law regulating job safety, the Occupational Safety and Health Act of 1970 (OSHA), imposes several reporting and recordkeeping obligations for employers.

**Federal OSHA**

Over the years, the Occupational Safety and Health Administration has issued reams of regulations and standards for workplace safety. If you have employees, you will need to consult an attorney, preferably one with OSHA expertise, to determine what, if any, steps you must take to comply with federal and state safety standards at your place of business. Otherwise, you may be subject to fines and other legal sanctions if any employee is injured on the job or OSHA inspectors find that you are not in compliance with applicable safety standards at your place of business.

You may also want to contact the nearest regional U.S. Department of Labor–OSHA office and request information on any free consultative services or publications the office may have available. Many state occupational safety and health agencies provide confidential, on-site consultations for no charge. These consultations point out state compliance issues at your place of business. These state agencies would also know if any federal OSHA consultants are available.

**Notices to Employees**

OSHA requires that you post a permanent notice to employees regarding job safety.[30] In addition, OSHA rules require the posting of a second official poster regarding the rights of employees who are punished for objecting to unsafe working conditions.

**Recordkeeping Requirements**

Under OSHA, it is necessary to keep a log of industrial injuries and illnesses.[31] The federal *Form 200* can be used to satisfy this requirement.[32] The information in the log must also be summarized and posted prominently in your workplace from February 1 to March 1.[33] This requirement was eliminated January 1, 1983 for most retail, financial, insurance, and service firms,[34] but not for:

- Building material and garden supply stores
- General merchandise stores
- Foodstores
- Hotels and other lodging places
- Repair, amusement, and recreation services
- Health services[35]

Under OSHA, a supplementary record must be prepared after a recordable injury or illness occurs, using federal *Form 101* or any of the substitutes state law permits to be used for this purpose.[36]

Neither of the above recordkeeping forms are ordinarily filed with the government. Instead, these records must be retained and kept available for inspection for five years.[37] In addition, special recordkeeping requirements will generally apply if your employees are exposed to toxic substances, asbestos, radiation, or carcinogens on the job. You can obtain more detailed information on OSHA recordkeeping requirements by calling the nearest OSHA office (usually listed in the phone book under U. S. Government – Department of Labor) and asking for the booklet entitled *Recordkeeping Requirements for Occupational Injuries and Illnesses.*

OSHA exempts any employer with 10 or fewer employees from most of its reporting and recordkeeping requirements;[38] however, these small employers are not exempt from keeping a log of all injuries and accidents or reporting job-related fatalities and multiple injuries.

**Exemption from Recordkeeping**

Federal OSHA reporting requirements include:

**Reporting Requirements**

- The Bureau of Labor Statistics may require certain selected employers, including small employers, to report certain summary information on job-related injuries and illnesses annually on an occupational injuries and illness survey form.[39]
- In the event of a fatality or an accident resulting in the hospitalization of five or more employees, you must notify the area OSHA director within 48 hours, describing the circumstances of the accident, the extent of any injuries, and the number of fatalities.[40] There are penalties in the event you fail to give notice as required.[41]

See Section 11.5 for a discussion of laws this state may have that govern employee health and safety.

**State Employee Safety and Health Regulations**

# 5.7 Employee Wage-Hour and Child Labor Laws

Not all businesses nor all employees of a given business are covered by federal and state wage-hour and child labor laws. The coverage of these laws is a crazy quilt patchwork of exceptions. Thus, there is no simple way to tell you whether your business will be subject to one or more of the federal and state laws relating to minimum wage, overtime pay, and child labor, or, if it is, which employees are covered and which are not. To find out which laws apply to your business, contact your attorney or the local wage-hour office.

The Federal Fair Labor Standards Act (FLSA) includes a number of requirements regarding compensation of employees covered under the act. There are two major requirements you need to know about.

**Federal Wage-Hour Laws**

The minimum wage provisions of the FLSA set an hourly minimum wage that you can pay to an employee. The current federal minimum wage is $4.25 per hour.[42] Certain states provide for a minimum wage in excess of the federal requirement or that applies to some employees who are not covered under the federal minimum wage law. Refer to Section 11.5 for the requirements in this state.

**Minimum Wage Requirement**

The overtime pay requirement rule states you must pay a covered employee at one and one-half times the employee's regular hourly rate

**Overtime Pay Requirement**

for any hours worked in excess of 40 in a week.[43] The regular hourly rate cannot be less than the minimum wage. For the overtime pay requirement, the FLSA takes a single workweek as its measuring period and does not permit averaging of hours over two or more weeks. For example, if an employee works 30 hours one week and 50 hours during the next, he or she must receive overtime compensation (time and one-half) for the 10 overtime hours worked in the second week, even though the average number of hours worked in the two weeks is 40. Note that the FLSA only requires overtime pay based on the number of hours worked during a week and not for working long hours on a particular day.

The above rules generally apply to salaried workers as well as to those paid on an hourly basis. To determine the regular hourly rate for a salaried employee, it is necessary to divide the employee's weekly salary by the number of hours in his or her regular workweek (40 or less).

**Employee Exemptions**

Executives, administrators, professionals, and outside salespeople are not covered and thus are not entitled by law to any pay for overtime hours worked.[44] The theory behind this exemption is apparently the view that these types of employees are independent and sophisticated enough to take care of themselves and do not need to be protected by the government from exploitation by their employers.

Under the Code of Federal Regulations (Section 541.5), an employee qualifying for the exemption as an outside salesperson must meet the two requirements listed below.

- The employee customarily and regularly works away from the employer's place of business while making sales or obtaining orders or contracts for services or for the use of facilities for which a consideration will be paid by the client or customer.
- The employee cannot do any other kind of work for the company (besides that of selling) for more than 20% of the usual workweek put in by the company's nonexempt employees; for example, the outside salesperson or exempted employee could do receptionist work for only 8 hours of each 40-hour workweek.

Various indicators of an employee's bona fide status as an outside salesperson include:

- A contractual designation or job title that reflects involvement in sales;
- Significant compensation on a commission basis;
- Special sales training; and
- Little or no direct or constant supervision in carrying out daily tasks.

**Small Enterprise Exemption**

Employees of certain small companies, other than those enterprises engaged in commerce, are exempt from coverage under the wage-hour laws. What this really means, translated from the legalese, is that certain smaller businesses that do not significantly affect the flow of goods and services in interstate commerce are exempted. An "enterprise engaged in commerce" is one that "has employees engaged in commerce or in the production of goods for commerce, or that has employees handling, selling, or otherwise working on goods or materials that have been moved in commerce or produced for commerce by any person," and "is an enterprise whose annual gross volume of sales made or business done is not less than $500,000."[45]

All of which means that, if your firm does less than a half million dollars in sales a year, it will generally be exempt from FLSA overtime and minimum wage requirements.[46]

Even if you are exempt from the FLSA wage-hour rules, state wage-hour laws may apply and may be more stringent than federal laws in many states.

Numerous other exemptions from the wage-hour laws are based on the type of business, the nature of the work performed by the employee, where the work is done, and other factors.[47] Before you assume that your employees are covered by the FLSA, you should consult your attorney, or at least call the local wage and hour office on an anonymous basis and ask for an informal and nonbinding opinion over the phone.

**Detailed Records Required**

Probably the most important thing you should be aware of, if you have employees subject to FLSA standards, is the need to keep detailed records of hours worked, the type of work, and wages or salary paid. Under the law, if an employee files a claim against you for alleged failure to pay required wages in the past, you will need to be able to produce proof that you met the statutory requirements. Keeping detailed pay and work records for each employee is the only way to protect yourself against such claims for back pay. In addition, the FLSA requires employers to preserve such records for up to three years.

**Poster Requirement**

If you have employees whose wages, hours, and working conditions are subject to FLSA regulations, you will need to post the official wage-hour poster provided by the U.S. Department of Labor.

**State Wage-Hour Laws**

Refer to Section 11.5 for a discussion of the basic wage-hour and other significant labor law requirements under state law.

**Child Labor Laws**

Both the FLSA and various state laws regulate or prohibit the employment of children in businesses, with very few exceptions. If you intend to hire children to work in your business — other than hiring your own children, which is usually permitted, except in hazardous situations — you need to be aware of the following basic child labor law provisions.

**Federal Child Labor Laws**

As a general rule, the FLSA prohibits the employment of children under 16 years of age;[48] although, there are a number of exceptions to this rule.[49] All children under age 18, however, are excluded from certain occupations that are designated as hazardous by the secretary of labor.[50]

Children under 16 years of age cannot be hired under any of the following circumstances:

- To work in any workplace where mining, manufacturing, or processing operations take place;
- To operate power machinery, other than office equipment;
- To operate or serve as a helper on motor vehicles;
- To work in public messenger services; and
- To work in the following occupations: transportation; warehousing or storage; communications or public utilities; or construction (except in sales or office work).[51]

Children 14 or 15 years of age can be hired in other occupations not considered to be hazardous, but there are numerous limitations on the hours and times when they may work, particularly when schools are in session. A few occupations, such as delivering newspapers and doing theatrical work, are exempt from the federal child labor laws, even for children under 14 years of age.[52]

**State Child Labor Laws**

Most states also strictly regulate the employment of children. See Section 11.5 regarding state child labor laws in this state. Thus, if you intend to employ children under 18 years of age in a business, you will probably need legal guidance as to the conditions under which they may work, if at all, under federal and state child labor laws.

# 5.8  Fair Employment Practices

As an employer, you will also need to be alert to your obligations under a number of federal and state laws that prohibit discrimination in employment on the basis of sex, age, race, color, national origin, religion, or on account of mental or physical handicaps. These anti-discrimination laws are not just limited to hiring practices, but relate to almost every aspect of the relationship between employer and employee, including compensation, promotions, type of work assigned, and working conditions.

In addition to outlawing discrimination in employment, companies contracting for business with the federal government are generally required to adopt affirmative action programs in employment of minorities, women, the handicapped, and Vietnam veterans. Affirmative action programs are employment programs that go beyond elimination of discrimination. Under such programs, employers consciously make an effort to hire more women and minority group members and to upgrade the pay and responsibility levels of women and other groups that have historically been subject to patterns of discrimination.

Affirmative action programs are generally required for businesses that are government contractors. Most businesses are only required to refrain from discriminating in employment.

There are several anti-discrimination requirements that, as a small business owner, you should be aware of; however, if your small business employs less than 15 employees and is not working on government contracts or subcontracts, the federal anti-discrimination laws listed below generally do not apply to you. The one exception to this would be the Equal Pay Act of 1963 which provides equal pay for equal work for women. This act is applicable to employers with two or more employees.

**Federal Anti-Discrimination Laws**

## Employers Subject to Federal Anti-Discrimination Laws

| Name of Law | Employers Who Are Covered | What the Law Requires |
|---|---|---|
| Title VII of the Civil Rights Act of 1964 and Americans with Disabilities Act (ADA) | Employers with 15 or more employees during 20 weeks of a calendar year (25 employees under ADA until 1994) | No discrimination in employment practices based on race, religion, disability or national origin |
| Pregnancy Discrimination Act | Same as for Title VII above | Equal treatment for pregnant women and new mothers for all employment-related purposes, including fringe benefits |
| Executive Order 11246 as amended | Employers with federal contracts or subcontracts of $10,000 or more | No discrimination in employment practices based on race, sex, color, religion, or national origin |
| Equal Pay Act of 1963 | Nearly all employers with two or more employees | Equal pay for women |
| Age Discrimination in Employment Act of 1967 | Employers with 20 or more employees, 20 or more weeks in a calendar year | No discrimination in hiring or firing on account of age, for persons age 40 to 70 |
| Rehabilitation Act of 1973 | Employers with federal contracts or subcontracts of $2,500 or more | No discrimination in employment practices on account of mental health or physical handicaps |
| Vietnam-Era Veteran Readjustment Assistance Act of 1974 | Employers with federal contracts or subcontracts of $10,000 or more | Affirmative action programs for certain disabled veterans |

Employers who violate any of the above laws may be sued by either the complaining individuals or by the various government enforcement agencies, or both.

**Formal Compliance Requirements**

Small businesses are not required to do a lot of paperwork or filling out of forms when it comes to federal anti-discrimination laws. An employer with more than 100 employees, however, must file *Form EEO-1* with the Equal Employment Opportunity Commission (EEOC) each year.[53]

As an employer you are required to keep detailed records — and should, for your own protection — as to reasons for hiring or not hiring, promoting or not promoting, any employee or job applicant. In the event it is ever necessary to demonstrate that your firm has not discriminated against any group or individual member of a group in violation of federal laws, these records will provide the needed documentation.

Besides these requirements, there are a number of official posters you may be required to post in your place of business. These may include:

**Display Posters**

| Type of Poster | Who Must Post | Source of Poster |
|---|---|---|
| Civil rights poster regarding sexual, racial, religious, and ethnic discrimination or because of physical or mental disability (*WH Publication 1088*) | Employers with 15 or more employees during 20 weeks of the year or with federal contracts or subcontracts of $10,000 or more[54] | EEOC offices, the nearest Office of Compliance |
| Age discrimination poster | Employers with 20 or more employees who work 20 or more weeks a year[55] | EEOC offices |
| Notice to employees working on government contracts (*WH Publication 1313*) | Any employer performing government contract work subject to the Service Contract Act or the Public Contracts Act | U.S. Department of Labor, Employment Standards Division |
| Poster required under the Vietnam Era Veterans Readjustment Assistance Act | Employers with federal contracts or subcontracts of $10,000 or more | From the federal contracting officer administering the contract |

To obtain these posters, you can contact each of the appropriate federal agencies and request a copy of their required poster.

The civil rights poster and the age discrimination poster — plus two other required posters mentioned earlier, the Fair Labor Standards Act (FLSA) and the Occupational Safety and Health Act (OSHA) posters — are available through a company called Remarkable Products. This company has conveniently laminated these four posters onto one, easy-to-mount poster.

These laminated posters are available for a nominal fee. For more information on these posters, contact:

**Remarkable Products**
(201) 784-0900

You need to be keenly aware of your potential liability for sexual harassment in the workplace, another increasingly significant area of the anti-discrimination laws, under Title VII of the Civil Rights Act. While the federal Civil Rights Act does not specifically refer to sexual harassment as a form of discrimination, the courts and the Equal Employment Opportunity Commission (EEOC) have long accepted it as such. There are two types of sexual harassment under Title VII, as it has been interpreted over the years.

One type of sexual harassment is where tangible job benefits are granted or withheld based on an employee's receptiveness to unwelcome requests or conduct. For example, a male supervisor tells a female employee to meet him in the hot tub of his mountain chalet on a Saturday afternoon to discuss a business contract. She refuses to meet him at his place and later receives a bad rating from him for "poor attitude and unwillingness to work overtime," which costs her a raise or promotion. The female employee in such a case has been denied a tangible job benefit due to sexual harassment.

The second type of sexual harassment involves a hostile work environment; that is, a situation in which the work environment is oppressive and hostile to members of one sex. This occurs when such conditions either unreasonably interfere with the individual's work performance or create an intimidating, hostile, or offensive environment. This type of harassment may not have any economic effects on the individual, and management or supervisory personnel may not be involved. Nevertheless, an employer who allows such a condition to persist may still be liable if management was aware of the harassment by co-workers (or even by customers) and fails to take appropriate actions to remedy the situation.

Merely having a company policy that prohibits sexual harassment at your company won't automatically stop such activity or protect the firm from liability if harassment occurs, but the absence of such a policy makes such conduct somewhat more likely to occur and will also tend to strengthen an employee's claim against you if your firm is sued for allowing such acts to occur. Adopt a sexual harassment policy that not only prohibits such conduct, but which sets up a grievance mechanism for employees who are victims of any such harassment, and communicate this company policy strongly and clearly to your employees.

Note that, in addition to federal civil rights case law, the statutes of many states, or the regulations of many state civil rights commissions, now specifically prohibit sexual harassment in the workplace, and some of these laws go well beyond the protections afforded under federal law.

Many states have additional statutes or regulations, which may go beyond federal laws. For a more detailed discussion of anti-discrimination laws in this state, refer to Section 11.5.

# 5.9  Immigration Law Restrictions on Hiring

The Immigration Reform and Control Act of 1986 represents a major governmental requirement regarding the relationship between the employer and employee. Under this law, you are prohibited from hiring illegal aliens and, depending on the number of any prior violations, are subject to fines of $250 to $20,000 for each illegal alien hired after November 6, 1986. At the same time, the act also prohibits employment discrimination on the basis of citizenship status and national origin; you may not fire or fail to hire anyone on the basis of foreign appearance, language, or name.

For all employees hired after November 6, 1986, you are required to verify their eligibility for employment within three business days of each new hire. As an employer, you will need to fill out and retain *Form I-9*. The employee fills out the top portion of the form, indicating whether he or she is a citizen or national of the United States; an alien lawfully admitted for permanent residence; or an alien authorized by the U.S. Immigration and Naturalization Service (INS) to work in the United States.

On the bottom portion of *Form I-9*, there are three separate lists of various forms of identification and employment eligibility documents the employee must provide for you. You must check off the documents you have examined, such as passport, certificate of naturalization, etc. These papers must include either one document in List A or one each in lists B and C. Both you and the employee must sign the form under penalty of perjury, and you must retain the completed form and make it available if the INS or U.S. Department of Labor requests it during an inspection.

You may obtain copies of *Form I-9* and a related *Employer's Handbook* from the nearest office of the U.S. Immigration and Naturalization Service. A sample *Form I-9* is also included at the end of this chapter. For more information on employer responsibilities, call and request Category 3.

**U.S. Immigration and Naturalization Service**
(800) 755-0777

# 5.10  Restrictions on Layoffs of Employees

**The WARN Act**

If your business grows to the size where you have 100 or more full-time employees — or the equivalent, based on 40-hour workweeks — at a single location, you may be subject to the potentially onerous provisions of the plant closing bill that was enacted by Congress in 1988 and went into effect on February 4, 1989. This law, called the Worker Adjustment and Retraining Notification Act, or WARN Act,[56] would affect you if you laid off 50 or more employees, or one-third of the work force, in a 30-day period. It applies to virtually any plant closing or major layoff for any reason, with a few obvious exceptions, such as due to an earthquake or flood, or due to a labor dispute, e.g., a strike or lockout for which no notice need be given.

A "layoff" under this act includes any of the following:

- A permanent termination of employment;
- A layoff of an employee for more than six months; or
- A loss of half the employees' working hours for six consecutive months.

In case of any major layoff or shutdown, the law requires you to give at least 60 days advance notice. If you give less than that, you are required to pay the laid-off workers for 60 days minus the actual number of days' notice you gave. The law requires you to notify the labor union that represents the employees, or, if none, the individual employees by mailing the notice to their last known address or including it in their pay envelope. You must also notify the local city or county government and state labor agency of the planned shutdown or cutback.

The WARN Act doesn't generally prohibit a company from making layoffs or shutting down a money-losing plant, but it makes it more costly for the employer to do so, and also gives local unions and politicians time to find some way to attempt to coerce a company into maintaining an antiquated facility that may no longer be economically viable.

The WARN law does impose stiff restrictions on a firm's ability to sell off, reorganize, merge, or consolidate operations, if such a decision would adversely affect the jobs of 50 or more employees. In other words, if your Japanese competition renders your plant obsolete, you will not be allowed to sell it off to a competitor, if doing so would cost 50 or more employees their jobs. The act has made it much more costly to take a risk on building a plant in the United States — if it fails, you may have to close shop rather than restructure or sell.

As a result, there is expected to be a great deal of litigation over what does and does not constitute a mass layoff or shutdown under WARN.

# 5.11 The Americans with Disabilities Act

In July of 1990, Congress enacted a revolutionary and wide-reaching piece of legislation, the Americans with Disabilities Act (ADA), which is designed to make both the workplace and most public facilities much more accessible to disabled persons.

This new law[57] and related regulations,[58] which are being phased in over several years, will have a significant impact on a great many businesses, both in terms of employment practices and in terms or removing architectural barriers and other physical features that have limiting effects on the lives of disabled persons.

## Anti-Discrimination Rules Regarding the Disabled

Title I of the ADA, which is effective for larger firms on July 26, 1992, prohibits discrimination against any "qualified individual with a disability" in all aspects of employment, including hiring and discharge of workers, compensation and benefits. In addition, you must reasonably accommodate employees' or applicants' disabilities, which may mean modifying facilities, restructuring work schedules, or transferring disabled workers to vacant positions for which they are qualified, in appropriate circumstances. You are not required to accommodate a disabled worker, however, if doing so would impose an "undue hardship" on yourself.

## Medical Screening Tests

One area that will be significantly affected in the hiring process is the limitation on medical screening of applicants. Under the ADA, companies can no longer screen out prospective employees with disabilities because the applicant has an elevated risk of an on-the-job injury or a medical condition that might be aggravated because of job demands. The law specifically bans questions about a job applicant's physical or mental condition either on an employment application form or during a job interview. This would include general questions such as, "Do you have any mental or physical conditions that would prevent you from performing your job functions?"

Medical exams are still allowed, but they are greatly restricted. Pre-offer exams are prohibited, but an offer may be conditioned upon the satisfactory results of a medical examination. Results, however, cannot be used to withdraw an offer, unless they show that the individual in question is not able to perform the tasks required by the position.

You should be aware that the definition of "disabled" under the ADA includes people with AIDS, those who test positive for the HIV virus, and rehabilitated drug abusers and alcoholics; however, you should also note that the ADA does not:

- Prohibit voluntary tests, such as employer-sponsored cholesterol or blood pressure tests; nor
- Require employers to hire persons who are drug users or who have contagious diseases.

The ADA is neutral on the issue of drug testing of employees, in effect leaving that up to regulation by the states.

## Effective Dates

The ADA's employment-related rules become effective on the following dates:

- July 26, 1992 — Equal employment rules with regard to the disabled, effective for employers with 25 or more employees during 20 weeks of the year;

- January 26, 1993 — Newly built facilities must be accessible to both disabled employees and customers; and
- July 26, 1994 — Equal employment rules with regard to the disabled, effective for employers with 15 or more employees during 20 weeks of the year.

Title III of the ADA requires practically all businesses to make their facilities accessible to disabled employees and customers. Examples of various accessibility requirements with regard to public accommodations include: **Public Accommodations for the Disabled**

- One designated parking space for the disabled must be provided for every 25 or fewer spaces. A lesser ratio applies if there are more than 100 total spaces.
- Hotels and motels must have 5% of their rooms accessible to wheelchairs and another 5% must be equipped with devices such as visual alarms for the hearing-impaired.
- Access ramps must be in place where the floor level changes more than one-half of an inch.
- Elevators must be provided in three-story or taller buildings and in those with more than 3,000 square feet per story.
- In retail or grocery stores, checkout aisles must be at least 36 inches wide. This is wide enough for wheelchairs.
- Theaters and similar places of assembly for 50 or more persons must have at least three wheelchair spaces dispersed throughout the seating area.

The new public access requirements will become effective: **Effective Dates**

- January 26, 1992 — For all larger employers with more than 25 employers or more than $1 million of gross annual receipts;
- July 26, 1992 — For companies with 25 or fewer employees and gross annual receipts of $1 million or less; and
- January 26, 1993 — For companies with 10 or fewer employees and gross annual receipts of $500,000 or less.

Companies spending money to remove architectural and transportation barriers to the disabled can deduct up to $15,000 a year of such expenses.[59] In addition, small firms — those with gross receipts under $1 million or fewer than 30 full-time employees — who spend between $250 and $10,250 a year on access for the disabled, can claim a tax credit for up to 50% of the cost of such expenditures, a maximum annual credit of $5,000.[60] For more information on the ADA, contact: **Tax Incentives**

**Equal Employment Opportunity Commission**   or   **U.S. Department of Justice**
2401 E Street                                  (202) 514-0301
Washington, DC 20506
(202) 663-4264

For further information on these new regulations and other hiring issues, you may want to read *People Investment* by E. R. Worthington & Anita E. Worthington, which will soon be available from your book source or:

**The Oasis Press**
(800) 228-2275

# Footnotes

1. Treasury Decision 7701, 1980-28 I.R.B. 20.
2. Treas. Regs. §31.6302(c)-1(a)(1)(i)(a).
3. Treas. Regs. §31.6302(c)-1(a)(1)(i)(b).
4. I.R.C. §6302(g).
5. I.R.C. §7502(e)(3).
6. I.R.C. §§3301(1) and 3306(b)(1).
7. I.R.C. §§3301(1) and 3302(b).
8. I.R.C. §3306(a)(1)(A).
9. I.R.C. §3306(a)(1)(B).
10. 29 U.S.C. §1131.
11. 29 U.S.C. §1132; I.R.C. §§4971, 4975, 6057–6059, and 6652.
12. 29 U.S.C. §1002(2); 29 C.F.R. §2510.3-2.
13. 29 U.S.C. §1002(1); 29 C.F.R. §2510.3-1.
14. 29 C.F.R. §2510.3-1(b); 29 C.F.R. §2510.3-2(b).
15. 29 C.F.R. §2520.104b-2.
16. 29 C.F.R. §2520.102-3.
17. 29 C.F.R. §2520.104b-2(a)(2).
18. 29 C.F.R. §2520.104b-2(a)(1).
19. 29 C.F.R. §2520.104-20.
20. 29 U.S.C. §1024(b)(4); 29 C.F.R. §2520.104b-1.
21. 29 C.F.R. §2520.104a-3.
22. 29 C.F.R. §2520.104a-5.
23. 29 C.F.R. §2520.104b-10.
24. 29 C.F.R. §§2520.104a-4 and 2520.104b-3.
25. 29 U.S.C. §1021(c).
26. 29 U.S.C. §1112.
27. I.R.C. §3405(a).
28. I.R.C. §6039 D.
29. Announcement 86-20, I.R.B. 1986–87, 34.
30. 29 C.F.R. §1903.2.
31. 29 C.F.R. §1904.2.
32. 29 C.F.R. §1904.10.
33. 29 C.F.R. §1904.5.
34. 29 C.F.R. §1904.16.
35. 29 C.F.R. §1904.12.
36. 29 C.F.R. §1904.4.
37. 29 C.F.R. §1904.6.
38. 29 C.F.R. §1904.15.
39. 29 C.F.R. §§1904.15 and 1904.21.
40. 29 C.F.R. §1904.8.
41. 29 C.F.R. §1904.9.
42. 29 U.S.C. §206(a)(1).
43. 29 U.S.C. §207(a)(1).
44. 29 U.S.C. §213(a)(1).
45. 29 U.S.C. §203(s).
46. 29 U.S.C. §207(a)(1).
47. 29 U.S.C. §213.
48. 29 U.S.C. §§203(1) and 212.
49. 29 U.S.C. §213.
50. 29 C.F.R. §570.50–570.71.
51. 29 C.F.R. §570.33.
52. 29 U.S.C. §213(c) and (d).
53. 29 C.F.R. §1602.7.
54. 29 C.F.R. §1601.30.
55. 29 U.S.C. §627 and 29 C.F.R. §1627.10.
56. 29 U.S.C. §§2101–2109.
57. 42 U.S.C. §12101 *et seq.*
58. 29 C.F.R. §1630.
59. I.R.C. §190.
60. I.R.C. §44.

# EMPLOYMENT ELIGIBILITY VERIFICATION (Form I-9)

**1** **EMPLOYEE INFORMATION AND VERIFICATION:** (To be completed and signed by employee.)

| Name: (Print or Type) Last | First | Middle | Birth Name |
|---|---|---|---|
| Address: Street Name and Number | City | State | ZIP Code |

| Date of Birth (Month/Day/Year) | Social Security Number |
|---|---|

I attest, under penalty of perjury, that I am (check a box):

☐ 1. A citizen or national of the United States.

☐ 2. An alien lawfully admitted for permanent residence (Alien Number A _____ ).

☐ 3. An alien authorized by the Immigration and Naturalization Service to work in the United States (Alien Number A _____ , or Admission Number _____ , expiration of employment authorization, if any _____ ).

I attest, under penalty of perjury, the documents that I have presented as evidence of identity and employment eligibility are genuine and relate to me. I am aware that federal law provides for imprisonment and/or fine for any false statements or use of false documents in connection with this certificate.

| Signature | Date (Month/Day/Year) |
|---|---|

PREPARER/TRANSLATOR CERTIFICATION (To be completed if prepared by person other than the employee). I attest, under penalty of perjury, that the above was prepared by me at the request of the named individual and is based on all information of which I have any knowledge.

| Signature | Name (Print or Type) | | |
|---|---|---|---|
| Address (Street Name and Number) | City | State | Zip Code |

**2** **EMPLOYER REVIEW AND VERIFICATION:** (To be completed and signed by employer.)

Instructions:

Examine one document from List A and check the appropriate box, **OR** examine one document from List B **and** one from List C and check the appropriate boxes. Provide the *Document Identification Number* and *Expiration Date* for the document checked.

| List A — Documents that Establish Identity and Employment Eligibility | List B — Documents that Establish Identity | and | List C — Documents that Establish Employment Eligibility |
|---|---|---|---|
| ☐ 1. United States Passport | ☐ 1. A State-issued driver's license or a State-issued I.D. card with a photograph, or information, including name, sex, date of birth, height, weight, and color of eyes. (Specify State)_____ ) | | ☐ 1. Original Social Security Number Card (other than a card stating it is not valid for employment) |
| ☐ 2. Certificate of United States Citizenship | | | ☐ 2. A birth certificate issued by State, county, or municipal authority bearing a seal or other certification |
| ☐ 3. Certificate of Naturalization | ☐ 2. U.S. Military Card | | |
| ☐ 4. Unexpired foreign passport with attached Employment Authorization | ☐ 3. Other (Specify document and issuing authority) _____ | | ☐ 3. Unexpired INS Employment Authorization Specify form # _____ |
| ☐ 5. Alien Registration Card with photograph | | | |
| *Document Identification* # _____ | *Document Identification* # _____ | | *Document Identification* # _____ |
| *Expiration Date (if any)* _____ | *Expiration Date (if any)* _____ | | *Expiration Date (if any)* _____ |

CERTIFICATION: I attest, under penalty of perjury, that I have examined the documents presented by the above individual, that they appear to be genuine and to relate to the individual named, and that the individual, to the best of my knowledge, is eligible to work in the United States.

| Signature | Name (Print or Type) | Title |
|---|---|---|
| Employer Name | Address | Date |

Form I-9 (05/07/87)
OMB No. 1115-0136

U.S. Department of Justice
Immigration and Naturalization Service

# Employment Eligibility Verification

**NOTICE:** Authority for collecting the information on this form is in Title 8, United States Code, Section 1324A, which requires employers to verify employment eligibility of individuals on a form approved by the Attorney General. This form will be used to verify the individual's eligibility for employment in the United States. Failure to present this form for inspection to officers of the Immigration and Naturalization Service or Department of Labor within the time period specified by regulation, or improper completion or retention of this form, may be a violation of the above law and may result in a civil money penalty.

## Section 1. Instructions to Employee/Preparer for completing this form

### Instructions for the employee.

All employees, upon being hired, must complete Section 1 of this form. Any person hired after November 6, 1986 must complete this form. (For the purpose of completion of this form the term "hired" applies to those employed, recruited or referred for a fee.)

All employees must print or type their complete name, address, date of birth, and Social Security Number. The block which correctly indicates the employee's immigration status must be checked. If the second block is checked, the employee's Alien Registration Number must be provided. If the third block is checked, the employee's Alien Registration Number *or* Admission Number must be provided, as well as the date of expiration of that status, if it expires.

All employees whose present names differ from birth names, because of marriage or other reasons, must print or type their birth names in the appropriate space of Section 1. Also, employees whose names change after employment verification should report these changes to their employer.

All employees must sign and date the form.

### Instructions for the preparer of the form, if not the employee.

If a person assists the employee with completing this form, the preparer must certify the form by signing it and printing or typing his or her complete name and address.

## Section 2. Instructions to Employer for completing this form

(For the purpose of completion of this form, the term "employer" applies to employers and those who recruit or refer for a fee.)

Employers must complete this section by examining evidence of identity and employment eligibility, and:
- checking the appropriate box in List A *or* boxes in both Lists B and C;
- recording the document identification number and expiration date (if any);
- recording the type of form if not specifically identified in the list;
- signing the certification section.

***NOTE: Employers are responsible for reverifying employment eligibility of employees whose employment eligibility documents carry an expiration date.***

Copies of documentation presented by an individual for the purpose of establishing identity and employment eligibility may be copied and retained for the purpose of complying with the requirements of this form and no other purpose. Any copies of documentation made for this purpose should be maintained with this form.

Name changes of employees which occur after preparation of this form should be recorded on the form by lining through the old name, printing the new name and the reason (such as marriage), and dating and initialing the changes. Employers should not attempt to delete or erase the old name in any fashion.

### RETENTION OF RECORDS.

The completed form must be retained by the employer for:
- three years after the date of hiring; or
- one year after the date the employment is terminated, whichever is later.

---

Employers may photocopy or reprint this form as necessary.

---

U.S. Department of Justice
Immigration and Naturalization Service

OMB #1115-0136
Form I-9 (05/07 87)
☆ USGPO 1987- 183-918/69085

For sale by the Superintendent of Documents, U.S. Government Printing Office
Washington, D.C. 20402

Chapter 6

# Businesses that Require Licenses to Operate

*The bureaucrat who smiles when something serious has gone wrong*
*has already found someone to blame it on.*

— Anonymous

## 6.1  General Licensing

Almost any kind of business activity you engage in will require a city or
county business license, which is usually fairly simple to obtain. In addition, some types of businesses will have to obtain licenses from the federal government to operate; while other businesses, occupations, and professions are also licensed and regulated by the state.

Even though there are tremendous variations regarding the requirements
for obtaining necessary federal and state licenses, these requirements
generally relate to educational attainments, experience in the particular
field, passage of examinations, submission of detailed applications,
meeting financial or bonding requirements, or some combination of the
foregoing, plus payment of a licensing fee or tax.

In addition to the federal and state licensing requirements, you need to be
aware of certain local city or county permits that you may have to obtain.
For example, if you will be in the food business, you may have to get a
license from the county health department; or, if your business would
like to do any construction or remodeling, you might have to get approval from your local planning commission.

Before you begin to operate any kind of business, find out whether you
will be required to obtain any special government licenses or permits,
since in most cases you must obtain the particular license before commencing operation.

This chapter and Section 11.6, respectively, provide a partial listing of the federal and state licensing requirements you are most likely to encounter as a small business owner. Because the number of activities that may require federal or state licenses is so large, no attempt has been made to try to list all of them in this book.

Thus, the lists of licensing agencies and businesses that require licenses found in this chapter and in Chapter 11 should be helpful in alerting you, as a small business owner, to possible licensing needs, but you should remember that these lists are not complete and are not a substitute for individualized legal advice.

# 6.2  Federal Licenses

If you are starting a small business, it is relatively unlikely that you will need any type of license or permit from the federal government; however, the following is a list of the federal licensing requirements you might possibly encounter:

### Federal Licensing Requirements

| Activity | Federal Agency |
| --- | --- |
| Rendering investment advice | Securities and Exchange Commission |
| Providing ground transportation as a common carrier | Interstate Commerce Commission |
| Preparation of meat products | Food and Drug Administration |
| Production of drugs or biological products | Food and Drug Administration |
| Making tobacco products or alcohol | Treasury Department, Bureau of Alcohol, Tobacco, and Firearms |
| Making or dealing in firearms | Treasury Department, Bureau of Alcohol, Tobacco, and Firearms |
| Radio or television broadcasting | Federal Communications Commission |

# 6.3  State Licenses

For a partial listing of businesses and professions required to be licensed in this state, see Section 11.6.

# Operating the Business

# Chapter 7

# Excise Taxes

*Taxation without representation is tyranny.*

— Patrick Henry

*Taxation with representation is worse.*

— Will Rogers

## 7.1 General Considerations

Both federal and state tax laws impose excise or similar taxes on a number of different types of businesses, products, services, and occupations. These taxes are usually imposed without any assessment or notice to the taxpayer. Thus, it is up to you to find out if you are subject to any of these taxes and, if so, to obtain the proper tax return forms and pay the tax on time.

It is not uncommon for a small business to operate for several years without the owner ever being aware of the need to pay excise taxes. Then comes the day of reckoning, when a formal notice is received from the government demanding immediate payment of several years' worth of back taxes on some particular item subject to excise tax, plus interest and penalties for not filing the returns and not paying the tax. This can be a disastrous surprise, especially since the business owner has not factored the cost of paying the excise into the price of his or her goods or services.

Therefore, this chapter is designed to alert you in advance to the types of federal and state excise — and similar — taxes that you may need to know about. Some excise taxes, such as those on telephone service and insurance companies, are not discussed below since they are passed along or absorbed by the telephone company, insurance company, or other large institution with which your business may deal, and you have no obligation to file any returns or make any direct payment to the government of such taxes.

# 7.2  State Excise Taxes

See Section 11.7 for a summary of various state excise taxes that may affect your business.

# 7.3  Federal Excise Taxes

Federal excise taxes on many products and transactions have been repealed over the last 20 years, so these taxes are much less pervasive now than in the past. The excise tax that the largest number of small businesses are likely to be subject to is the motor vehicle highway use tax on vehicles of more than 55,000 pounds gross weight.[1] *Form 2290* must be filed by owners of trucks and buses subject to the highway use tax. If you want information about the highway use tax, you should request a copy of IRS *Publication 349* from any IRS office. The federal government imposes a number of excise taxes on various types of business activities. Some excise taxes are on the production or sale of certain goods. Some are on services or the use of certain products or facilities. Still others are imposed on businesses of a certain type. Most federal excise taxes are reported on *Form 720, Quarterly Federal Excise Tax Return*, the most common excise tax form.

Environmental taxes on petroleum and 42 designated chemical substances are reported on *Form 6627* and attached to *Form 720*. The windfall profits tax on crude oil was repealed by Congress in 1988.

Federal excise taxes can be broken down into several major categories:

- The motor vehicle highway use tax — This tax is imposed on vehicles of more than 55,000 pounds gross weight.[2]
- Retailer taxes on certain fuels[3] — The federal gasoline tax is now $0.14 (14 cents) per gallon on gasoline, and the tax on diesel is $0.20 (20 cents) per gallon. In addition, both of the taxes are increased by $0.01 ($1/10$ of a cent) per gallon to create a Leaking Underground Storage Tank Trust Fund. A reduced tax rate applies to qualified methane and ethanol fuel.
- Other retail excise taxes are now imposed on sales of:

- Heavy trucks and trailers;[4]
- Tires and tubes;[5]
- Recreation equipment such as bows, arrows, fishing rods, reels, lures, and creels;[6] and
- Firearms and ammunition.[7]

- Transportation taxes on air transportation[8] — If you are in the business of transporting people by air, you may have to collect an excise tax.
- Communications taxes on telephone and teletype services.[9]
- Wagering taxes.[10]
- Tax on coal mined in the United States.[11]
- Environmental taxes on petroleum products, various chemicals, and hazardous wastes.[12]
- Taxes on alcohol, firearms, ammunition, and tobacco products.[13]
- Manufacturer's excise tax on vaccines — Certain vaccines manufactured or imported into the United States are subject to an excise tax in order to create a Vaccine Injury Compensation Trust Fund, a no-fault program for compensating persons who are injured by, or die from, certain vaccines.[14]

The Revenue Reconciliation Act of 1989:

- Created an excise tax on ozone-depleting chemicals; and
- Increased the oil spill liability excise tax to $0.05 (5 cents) a barrel.[15]

## Luxury Taxes

So-called luxury taxes, which were all repealed in 1965, have come back to life in the Revenue Reconciliation Act of 1990. In general, the newly enacted luxury taxes apply to retail purchases of certain items after December 31, 1990 and apply at a rate of 10% of the amount by which the retail price exceeds certain exempt amounts.[16] The new luxury taxes are as follows:

- Automobiles — The 10% tax applies to the portion of the retail purchase price in excess of $30,000. It does not apply to vehicles of more than 6,000 pounds unloaded gross weight, or to any vehicle, such as a taxicab, that is used exclusively in the active conduct of a trade or business of transporting people or property for compensation or hire.
- Boats — The 10% tax applies to the portion of the retail purchase price that exceeds $100,000, but not to boats used commercially for fishing or transporting persons or property for compensation or hire.
- Aircraft — The 10% tax applies to the portion of the retail purchase price that exceeds $250,000. The tax can be avoided if the aircraft is to be used at least 80% for business.
- Furs and Jewelry — The 10% tax applies to the portion of the retail purchase price that exceeds $10,000 per item.

The new luxury taxes, which are collected by the retailer who sells the item, apply only to the first retail sale of an item. Thus, for example, if you buy a used $50,000 automobile, there is no luxury tax on the purchase.

For further information on excise taxes and other federal taxes, you may wish to obtain IRS *Publication 334, Tax Guide for Small Business,* or, for more detailed information on excise taxes, IRS *Publication 510, Excise Taxes.*

# Footnotes

1. I.R.C. § 4481(a).
2. Id.
3. I.R.C. §§ 4041, 4081, and 4091.
4. I.R.C. § 4051.
5. I.R.C. § 4071(a).
6. I.R.C. § 4161(a) and (b).
7. I.R.C. § 4181.
8. I.R.C. §§ 4261(a) and 4271(a).
9. I.R.C. § 4251.
10. I.R.C. §§ 4401 and 4411.
11. I.R.C. § 4121(a).
12. I.R.C. §§ 4611 and 4661.
13. I.R.C. §§ 5001, 5041(b), 5701, and 5801–5822.
14. I.R.C. §§ 4131–4132.
15. I.R.C. §§ 4611(c)(2) and 4681.
16. I.R.C. §§ 4001–4012.

Chapter 8

# Planning for Tax Savings in a Business

*The words of such an act as the income tax merely dance
before my eyes in a meaningless procession: cross-reference
to cross-reference, exception upon exception — couched in
abstract terms that offer no handle to seize hold of — leave in
my mind only a confused sense of some vitally important, but
successfully concealed, purport, which it is my duty to extract,
but which is within my power, if at all, only after the most
inordinate expenditure of time. I know that these monsters are
the result of fabulous industry and ingenuity, plugging up this
hole and casting out that net against all possible evasion; yet
at times I cannot help recalling a saying of William James'
about certain passages of Hegel: that they were no doubt
written with a passion of rationality; but that one cannot help
wondering whether to the reader they have any significance
save that the words are strung together with syntactical
correctness.*

— Judge Learned Hand

referring to the 1939 Internal Revenue Code, a statute which was
almost childlike in its simplicity compared to our current tax law.

## 8.1 General Considerations

One of the most shocking and unpleasant realizations of many successful
small business owners comes when they finally grasp the fact that they
have acquired an unwanted silent partner — a partner who contributes
nothing to the business but who often lays claim to half or more of the

owner's hard-earned profits. That silent partner, of course, is the government income tax collector, and this chapter is a summary of many of the best and most effective legal ways to reduce that silent partner's share of the profits from your business.

This chapter is not intended to be a substitute for professional tax advice regarding your individual situation. Because the tax laws are so enormously complex, a technique that may work brilliantly in most cases might be useless or even disastrous in your particular tax situation. This chapter will provide you with a working understanding of some of the key ways to plan for tax savings and to avoid tax pitfalls in your business.

After you have read this chapter, you may want to talk to your tax adviser about one or more of the ideas discussed, if you feel they might be useful for applying to your business. Your tax adviser should be able to tell you whether a particular idea will work in your situation. If it will, he or she can help you implement it.

Tax attorneys and accountants, particularly the most competent ones, often have a very heavy workload and a large number of clients to serve. An unfortunate result of this situation is that your tax adviser may tend to spend most of the time responding to inquiries by clients and meeting tax deadlines rather than taking the initiative in seeking out ways to minimize your taxes. Thus, by having some understanding of what you would like to do in the way of reducing taxes on your business income, you can propose ideas to your tax advisers and maximize the effectiveness of their expert knowledge and advice. In tax planning, as in so many areas of life, it pays to be assertive. "The wheel that squeaks is the one that gets the grease."

# 8.2  Using a Corporation as a Tax Shelter

One of the most effective ways to reduce your taxes, in many cases, is to incorporate your business. Incorporation is most likely to be advantageous if the business is generating about $75,000 or less in annual profits and salary for the owner — or per owner, if there is more than one. There are three basic ways, other than the adoption of employee fringe benefit plans, that incorporation can reduce your taxes on business income:

- Leaving profits in the corporation;
- Income-splitting; and
- Investing in stock.

**Leaving Profits in
the Corporation**

By leaving your first $75,000 of profits in your corporation, they are taxed at corporate rates — 15% for the first $50,000 and 25% for the next $25,000 — that are lower than the current individual income tax rate of 31%. Note that after the first $75,000 of profits, the corporate tax rate jumps to 34%, 3% more than the individual rate. An additional 5% is added on profits over $100,000, making the tax rate 39%. Keep this in mind when deciding how much of your profits to leave in your corporation. In Section 2.4, there is more information on federal corporate income taxes and a tax table. Sections 8.5 and 8.9 discuss the potential benefits and risks of having your profits accumulate in your corporation.

**Income-Splitting**

Splitting income between you and the corporation is done by paying yourself a salary and leaving the remaining profit after salary in the corporation, so it can be taxed at lower corporate rates, if less than $75,000. Thus, both you and the corporation may be taxed at relatively low tax brackets on the business income. More details are located in Section 2.4.

**Investing in Stocks**

By investing accumulated corporate funds in dividend-paying stocks, you can take advantage of the 70% deduction corporations are entitled to on dividends they receive.[1] Because this special deduction makes most dividends received by a corporation — other than an S corporation — practically tax-free to the recipient corporation, your incorporated business can be an excellent place to hold stocks you wish to invest in, if you do not need the dividend income to live on.

Before you get too excited about putting your whole stock portfolio into your incorporated business, you should be aware of several potential drawbacks:

- If you decide to later withdraw your corporate dividends or the stocks themselves, the withdrawal will usually be taxable to you as ordinary income[2] or perhaps, if you liquidate the corporation, as capital gains.[3] After 1990, capital gains are taxed at a maximum rate of 28% for individuals;[4] although, proposed legislation may change this rate in 1992 or 1993.

- If you should accumulate more than $250,000 — $150,000 for professional and certain personal service firms — in after-tax earnings in your corporation, including the 70% of dividends that the corporation doesn't pay income tax on, and invest part of those earnings in liquid, nonbusiness investment assets like stocks, you may be inviting an IRS audit and a potential penalty tax[5] for unreasonably accumulating earnings and profits in the corporation. See the discussion of the accumulated earnings tax in Section 8.9.

- If too much of your corporation's income is in the form of dividends and other passive types of investment income, the corporation may be classified as a personal holding company[6] for tax purposes, and this can have drastic tax consequences, as outlined in Section 8.9. As long as more than 40%[7] of your corporation's gross income is from sales of goods and services, however, as a general rule, you should not have to be concerned about personal holding company taxes.

- Putting your personal assets that are not needed in the business into your corporation will subject those assets to the risk of the business. That is, anything you put into the corporation will be subject to the claims of the corporation's creditors if it goes bankrupt. If you put all of your assets into the corporation, you will in effect have given up the benefits of limited liability.
- If your corporation borrows money to invest in or carry stock investments, the 70% dividend exclusion will be reduced in part by the interest paid on the borrowed funds.[8]

Your accountant will probably be the best person to consult for determining how and whether you can use a corporation to reduce taxes on your business profits.

# 8.3  Retirement Plans and Other Fringe Benefits

One advantage of being your own boss, either as a sole proprietor, a partner, or a shareholder of a closely held corporation, is the opportunity to be able to set up a Keogh plan or corporate retirement plan. In a corporation, other than an S corporation, you can obtain insurance and other important fringe benefits as an officer and employee of the corporation on a tax-favored basis. At this point, you may wish to refer to Section 2.4, where retirement plans for businesses and corporate fringe benefits are discussed in greater detail.

In the past, corporate retirement plans offered very substantial tax and practical advantages to corporation owners compared to the Keogh plans available to unincorporated owners; however, since 1984, it has become a whole new ball game. You should be aware that corporate and Keogh retirement plans are now almost identical under the tax law in all major respects, except for the ability to borrow one's retirement funds from the plan, which still will be subject to an excise or penalty tax in the case of a Keogh. It no longer pays to incorporate your business just for pension and profit-sharing plan purposes.

If you decide to establish a retirement plan, there are several practical points you should consider before reaching a decision.

**Model SEP Plans from Financial Institutions**

If you are setting up a Simplified Employee Pension (SEP) plan for yourself, or a Keogh plan, you should consider obtaining a "canned" plan from a bank, savings and loan, insurance company, or mutual fund. Usually, these preapproved plans will be suitable for you unless you have a significant number of employees to cover under your Keogh, in which case you probably should be incorporated anyway. The great advantages of getting a canned SEP or Keogh plan from a financial institution are cost and simplicity. Most such institutions will charge you only $10–$25 to adopt their plan. Their profit comes from investing your funds for a management fee, in the case of a mutual fund; or maintaining your deposits in interest-bearing accounts, in the case of a bank or savings and loan.

By contrast, hiring a lawyer or benefit consultant to draw up a customized SEP or Keogh plan for you could cost anywhere from a few hundred to a few thousand dollars in fees. In addition, since the pension laws seem to be rewritten every time Congress meets, you may find yourself paying hundreds or even thousands of dollars each year to your attorney or benefit consultant to revise or amend a custom-designed plan, just to keep it in compliance with the never-ending changes in the tax and other laws affecting pension plans.

**Model SEP and Keogh Plans from Stockbrokerages**

If you are not content to invest your SEP or Keogh funds in or with a financial institution, you can still participate in a canned plan offered by some stockbrokerage firms. These plans usually permit you to direct your own stock and bond investments.

**Model Corporate Plans**

If you are setting up a corporate retirement plan, it is also possible to obtain canned prototype plans from banks, if you allow them to act as trustee — or from insurance companies, if you buy their insurance or managed fund accounts through the plan. These plans usually have variable terms that can be tailored somewhat to suit your needs, unless you want to do something out of the ordinary, such as allow each participant to direct the investment of his or her portion of the plan's funds. Other institutions, such as stockbrokerages and mutual funds, also offer corporate plans.

**Customized Plans**

Even if you do need something unusual that requires a customized retirement plan for your corporation, you will probably find it more cost-effective to have a benefit consulting firm draw up the plan for you. This way, your attorney would only be involved in reviewing the plan and obtaining approval of the plan from the IRS. Typically, benefit consultants or pension consultants will charge only a fraction of what a law firm would charge to draw up the plan, and the larger benefit consulting firms are generally quite competent. Most of their fees come from helping you administer the plan under ERISA after it is set up — a service you will need anyway.

**Saving with SEPs**

Simplified Employee Pension (SEP) plans have gotten very little use since they were created by Congress several years ago; however, they now offer most of the attractive features of typical Keogh and corporate plans with virtually no administrative costs, unlike a Keogh or corporate plan that may cost up to $2,000 or $3,000 a year to maintain for only 5 or 10 employees.

A SEP is basically a glorified individual retirement account (IRA), but it is one where you contribute to each employee's IRA account an amount of up to 15% of an employee's compensation with a maximum of $30,000.

The amount contributed is not taxed to the employee and can be invested in any type of IRA account the employee chooses. SEPs can be set up by corporations, partnerships, or sole proprietorships. Participants can still contribute up to $2,000 a year to their SEP/IRA or to another IRA plan.

SEP participants with taxable income in excess of $25,000 (single) or $40,000 (married filing jointly), however, will have their IRA deductions reduced or eliminated.

The main existing drawback of an SEP is that any distributions from the plan at retirement are taxed as ordinary income. The special five-year averaging — which can result in a lower tax rate — for lump sum distributions from a Keogh or corporate qualified plan is not available for IRAs or SEPs. Even so, they strongly merit consideration as an alternative to Keogh or corporate retirement plans, due to their relative simplicity.

## Section 401(k) Plans

An increasingly popular form of qualified retirement plan is the Section 401(k) plan. This type of plan generally permits employees to elect to have a percentage of their salary — with various limitations — deducted from their paychecks, free of income tax, and deposited on their behalf in a profit-sharing-type plan. In many cases, as an additional incentive to employees to make such tax-favored savings, you, as an employer, may provide some degree of matching contribution to the plan on behalf of the employee.

For example, a typical situation would be where you contribute $0.50 (50 cents) for every dollar the employee elects to have withheld from his or her pay. Your contribution is placed in the 401(k) plan and is tax-free to the employee.

## Various Nonretirement Fringe Benefit Plans

The federal tax laws are replete with a whole host of tax-favored employee fringe benefits, which are characterized as being deductible to you and nontaxable to the employee. In addition to the fairly standard health care, disability, and group-term life insurance plans discussed in Chapter 2, some of the other most common and important nontaxable fringes are discussed below.

## Section 132 Excludable Fringe Benefits

The following fringe benefits are excludable both from income and employment taxes (FUTA and FICA) for you and the employee:

- No-additional-cost services provided to an employee — These services consist of benefits such as free airline, rail or bus transportation, provided by companies in those industries; rooms for hotel employees; or free phone service for telephone company employees.

- Employee discounts — Service companies can provide their services to employees at up to a 20% discount. For companies selling goods, the discount may not exceed the employer's gross profit percentage multiplied by the usual selling price of the item to customers.
- Working condition fringes — These fringe benefits are tax-free, up to the amounts that would have been deductible if paid by the employee. Benefits include such items as a company car or plane used for business purposes; subscriptions to trade or professional publications; on-the-job training; business travel; parking; and others.
- Minor fringes — These benefits are items that are considered to be minimal to justify the administrative costs for them, such as using the company's copier machine or having a secretary type a personal letter.
- On-premises athletic facilities — Providing and operating facilities such as gyms, pools, tennis or golf courses on the business premises, for employees, their spouses, and dependents is a nontaxable fringe benefit.[9]

**Meals on Premises**

If meals are provided on-premises to employees, for your convenience as the employer, the value of such meals is usually not taxable to the employee for income tax purposes;[10] however, you can only deduct 80% of the cost of furnishing such meals.

**Educational Assistance Plans**

You may pay educational expenses on behalf of an employee — free of employment taxes or income tax to the employee — if the purpose of such education meets one of the two following tests:

- The education maintains or improves skills required by the job.
- The education meets requirements set by you or applicable laws, where such requirements are imposed as a condition of the retention of employment or rate of compensation.

You may also set up tax-qualified educational assistance plans to provide other — not necessarily job-related — educational benefits for employees, in amounts up to $5,250 a year per employee.[11] To qualify, such a plan must be in writing, disclosed to employees, and no more than 5% of benefits paid under the plan can go to 5% owners of the firm or their spouses or dependents.

This tax benefit is scheduled to expire after June 30, 1992, unless extended again by Congress, which has routinely occurred several times during recent years.

**Legal Services Plans**

As an employer, you may also set up a qualified group legal services plan, whereby prepaid legal services are provided to employees. If the value of such coverage is no more than $70 a year to the employee, no part of any legal services actually provided to the employee under the plan — which may be worth thousands of dollars in some instances — is taxable to the employee.[12] If the value of such coverage exceeds $70, then a proportional part of benefits are taxable. Under a group legal services plan, benefits may not be provided to highly compensated employees on a discriminatory basis, and not more than 25% of amounts contributed under the plan may be on behalf of 5% owners of the company or their spouses or dependents.

Similar to the educational assistance plans, this tax benefit is scheduled to expire after June 30, 1992, unless extended again by Congress.

## Dependent Care Plans

Dependent care plans are one of the most popular and rapidly growing types of employee fringe benefit plans in recent years, providing up to $5,000 a year of dependent care benefits for children or elderly dependents per employee. Not more than 25% of benefits provided, however, can be on behalf of 5% owners of the employer company, and other technical nondiscrimination rules also apply.[13]

## Stock Option Plans

Companies have devised, or Congress has provided, a number of different stock option plans with various tax advantages, all of which are designed to encourage employees to acquire a proprietary stake in the companies they work for. Major types of such plans include:

- Nonqualified stock options — In this plan, you usually grant favored employees options to acquire stock of the company at a bargain price during a period of several years. Such an option is usually not a taxable event, although the excess of the value over the option price of the stock received, when the option is eventually exercised, is then taxed as ordinary compensation income in most cases — unless the stock is restricted or forfeitable.

- Incentive stock options (ISOs) — ISOs are options granted under a plan that meets IRS requirements, where the term of the option is limited and the option price is not less than the value of the stock at the day the option is granted. That is, with an ISO, there is no bargain element built into the option. If the stock is worth, say, $20 a share the day the option is granted to the employee, the option must be at an exercise price of no less than $20. Thus, the employee will not stand to profit from exercising the option unless the value of the stock subsequently rises to above $20 a share — which is good incentive for the employee to help make the company as profitable as possible, so its stock goes up. If certain requirements are met, the employee does not recognize taxable income when he or she exercises an ISO and may qualify for subsequent capital gains treatment if the stock received from exercise of the option is sold at a gain.[14]

- Employee stock purchase plans — Under a tax-qualified employee stock purchase plan, a company may allow employees to purchase its stock, directly from the company, for up to a 15% discount from the fair market value of the stock. The employee is not taxed when exercising the right to purchase stock under such a plan and may receive capital gain treatment when the stock is eventually sold at a gain.[15]

In the last few years, the flexible spending plan, or flex plan, has become another increasingly popular type of tax-favored employee benefit plan. Each of the three flex plans below are designed to permit employees to choose how much to spend on a tax-free basis for various employee benefits, such as health care or dependent care. Please note that flex plans are for employees only and cannot cover sole proprietors, partners in a partnership, or 2% shareholders in an S corporation.

**Flexible Spending Plans**

- Premium-conversion accounts — This is the simplest kind of flex account. It primarily is set up to allow employees to pay for their share of health, disability, or group-term life insurance premiums with untaxed dollars by deducting specified amounts out of their regular paychecks to pay for such coverage. The amounts the employees agree to have withheld from their salaries or wages to pay such insurance premiums are excluded from their taxable income, but deductible by the corporation or unincorporated employer. Such plans, in effect, convert part of wages directly into insurance payments, without having the government first remove a slice for taxes. Premium-conversion accounts are practical for even the smallest companies with only one or two employees.

- Flexible reimbursement accounts — Flexible reimbursement accounts are accounts where an employee may agree to contribute a specified amount to each year and draw on the account to pay for health care expenses not covered by the company. Health care expenses could include medical insurance deductibles, vision care, dental coverage, etc., or for up to $5,000 a year for dependent care expenses.

  Here's how these accounts work: Before the start of each year, the employees must estimate their medical and dependent care costs for the coming year that they want paid out of their accounts. The amount designated by an employee is withheld from his or her paycheck during the year (tax-free). As expenses are incurred during the year for health and dependent care, the employee submits requests for reimbursement out of the account to the plan administrator, up to the specified maximum. Employers may choose to supplement or match amounts employees choose to have withheld from their pay, as an additional tax-free benefit to the employee.

  Flexible reimbursement accounts may stand alone, or may be combined with premium-conversion accounts. They are feasible for fairly small employers, as well, although administrative costs may tend to be greater than for premium-conversion accounts.

- Cafeteria plans — Cafeteria plans are more complex and are rarely adopted by companies with fewer than 50 employees. Under a cafeteria plan, a company gives employees a menu of benefit choices, provides a fixed number of tax-free dollars per employee each year, and allows the employees to each select or buy the particular benefits desired, such as:

  - 401(k) contributions
  - Health insurance

- Life insurance
- Disability insurance
- Vision or dental care, or both
- Vacation time

If the costs of the benefits selected exceeds the dollar amount provided by you, the employee may fund the balance with salary reduction amounts through premium-conversion or reimbursement accounts, or both, also on an untaxed basis.

Under flex plans, the golden rule is "use it or lose it." Any amount in an employee's account that is not utilized by the employee during the year is forfeited, and reverts back to you at the end of the year. Note that flex plans are required to meet nondiscrimination tests to ensure that highly compensated employees do not receive a disproportionate share of the benefits provided.[16] For more information on flex plans, contact:

**Employers Council on Flexible Compensation**
927 15th Street NW, Suite 1000
Washington, DC 20005
(202) 659-4300

# 8.4  Sheltering Profits on Export Sales

Many small and large American businesses have an unfortunate tendency to look at the United States as their only market and to ignore the vast potential markets for their products or services that lie outside the borders of this country. One way in which Congress has taken constructive steps to encourage more exports and to make American goods and services more competitive in foreign markets is to provide a form of indirect tax subsidy to American firms that export.

While this export subsidy has not succeeded in stemming the unfavorable trend in the balance of trade the United States has experienced in recent years, it does provide a very attractive tax benefit for U.S. companies that export.

If your business is one of the many small firms that does sell its goods or services overseas, you may be able to qualify for this tax incentive by setting up either a Domestic International Sales Corporation (DISC) or another type of entity permitted by the Tax Reform Act of 1984, called a Foreign Sales Corporation (FSC).

In general, a DISC will allow you to accumulate profits earned from export sales in a specially treated corporation, free of U.S. taxes until you eventually choose to distribute the deferred income. An FSC will allow you to accumulate such income, whether or not distributed, free (in part) of U.S. corporate taxes. For an FSC, the exempt foreign trade income will not even be taxed when paid out as a dividend, if the shareholder is a corporation.[17] For small companies, DISCs may often be much simpler to operate and preferable to the FSCs, at least for the first few years of operation.

**DISCs — In a Nutshell**

A DISC is usually just a dummy corporation that has no employees and does not carry on any sort of business, except on paper.

The tax law allows a U.S. firm that has qualified export receipts to set aside part of its profits on the export transactions by paying a so-called sales commission to a DISC.[18] As a corporation without any employees, the DISC does not actually do anything to earn the commissions; your firm pays the DISC the largest commission permitted by the tax law on each qualifying export sale. It is usually advisable to have a written commission agreement between your firm and the DISC for legal purposes, although not required for tax purposes.

The commission that can be paid to the DISC on an export sale is the larger of 4% of the gross sales price or 50% of the profit on the sale[19] — so long as the commission does not create a loss on the sale for your firm.[20] In addition, the DISC's commission income can be increased by 10% of certain export promotion expenses, if any, incurred by the DISC.[21] As you might suspect, some fairly elaborate tax accounting rules[22] determine how much profit you have on an export sale, for purposes of computing the DISC's maximum commission.

The tax benefits for your business arise from the fact that you or your business owns the DISC stock, and the commissions your business pays to the DISC are deducted from the business taxable income, while the DISC pays no tax on income it receives.

However, about 6% (or $1/17$) of the DISC's income each year is taxed to its corporate (but not individual) shareholders,[23] so the DISC will usually pay about 6% of its income back as a dividend to the business that owns the stock of the DISC — which is usually, but not necessarily — your corporation that paid the DISC the commissions. Thus, 94% (or $16/17$) of the income that is shifted to the DISC as export sales commissions escapes federal income tax indefinitely, until the DISC either pays out the accumulated income as dividends or is disqualified and loses its status as a DISC.[24]

For deferred DISC income that accumulates after 1984, however, each DISC shareholder must compute the amount of additional tax it would pay each year if all the deferred DISC income were taxed and pay the IRS interest on the deferred tax.[25] This interest will apparently be tax-deductible if paid by a corporation. The interest rate is based on the going rate for one-year T-bills.

Conceptually, having a DISC can be thought of as taking $100 of pre-tax income out of your left-hand pocket and putting it in your right-hand pocket, then putting $6 back into the left-hand pocket. You do not have to pay tax on the $94 that remains in the right-hand pocket as long as you leave it there. In fact, there are even legal ways in which you can borrow the $94 and put it back in the left-hand pocket (your business) without paying tax on it — another example of having your cake and eating it, too.[26] But as long as you keep the $94 in the right-hand pocket, you pay interest on the tax saved.

Another advantage of having a DISC is that the DISC can continue to accumulate its undistributed profits year after year without fear of incurring an accumulated earnings tax, since a DISC is exempt from the accumulated earnings tax as well as the regular federal income tax.[27]

## FSCs — In a Nutshell

A Foreign Sales Corporation (FSC) is somewhat similar to a DISC, but will probably be too great of an administrative burden for it to be worthwhile for your small business to consider.

Unlike a DISC, an FSC cannot be a dummy or paper corporation set up in the United States. Instead, it must meet all of the following requirements:

- It must be a foreign corporation, incorporated in a U.S. possession or in a foreign country that, in general, has arrangements to swap tax information with the IRS.
- There can be no more than 25 shareholders in an FSC.
- An FSC cannot issue preferred stock.
- An FSC must maintain a foreign office, at which there is a permanent set of tax records, including invoices.
- The FSC's board of directors must include at least one person who is not a resident of the United States — although the nonresident member can apparently be a U.S. citizen.
- An FSC cannot be part of a controlled group of corporations that also includes a DISC. That is, you can set up either an FSC or a DISC, but not both.[28]

## Summary

Here is a brief summary of this section on DISC and FSC tax benefits.

- If your business will be engaged or is engaged in selling goods or services abroad, you should consult your tax adviser as to the advisability of establishing a DISC or FSC to shelter a large portion of your export profits.
- Both DISCs and FSCs are extremely complex entities to establish and administer, although a DISC will probably be much less of a headache for a small business to operate than an FSC. In either case, you will need to hire some very sophisticated accounting talent, so unless you earn some fairly substantial export profits, the administrative costs of having a DISC or FSC may well exceed any tax savings you will generate.
- State tax treatment of DISCs and FSCs is discussed in Section 11.8.

## 8.5  Planning for Withdrawal of Corporate Funds with Minimum Tax Cost

Because of the many tax and other advantages of operating a corporation, there is a good chance you will choose, either initially or later on, to incorporate your business. If you do, and your business becomes profitable to the extent that it has significant profits even after paying you the largest salary that can be justified as "reasonable compensation" under the circumstances, you will eventually be faced with the problem of how to remove the accumulated profits from the corporation without excessive tax costs. That is, unless you decide to liquidate the corporation at some point and operate as an unincorporated business or decide to sell your stock to someone else. The proceeds you receive from liquidation or selling your stock would probably result in capital gains tax in most cases, in addition to a tax at the corporate level upon liquidation. For a definition of unreasonable compensation, see Section 8.9.

If the corporation simply pays dividends to you, that will normally be a tax disaster, since the dividends you receive will probably be taxable to you as ordinary income at federal income tax rates up to 31% or somewhat more. Since the corporation will have already paid tax on the money it distributes to you as dividends, double taxation will result. If both you and the corporation are in the maximum tax brackets, the result can be an effective tax rate of approximately 58% (federal corporate and individual taxes) on the income that is paid out as dividends and an even higher rate if there are also state income taxes. There are better ways to get the money out of the corporation.

**Personal Loans from the Corporation**

Your corporation can often serve as a bank for your short-term financial needs; however, if you continually borrow from your corporation, the IRS can in some cases treat the loans as dividends to you, which is just what you want to avoid. Or, if your corporation has an accumulated earnings problem, as described in Section 8.9, the existence of loans to shareholders can make it very difficult to argue that the corporation is accumulating earnings for the reasonable needs of the business. So, while a loan from your corporation can be a very good way to tap its funds on a temporary basis, it is not a long-term solution.

If you do borrow, you should normally pay interest if the loan is greater than $10,000. The interest rate should not be less than the applicable federal rate established by the IRS.[29] This rate is announced by the IRS each month of the year for transactions that occur during the following month.

**Preliminary Structuring**

A number of different ways of structuring your corporation at its inception can give you a great deal of potential flexibility in getting money out of the corporation for yourself or family members later at no tax cost or, at worst, as only partially taxable. Some of these approaches can also make it possible to keep a great deal of the value of the corporation's stock out of your taxable estate for estate tax and inheritance tax purposes. Discuss the structuring of your corporation with your tax adviser before you form the corporation. Here are some of the strategies you might explore.

## Putting Stock in Names of Spouse and Children

When the corporation is formed, consider putting a substantial part of the stock in the name of your spouse or children, or both. Later, when or if the business has prospered and the stock has become valuable, it may be possible to bail out a large chunk of the corporation's accumulated profits at a child's lower tax rates by having the corporation redeem (purchase) all of the stock of your spouse or child.

The redemption will usually be treated as a sale for a capital gain if your spouse or child agrees to notify the IRS if he or she reacquires any interest in the corporation within 10 years after the redemption.[30] Working as an employee of the corporation would be an "interest" that would prevent the spouse or child from receiving favorable capital gains treatment. So if you want your son or daughter to work for you in the business, do not count on being able to redeem his or her stock as a capital gain.

Note that while capital gains are taxed at only slightly lower rates than ordinary income after 1990, it is still very desirable to have a stock redemption qualify for capital gains treatment, since part of the money received will be a nontaxable recovery of the shareholder's tax basis in the stock that is being redeemed. This is usually not the case if the redemption payment is treated as an ordinary income dividend.

Such redemption of stock as a capital gain could even be made on an installment basis.[31] For example, if your daughter had all her stock redeemed by the corporation for $150,000, the corporation could pay the $150,000 price, plus interest, in 15 annual installments of $10,000 each, so that your daughter would not have a "bunching" of all the capital gain on the sale in one tax year. Instead, the capital gains tax would be spread over a 15-year period, and the corporation should be able to deduct interest paid on the note held by the daughter.

## Constraints in Community Property States

Unfortunately, this tactic does not work as well in community property states if you attempt to redeem your spouse's stock. Under the community property laws, half of your stock will generally be treated as owned by your spouse. This makes it difficult to completely terminate his or her interest, unless all of the stock that is community property is first split in half between you by agreement, so that you each own your shares as separate property.

Even in that case, your spouse may be considered to have reacquired a community property interest in your separately owned stock if you continue to work for the corporation and the value of the stock increases on account of your efforts. Thus, if you live in a community property state, you probably should not count on trying to redeem your spouse's interest in the corporation as a capital gain. The states that have community property laws are Arizona, California, Idaho, Louisiana, Nevada, New Mexico, Texas, Washington, and Wisconsin.

Even if the corporation never redeems your children's stock, it is useful to put some of the stock in their names when you form the corporation — especially at a time when a gift to them of the stock will be subject to little or no gift tax because of its low value. When you die many years later, the stock owned by your children may then be very valuable and will not be included in your estate in most instances, which could save your children a great deal in estate and inheritance taxes. The federal gift tax laws now permit you to make gifts worth up to $10,000 per child per year free of federal gift tax. If you are married, you and your spouse can jointly make gifts of up to $20,000 per year per child; however, you may be subject to state gift taxes in some states.

**Gifts of Stock to Children**

Until the Revenue Reconciliation Act of 1989 was passed, it was considered astute tax planning — when setting up a new corporation — to capitalize the company with both equity capital (stock) and debt capital (an interest-bearing note from the corporation to you); however, such a tactic can now be a tax trap.

**Debt Capitalization Drawback**

This type of structuring can still be done without adverse tax consequences, but only if the assets you are transferring to the corporation are cash or other assets on which you would not have a taxable gain if sold at current fair market value. Otherwise, under the 1989 law, any notes or other debt capital you take back from the corporation will cause you to pay tax on appreciated assets (land, equipment, etc.) that you transfer to the corporation in return for the stock and debt instruments.

If, however, the only asset you are putting in the corporation to start it up is, for example, cash, you will not be affected by the 1989 tax law change mentioned in the preceding paragraph. As an illustration, if you plan to put $10,000 in the corporation to get the business started, you might take back stock for $5,000 and a $5,000 note when the corporation is set up, rather than having the corporation issue you stock for the whole $10,000. While the note is outstanding, you will be able to siphon off some funds from the corporation as interest on the note, which the corporation can deduct. By contrast, if the corporation distributed profits to you as dividends on its stock, it would result in double taxation of those profits, since, unlike interest, the corporation cannot deduct dividends it pays.

**Debt Capitalization Still Can Be Advantageous**

More importantly, when the note becomes due, the corporation will repay you the $5,000 principal of the note; if things have been handled properly, you should pay no tax on that $5,000. In contrast, if the corporation attempted to return part of your investment in the stock, whatever you received would probably be fully taxable to you as a dividend, even if you surrendered some of your stock in a redemption. Lending the corporation part of its start-up capital allows you to withdraw part of your investment without paying tax.

Thus, there are considerable advantages in partially capitalizing your corporation with debt in the form of a note or notes that you will hold from the corporation. You will need competent tax advice before you do so, however, since there are hundreds of court cases that have tried to define when debt instruments will be considered debt and when they will be considered stock.

For example, if you capitalize your corporation with more than $3 of debt for each $1 of stock — say a $6,000 note and $2,000 of stock — the note (debt) may be treated as though it were stock for tax purposes. Thus, if the corporation paid you interest or principal on the note, whatever payments you received would be treated as dividends to you, and the corporation's deduction for the interest payments would be disallowed. So you must tread very lightly in lending money to your corporation. See the discussion of the distinction between debt and equity for tax purposes in Section 8.9.

## Post-Incorporation Planning

Whether or not you take advantage of the above planning suggestions at the time you incorporate, there are a number of other ways you can get cash out of your corporation at a low tax cost later on.

## Leasing to the Corporation

One way is to lease real property or equipment to the corporation. Instead of putting enough of your own money into the corporation for it to buy property it needs for its business, keep the money outside the corporation, and buy the property yourself and lease it all at a reasonable rental to the corporation. This way, you will be able to directly obtain the tax depreciation and other benefits of owning the property. At the same time, by keeping the property out of the corporation, you will be putting less of your assets at risk in the business, especially if the corporation goes broke. Also, if the leased property is real estate, it will probably appreciate in value.

You can personally and directly benefit from that appreciation, including the increased rent you will be able to charge the corporation as inflation continues. Furthermore, if you have used straight-line depreciation and sell the property at a gain, all of the gain will be capital gain. By contrast, if the corporation sells real property at a gain, 20% of the straight-line depreciation is recaptured as ordinary income.[32] Although a corporation's capital gains are currently taxed at the same rate as ordinary income, Congress restored preferential tax rates for capital gains in 1990 tax legislation. It may do the same for corporations in the near future, if regular corporate tax rates are increased.

## Trusts for Your Children

You could make a gift of business property — or the funds to buy it — to a trust and have a bank or other independent trustee negotiate a reasonable lease of the property to the business, with the rental income going to the trust for distribution to your children. Upon the trust's termination, the property can be distributed to the children, revert to the trust grantor, or be distributed in accordance with the trust terms.

This can be a useful way of taking cash out of the corporation for the benefit of your children, who have lower tax brackets; however, since the IRS regularly attempts to attack these types of arrangements, you should go into this only with the help of an astute tax adviser. Be aware that the Tax Reform Act of 1986 eliminated nearly all the tax advantages of trusts for children under 14 years of age.

Consider setting up a DISC corporation if your corporation has foreign sales. You can then hold the DISC stock yourself or give it to your children. This will not only enable you to indefinitely defer federal income taxes on part of the profits from export sales, it will also, in effect, allow you or your children to siphon off part of the profits on export sales — dividends paid by the DISC — in a manner that allows your corporation to deduct those dividends, thereby avoiding double taxation.

**DISC Deferrals**

Consider adopting corporate pension or profit-sharing plans and various corporate fringe benefit plans. These types of benefit plans, in appropriate circumstances, can provide deferred retirement benefits or current insurance benefits to you tax-free — or on a tax-deferred basis, in the case of retirement plans — while reducing the corporation's current taxable income. See the discussion of these kinds of employee benefit plans in Section 8.3.

**Benefit Plans**

## 8.6 Deducting Expenses Related to Your Business

One major advantage of operating your own business is the opportunity it may give you to enjoy certain luxuries as deductible business expenses. Some of the tax benefits that were available in the past, however, such as costs of attending foreign conventions[33] and treating part of your home as a business office,[34] have been severely curtailed, and there are strict recordkeeping requirements[35] for others.

Deductions for attending foreign conventions are now completely disallowed, unless you can show that:

- It is just as reasonable for the convention to be held abroad as it would be to hold it in North America; and
- The meeting is directly related to your trade or business.

If these two requirements are met, you must then meet the general requirements for traveling outside the United States. Deductions for conventions or seminars on cruise ships are limited to $2,000, and other travel by "luxury water transportation" is deductible only up to certain per diem amounts.[36]

Some other items you may be entitled to write off as business expenses for tax purposes are discussed on the following page.

## Travel, Entertainment, and Meal Expenses

It is still possible to deduct business travel expenses, entertainment of your clients or customers, and business-related meals, but only 80% of qualifying business meals and entertainment are deductible. This 80% rule considerably complicates recordkeeping for expenses. For instance, if you stay in a hotel on a business trip and charge your meals to your room, you are required to separately break out your meal expenses from the rest of your hotel bill for tax purposes, since your meal expenses are only 80% deductible.

Note that if you are an employee of your business, the 20% disallowance of meal and entertainment expenses does not apply to you individually, if your company reimburses you for the expenses; it applies only at the company level.

## Detailed Records Required

To claim any of these kinds of deductions, you must keep daily, detailed records of such expenditures, including bills, receipts, and the following information for each expense:

- The relationship of the expenditure to the business;
- The time when the expense was incurred;
- Where the money was spent, and to whom it was paid;
- The amount of the expenditure; and
- The identities of the persons involved, including persons entertained.[37]

It is strongly recommended that you pick up a daily expense record book or diary and enter all expenses for travel, meals, and entertainment you think should be deductible. Include the above information for each item.

The Tax Reform Act of 1984 would have required contemporaneous written records to substantiate all such travel and entertainment expenses, beginning in 1985. The issuance of IRS regulations on October 15, 1984, however, provoked a massive outcry among taxpayers that was heard all the way to the District of Columbia. Senator William Roth (R–Del.) said, "I've never had an outrage at home as I've had with this legislation."

Accordingly, by mid-1985, Congress retroactively repealed the contemporaneous part of the recordkeeping requirement for travel and entertainment deductions, replacing it with the requirement that taxpayers keep "adequate records or . . . sufficient evidence corroborating the taxpayer's own statement."[38]

This is a return to the old substantiation requirements as they existed before the 1984 act, except that these substantiation requirements now also apply to local travel expenses, which was not the case in the past.

## Not All Expenses Deductible

Not all expenses for entertaining clients or customers will be deductible, even if you keep meticulous records. As a general rule, your records must show that you were engaged in a substantial and bona fide business discussion during or immediately before or after the entertainment.[39] Expenses of entertaining people just to create a good impression on them, in the hope they might send some business your way someday, are classified as goodwill entertainment and are not deductible.

The rule allowing quiet business meals with clients or potential customers to be deductible, even if no business is discussed, has been repealed.[40] For more information on business-related expenses you can deduct, contact your local IRS office and request *Publication 463, Travel, Entertainment, and Gift Expenses*.

**Automobile Expenses**

If you use an automobile more than 50% of the time for business purposes, you will generally be able to deduct a percentage of the costs of owning and operating the car, if you can substantiate the business mileage. The expenses of using the car for commuting to and from work and for personal travel are not deductible.[41] For example, if your business purchases a new car for your use as a business car, and 80% of the mileage on the car can be shown to be for business trips, and only 20% for commuting to work and other personal use, you should be able to deduct 80% of the gas, oil, insurance, and maintenance costs relating to the car. You can also depreciate the cost of the car, less 20% for personal use.

Rules are even more drastic for any automobile, airplane, boat or computer not kept in your place of business if you can't establish a business-use percentage in excess of 50%. Automobile depreciation is stretched out over at least six years, straight-line: 10% the first year; 20% a year thereafter, for four years; and 10% the final year. For boats, planes, or computers, it can be stretched out for longer periods.[42]

For luxury automobiles placed in service after 1986, the maximum annual depreciation deduction allowed is limited to the amounts below.

**Luxury Automobile Depreciation**

| 1991 Acquisitions | 1989 or 1990 Acquisitions |
| --- | --- |
| $2,660 for the first year | $2,660 for the first year |
| $4,300 for the second year | $4,200 for the second year |
| $2,550 for the third year | $2,550 for the third year |
| $1,575 for each succeeding year[43] | $1,475 for each succeeding year |

**Exemptions**

These restrictions don't apply to business vehicles such as ambulances, hearses, taxis, delivery vans, or heavy trucks.[44]

**Mileage Deduction**

If you drive an inexpensive economy car on business, it may be simpler and better to elect to deduct a flat $0.28 (28 cents) per mile for 1991[45] for your business mileage rather than keep records of your various kinds of automobile expenses. You will, however, still be required to keep records to substantiate that the car was used for business purposes for the mileage you claim. If you use this method, you can still deduct tolls and parking incurred on business trips. If you drive an expensive car, you will probably get much larger tax deductions by reporting your actual operating expenses, plus depreciation, than by electing the mileage allowance.

*Form 4562* of your annual tax return requires you to answer certain questions if you claim an automobile deduction.

---

**Questions to Be Answered if You Claim an Automobile Deduction:**

Total miles driven during the year:                                        _____

Total business miles driven during the year:                        _____

Total commuting miles driven during the year:                     _____

Total other personal (noncommuting) miles driven:             _____

Was the vehicle available for personal use during off-duty hours? Yes ☐  No ☐

Was the vehicle used primarily by a more than 5% owner or related person?  Yes ☐  No ☐

Is another vehicle available for personal use? Yes ☐  No ☐

Do you have evidence to support the business-use percentage claimed? Yes ☐  No ☐

If yes, is the evidence written? Yes ☐  No ☐

---

# 8.7  Choosing the Best Taxable Year for a Corporation

If your business is an S corporation or is considered a personal service corporation, you will generally have no choice but to operate on a calendar-year basis, and you can skip over the following discussion of how to select a taxable year. If, however, your business is incorporated and is neither an S corporation or a personal service corporation in which the services performed are "substantially performed" by owner/employees,[46] you will have an opportunity to choose any tax fiscal-year period you desire during your initial year of operation as a corporation. There are significant tax deferral and savings opportunities in selecting the right year end.

Unfortunately, in some cases, it will be necessary to be able to project with some accuracy how much your corporation will earn or lose each month for several months to a year ahead. If you expect to have start-up losses and show an overall net profit for your first year as an incorporated business, one good rule is to cut off your first taxable year at the end of the month in which you first get back to break even for the year-to-date.

For example, assume your first tax year starts on January 1, 1991, and you show a cumulative tax loss of $20,000 at the end of June. You then have taxable income of $10,000 a month in July, August, and September, and expect profits to continue. If you chose June 30 as your tax year end, you would have a $20,000 loss for your first tax period ending June 30,

1991. For federal income tax purposes, it's no problem, since you can carry over the loss and use it to offset $20,000 of taxable income during the next tax year. Some states, however, do not allow a carryover of losses.

Another approach would be to choose an August 31 year end, so that you would show no taxable income for your first year, assuming the corporation continued to net $10,000 a month.

If you do not mind paying some tax earlier, it might pay, in the above example, to wait until the end of October, November, or even December to cut off the first tax year. This would enable the corporation to isolate $20,000 to $40,000 or so of profit in a tax period subject to low federal corporate income tax rates, which are only 15% on the first $50,000 of corporate income.

If you do so, however, you are making an assumption that the corporation will be in a higher tax bracket in the following year, which cannot be known with any certainty. Also, the existence of tax credits would somewhat complicate the simple picture portrayed above. Obviously, your accountant can help you decide which tax year will produce the best result.

## Start-up Losses Must Be Capitalized, Not Deducted

Remember, when projecting your start-up losses, you can't immediately deduct preopening expenses; instead, you must capitalize those costs and write them off (straight-line) over 60 months.[47] For example, if you are starting a restaurant and are paying salaries, etc. to a manager and to employees being trained prior to the day the restaurant opens for business, you might well think those expenses are immediately deductible. Not so! All such preopening expenses must be capitalized, and you can't begin to amortize them until opening day.

## Benefits of Adopting January 31 Year End

Another planning approach in adopting a year end, which may sometimes conflict with the above strategy, is to adopt a January 31 year end. If you structure your employment contract with your corporation so that you receive a substantial part of your compensation in January each year, you can, in effect, defer the bonus to your following tax year, while the corporation can deduct it — if paid in January — for its fiscal year ending just after the bonus is paid. Naturally, the corporation will be required to withhold income tax from your bonus, but at reduced rates, compared to regular monthly salary payments. Federal income tax withholding on bonuses is at a flat rate of only 20%.

## Seasonal Businesses

If you have a seasonal business, you may want to defer taxes by selecting a tax year that ends just before your most profitable season begins. For example, if you are in the business of selling Christmas tree ornaments and do most of your business from October through December each year, you might choose a September 30 tax year end.

Remember, though, that tax considerations are not the only factors to take into account in choosing a fiscal year. If taking an annual inventory is a major task, consider adopting a year end that occurs when inventory is at a low ebb and when business is slow, if possible. You may also find that you will get somewhat quicker and better service from your CPA firm for annual tax returns, audits, etc. if you pick a fiscal year that ends several months before or after December. Most CPAs are at their busiest during their annual tax season from about February to May, preparing 1040s and doing audits for their many clients who have December year ends.

# 8.8　Selecting Tax Accounting Methods

Rely on your tax accountant's advice when choosing which tax accounting methods you should adopt in your business. This section is provided for your information in case you are not sure whether your accountant has recommended the method that will produce the best results for you.

The two overall tax accounting methods most commonly used are the cash method and the accrual method. There are, however, other special overall methods, plus a number of special kinds of accounting elections a business can make with regard to particular items, such as installment sales, inventory valuations, and deduction of accrued vacation pay.

**Cash Method**

The cash receipts and disbursements method of accounting, called the cash method, is the simplest accounting method in use. Under this method, you include income only as it is actually or constructively received.

Likewise, you only become entitled to deductions when you actually pay expenses — except for certain special items like depreciation or amortization of certain kinds of expenditures — rather than when you receive bills for the expenses. Thus, you usually do not have to report your year-end accounts receivable in income for the year and cannot deduct your year-end accounts payable. This will normally allow you to defer some taxable income each year if your year-end receivables are larger than accounts payable and other accrued but unpaid expenses. Obviously, this gives you some flexibility, too, if you want to pay off a number of payables at year end to reduce your taxable income for the current year.

The cash method is the method used by most individual taxpayers and by businesses in the real estate, financial, and service fields, where inventories of goods are not material factors in producing income.

Businesses with significant inventories, such as manufacturers and wholesale or retail firms, are usually required to use an accrual method of tax accounting.[48] In some cases, however, it is possible even for those businesses to use a hybrid accounting method — accounting for income and the cost of goods sold on an accrual method — while using the cash method to report selling expenses and administrative expenses.

The Tax Reform Act of 1986 disallowed use of the cash method for C corporations — regular corporations — and for partnerships that have C corporations as partners. One exception is for small firms with an average gross receipts of $5 million or less during the three preceding years.[49] Another exception is made for larger firms in the farming business and for certain employee-owned qualified personal service corporations in fields such as law, medicine, accounting, architecture, or consulting.

Sole proprietorships, S corporations, and partnerships with no C corporation partners are not affected by these restrictions, unless they are considered tax shelters, and may remain on the cash method if that is a permissible accounting method for their particular type of business. Firms that are forbidden from using the cash method must adopt the more complex accrual method of accounting.

As noted above, most large corporations and businesses with significant inventories are required to report income on the accrual method of accounting for tax purposes. This method requires you to report income when income is earned rather than when you receive it. Similarly, expenses can be deducted when all events have occurred that fix the amount and the fact of your business' liability for a particular expense, even if it is paid in a subsequent tax year. However, if economic performance required of the other party does not occur until a subsequent tax year, you may not be able to deduct an accrued expense until economic performance occurs.

**Accrual Method**

For example, if you sign a contract with your accountant in 1991 to prepare your tax return in 1992, "economic performance" does not occur until 1992, and you may be unable to accrue the deduction in 1991, unless you meet several requirements — recurring expenses, performance occurs within a reasonable time after the end of the tax year, etc.[50]

A once-in-a-lifetime tax election was required to be made on your first tax year after 1989 — the 1990 tax return for existing businesses. Under the economic performance rules, if you wish to deduct, in advance, items that you prepay under the recurring items exception, you must elect to deduct such items on the first return on which the item recurs, or you will be unable to use that exception for the item in question, forever.

The new tax regulations covering this exception to the economic performance rules went into effect for tax years that began after 1989. This means that if you had some recurring item that you were in the habit of prepaying before year end each year, you had to deduct it on your 1990 tax return. If you didn't, you will never again be able to deduct it in advance in any subsequent year. The IRS announced in 1991 that the one-time election that was required to be adopted on 1990 tax returns has been delayed for one more year, for certain types of expenses.[51]

Even though the accrual method may not be required for your business, you may find it preferable to use, if most or all of your income is from cash sales and you pay a large part of your expenses on a delayed credit basis. In this case, you would have few, if any, receivables at year end but might have substantial accrued payables you could deduct in the current year without having to actually make payment before year end.

Accrual of bonuses to employees, in an incorporated business, is a good example of a deduction that can be accelerated by a business using the accrual method. But expenses owed to you or a related owner of the business can't be deducted until actually paid.[52]

## Special Accounting Methods Long-term Contracts

If your business is engaged in heavy construction work on a long-term contract basis, it may be difficult to tell in advance whether a particular contract will result in a profit or loss, since many unforeseen difficulties may arise. The tax regulations recognize this problem and allow such contractors to utilize special methods of accounting which may delay the time at which profit or loss is recognized on a long-term contract. They are:

- The percentage of completion method; and
- The completed contract method.[53]

The Tax Reform Act of 1986, however, and subsequent legislation has eliminated the use of the completed contract method of accounting for most large companies, except for certain ship contracts and for some home construction and other residential building contractors. Fortunately, small businesses, whose average annual gross receipts for the three preceding years do not exceed $10 million, are still allowed to use completed contract accounting for tax purposes, at least for contracts that are estimated to take no more than two years to complete.[54]

Even those completed contract method deferrals that survive the new restrictions are now mostly considered tax preference items under the alternative minimum tax rules.[55] In other words, heads you lose, tails the tax collector wins.

## Installment Sales

If your business makes casual or occasional sales of personal property — other than merchandise held for sale — or makes sales of real estate it owns, the profit on any such sale can, in general, be reported on the installment basis as and when payments are received, rather than in the year of sale.[56] The installment method of reporting, however, is not available for "dealers," such as retailers, in personal or real property, except for certain dealers in real property. This is an election that sellers of residential lots or time-shares may make to use the installment method. The catch is that the dealer making such an election must agree to pay interest on any tax that is deferred by using installment reporting.[57]

In the case of nondealer sales of property for more than $150,000, if the total face amount of all installment notes exceeds $5 million for the year, at the end of the year, the seller must pay interest on the deferred tax liability.[58]

Sales of personal-use property or of farm property, for any amount, are exempt from the interest-on-deferred-tax provisions.[59]

If you maintain substantial inventories, discuss with your accountant the pros and cons of using the last-in-first-out (LIFO) method of valuing year-end inventories[60] versus the more common and simpler first-in-first-out (FIFO) method.

**Inventory Valuation Methods**

Under the FIFO method, the cost of ending inventory is calculated under the assumption that the first items of inventory bought were the first ones to be sold, so that only the most recently purchased items are assumed to be left in inventory at the end of each year. This usually means the highest-cost items, in times of inflation. That is, if a company turns all its inventory over every three months each year, FIFO assumes, in effect, that the inventory remaining on hand at December 31 was all bought in the last three months of the year, rather than at some earlier date when prices may have been lower.

**FIFO Method**

Most companies use the FIFO method because:

- FIFO is much simpler to use in terms of maintaining accounting records;
- When prices of goods are generally rising, FIFO has the effect of making a company's net income appear to be greater than if the more conservative LIFO method were used — but it also tends to inflate the amount of a company's taxable income; and
- Their accountants never mention to them that there is an alternative method (LIFO) of inventory accounting that can be used.

In contrast to FIFO, the LIFO method assumes that the items in your ending inventory are the first or oldest ones that were acquired. Thus, under LIFO, ending inventory values for many of the items of inventory will be based on what that item cost in the very first year in which the business began using the LIFO method. The difference in inventory valuation can be dramatic if, for example, a business using LIFO for 10 years was paying $10 each 10 years earlier for the widgets it keeps in inventory versus a current price of $75 per widget. Under LIFO, the widgets would still be carried on the accounting records at a cost of $10 apiece versus $75 under FIFO.

**LIFO Method**

Accordingly, the difference in inventory cost, or $65 per widget in the above example — called the LIFO reserve — would be the amount of taxable income per widget that the company has deferred over the 10 years. Thus, for a company with large amounts of capital invested in inventories, it is easy to see how LIFO can result in a huge tax saving.

At present, using the LIFO method is extremely complex, and the tax savings may in some cases be offset by increased accounting fees incurred and additional management time spent in attempting to comply with the LIFO tax regulations. The tax requirements for using LIFO, however, are somewhat relaxed for those small businesses with less than $5 million a year in sales.[61]

Any firm with inventories may elect to use either FIFO or LIFO. If a firm is already using FIFO, it may be able to change over to LIFO, if a number of technical requirements set by the IRS are met. Or, a company using LIFO may also change over to FIFO. Note, however, that if a firm uses LIFO and changes to FIFO for some reason, it will usually have to pay a large amount of tax, when it recaptures the LIFO reserve described above, at the time of the changeover. Any such changes in inventory accounting methods should not be attempted without the assistance of a competent tax advisor. If your C corporation already uses LIFO inventory accounting and elects S corporation status, your corporation will be required to pay tax, in four annual installments, on the LIFO reserve at the time of the changeover to an S corporation.[62]

Regardless of whether a company uses LIFO or FIFO for inventory accounting, it generally must allocate a wide range of its indirect costs to inventory, rather than simply deducting them as expenses, under the IRS's uniform capitalization rules. The practical effect of this is that any such costs that have been absorbed into the cost of inventory on hand at the end of the tax year do not get deducted currently for tax purposes. Manufacturing and processing operations of any size are subject to these complex capitalization rules. Fortunately, the uniform capitalization rules do not apply to a wholesale or retail business in any year when the company's annual gross receipts for the preceding three years have averaged $10 million or less.[63]

## Vacation Pay Accrual Method

If you accrue employees' vacation pay for internal business purposes, you normally can only deduct your liability for such accruals when an employee actually uses his or her vacation pay. Before 1988, under certain circumstances, you were able to deduct the vacation pay liability that was accrued as of the end of each year;[64] however, this method of accounting was repealed in 1987. Vacation pay is now generally deductible only in the year it is paid out. The exception is for accrual-basis taxpayers, where vacation pay is vested at the end of a tax year and paid within two-and-a-half months afterwards.

## Bad Debt Deductions

Before 1987, if your business extended credit to customers you could accelerate your business' bad debt deductions by electing to create a bad debt reserve for tax purposes. By doing so, you could deduct the amount that you expected to have to write off in the future, without waiting until the debts became uncollectible.

Since 1987, the reserve method of accounting has been abolished except for certain small financial institutions.[65] For all other taxpayers, bad debts are now only deductible when they actually become uncollectible.

# 8.9  Tax Problems Unique to Corporations

While this book has outlined some of the many tax and other advantages inherent in operating a corporation, you need to be aware that there are a number of traps in the tax law if you go overboard in trying to take advantage of the tax benefits bestowed on corporations.

For many years, the most basic goal in corporate tax planning for many high-income individuals was to leave as much profit in the corporation as possible so it could be taxed at the relatively low corporate tax rates and later withdrawn tax-free or at capital gains rates, such as by selling or having the corporation redeem the stock or by liquidating the corporation.

The government's role is to prevent the taxpayer from reaching these goals except where the corporation has good business reasons — as opposed to the individual's tax and investment reasons — for virtually everything it does. In attempting to plug up all the possible loopholes taxpayers might use to take advantage of low corporate rates, the tax law contains a whole array of penalties for corporations:

- That unreasonably accumulate earnings;[66]
- That are used as "incorporated pocket books" for holding personal investments;[67] or
- That are capitalized too heavily with debt.[68]

These and other operating problems of corporations under the tax law are briefly outlined below to give you a sense of what the limits are and how far you can go in utilizing corporate tax advantages.

**Tax Problems Specific to C Corporations**

None of the pitfalls and problems discussed below are of concern if your business is not incorporated or taxed as a corporation, and most of them are not applicable or are of only minor concern to corporations operating under S corporation elections.

**Penalty Tax on Accumulated Earnings**

The accumulated earnings tax[69] might well be called the scourge of the overly successful small corporation. This tax potentially applies to almost every corporation that accumulates more than $250,000[70] in after-tax profits (with certain adjustments),[71] unless the corporation can demonstrate that it needs to retain the profits for use in its business operations.[72]

Your corporation can accumulate up to $250,000 — $150,000 for professional and certain personal service firms — in earnings without having to be concerned about this penalty tax.[73] If additional accumulations cannot be justified as being made for the "reasonable needs of the business," however, the corporation will be faced with the choice of paying out the excess earnings as dividends or paying the accumulated earnings tax. The tax is imposed at the rate of 28% on the improperly accumulated earnings.[74] Since this is a tax that is imposed in addition to the corporate income tax, it is one you probably do not ever want to be forced to pay.

As long as you are able to keep plowing profits back into your business, buying more facilities, equipment, and inventory, and maintaining needed working capital, you will not have much cause for worry about the accumulated earnings tax. If, however, you reach a point where the corporation has more liquid funds than it needs, and you are beginning to look for places to invest the surplus cash, like real estate or the stock market, that should serve as a signal to you that there may be a potential accumulated earnings problem. In that case, you will need some good tax advice as to what you can do to protect the corporation from imposition of the penalty tax.

## Justifiable Accumulations

Fortunately, there are a number of acceptable reasons that can justify accumulating funds that are not currently being used in the corporation's business. Some of the more important ones include:

- Setting up a reserve to redeem enough of the stock of a shareholder (yourself, for example) who dies, in order to enable the individual's estate to pay certain expenses related to his or her death — estate and inheritance taxes, funeral expenses, and expenses of administering the estate.[75] This reserve can only be created by the corporation after the death of a shareholder, prior to the repurchase of the shareholder's stock;

- Creating a fund to allow for a bona fide plan to replace facilities or expand the business, including the acquisition of another business;[76]

- Creating a reasonable reserve fund to pay potential uninsured product liability claims;[77]

- Accumulating funds to retire indebtedness created in connection with the business of the corporation;[78] and

- Setting up a defined benefit pension plan with an initial "past service liability" to be funded over a number of years.

A number of ways also exist to reduce the accumulated earnings without paying them out as dividends. Some typical examples would be to redeem part of the stock of the corporation, such as the stock of one of your children. This will not only reduce accumulated earnings but will reduce the amount of excess cash not needed in the business.

Another useful approach is to have the corporation purchase real estate that it might currently be leasing. This can sometimes be particularly advantageous where you are the landlord who is leasing the property to the corporation, as suggested in Section 8.5. This tactic technically will not reduce the corporation's accumulated earnings, but will use up excess cash that would otherwise raise questions by IRS auditors.

## S Corporations

S corporations are not subject to the accumulated earnings tax because all their earnings are deemed to be distributed to shareholders. Thus, in some cases, an S corporation election may be a solution to the accumulated earnings problem. In the past, one frequent objection to electing

S corporation status was that it limited pension plan contributions for shareholder/employees to the lesser limits allowed for Keogh plans. Since 1984, this has ceased to be a problem since pension and profit-sharing plans of S corporations are treated almost exactly like those of regular corporations.

**Penalty Tax on Personal Holding Company Income**

If a closely held corporation gets a large proportion of its gross income, usually 60% or more, in the form of personal holding company income,[79] such as dividends, interest, rents, and royalties, it will generally be considered a personal holding company for tax purposes.[80]

Other kinds of income considered personal holding company income include income received by a service business from anyone (other than the corporation) who has the right under a contract to designate a particular individual to perform the contracted services. The person designated, however, must own at least 25% of the corporate stock.[81] Also, payments a corporation receives from a 25% shareholder for use of its property is personal holding company income.[82] This puts a damper on schemes such as having your corporation buy a yacht and charter it to you.

As a rule, if a corporation comes within the definition of a personal holding company, the tax law imposes a 28% penalty tax on any personal holding company income not distributed as a dividend.[83] This tax rate is expected to be raised to 31% by Congress in the very near future.

Most actively conducted small businesses will not need to be very concerned about being treated as personal holding companies since they will seldom get 60% or more of their gross income from passive sources like dividends and interest.

The kind of small business most likely to have a personal holding company problem is the incorporated personal service business — when the corporation enters into contracts and agrees to provide the services of an employee who is a major shareholder.

The best way to avoid this problem is to specify in the contract that the corporation reserves the right to designate the person who will provide the services. You will need to consult your tax adviser, however, before entering into any such personal service contract since the tax rules in this area are quite subtle and the tax penalty is very heavy if the income under the personal service contract is considered to be personal holding company income.

Another type of operating company that frequently encounters personal holding company tax problems is the developer of computer software that generates much of its income from software licensing agreements.

While the Tax Reform Act of 1986 included a special exemption from the personal holding company provisions for corporations actively engaged in the computer software business, the terms of this exception[84] are quite technical and many software firms will not be able to qualify for this relief without very careful planning.

## Possible Treatment of Corporate Debt as Stock

As discussed in Section 8.5, there are two significant advantages to putting part of your investment in an incorporated business into the corporation in the form of debt, rather than all of it in exchange for stock. These advantages are:

- The interest paid to you is normally deductible by the corporation, unlike dividends paid on its stock.
- Repayment of the money you loaned to the corporation allows you to take part of your investment out of the corporation free of tax.

Because the use of debt in structuring a closely held corporation is so advantageous, Congress[85] has taken steps to limit the extent to which you can use debt to capitalize a corporation and still enjoy these advantages.

Over the last few years, the IRS has proposed several sets of new and complex regulations as to when loans to a corporation by its shareholders will be treated as equivalent to an investment in its stock — in which case interest payments will not be deductible by the corporation and principal payments would be taxable to the recipient.

## Debt-Equity Distinction

These regulations raised such a storm of protest each time they were proposed that the IRS has finally withdrawn them. So, to determine what constitutes debt and stock, guidelines are used from hundreds of different court decisions. Nevertheless, there are a few generally accepted ground rules that you should follow to avoid having corporate debt reclassified by the IRS as equity or stock:

- The loan should not have any equity-type features, such as interest or payments, pegged to the corporation's income.
- The loan should be made at a reasonable interest rate, such as the rate at which the IRS imputes interest between related parties.
- The corporation's total debts — other than trade accounts payable — should not be more than about three times its net worth.
- The loan should be documented by a written note and should have a specified maturity date. All interest and principal payments on the note should be made on time.

If you follow each of the above rules, you will generally avoid the problem of having debt reclassified as stock. If you fail to comply with one or more of those rules when lending money to your corporation, the loan may be treated as a stock investment. This can be a serious tax trap if, when the loan is to be repaid, you are unaware that the repayment to you may constitute taxable income.

## Double Taxation of Corporate Income

The most basic tax problem resulting from incorporating a business is the possibility of double taxation of the business income if it is paid out as dividends. That is, if the corporation has any profit after payment of salaries and other expenses, it must pay tax on those profits, unless it is an S corporation. Then, if those profits left after taxes are distributed to stockholders as dividends, the stockholders must also pay tax on the dividends they receive.

Fortunately, the problem of double taxation is generally quite manageable and most small incorporated businesses never pay dividends. The owners normally are also the officers of the corporation and can take enough income out in the form of salary and fringe benefits to live on, usually leaving some profit in the corporation to be plowed back into the business.

Also, as outlined briefly in Section 8.5, there are a number of better ways to get the accumulated profits out of the corporation than by paying dividends.

## Unreasonable Compensation

If you own an incorporated business or own a portion of its stock and are actively involved in operating the business, you will be an employee of the corporation and will draw a salary. Drawing a large salary from the corporation may enable you to withdraw much of the profits of the business without any problem of double taxation, since the corporation can deduct reasonable compensation it pays to you as your salary.[86]

Thus, taking salary out of the corporation is preferable to taking money out in the form of dividends, since the corporation cannot deduct dividends it pays. The salary you receive, if reasonable, is deductible by the corporation; however, the key word here is reasonable. If you try to take too much income out of the corporation as salary, including bonuses and fringe benefits like pension and profit-sharing contributions, the IRS may try to treat part of your salary as unreasonable compensation.

There are no hard and fast rules as to how much compensation is reasonable, but if you are taking no more than the officers in similar businesses of the same size are paid, you should not have any problem establishing that your compensation from the corporation is reasonable under the circumstances.

If, however, the IRS does succeed in treating part of your compensation as excessive, there will be two serious tax consequences:

- The deduction by the corporation for the unreasonable portion of your salary will be disallowed.
- Part of your salary will be reclassified as dividend income, and thus pension and profit-sharing plan contributions based on that salary may not be fully deductible, which could even result in disqualification of your pension or profit-sharing plan.

# 8.10  Estate Planning in Connection with Your Business

As the owner of part or all of even a moderately successful business, you may find that after a few years the value of your business accounts for a very large portion of your personal net worth. As such, your business will probably be the most important single asset you have to be concerned with for estate planning purposes, both during your lifetime and at the time of your death. No attempt will be made here to go into the intricacies of the estate-planning possibilities that may be available; instead, the fundamental approaches you need to be aware of are outlined below. Discuss how to relate these concepts to your own situation with your tax adviser and attorney.

**Income-Splitting**

A useful method of reducing lifetime income taxes is to split the taxable income from your business between two or more persons or entities. Usually a corporation, particularly an S corporation, is a useful vehicle for doing this; you can split income between you and your children by giving them stock in the corporation. A corporation that has not elected S corporation treatment can also be used to split income between you and the corporation. See Section 2.4.

Remember, however, that income-splitting only works if your children are 14 years of age or older. Otherwise, any unearned income of your children in excess of $1,000 a year is taxed at your marginal tax bracket, eliminating any tax savings.[87]

**Reducing Estate and Gift Taxes**

Often the best time to remove potential wealth from your taxable estate at death is by giving your children part of the stock in your incorporated business when the business is formed — when the value of the stock is likely to be negligible. If you wait until the business has become a valuable and profitable enterprise, gifts of stock at that time may result in substantial taxable gifts for gift tax purposes, even though the tax cost of those gifts may not be felt until you die, in some cases. You can now make gifts of up to $10,000 ($20,000 if married) per year to each of your children completely free of federal gift taxes.

Assuming that you want part of your stock in your incorporated business to pass to your children at your death, it obviously makes sense to give them a portion of the stock — but not enough to affect your control of the corporation — during your lifetime. By doing this, there will be little or no gift tax cost if it is done when the business is started. Thus, they will already own the stock when you die, and that valuable asset will have passed to them free of death taxes in most instances. Also, as noted above, lifetime gifts of stock to your children may also save income taxes.

**Buy-Sell Agreements**

If you have one or more partners or business associates who also own a part of the business, it is highly important that you enter into a buy-sell agreement with them that spells out what happens if one of you dies, becomes disabled, or wants to sell his or her interest in the business.

Often these agreements are funded by life insurance on the owners, so that if you die, the business or the other owners will collect the life insurance proceeds and use those funds to buy out your interest in the business. Otherwise, your surviving family members might find it very difficult to sell the interest in the business they inherit from you, except at a give-away price.

Many small business owners ignore the need for buy-sell agreements or, like having a will drawn up, they keep putting it off. When one of the partners or shareholders dies, the survivors may have a problem in raising enough cash to pay the death taxes. This is only one of the problems that may arise when there is no buy-sell agreement.

The few hundred dollars you may spend in legal fees to have a buy-sell agreement with your business partners or associates drawn up is probably one of the best investments you and your associates will ever make.

**Retirement Plan Exemptions**

Prior to 1983, there were unlimited statutory exemptions from the estate tax for retirement plan benefits if you left your interest in any such plan or IRA to a designated beneficiary, other than your estate, and if certain other requirements were met;[88] however, Congress repealed this exemption entirely in 1984.

Accordingly, if you have already done some estate planning based on obtaining this estate tax exemption for retirement benefits you planned to leave to a beneficiary other than your spouse, you had better go back to the drawing board now that this exemption has expired. If, however, you were already receiving retirement benefits before 1984, the benefits may still be eligible for the above exclusions — if you don't change the form in which benefits are being paid.

**Unlimited Estate Tax Marital Deduction**

Since 1982, it has been possible to leave your entire estate to your surviving spouse free of federal estate taxes. In some cases, however, it is not the best strategy to fully use the unlimited estate tax marital deduction, so see a lawyer to get a current will that takes the best approach for your situation.

This exemption from the estate tax also applies to pension benefits you leave to your spouse when you die, unless the accrued value of your pension benefits exceeds $750,000 (less in some instances). If so, your estate will have to pay a special 15% excise tax on the amount over $750,000.[89]

Since not all state inheritance tax laws permit an unlimited marital deduction, it can create inheritance tax problems in those states if you leave too much property to your spouse. Refer to Section 11.8 for details regarding this state's marital deduction rules under its inheritance tax laws.

Wills or trusts executed before September 13, 1981 may not qualify for the unlimited estate tax marital deduction.[90] If you have such a will or trust, have it updated immediately. See the discussion in Section 2.4 under the sidehead, Exemptions from Estate Tax, for more information.

# 8.11  Targeted Jobs Tax Credit

Are you aware that if you hire members of certain economically disadvantaged groups, the federal government will pay you a subsidy of up to $2,400 in the form of tax credits per employee? Unfortunately, most employers, particularly small businesses, seem to be unaware of this substantial tax subsidy.

Part of the reason so many employers fail to take advantage of this tax incentive appears to be on account of a Catch-22 in the way the program works. To qualify for the targeted jobs tax credit for hiring a disadvantaged category person, he or she must be certified as such by a designated state employment security agency, and the certification must be received by the employer (or requested in writing) at least one day before the employee begins work.[91]

At the same time, state and federal anti-discrimination laws make it very difficult for you as an employer to ask prospective job applicants if they belong to any of the disadvantaged groups that are eligible for the targeted jobs tax credits, since to do so could be considered a discriminatory hiring practice.

Your best bet is to check first with your local state employment department or division to find out how to take advantage of state and federal job credit programs. The department will either refer you to the proper agency or organization that can assist you, or the department itself will help you find an individual who qualifies under this program and matches your specific job requirements.

**Targeted Groups**

The targeted group individuals for whom you can claim the jobs tax credit are:

- Vocational rehabilitation referrals — These referrals are for certain handicapped individuals who have completed rehabilitation programs. Tax credits aside, handicapped individuals often are extremely good and conscientious employees.
- Economically disadvantaged youths — These individuals are between 18 and 22 years of age and are certified as members of economically disadvantaged families.
- Economically disadvantaged Vietnam veterans.
- Supplemental Security Income (SSI) recipients — SSI recipients are people who are 65 or older, or blind, or have a disability and who don't

own much or have a lot of income. SSI payments are not just for adults; they can also go to disabled and blind children.

- General assistance recipients — These persons receive state or local welfare payments.
- Economically disadvantaged ex-convicts.
- Youths participating in a cooperative education program — Youths in this category are 16–20 years of age and have not finished high school.
- Eligible work incentive program employees.
- Qualified summer youth employees — These economically disadvantaged youths are 16 or 17 years old and are hired to work between May 1 and September 15, and they were not previously employed by you.

On the first $6,000 you pay an eligible target group employee, you will earn tax credits of 40% of the wages. This is limited to $3,000 of wages for qualified summer youth employees during the first 90 days they work for you.

Here is how the federal targeted jobs tax credits apply for eligible and certified new employees:

| Category of Employee | Federal Tax Credit | Minimum Work Period |
|---|---|---|
| All qualified employees as listed above | 40% of wages on first $6,000 of wages or a maximum credit of $2,400 per employee | 90 days or 120 hours |
| Qualified summer youth employees | 40% of first 90 days' wages for up to $3,000 of wages or maximum credit of $1,200 | 14 days or 20 hours |

One drawback with all of these tax credits is that you must reduce the wages you can deduct dollar-for-dollar for credits you claim.[92] That is, if you pay someone $1,000 and claim a $400 targeted jobs tax credit, you can only deduct $600 for wage expense, not the full $1,000. The credit is not allowed for wages paid to strikebreakers.

**Drawbacks**

The targeted jobs credit expires on June 30, 1992, but it is likely to be extended again by Congress.

## 8.12 Hiring a Spouse as an Employee

If you run an unincorporated business and your spouse works with or for you, there are three ways your spouse can be treated for tax purposes:

- As an employee;
- As a partner in the firm; and
- As an uncompensated employee — probably the most common approach.

**Social Security Tax**

Congress, by enacting the Omnibus Budget Reconciliation Act of 1987, ended the exemption from Social Security (FICA) taxes for wages paid to a spouse, parent, or minor child — with the exception of a child under 18 years of age. There are, however, still some advantages to having your spouse be a paid employee of your proprietorship, as described below.

**Individual Retirement Account for Spouse**

If your spouse works for you without pay and has no other income from an outside job, the most the two of you can put into an individual retirement account (IRA) is $2,250. If you start compensating your spouse, even as little as $2,000 a year, you should each qualify for a $2,000 IRA deduction or a total of $4,000 a year, rather than only $2,250. Note that IRA deductions may be limited if either of you is an active participant in another retirement plan.

**Medical Insurance**

You can deduct any medical insurance premiums that you pay for employees, but you can only deduct 25% of your own medical insurance premiums. If your spouse works for you, however, you can put your spouse on the payroll and provide a medical expense reimbursement plan or medical insurance for your spouse and his or her family — which includes you — you can then deduct the payments or premiums in full since your spouse is an employee.[93] See Section 11.8 regarding state tax exemptions and other implications of hiring a spouse as an employee.

## 8.13  How to Save on Unemployment Taxes

The unemployment tax rate you pay as an employer is one of the few taxes where you have some control over the rate you pay. The state maintains a reserve account for each employer, in which it monitors the unemployment taxes you pay in and the unemployment benefits it pays out to your former employees. The more benefits the state pays to your former employees, the higher your individual company's tax rate will be and vice versa. So it pays for you to have as few former employees as possible who are collecting unemployment benefits, since these are charged to your reserve account.

To succeed in keeping down the unemployment claims charged to your account, you need to challenge any former employees' claims that appear to be unjustified. Often you will be surprised to learn that an employee you had fired for stealing or who had quit on you has filed for benefits and has lied about his or her reasons for leaving. In general, an ex-employee can't collect unemployment from you if he or she left your employment for one of these reasons:

- Refusal to work;
- Voluntarily quitting;

- Inability to continue work due to illness, injury, etc; or
- Misconduct, such as theft, not showing up for work, or the like.

An employee who leaves your employ for virtually any other reason, such as being fired for incompetence, can generally collect benefits, which will cost you money by raising your unemployment tax rate. Here are some tips on how you can keep down the number of unemployment claims filed against your account.

- When you are hiring, be aware of the cost you may have if you lay off these people in the future. You may hire a number of new employees for an expansion or new project with the view that if things don't work out as planned, you will simply lay them off and cancel the project with no further cost. Count the cost. Remember that if you do have to lay them off, you may pay a much higher unemployment tax rate for several years.
- Document in writing your reasons for firing an employee, if for reasons such as theft, insubordination, absence, or intoxication on the job. This will buttress your argument that the fired employee is not entitled to benefits if he or she should file a claim.
- Be aware that if you change an employee's hours of work and he or she quits as a result, it will be considered involuntary dismissal and the employee will probably be eligible for benefits. So it pays to have a written agreement signed by the employee to work any shift, hours, weekends, etc., that are required, if needed. Then if the employee quits it will not be due to a change in job conditions, in the eyes of the law.
- If you decide to fire someone for misconduct, do it on the spot. If you keep them on at your convenience until you find a replacement, it will not usually be considered a discharge for misconduct, and the fired employee will most likely be eligible for benefits.
- If new employees do not work out, consider firing them before they have worked three months. In most states, a person has to work for you at least three months before they can earn unemployment benefits that are chargeable to your reserve account.

In general, it pays to keep a close eye on your employer reserve account and be aware of who is filing benefit claims that will cost you money. Contest any claims that you do not feel are legitimate.

# 8.14 Deductions for Office-in-the-Home Expenses

If you use part of your residence for business purposes, you may be able to deduct part of your office-in-the-home expenses; however, the rules are rather stringent, and the general rule is that office-in-the-home expenses are not deductible for tax purposes, unless you meet a number of quite technical requirements. There are several types of situations under which you may be able to claim deductions for part of your rent or expenses related to ownership of your residence, as well as other occupancy expenses, despite the home-office deduction limitations.

## Exclusive-Use Tests

If you use part of your residence exclusively for business purposes and on a regular basis, you may be able to claim office-in-the-home deductions, if you also qualify under one of these tests:[94]

- You use a portion of your home as your principal place of business.
- You use your home as a place to meet clients, customers, patients, etc.
- Your home office is a separate structure that is not attached to your house or living quarters.

Note, however, that the definition of "principal place of business" will be reviewed by the Supreme Court at the end of 1992.

## Nonexclusive Uses that Qualify

Two special exceptions are made where part of a home is regularly, but not exclusively, used for business purposes.

- Storage of inventory — A wholesaler or retailer who uses part of a home to store inventory that is being held for sale; if the dwelling unit is the taxpayer's sole fixed location of the trade or business; or
- Day care facility — Part of the home is used for day care of children, physically and mentally handicapped persons, or individuals age 65 or older.

If you can show that a portion of your residence qualifies as a home office, you have cleared the first hurdle. But note that, even if you don't meet any of the above requirements, these rules will not disallow your deductions that are otherwise allowed for tax purposes, such as interest on your home mortgage, real estate taxes, or casualty losses from damage to your residence. Also, business expenses that are not home-related, such as business supplies, cost of goods sold, wages paid to business employees, and other such operating expenses, are not affected by the limitation on home office-related deductions.

If the business use of your home qualifies under one of the above tests, then you may be able to deduct part of the home office expenses that are allocable to the portion of your home that is used in your business, in addition to home mortgage interest, property taxes, and casualty losses.

For example, if 15% of your home is used exclusively and regularly as your principal place of business, you could possibly deduct up to 15% of your occupancy costs, such as gas, electricity, insurance, repairs, and similar expenses, as well as 15% of your rent or depreciation expense on 15% of the tax basis of your house. The IRS and the tax court don't agree on the deductibility of certain other types of expenses, e.g., lawn care.

Note, however, that the amount of qualifying home office expense you can actually deduct for the year is limited to the gross income from your home business, reduced by regular operating expenses (wages, supplies, etc.) and an allocable portion (15% in the above example) of your mortgage interest, property taxes, and casualty loss deductions. If you still have net business income after taking those deductions, then you may deduct the allocable portion of your home office expenses, up to the amount of such net income.

Any portion of your home office expenses that aren't deducted due to the income limit in one year can be carried over to future years until usable, if ever. Thus, it pays to keep track of any such disallowed expenses, in case your home-based business becomes more profitable in the future, and you are then able to deduct the carried-over expenses from earlier years.

On 1991 individual returns, the *Schedule C* no longer asks you whether expenses for business use of a home are being deducted. Instead, you must determine a tentative profit or loss on *Schedule C*, without taking into account home use expenses. Home office expenses will be computed separately on a new schedule, *Form 8829*, on which you must compute the amount of deductible expenses for business use of the home, which (if any) can then be deducted from the net *Schedule C* income. This will make it impossible, or at least illegal, for taxpayers filing *Schedule C* to simply bury the home office expenses in with other business expenses.

**Deductions Limited to Income**

The downside of taking home office deductions is a potential tax bite when you sell your home. For example, if 15% of your home has been used for business and you sell your home for a gain, you will have to pay tax on 15% of the gain, even if you reinvest in a new house, or even if you qualify for the once-in-a-lifetime $125,000 exclusion of gain — for persons over age 55 — when you sell the house. Thus, a few hundred dollars of home office deductions now, could later result in many thousands of dollars of tax on the "business" part of your house, if you sell it for a gain a few years down the road.

**Potential Tax Trap**

# Footnotes

1. I.R.C. §243(a).
2. I.R.C. §§301 and 302(d).
3. I.R.C. §331.
4. I.R.C. §1(h).
5. I.R.C. §531.
6. I.R.C. §542.
7. I.R.C. §542(a)(1).
8. I.R.C. §246A.
9. I.R.C. §132.
10. I.R.C. §119.
11. I.R.C. §127.
12. I.R.C. §120.

13. I.R.C. § 129.
14. I.R.C. § 422.
15. I.R.C. § 423.
16. I.R.C. § 125.
17. I.R.C. § 245(c)(1).
18. I.R.C. §§ 991–997.
19. I.R.C. § 994(a).
20. Treas. Reg. § 1.994-1(e).
21. I.R.C. § 994(a).
22. Treas. Reg. § 1.994.
23. I.R.C. § 995(b)(1)(F)(i) (as amended by The Tax Reform Act of '86).
24. I.R.C. § 995.
25. I.R.C. § 995(f).
26. Rev. Rul. 75-430, 1975-2 C.B. 313; Rev. Rul. 76-284, 1976-2 C.B. 236.
27. Treas. Reg. § 1.991-1(a).
28. I.R.C. § 922(a)(1).
29. I.R.C. § 7872.
30. I.R.C. § 302(c)(2) permits the complete termination of the interest of a family member in a corporation by means of a stock redemption to qualify for capital gains treatment, if certain conditions are met.
31. I.R.C. § 453(g).
32. I.R.C. § 291(a).
33. I.R.C. § 274(h).
34. I.R.C. § 280A.
35. I.R.C. § 274(d).
36. I.R.C. § 274(m)(1).
37. I.R.C. § 274(d).
38. I.R.C. § 274(d), as amended by Pub. L. No. 99-44.
39. I.R.C. § 274(a)(1)(A).
40. I.R.C. § 274(e)(1). (Repealed as of 1-1-87.)
41. I.R.C. § 262.
42. I.R.C. § 280F(b)(2).
43. I.R.C. § 280F(a)(2)(A) as amended in 1986 by Pub. L. No. 99-514.
44. I.R.C. § 280F(d)(5)(B).
45. Rev. Proc. 89-66, 1989-2 C.B. 792.
46. I.R.C. § 441(i).
47. I.R.C. § 195.
48. Treas. Reg. § 1.446-1(c)(2)(i).
49. I.R.C. § 448.
50. I.R.C. § 461(h).
51. Notice 91-10, 1991-11 I.R.B.
52. I.R.C. § 267(a)(2).
53. Treas. Reg. § 1.451-3.
54. I.R.C. § 460.
55. I.R.C. § 56(a)(3).
56. I.R.C. § 453(b).
57. I.R.C. §§ 453(1)(2)(B) and 453(1)(3).
58. I.R.C. § 453A(b).
59. I.R.C. § 453A(b)(3).
60. I.R.C. § 472.
61. I.R.C. § 474.
62. I.R.C. § 1363(d).
63. I.R.C. § 263A(b)(2)(B).
64. I.R.C. § 463(a). (Repealed by '87 Act.)
65. The Tax Reform Act of 1986 § 805.
66. I.R.C. § 531.
67. I.R.C. § 541.
68. I.R.C. § 385.
69. I.R.C. § 531.
70. I.R.C. § 535(c)(2).
71. I.R.C. § 535(a) and (b).
72. I.R.C. § 537(a).
73. I.R.C. § 535(c)(2).
74. I.R.C. § 531.
75. I.R.C. § 537(a)(2).
76. Treas. Reg. §§ 1.537-1(b)(1) and 1.537-2(b)(2).
77. I.R.C. § 537(b)(4).
78. Treas. Reg. § 1.537-2(b)(3).
79. As defined in I.R.C. § 543.
80. I.R.C. § 542.
81. I.R.C. § 543(a)(7).
82. I.R.C. § 543(a)(6).
83. I.R.C. § 541.
84. I.R.C. § 543(d).
85. I.R.C. § 385.
86. I.R.C. § 162(a)(1).
87. I.R.C. § 1(g).
88. I.R.C. § 2039(c) and (e). (Repealed after 1984.)
89. I.R.C. § 4980A(d).
90. Economic Recovery Tax Act of 1981, Pub. L. No. 97-34, § 403(e)(3).
91. I.R.C. § 51.
92. I.R.C. § 280C(a).
93. Rev. Rul. 71-588, 1971-2 C.B. 91.
94. I.R.C. § 280A(c)(1).

Chapter 9

# Miscellaneous Business Pointers

*Money is not the root of all evil. The lack of money is the root of all evil.*

— Reverend Ike

## 9.1 General Considerations

This chapter provides a number of general pointers and suggestions in connection with operating a small business, some of which may be of interest to you.

## 9.2 Accounting — Some Basics

Maintaining good accounting records is a must for any small business. Without accurate and up-to-date records, you will be operating your business without vitally important information. Meaningful financial statements can only be prepared if the underlying records of transactions are accurate and current.

**Accounting Systems**

It may help to think of your accounting system as being like an airplane's radar system. If you are not getting current and correct feedback from either system, you will not have enough time to react to prevent a potential crash.

While most schools and colleges teach only the double-entry method of bookkeeping, which provides a series of checks and balances in recording

**Single-Entry Method**

income and expenditures, some small business owners use a single-entry method of accounting.

If you are not knowledgeable about double-entry bookkeeping and handle most of the funds directly yourself, you may find that a single-entry system is acceptable for your needs and much simpler to use. The single-entry method is only slightly more involved than keeping a checkbook record of cash income and disbursements and usually consists of three basic records:

- A daily cash receipts summary, which may come from a cash register tape or sales slips. This will not only give you a total of your daily cash receipts, but it will break down your sales by product, by salesperson, by store, etc., depending on how much detail you need.
- A monthly cash receipts summary, which is simply a summary of the daily summaries.
- A monthly cash disbursements report of expenses and other payments, such as debt repayments, purchases of capital assets or distributions of profits.

A number of simplified write-it-once systems for all different kinds of businesses are available at office supply stores.

## Double-Entry Method

Be aware that while a single-entry system is easy to use, it is not a complete accounting system since it focuses mainly on profit and loss and does not provide a balance sheet. For all but the very smallest of businesses, a single-entry accounting system is likely to be inadequate. Even if your business is very small, but expects to grow, it is usually advisable to start out with a full set of books, using the double-entry method.

You can avoid many future problems if you get a CPA to help you set up the accounting system for your business. He or she will tailor a chart of accounts to your specific needs and build in internal controls to record all transactions and to reduce the possibilities of employee theft or embezzlement that might go undetected with a poorly designed system.

If you use a personal computer in your business, there are any number of general ledger accounting software packages you can buy if your accounting needs are fairly straightforward and if you have a reasonable understanding of how double-entry accounting works. For a very small business, there are adequate software packages available for under $100.

*Business Owner's Guide to Accounting & Bookkeeping,* published by The Oasis Press, is a valuable resource for the beginning small business owner, manager, or accountant. This book explains the why's and how's of small business accounting, from preparing financial statements to interpreting the numbers. To obtain this book, contact your book source or:

**The Oasis Press**
(800) 228-2275

If you are going to use an outside accounting firm to prepare financial statements, you need to be aware of the three different levels of service that they will provide: compilations, reviews, and audits.

**Accounting Firm Services**

Most financial statements prepared for small businesses are compilations for the simple reason that a compilation is far less expensive than an audit or review. In a compilation, the outside accountant has no obligation to do any investigation unless he or she becomes aware of something that looks suspicious or that could be misleading. Generally, all an accountant is required to do in preparing compilation statements is to take the financial data you give him or her and present it in a manner that conforms with generally accepted accounting principles (GAAP).

**Compilations**

In a compilation, the accountant expresses no opinion on the accuracy of the information presented. The accountant is simply taking what you gave him or her and putting it in a proper financial statement format. It is important for you to remember that regardless of what type of assurance your accountant expresses, they are your financial statements and it is your ultimate responsibility to see that they are accurately prepared.

A review involves some limited analysis or testing of the financial records, but the certified public accountant (CPA) expresses only a very limited opinion as to the accuracy of the information in the financial statements. A review is somewhat less expensive than an audit but more expensive than a compilation. Most small businesses hire a CPA firm to do a review only if their bankers or other lenders or financial backers insist on a review rather than a compilation.

**Reviews**

An audit is invariably the most involved and most expensive level of service in connection with financial statements. An accounting firm that audits financial statements must not only verify that your financial statements are presented fairly and in accordance with GAAP, but it also checks and verifies some or all of the actual accounts to satisfy itself that they are for real. It does this, for instance, by requesting confirmations of bank accounts or receivable and payable account balances from banks, customers, and vendors to uncover possible errors or fraud in record-keeping. Because audits are relatively expensive, many small businesses elect to have review or compilation statements done; however, lenders or bonding companies often insist that you have a certified audit.

**Audits**

The Tax Reform Act of 1986 effectively repealed the highly favorable accelerated cost recovery system (ACRS) tax depreciation system that was in force from 1981 until the end of 1986. In January 1987, taxpayers learned to live with another whole new complex system of depreciation. Unfortunately, it is still necessary to know the former ACRS rules for assets acquired during the 1981–86 period, as well as the old depreciation rules for items acquired before 1981, to compute current depreciation on those assets.

**Depreciation**

## The Modified ACRS System

The modified ACRS (MACRS) law from 1986 does not provide depreciation tables, unlike the previous ACRS system. Instead, all assets (with a few special exceptions) placed in service after 1986 are assigned to 3-, 5-, 7-, 10-, 15-, or 20-year recovery period categories, except for real estate, which must be depreciated over 31.5 years — 27.5 years for residential rental property.[1]

Under the MACRS system, all personal property is depreciated under the 200% declining balance method over its recovery period, except for 15- or 20-year property, for which the 150% declining balance method is used. Real estate may only be depreciated under the straight-line method.

Assets other than real estate are mostly assigned to the various recovery periods based on the former asset depreciation range (ADR) "midpoint" class lives,[2] which were published by the IRS back in the 1970s. These ADR class life guidelines vary from industry to industry and are far too voluminous, technical, and detailed to reproduce in a book of this nature. The MACRS, however, specifically assigns some types of assets to recovery classes. For example, autos and light trucks are five-year property. The MACRS provisions have also reduced the maximum annual depreciation deductions on luxury automobiles as discussed in Section 8.6.

One small ray of sunshine in the MACRS tax depreciation nightmare is a liberalization of the former $5,000 first-year expending election for tangible personal property. You may elect to expense up to $10,000 in cost of furniture, equipment, etc. in the year such assets are placed in service.[3] For example, if the only depreciable items you buy in 1992 are $10,000 of office equipment, you may be able to deduct the full $10,000 in 1992. Note, however, that this special deduction is not allowed to the extent that it would create a loss for your trade(s) or business(es) for the year. Also, the deduction is phased out if you acquire more than $200,000 of eligible property during the tax year.

## The Previous ACRS System

The previous accelerated cost recovery system of depreciation applied to all tangible depreciable property acquired after 1980 and before 1987, except certain pre-1981 assets acquired from a related person or entity.

## Property Other Than Real Estate

Under the previous ACRS system, depreciation calculations for most kinds of property were extremely simple. Assets other than real property fell into several categories, each with a prescribed percentage for each year of the recovery period:

- Three-year property
- Five-year property
- Ten-year property
- Fifteen-year public utility property

## Fifteen-, Eighteen-, or Nineteen-year Real Property

The previous ACRS system allowed buildings to be depreciated over 15, 18, or 19 years, compared to the 27.5 or 31.5 years required after 1986.

Real estate acquired during the period from 1981 through March 15, 1984 is depreciable over 15 years. In general, real estate acquired or constructed after March 15, 1984 and before May 9, 1985 must be written off in 18 years. Real estate acquired or constructed on or after May 8, 1985 and before 1987 generally must be written off over a period of 19 years. A taxpayer could either elect straight-line depreciation or use accelerated depreciation tables for real property — that is, other than for low-income housing units.

## Internal Accounting Controls

Poor internal controls and recordkeeping procedures are a weakness for many small business owners. Lax procedures are frequently to blame when a secretary or bookkeeper departs for Brazil with thousands of dollars of stolen or embezzled funds belonging to his or her employer. Ideally, you would consult a good accountant to set up and review your internal financial controls; however, that will cost you a good deal of money, so before you do so, you may want to do your own review of your internal controls, utilizing this checklist.

---

**Internal Controls Checklist**

☐ The same person who handles your cash receipts should not be the same person who makes the bank deposits. Cash is too easily misappropriated. Don't tempt an employee by letting him or her handle both of these duties.

☐ The person who writes checks should not also sign them or have the authority to sign checks. A different person should sign checks.

☐ Whoever signs checks should only sign them when the bill that is being paid is presented at the same time. The check number should be written on the bill to avoid double payments or payments to a nonexistent vendor. When you sign the check, be sure you know what the bill is for.

☐ Consider using some type of mechanical check imprinting equipment for all checks that are written, as a further means of preventing unauthorized payments. Such machines keep a record of the amount of any checks written.

☐ Use only prenumbered checks and keep all of the cancelled or voided checks in your records. This will help make it readily apparent if any additional checks are written without your knowledge.

☐ Complete a monthly bank reconciliation yourself or have your outside accountant do it. Never let the person who writes checks do the reconciliation.

☐ Deposit your daily cash receipts in the bank each day. Do not let cash collections for one day get mingled with the next day's collections.

☐ Use prenumbered sets of sales checks, invoices, and receipts to keep control of payments made and received. Duplicates will be kept track of by the individuals making sales, etc., and the master copy will enable you to make sure they account for all of their transactions.

(continued)

---

---

**Internal Controls Checklist** (continued)

☐ Use a petty cash fund and voucher system for stamps, small bills, and other small cash outlays. Do not use cash from the day's receipts to pay bills! Put a voucher or bill in the petty cash box each time money is taken out. When the fund is depleted, write a check to bring it back up to the maximum amount (say $50), and record all the vouchers at the time the check is cashed to replenish the fund.

☐ Maintain a master or control account for all of your accounts receivable, and reconcile it each month to the subsidiary accounts receivable. If someone is stealing money from customer payments, it will be easier to spot if the master and subsidiary accounts are reconciled regularly.

---

# 9.3  Cash-Flow Management

Cash flow is the lifeblood of any business organization; yet, often small business operators are so concerned with other matters that they fail to pay proper attention to managing their cash resources properly. Good cash management can make a significant contribution to the competitiveness and profitability of your business. Poor cash management is one of the main causes of business failures, particularly among smaller firms, since a cash shortage due to poor planning can set off a chain reaction of disastrous consequences, even in a profitable business.

Cash-flow management has two aspects: projecting future cash flow and controlling and maximizing the cash available from operations at all times.

**Projecting Cash Flow**

Perhaps the most important part of cash-flow management is accurately projecting your business' near- and long-term cash needs and making your business decisions reflect those needs. Often, to project what your sales will be in coming months, it will be necessary to rely on what has happened in the past — what percentage will be credit sales and when your receivables are likely to be collected. Similarly, you have to estimate and project what you will have to pay out in the way of payroll, rent, taxes, servicing debts, purchasing inventory, and paying off existing payables, plus extraordinary outlays you can anticipate.

The purpose of making these detailed projections of expected cash inflows and outflows is to point out any future cash shortages or deficits, so you can take steps in advance to prevent such occurrences. For example, if your projections indicated that you were going to experience a severe cash crunch in about three months, you might take any of a number of steps to avert it, such as:

- Seeking to raise new capital;
- Borrowing money;
- Liquidating some of your inventory by cutting prices; or
- Cutting back on planned expenditures.

If you have a computer, be aware that there are microcomputer models available to assist in preparing projections of cash flows. If you don't own a computer, your accountant may have such models available to assist you.

PSI Successful Business Software has developed an inexpensive and simple-to-use program that can help you manage all financial aspects of your business. *Financial Templates for Small Business* lets you monitor cash flow; generate financial statements; track monthly, quarterly, or three-year cash flow and income; and plan for the future by analyzing past and present performance. These multipurpose templates run on either IBM PC (or compatible) or with Macintosh computers, along with spreadsheet programs, such as Lotus 1-2-3 or Excel. For more information, contact:

**PSI Successful Business Software**
(800) 228-2275

**Controlling and Maximizing Cash Flow**

If you are able to increase available cash by speeding up collections, delaying payments, or by other means, you can use the extra cash to reduce your borrowings — thus saving interest expenses — or you can invest the surplus cash to earn interest. Either way, improving your cash flow should increase your net earnings and should also help you avert cash shortages.

Here are some basic ways to improve your business' cash flow.

- Bill your customers promptly. The later they receive the bill, the later you will usually collect for a particular sale.
- If you know that certain large customers must receive bills by certain days of the month so you can get paid in that month, try to bill them before those deadlines.
- Deposit your cash receipts daily, if possible.
- Keep close tabs on credit customers. Send them past due notices as soon as payments become overdue.
- If you can do so without hurting business, add late charges to overdue accounts.
- Never pay bills until just before they become due, unless there is a worthwhile discount for quick payment.
- Try to keep inventories as lean as possible. Even if you occasionally lose a small sale because you are temporarily out of an item, you should be far ahead of the game by substantially reducing the amount of cash you have tied up in inventory.

- Look for items in your inventory that are moving slowly or not at all. Consider slashing the price on those articles to convert them to cash and also to reduce the cost of storing them or taking up valuable shelf space.

- Consider leasing equipment items instead of buying.

- Be sure that you are not paying more on your estimated income taxes than you have to. You may qualify — without incurring interest charges or late payment penalties — under one or more exceptions that will allow you to delay paying much of your tax for the year until the tax return is due. If you realize that you have already overpaid your corporate estimated tax for the year, there is a procedure for obtaining a refund prior to the time when you can file a return.[4]

- If your business has a net operating loss for tax purposes that can be carried back to prior years, a procedure exists for filing a claim for a quick refund of the prior years' taxes. And file it as early as you can, since the IRS no longer pays interest on these refunds.

- Instead of keeping all your business cash in a local bank account, consider putting a significant portion of your cash in an out-of-town money market-type fund that pays interest and allows you to write checks against the account. Since you continue to earn interest on funds on deposit until the checks clear, consider using a fund in a distant part of the country, since it will take longer for your checks to clear when you make payments to local firms.

# 9.4  Protecting Your Assets

Starting a new business is almost always a risky proposition, and you should not overlook the fact that, if the business fails, you may be forced into bankruptcy and could lose everything except what the bankruptcy laws allow you to keep. This is one reason why many small businesses incorporate at the outset, since a corporation will generally limit your liability to business creditors to the amount you invest in the corporation, plus any loans to the corporation you guarantee.

Accordingly, if you incorporate, you should be cautious about unnecessarily committing too much of your personal assets to the business. For example, instead of putting a building or piece of land you own into the corporation, it may be better — and may save income and property taxes — for you to keep the property and lease it to the corporation.

Even if you incorporate, the leases or bank loans you find it necessary to guarantee on behalf of the corporation could still wipe out your personal assets if the business folds. Thus, it often makes sense to have your corporation set up a tax-qualified pension or profit-sharing plan and to have it contribute as much as possible to the plan on your behalf. Not only does this provide substantial tax savings and deferral, but the law in most states will in many cases protect your account under such a plan from your creditors or the corporation's creditors.

So, if you can build up a significant retirement fund in your corporation's pension plan, you have at least some degree of assurance that the failure of the business or a disastrous lawsuit will not touch that nest egg — but in a divorce, your spouse may be able to claim his or her share of the pension plan account.

# 9.5 Protecting Trade Names and Trademarks

If you intend to use some type of distinctive trade name for your business or trademark for your product or in advertising your services, it will usually be advisable to consider taking steps to protect the use of the name or mark by registration under state or federal law, or both. Also, it may be necessary to perform a search, which can be expensive, to determine whether someone else has already registered the same or a very similar name or symbol.

You do not want to open yourself up to a lawsuit for infringement. Since not every trade name can be registered, you will need to consult a trademark attorney if you are interested in protecting a particular name used by your business. Federal registration of a name confers a number of significant benefits, including:

- Nationwide notice to others of your exclusive right to use the name or mark.
- *Prima facie* evidence of the validity of the registration and your exclusive right to use the mark throughout the country.
- With certain exceptions, registration gives you an unquestionable right to use the name or mark.
- If you prove in court that someone violated your rights under the Trademark Act of 1946,[5] you will be entitled to recover their profits and damages from its use.
- The right to sue in federal court for trademark infringement regardless of the amount at stake and whether or not there is diversity of citizenship, i.e., regardless of whether you and the defendant operate in the same or different states.
- The right to have customs officials halt importation of counterfeit goods using your trademark.

The Oasis Press' *How to Develop & Market Creative Business Ideas* can explain, step-by-step, how to protect your ideas, as well as, trademarks and names. To obtain this book, contact your book source or:

**The Oasis Press**
(800) 228-2275

## 9.6  Section 1244 Stock

If you invest directly in a small corporation by transferring money or property (other than securities) to the corporation in exchange for its common stock — or preferred stock, if issued after July 18, 1984 — the stock will usually qualify as Section 1244 stock.[6] If it does, and the stock later becomes worthless or you sell it at a loss, Section 1244 of the Internal Revenue Code permits you to deduct up to $50,000 of your loss — $100,000 for a couple filing a joint return — as an ordinary deduction instead of as a capital loss for that year.

This can be very important, since you can fully deduct an ordinary loss from your taxable income, while capital losses can only be used to offset capital gains, if you have any, or $3,000 of ordinary income per year until your capital losses are used up.[7]

Any stock issued by a small business corporation will generally qualify as Section 1244 stock unless the corporation obtained half or more of its gross receipts from passive kinds of income, such as interest, dividends, and the like, in the five years before your loss is incurred.[8] A corporation qualifies as a small business corporation if the total invested in its stock is $1 million or less.[9]

In the past, for its stock to qualify for this special tax treatment, it was necessary for a corporation to adopt a plan to issue Section 1244 stock. This is no longer required. If the stock issued by your corporation meets the requirements of Section 1244, it will automatically qualify for ordinary loss treatment, up to the first one million dollars of stock issued. You should be aware, however, that capital contributions you make, where no stock is received by you for such money, will not qualify for ordinary loss treatment.[10]

Note that the $50,000/$100,000 limit on the amount of loss that can qualify for ordinary loss treatment is an annual limitation. Thus, if you sell part of your stock for a loss in each of several years, you could theoretically claim up to $50,000 or $100,000 of your loss each year[11] as an ordinary deduction under Section 1244. See Section 11.9 as to whether state law also provides favorable tax treatment for losses on stock in a small business corporation.

## 9.7  SBA and Other Government Loans

If you need to borrow money for your business and cannot obtain regular bank financing, you should not overlook the possibility of obtaining a loan through the U.S. Small Business Administration (SBA). While many small business owners are under the impression that it is virtually impossible to obtain an SBA loan unless a member of a minority group, this is not the case. Although the SBA does make special efforts to provide financing for minority-owned businesses, only a relatively small percentage of SBA loans are made to minority firms. Furthermore, a very high percentage of applications for SBA loans are approved when applications are properly submitted.

To apply for an SBA or conventional loan, you will most likely need to include a complete, well-documented business plan in your financial request presentation. To take you step-by-step through the business plan writing process, get a copy of Rhonda M. Abrams' recent book, *The Successful Business Plan: Secrets & Strategies*. Not only will you learn to write a strong business plan, you will also gain special insight into the financing request process by reading the numerous tips and suggestions provided by venture capitalists, bankers, and various business leaders. The book also features easy-to-follow financial worksheets and samples. For more information, contact your local book source or:

**The Oasis Press**
(800) 228-2275

## SBA Loan Programs

The SBA, an agency of the U.S. government, guarantees intermediate and long-term loans to small firms and, to a limited extent, also makes direct loans to some small businesses. The SBA is not allowed to grant such financial assistance unless the borrower is unable to obtain private-sector financing on reasonable terms. The SBA does not compete with banks or other lenders; instead, it works with private lenders to assure availability of capital to potentially profitable small firms.

For your firm to qualify for SBA financial assistance, it must come within the current definition of a "small business." In general, these are the types of small businesses eligible for SBA financing:

- Manufacturers with a maximum of 250 to 1,500 employees, depending upon the industry in which the applicant is engaged;
- Retailers with less than $2 million in annual sales — up to $7.5 million for some types of retailers;
- Wholesaling firms with gross annual sales ranging from $9.5 to $22 million, depending on the industry;
- General construction firms, whose annual sales have averaged less than $9.5 million for the last three fiscal years; lower limits apply to various special trade construction firms;
- Service firms with annual receipts not in excess of $2 to $8 million, depending on the industry; and
- Other definitions apply for businesses engaged in activities, such as agriculture and transportation.

Private lenders that are eligible to make SBA-guaranteed loans or participate in SBA financing packages include banks, savings and loans, and certain other lenders. The SBA has several types of loan programs for small businesses.

**Guaranteed Loans**

Most SBA financing actually consists of loans by banks or other lenders that are guaranteed by the SBA. This enables the small business to obtain such loans at reasonable interest rates because the bank's risk is largely eliminated.

As the borrower, you must put up a reasonable amount of equity or collateral. These loans are usually secured by fixed assets, real estate, and inventory and are limited in term to seven years for working capital loans or 10 years for purchasing fixed assets. Construction loans can be for as long as 25 years.

Under this program, the bank or other private lender deals with the SBA, and you deal with the bank, not the SBA. You will, however, need to do the following in applying for such a loan or any other SBA financing:

- Define the amount you need to borrow and the purposes for which the funds will be used.
- Describe the collateral you will offer as security.
- Determine from a bank that a conventional loan is not available.
- Prepare current financial statements, preferably with your accountant's assistance. These would include, at a minimum, a relatively current balance sheet and an income statement for the previous full year and for the current year up to the date of the balance sheet.
- Prepare personal financial statements of the owners, partners, or stockholders owning more than 20% of the stock of the company.

**Direct Loans**

If you are unable to obtain sufficient conventional financing or SBA guaranteed loan funds, you may in some cases be able to obtain a direct loan from the SBA of up to $150,000; however, these direct loans are hard to get, and can only be made if the SBA has funds available.

In recent years, the funds available for lending by the SBA have been quite limited, so that eligible borrowers are frequently turned away because the SBA simply doesn't have any money to lend. When made, these loans are usually offered on a participation basis with a bank or other lender, where the bank oversees the loan payments and loan servicing on behalf of itself and the SBA.

**Other SBA Programs**

New legislation frequently adds to and modifies the number and scope of SBA loan programs. Other such programs include:

- Seasonal lines of credit;
- Economic opportunity loans for entrepreneurs who are physically handicapped or members of a minority group;
- Short-term contract loan guarantees;
- Energy loans to small firms to install, sell, service, develop, or manufacture solar energy or energy-saving devices; and
- Disaster recovery loans to firms harmed by natural disasters.

Since the nature, scope, and availability of funds under these numerous programs are constantly changing, you should consult your bank or local SBA offices, if you think your firm may qualify under one of these special financial assistance programs.

The U.S. Department of Housing and Urban Development (HUD) makes Urban Development Action Grants (UDAG) to cities in economically distressed areas. The cities are then able to use these UDAG funds to make second-mortgage loans to private developers who are able to leverage these loans by borrowing at least five times such amounts — three times in small towns — from private sources. The purpose of such loans is to encourage new investment and development in depressed areas.

**U.S. Department of Housing and Urban Development**

The Economic Development Administration (EDA) of the U.S. Department of Commerce makes direct loans and offers loan guarantees to businesses, in areas with low family incomes or suffering from high unemployment, to promote creation or retention of jobs for residents of such areas.

**U.S. Department of Commerce**

To qualify for this financing, your business must be located in an EDA redevelopment area and you need to demonstrate that the venture will directly benefit local residents and will not create local over-capacity for the industry in question. Application for EDA loan assistance is a long and complex process, taking much longer for processing than typical SBA loans.

The Farmers Home Administration (FmHA) can perhaps be thought of as an SBA for rural areas. It offers insured and guaranteed loans to develop business and industry in nonurban areas with populations of under 50,000. Like the SBA program, FmHA loan guarantees are for up to 90% of the total amount of the loan and are made for up to 30 years for financing real estate acquisition, 15 years for machinery and equipment, and 7 years for working capital. FmHA loan guarantees are not available for agricultural production.

**Farmers Home Administration**

Unlike SBA loan guarantees, there is no dollar limit on FmHA loan guarantees, nor does the FmHA make direct loans. Applicants for FmHA loan guarantees must not only have adequate collateral and good business histories, they must also demonstrate that the project will have a favorable economic impact and will create new jobs in the area — not merely shifting business activity and jobs from one area to another. Preference is given:

- To businesses who are expanding, rather than transferring into an area;
- To projects in open country areas or towns with populations of under 25,000; and
- To business owners who are military veterans.

## Other Federal Loan Programs

Other major federal loan programs are provided through the Federal Land Bank Association, Production Credit Association, and the Federal Intermediate Credit Bank. These organizations offer loans to businesses that provide services to farmers. These loans can be for purchasing land and equipment and for obtaining start-up working capital.

## SBICs and MESBICs

In addition to direct loans and guarantees from government agencies, don't overlook possible loans or equity financing from Small Business Investment Companies (SBICs) and Minority Enterprise Small Business Investment Companies (MESBICs) as possible sources of financing. Both are licensed and regulated by the SBA to provide equity capital, long-term loans, and management assistance to small businesses.

SBIC and MESBIC loans are usually subordinated to loans from other creditors and are typically made for five- to seven-year terms. Both types of investment companies are privately owned and thus tend to favor loans to established companies with significant net worth rather than new business start ups.

Be aware that you may have to give up a large part of the equity in your business if you obtain SBIC financing. An SBIC is not permitted to control a company (50% or greater ownership) it lends to, but typically an SBIC lender will insist on debt that is convertible into common stock, warrants, and options, which may give it up to 49% ownership in your company.

An SBIC will also want seats on your board of directors, will impose controls and restrictions on the way your business operates, and may insist upon salary limits for the principal owners. SBIC financing does not come without a price.

MESBICs serve only those small firms that are owned by members of economically or socially disadvantaged minority groups.

## Business Development Corporations

Business Development Corporations are Local Development Companies (LDC), SBA Section 502, and Certified Development Companies (CDC), SBA Section 503, organized by local residents to promote economic development in their particular communities. These entities do not make working capital loans or loans to purchase free-standing equipment.

Instead, LDCs or CDCs will arrange for SBA-guaranteed bank loans and sale of SBA-guaranteed debentures for up to 90% financing for 25 years for land acquisition, building construction, or renovation and purchase of fixed assets such as machinery and equipment.

## State Loan Programs

For information on what state business loan programs may be available in this state, refer to Section 11.9.

# 9.8 Mail Order Sales

If your business involves selling goods by mail order, you need to be aware of a regulation by the Federal Trade Commission that deals with mail order sales, Rule 435.1.[12] This federal regulation requires any business soliciting mail order sales to be prepared to ship the merchandise within 30 days after an order is received, unless it has clearly stated in its solicitation that orders will not be shipped for a longer period, such as 60 days. Otherwise, the solicitation will be considered as an unfair and deceptive trade practice.

In addition, if you receive an order and for some reason you cannot ship it within 30 days, or the period stated in your solicitation, you must:

- Immediately notify the customer and offer to either cancel the order and receive a refund or consent to the delay in shipment.
- Indicate when you will be able to ship or that you do not know when you will be able to ship the order.
- Provide other required information to the customer, which will vary in content depending upon when you expect to be able to ship.

Rule 435.1 is fairly complex and difficult to understand, but you need to understand and be familiar with it if you sell goods by mail order. If you are going into the mail order business and want a single source of information on state and federal mail order laws, obtain the *Mail Order Legal Manual*, by Erwin J. Keup, from your book source or:

**The Oasis Press**
(800) 228-2275

**State Sales and Use Taxes**

If you sell across state lines to customers in states where you have no offices, employees, or other presence, the sale is usually not subject to sales tax in either state, since it is an interstate sale; however, technically, such sales are subject to use tax in the customer's state. A use tax is sort of a shadow of the sales tax and, in most states, applies where the sales tax doesn't.

The U.S. Supreme Court and other courts generally have not supported attempts of the various states to force out-of-state retailers to collect use tax on mail order or other sales made to residents of the taxing state, so that most mail order firms tend to treat such interstate sales as being tax-free, or tell the customers that it is up to them to report the purchase and pay the use tax, which they rarely do.

Unfortunately, in the last few years, many states have enacted new and broader sales and use tax laws. Many of these laws require out-of-state retailers, who advertise in the local media or send substantial amounts of direct mail/catalog solicitations into the state, to register as retailers subject to sales or use tax in the state and to treat such direct sales as taxable.

Some states are aggressively enforcing these new laws, which will definitely cramp the style of many mail order firms if these laws stand up in court. On the other hand, some states, like Massachusetts, have passed such legislation; but, because of doubts as to its constitutionality, these states will not attempt enforcement until proposed federal legislation is enacted.

Even if these new state laws are held to be unconstitutional, a bill has been working its way through Congress in recent years that would specifically grant states the right to require out-of-state sellers to collect use tax on sales made into the state, with certain restrictions. The bill, as it currently stands, would provide exceptions for small businesses, since having to file and pay sales or use taxes to all 50 states would be extremely expensive and onerous for small firms, and would effectively put small mail order firms out of business if they were not exempted.

Note that, unlike the proposed federal legislation, the new state laws adopted in recent years do not generally make an exception for small firms.

To summarize, don't assume that in many states interstate sales are still free of sales tax. If the proposed federal legislation passes, you will probably be required to collect and pay sales or use tax in all 50 states fairly soon after any such enactment.

# 9.9  Environmental Laws Affecting Your Business

As the world becomes more crowded and as the damaging effects of two centuries of unrestrained industrial development becomes more apparent on the environment, political attempts to remedy these problems, particularly the problems of pollution and toxic emissions, have resulted in a flood of legislation, regulations, and litigation involving environmental matters. While this is probably all to the good in the larger sense, some of the immediate effects of these new environmental restrictions have been to create another whole layer of complex and often conflicting government regulations on business, plus a virtual minefield of legal exposure for companies of all sizes.

For small businesses, most of which do not have in-house legal staffs and can hardly afford the large legal fees needed for professional guidance through this maze of regulations, the effect of the growing body of environmental laws is especially harsh. Small businesses are also disproportionately affected by the heavy costs of complying with various mandated emissions requirements, which often require large capital expenditures for sophisticated new pollution control equipment.

While this section cannot do much more than scratch the surface of the environmental law exposure and increased operational complexities most firms are going to be faced with from now on, the outline below explains some of the main problem areas that you need to be at least passingly familiar with. This section also provides a capsule description of the major areas of federal environmental law that may currently apply to your business or which may apply at some time in the future.

Perhaps the most pervasive of the environmental laws, with the most devastating potential consequences for the unwary, are the environmental clean-up laws, and the legal liability that these laws attach to real estate that has been contaminated by hazardous substances. The main laws that apply in this area are the Comprehensive Environmental Response Compensation and Recovery Act[13] (CERCLA or the Superfund law) and the Resource Conservation and Recovery Act (RCRA).[14]

**Environmental Clean-Up Laws**

CERCLA and RCRA apply to virtually every real estate transaction. While RCRA applies primarily to currently generated hazardous waste, including limits on creation of waste and requirements for disposing of it, CERCLA is more focused on cleaning up hazardous substances that have been spilled or dumped in the past.

CERCLA deals with all kinds of pollution: air, surface water, groundwater, and soil. It covers virtually every type of hazardous substances as defined under CERCLA, the Clean Water Act, the Clean Air Act, or the Toxic Substances Control Act. There are, however, major exceptions for petroleum and certain petroleum derivatives. The main thrust of CERCLA is to impose liability on private owners of property to clean up hazardous wastes that they have created. CERCLA would also apply to owners of the inherited property, if the property in question was already contaminated when it was acquired.

**CERCLA Liability**

In short, even if you were not responsible for creating a contamination problem, if you acquire real estate that is already contaminated — and it later becomes apparent that there has been a spill or dumping that requires an environmental clean up, possibly at astronomical cost — you are liable for the costs of the clean up, if you are the current owner. You can't simply walk away from the property and let the government take it in lieu of paying the clean-up costs.

Once the owner, you are the responsible party and may be held liable for costs that exceed the value of the property many times over. You may even become liable somewhere down the road if you sell a business — an existing corporation, for instance — that has formerly owned contaminated property. The government could eventually institute environmental proceedings against the current property owner, who then sues all the prior legal owners of the property, including you, for indemnity or reimbursement.

Of course, you may be able to sue the prior owner or anyone in the chain of prior owners for indemnification, if they are still in existence and can be found. However, since that is a pretty slim thread upon which to hang your financial survival, you need to take precautions up front, before acquiring any real property, to protect yourself from possible environmental liability for clean up under CERCLA.

The following are some things you can and should do to reduce your risk in any real estate or existing business acquisition:

- Exercise considerable diligence concerning the current condition and past uses of any real estate involved in a transaction. Also, if buying an existing corporation, you need to find out what properties it owned in the past and be concerned whether any such properties may have been contaminated by hazardous substances.

- Be particularly wary of any sites that have been used as gas stations, landfill areas, locations of dry cleaners, chemical or other industrial production processes, battery production, recycling, or metal plating. Be extremely cautious if the site contains underground storage tanks.

- Consider retaining an environmental audit firm to do detailed site inspections and evaluations to determine if there may be a contamination problem.

- In a business or real estate purchase agreement, require written representations and warranties about the site from the seller and include provisions under which he or she will indemnify you if there is a problem. Be mindful of the seller's financial viability, in case you should be forced to seek indemnity from him or her. A promise isn't worth the paper it's written on, if the seller doesn't have the wherewithal to make good on it.

Even though under the Superfund law there is an innocent purchaser defense, you must be able to demonstrate that you made appropriate inquiry before acquiring the property to determine any pre-existing contamination problem. There is little guidance in the law at this point as to what constitutes an appropriate inquiry, so perhaps you should not expect to escape liability under that rule. The best defense is to avoid purchasing property that is contaminated by taking the steps outlined above. Even if such steps fail to discover a lurking environmental problem, at least you will have a much stronger argument to make under the innocent purchaser defense if you have done a due diligence survey and had an environmental audit performed by a reputable firm.

**RCRA Requirements**

RCRA contains a comprehensive set of rules for managing hazardous wastes, including petroleum-based substances, and regulating those who generate hazardous wastes, transport them, and store, treat, or dispose of them. Penalties for violations include monetary penalties of up to $25,000 a day, plus imprisonment.

One important focus of the RCRA law is on underground storage tanks (USTs), many of which are known to be leaking gasoline or other contaminants into the surrounding soil and groundwater. Under RCRA, much of the regulation of USTs is left to state governments. Thus, under federal regulations, the owner of a UST must notify the state of the tank's existence, including tanks that were taken out of service after January 1, 1974.[15] New USTs must satisfy federal performance standards, which generally require that they be constructed of fiberglass-reinforced plastic or steel that is cathodically protected from corrosion.[16] Furthermore, all existing USTs must be upgraded to federal standards by December 22, 1998,[17] which will result in some major expenditures for many small businesses, such as service stations.

Under the Clean Water Act,[18] the federal Environmental Protection Agency (EPA) and individual states are the watchdogs of water pollution standards. It also allows private citizens to sue to enforce the act. Penalties for violations can be as high as $50,000 a day, and even negligent, but unintentional, violations can result in imprisonment. For certain existing facilities, this law provides for a system of EPA permits for discharging certain amounts of water pollutants.

**Clean Water Act**

Portions of the Clean Water Act require that all proposed development activities, which involve the dredging or filling of wetlands, obtain permits from the U.S. Army Corps of Engineers.[19] Thus, before you acquire real property that you plan to develop in any way, you need to do a careful survey to determine if the property lies within an area that is considered to be a wetland. Otherwise, you may end up with a piece of property which is undevelopable and which can hardly be sold at all, even for a huge loss. This has been a trap for more than one unwitting buyer of land in wetlands districts, since wetlands include much more than swamps and marshes. Many dry-looking parcels may also fall within the regulatory definition. Furthermore, be aware that many states have adopted wetlands restrictions, which may require you to also obtain state development permits.

**Wetlands Development**

The Clean Air Act of 1970, which was substantially amended and strengthened by the Clean Air Act of 1991, among other things, restricts the ability of stationary sources of air pollutants to emit various pollutants into the atmosphere at new or modified facilities.[20] States are allowed to implement their own rules for controlling air pollution levels. Recent amendments to this law in 1991 have greatly expanded its impact on small businesses. As they go into effect, these new amendments will require a diverse number of air pollution controls. Some will include:

**Clean Air Act**

- Gasoline stations will need vapor-recovery devices on gasoline pumps.
- Furniture makers may need incinerators to burn off hydrocarbons released from spray-paint booths.
- Restaurants in smoggy areas will have to install containment units that collect hydrocarbon emissions from charcoal grills.

- Many bakeries will have to install oxidation devices or catalytic converters to neutralize the gases produced by fermenting yeast when dough is baked.
- Auto-body paint and repair shops will have to install extremely expensive equipment to catch hydrocarbon emissions from spray painting.
- Print shops will have to neutralize or eliminate use of chemicals that contribute to ozone formation.

As the foregoing examples indicate, the new requirements under the Clean Air Act of 1991 are very pervasive and will affect many nonindustrial types of businesses who would never have considered themselves to be polluters in the past. Companies that are sources of air pollutant emissions will have to obtain state-issued construction and operating permits under EPA rules. Small businesses will have to apply for permits at least every five years and file reports of their compliance with the law every six months, if they produce more than 100 tons per year of any ozone-forming pollutant. Ozone-forming pollutants are the main targets of the new legislation.

According to some experts, once these rules go into effect, a small business' main cost of complying with the clean air regulations is likely to be all the required paperwork. Penalties for violations are also very severe, with civil penalties as high as $25,000 a day for each violation, plus felony imprisonment and huge fines for willful or negligent releases of hazardous air pollutants. In addition, the EPA has set emissions fees of $25 a ton for every ton of regulated pollutants that a firm emits, up to $4,000 per year.

## Toxic Substances Control Act

If your business is one that engages in the manufacturing, processing, or distribution of chemical substances, you may be required under the federal Toxic Substances Control Act (TSCA)[21] to report certain information to the EPA regarding the chemical substances and mixtures you use. The TSCA requires manufacturers to give a 90-day notification prior to producing a new chemical substance and, in some cases, for older chemicals. The EPA may require safety testing before approval of such a chemical. The TSCA also has extensive recordkeeping rules regarding use and disposal of toxic chemicals.

There are severe penalties for failing to make the required reports to the EPA, including civil and criminal penalties of $25,000 and up, plus up to a year's imprisonment for each violation. Each day the violation continues is considered a separate violation for purposes of the fines levied under the TSCA.

## Pesticide Regulations

The Federal Insecticide, Fungicide and Rodenticide Act (FIFRA),[22] which amends the Federal Environmental Pesticides Control Act of 1972 (FEPCA), regulates both the manufacture and distribution of pesticides.

The National Environmental Policy Act of 1969 (NEPA)[23] requires an environmental impact statement (EIS) to be prepared with respect to major federal actions that significantly affect the quality of the human environment. While this would not, at first impression, seem to directly affect you, as a small business owner, the EIS requirement also applies in any situation where a federal agency approves some action by other persons, such as a private company. Also, many states have adopted similar EIS requirements, so that, for instance, when a local planning board approves a real estate development, an EIS may be required under state law, if not federal.

**Environmental Impact Reports**

In recent years, as the severe lung disease, cancer, and other health risks attributed to exposure to asbestos have come to light, a number of state and federal laws have been enacted to deal with this problem. In addition, huge numbers of individual damage suits for alleged harm to individuals, who were exposed to asbestos in the workplace and elsewhere, have resulted in enormous judgments against many companies, even forcing a giant building materials firm, Johns-Manville Corporation, into Chapter 11 bankruptcy to protect itself from a host of asbestos-related lawsuits.

**Asbestos Regulation**

Recent federal amendments to the TSCA and the Asbestos Hazard Emergency Response Act of 1986 (AHERA) have given the EPA power to issue regulations regarding asbestos in school buildings. In addition, Occupational Safety and Health Administration (OSHA) regulations[24] have been issued to limit asbestos exposure in the workplace and to set construction standards regarding use of asbestos.

Both OSHA and the EPA have issued regulations on noise emission standards, ranging from aircraft noise to protections of workers from hearing impairment in the workplace.

**Noise Control**

# 9.10 Consumer Credit Laws and Regulations

Many of the largest and most successful companies in America have gotten where they are, in part, by providing consumer credit to persons who buy their products. Classic examples would include such giant companies as Sears and General Motors, although countless smaller companies have also found that financing their customers' purchases can be a major boon to sales and that the interest earned on such credit can also become an important profit center in its own right.

The definition of consumer credit does not refer to the practice of allowing a client or customer to charge it and pay you at the end of the month, which is largely unregulated by the government. Instead, the following discussion deals with the situation where your business extends credit and charges interest during the period over which the loan amount (or amount financed) is being paid off by the customer.

The three main areas of the law regulating the extension of consumer credit, which affects nearly all businesses that grant such credit, are: the federal Equal Credit Opportunity Act, the federal Truth-in-Lending Act, and state laws that prohibit usury.

## Equal Credit Opportunity Laws

If your business is engaged in providing consumer credit, note that you will most likely be subject to the provisions of the federal Equal Credit Opportunity Act (ECOA).[25] In general, the ECOA prohibits discrimination in credit transactions on the basis of race, color, religion, national origin, sex, age, or marital status.

The basic principle of this law is that each person applying for credit must be considered as an individual. This means, primarily, that there are very strict limits regarding what you may ask about marital status and about the spouse of the applicant. You may ask about marital status, but only to determine what rights and remedies you might have as a creditor — such as in a community property state — to refuse an applicant's credit.

The ECOA also forbids discrimination in providing credit because some or all of the applicant's income derives from public assistance programs, or because a person exercised a right, in good faith, under the Consumer Credit Protection Act.

## Truth-in-Lending Requirements

If your business activities involve lending money, or if you sell to consumers on credit terms, you may have to comply with the federal Truth-in-Lending Act[26] and state laws such as those that prohibit the charging of usurious interest rates on loans or other credit transactions.

Regulations under the Truth-in-Lending Simplification and Reform Act provide that a business is not subject to the Truth-in-Lending rules unless it extended consumer credit at least 25 times in either the previous year or the current calendar year.[27] For loan transactions, required disclosures include:

- The annual percentage rate of interest;
- When the finance charge begins to accrue;
- The total amount of the finance charge;
- The number of payments to be made and the dollar amount of each payment;
- When payments are to be made;
- The total dollar amount of all payments;
- How any prepayment penalty and any late charges are to be computed;
- The amount of any prepaid finance charges and any deposit, plus the sum of the two;

- The amount financed;
- The existence of any balloon payment and its dollar amount;
- Annual statements of billing rights;
- Other information regarding security interests and rights to rescind; and
- Periodic billings to credit customers must include a number of disclosures regarding outstanding balances, how finance charges have been computed, and other items.

The rules regarding the Truth-in-Lending Act are far too complex to cover satisfactorily in a book of this nature; it can only alert you to the possibility that you may be required to comply with those rules and give you some sense of what will be required if the rules do apply to you. If you plan to extend credit to consumers — other than sending out bills requesting payment in full, without interest charge, after you have provided goods or services — you need to consult an attorney experienced in this area.

Fortunately, recent legislation has considerably simplified the truth-in-lending rules, and the Federal Reserve Board has published model disclosure statements and billing rights statements that can be used to satisfy the requirements of the truth-in-lending regulations.

**Cash Discount Act**

The Cash Discount Act (Public Law 97-25) permits sellers to offer a discount of any amount to customers who pay in cash or by check without running afoul of the truth-in-lending rules. The discount, in this case, has to be clearly disclosed and made available to all customers.[28] In the past, if you offered more than a 5% cash discount, you were considered to be imposing a finance charge on credit customers and had to give them all the required truth-in-lending disclosures.

**Usury Laws**

See Section 11.9 for a brief description of how this state's usury laws may apply to your business.

# 9.11 Employee or Independent Contractor?

As was pointed out in Section 5.2, there are some major advantages in hiring independent contractors rather than employees to work in your business. Not only do you gain considerable payroll tax savings by retaining independent contractors, but there are far fewer administrative headaches.

You don't have to withhold income and payroll taxes from payouts, provide workers' compensation coverage, or cover independent contractors in your retirement plan or other employee fringe benefit plans.

Unfortunately, just because you agree with someone you hire that they will be an independent contractor does not make it so for tax and legal purposes.

Thus, before you hire anyone to work for you as an independent contractor, you need to take a hard look at whether the IRS or a court of law would consider that person to be your employee rather than an independent contractor. While the IRS uses a 20-factor test to evaluate whether a person is or is not an employee, a few major warning flags will indicate to you whether the person is your employee or not. These include:

- The person works mostly or only for your firm. That is, the person is not like a lawyer, for example, who has a number of clients besides you that he or she works for.
- The worker is subject to your control, and you have the right to direct how the work is done, not just to demand a particular result.
- The person works in your office or establishment and does not have his or her own place of business, business cards, business name, etc.
- The kind of work the person does for you is normally done by employees, such as secretarial work.
- The person is not a licensed professional of any type.

Unless you are quite clear that the work relationship will not be considered that of employer/employee, be very careful about hiring someone as a so-called independent contractor. The consequences of being wrong can be quite severe. Here are just a few of the things that can happen if your independent contractor is held to be an employee:

- You are liable for not only the employer payroll taxes you failed to pay, but also for a portion of the employee taxes you failed to withhold (income taxes, FICA).

  If you treat someone as an independent contractor, you should report payments of $600 or more a year to that person on IRS *Form 1099-MISC*. If you do, and the IRS later determines that the person was really an employee, the back taxes you are liable for are limited to the employer payroll taxes, 20% of the employee's FICA tax you failed to withhold, and income tax withholding equal to only 1.5% of the wages you paid the person.

  If you do not file *Form 1099-MISC* and the person is reclassified as an employee, you are liable for 40% of the employee's FICA tax and income tax withholding equal to 3% of the wages — twice as much as if you would have filed *Form 1099-MISC*. Furthermore, there is now a $100 penalty for failure to file *Form 1099-MISC* and you will owe interest on the taxes due. It is no longer a bargain to "borrow" from the IRS.

  You may also be assessed other penalties if you did not have a reasonable basis for treating the person as a nonemployee and may be liable for up to 100% of the employee's FICA and income tax which you failed to withhold.

- If the person is hurt on the job and you have not provided workers' compensation insurance coverage, you will be liable for extensive legal damages.
- If your firm has a qualified retirement plan and you have not contributed to the plan on behalf of the person because he or she was not thought to be an employee at the time, the retirement plan could be disqualified for tax purposes for failing to cover the employee in question.

Thus, do not get stampeded into the independent contractor game by your friends and business associates who tell you how simple it is to avoid all those payroll taxes.

Note that the foregoing discussion of independent contractors summarizes federal rules only. Many states take an even more restrictive view than the IRS on the employee/independent contractor issue.

## Independent Contractors Treated as Employees

There are a number of steps you may be able to take to make a stronger case for someone who works for you to be treated as an independent contractor. Obviously, not all of the following will necessarily be feasible in every case, and a number of these steps, if implemented, may require some significant changes in the way you do business. But if you can follow most of the suggestions below with regard to a given worker, you will improve your odds against having that worker reclassified as an employee by the IRS.

- Have a written agreement, signed by both parties, that makes it clear that the company doesn't have the right to control the methods or procedures for the worker to accomplish the work contracted for. Include language in the agreement that it is the worker's obligation to pay income and self-employment taxes on amounts earned, and that he or she will receive a 1099 reflecting amounts earned, if $600 or more.
- Try to avoid setting working hours by hour or week. It would be all right to specify starting and completion dates for the work.
- Make it clear that if additional workers are needed to help, the contractor will hire and pay them.
- The arrangement should make it clear that the contractor is not limited to working exclusively for you, but is free to take on other work from other customers.
- Compensation should be based on what work is performed rather than the time spent to do it. This may require careful estimates so that the worker is fairly paid, not overpaid, for the work done.
- Avoid providing office space to the contractor on a regular basis.
- Let the workers be responsible for their own training, if that is possible.
- Each worker should be advised, in writing, to provide for their own liability, workers compensation, health, and disability insurance coverage.

- Costs such as meals, transportation, and clothing should be built into the contract price of the job, rather than being billed directly to your account.
- It should be clear in your agreement with the worker that he or she can't be fired and can't quit. The worker's job is to fulfill a given work contract.
- Don't give the worker other work to fill in during downtime. This may mean, of course, that you will have to pay the worker somewhat more for the work done than you otherwise would, if you wish to keep him or her happy.
- Don't pay bonuses to a person you treat as an independent contractor.

# 9.12  Whether You Should Incorporate Outside Your State

For most small businesses, there is little reason to consider incorporating your business under the laws of some state other than where you live. In fact, there are a few very good reasons why you should not incorporate in a different state:

- Your corporation may have to pay a qualification fee to transact business in your home state as a foreign corporation. See Section 11.9 on this point.
- If your attorney is a local lawyer, he or she is likely to be much less familiar with the corporate law rules of some other state than those of your state. Thus, your attorney is likely to either charge you more for corporate law advice if he or she has to research the law of an unfamiliar jurisdiction or give you less accurate advice than he or she could about your state's corporation laws.
- In many states, your corporation will have to pay some sort of minimum annual franchise tax or capital tax to the state of incorporation, even if you do no business there.

Also, don't believe the newspaper ads that tell you to incorporate in wonderful, tax-free Nevada or some other state and avoid your state's corporation income or franchise taxes. It doesn't work. If your corporation does business in your state, it pays the same taxes on its taxable income regardless of whether it is incorporated in your state, Nevada, or in the Grand Duchy of Luxembourg.

Perhaps the only valid reason why you might want to incorporate elsewhere would be to take advantage of some particular provision or flexibility available under the corporate laws of a particular state. If you own all the stock of your company, it is unlikely you would ever need to take advantage of any such provisions, which are usually more important where different groups are struggling for control of a corporation's board of directors or the like.

## 9.13 Foreign Investment in U.S. Businesses

Under the Foreign Direct Investment and International Financial Data Improvements Act of 1990, foreign individuals owning or acquiring 10% or more voting interest in U.S. businesses, including interests in U.S. real estate, must report certain information, including annual financial and operating data, to the U.S. Department of Commerce. Failure to file can result in civil penalties of $2,500 to $25,000.[29]

Reporting requirements under this law may be summarized as follows:

- *Form BE-13*, *Form BE-13C*, and *Form BE-14* — These forms are initial investment reports representing the establishment or acquisition of a U.S. affiliate.

  A person is excused from filing these reports only in the case of purchases of U.S. real estate to be used exclusively for personal, non-business purposes.
- *Form BE-605* and *Form BE-606B* — These forms are used as quarterly reports for qualifying reporters.
- *Form BE-15* — This is an annual reporting form.
- *Form BE-12* — This form is for quinquennial (five-year) reporting in benchmark surveys.

For more information on this new law, write to:

**Bureau of Economic Analysis**
**U.S. Department of Commerce**
BE-50 (IN)
Washington, DC 20230
(202) 523-0547

## 9.14 Emerging Trends and Issues

Today, businesses of every size and type are being buffeted by the ever-accelerating rate of change in the business, economic, social, and political environment in which they must operate. Part of the reason, is that Congress, along with 50 state legislatures and countless government agencies, spew out reams of new laws and regulations all year long, in ever greater volume. As Benjamin Franklin once put it, "No man is safe in his bed when the Congress is in session."

To blame all of the disorienting changes that are occurring on lawmakers, however, is unfair since it seems that life in general is becoming more complex and unpredictable by the day. Accordingly, this section attempts to provide you, as a business owner, with a brief overview of developing and current trends in the business environment.

## The Changing Economic Environment

Changes in the global economic structure in the wake of the collapse of communism throughout Eastern Europe and the break up of the Soviet Union, and the shift toward more efficient, free-market-oriented economies in places like Poland and Argentina, are creating a world that will soon look very different from the one you have become accustomed to since 1945.

While many applaud the changes taking place abroad, the net result seems to be the creation of a far more competitive world. U.S. businesses, even relatively small ones, are running up against increasingly severe international competition. Many firms that never gave a thought to export markets may have to get involved in doing business overseas if they wish to continue as viable operations in the global economy. Furthermore, even if your business is of a type or size that seems to make foreign competition seem irrelevant, you are still unlikely to completely elude its indirect effects, such as labor rates, increased automation, and downsizing.

## Labor Rates

Low labor rates abroad are causing the permanent shutdown of many large and small U.S. manufacturers, who can no longer meet the competition from Japan, Mexico, and elsewhere, or from U.S. manufacturers who move their operations overseas to places like Indonesia or Thailand, where wages are lower. This trend seems likely to continue and will have a rippling effect throughout the U.S. economy, adversely affecting many of the small firms that are either suppliers to large U.S. manufacturers or whose service operations (restaurants, retail shops and the like) will be drastically affected as larger companies close plants and make massive and permanent layoffs of thousands of employees. This is a rude fact of modern life of which almost anyone doing business in the so-called "Rust Belt" is already acutely aware, and which the recession that began in 1991 is rapidly introducing to the parts of the country that have, up until now, escaped the brunt of the effects of increased foreign competition.

## Automation

Increasing automation, both here and abroad, is also likely to have a dramatic effect on employment and competitiveness in this country and throughout the world. Automation has been a factor in replacing blue-collar labor for decades now. With the recent and continual explosion in computing power and sophistication, vast numbers of middle managers and other white-collar workers are beginning to be displaced. With the advent of expert systems and "artificial intelligence," which are still in their infancy, but rapidly coming into their own, it is difficult to say whose job, if anyone's, will be safe in a few years.

While the ability to replace workers with computers or computer-driven machinery may be very attractive, from a cost-savings standpoint to you as an employer, its societal effects are hard to predict and may prove to be very adverse to the overall business environment. The field of information processing is moving rapidly, and it is difficult to visualize how the world and the U.S. economy may look in as little as five or six years.

**Downsizing**

Largely in response to ever-fiercer foreign competition, employer downsizing continued at a rapid pace in 1991, up sharply from 1990. According to an American Management Association (AMA) survey for the year ending in June 1991, 55.5% of the organizations polled engaged in downsizing and 60% of those firms had also made significant staff cutbacks in the previous year, suggesting that firms are now cutting even deeper and deeper. The survey revealed that the cuts were heaviest on the Pacific Coast, averaging 12.6% of the workforce among firms reporting downsizing. Middle management jobs, which are estimated to make up something like 5% to 8% of the total work force, accounted for more than 16% of the jobs cut in the 1991 survey period.

While much of this change seems frightening to business people, as well as to their employees — the hundreds of thousands, perhaps even millions, of skilled management and white-collar workers who are being given their pink slips and severance packages by downsizing corporations over the next few years — it may also give rise to fantastic new opportunities.

Many of these people are likely to start their own smaller businesses due to the permanent disappearance of so many middle management or automatable jobs. Many may even keep working for their former firms as independent contractors or consultants. In addition to enriching the overall business environment by creating a major upsurge in the formation of new, small, and flexible business entities, firms that cater to the needs of other small businesses may find the coming decade to be one of explosive growth and unparalleled opportunity.

**Telecommuting**

One of the most predictable trends, which is already well under way, is the growth of telecommuting, where more and more people work out of their homes, communicating with their clients or employers by use of personal computers, modems, faxes, or multiple phone lines. Already, some employers, like certain government agencies in Washington, D.C., are taking an intermediate step by setting up satellite telecommuting offices in suburban areas. By going to these nearby satellite offices, equipped with computer workstations, many workers can, on most days, avoid long and arduous commutes to downtown offices by piping their work product electronically to the main office instead.

A 1991 survey by Link Resources Corporation, a research and consulting firm, showed telecommuting has become a major factor in the economy almost overnight. The survey estimated that company employees who work at home part- or full-time increased in 1991 by 38%, over 1989, to 38.4 million individuals, most of whom are believed to be telecommuting. The survey apparently did not even take into account home-based businesses, which are also believed to be proliferating at truly startling rates.

The enormous changes in the workplace that are already taking place will obviously create tremendous new business opportunities, as well as problems, in the coming years. These should include the obvious ones such as sales of more fax machines and other equipment and supplies for home office use, as well as less obvious opportunities like restaurants that deliver meals to busy home workers, and doubtless many other novel kinds of services and products that no one has even conceived of yet.

**Pending Law Changes**

The abrupt plunge in the U.S. economy in late 1991 and early 1992 is likely to lead to significant tax law changes in 1992, particularly with a presidential election coming up in November. Because of this election, politicians will try to jump start the flagging economy to give voters the impression that they are working to get the country out of the economic doldrums. Some of the major tax changes you should be looking out for, which may have already passed by the time you read this, would include:

- Mandatory health care coverage — This is likely to be the biggest item on the entire legislative agenda in Congress this year, as the battle over what to do about the increasing inaccessibility of medical care to large segments of the population gets fought out on Capitol Hill. Most of the legislative proposals that have been floating around Congress for the last year or two would involve a combination of:

  - Requiring that most, or all employers, provide some level of medical coverage for their full-time employees, and

  - Additional payroll taxes to finance the cost of government-provided health care for individuals outside of the work force. In some of the proposals, the employer would be given a choice of paying a hefty tax for national health insurance or providing coverage for employees; other proposals would require both, which could be a very difficult financial burden for many small businesses, even those that already provide medical insurance for their employees.

  In a related issue, close to the hearts of all self-employed individuals, some of the proposals would also put self-employed persons and S corporation shareholder/employees on the same footing as incorporated business owners, by increasing the deductible amount of medical insurance for such business owners from 25% of the amount incurred to 100%.

- Capital gains tax relief — The United States is one of the few countries that taxes capital gains at nearly the same rate as other income. Many of the fastest growing companies in the world don't tax capital gains at all, and much of the available evidence indicates that reducing capital gains in the late 1970s and early 1980s had a remarkable effect on stimulating capital investment and boosting economic growth in this country. Perhaps Congress will see this message this year and cut capital gains tax.

- Other incentives — Look for various other business tax incentives to be resurrected, such as restoring the investment tax credit, accelerated depreciation, or new jobs credits. Since the government has a history of taking such tax gifts back after a year or two, you may want to act fairly quickly to find out more about and take quick advantage of any such capital investment incentives that may be enacted.

## New Civil Rights Laws

The new federal Civil Rights Act of 1991 (CRA91), which became immediately effective upon enactment on November 29, 1991, is certain to make life a lot more complicated for all covered employers in the area of employment practices.

The new law's most controversial aspect will be in the "disparate impact" cases, where a company's employment practices, although not shown to be intentionally discriminatory, have a disparate (unequal) impact on employment of protected groups.

For example, if a company is located in an area where 80% of the population consists of Native Americans, but only 5% of its employees are Native Americans, there may be grounds for a disparate impact claim against the employer, under prior civil rights law as well as the new CRA91 provisions, regardless of employer intent.

Under prior law, the U.S. Supreme Court held that the burden of proof was on the employee who alleged discrimination. The employee had to identify the particular business practice of the employer that resulted in the disparity. By contrast, under the new CRA91, the employee is relieved of this burden of proof if he or she can simply show that the employer failed to select an alternative employment practice (such as hiring quotas), that would not have had a disparate impact — that is, that would not have had a negative impact on the minority or other protected group. Instead, the burden of proof in these cases is now shifted to the employer, who must show that the challenged employment practice regarding hiring, promotions, pay, or other aspects of employment is job-related for the position in question and consistent with business necessity.

This vagueness regarding job-relatedness business necessity is what President Bush initially expressed concerns over, arguing that many firms would find it easier to simply adopt minority hiring quotas than to attempt to prove the "business necessity" defense in court. There are no easy answers as to what policy a company should adopt in this regard. It may seem that one safe way to avoid discrimination suits under the new law would be to adopt some sort of quota system; yet, using the quota system generates issues of unfairness and possible employee morale problems.

CRA91 also considerably expands the monetary damages that can be awarded in cases of intentional discrimination. Before, an employer who lost such a discrimination suit was usually liable only for back pay, front pay, lost benefits, attorney's fees, and court costs. Now, under CRA91 — which may even be retroactive in effect — compensatory damages may also be allowed in addition to other monetary damages. CRA91 also overrides a U.S. Supreme Court case that had limited fees — a flat $40 — recoverable by a claimant for expert witness fees.

In light of the foregoing changes in the Civil Rights Act of 1991, the odds, as well as the costs, of losing a discrimination action have increased significantly for employers. The new rules will make it much more attractive for plaintiffs to file such suits, both for claims of intentional discrimination and in disparate impact cases. Employers can now expect a great many more such claims to be filed. Thus, however fair you may feel your firm's employment practices are, if you are a large enough firm — generally 15 or more employees — to be subject to the Civil Rights Act, this may be a good time to consult an attorney who is familiar with employment discrimination matters to see what, if any, steps you may need to take to protect your business from liability in this area.

## Sexual Harassment

The Clarence Thomas–Anita Hill hearings brought the issue of sexual harassment to a new and heightened level of awareness among the public. While sexual harassment, as such, is not mentioned anywhere in Title VII of the federal Civil Rights Act, the Equal Employment Opportunity Commission (EEOC) and the courts have long accepted such harassment as being illegal and discriminatory. In addition, many states have adopted specific laws banning sexual harassment.

Because this is now such a highly topical issue, many employment law experts expect an upsurge in litigation involving sexual harassment claims, so you should probably take a fresh look at your firm's policies regarding this subject. See Section 5.8 for a discussion of the federal sexual harassment law and steps you can take to protect your firm from being sued for failing to take proper steps to prevent such acts from occurring.

## Other Legal Trends and New or Pending Legislation

Listed and discussed below are several other legal trends and new or pending legislation you should know about for future reference. This information provides possible tips for issues or rules which may affect your business.

## Family Leave Legislation

Congress attempted in both 1990 and 1991 to pass a parental and family leave act. Both times, the legislation was vetoed, but President Bush's veto was barely sustained in 1991. This act, or similar legislation, is almost certain to come up again and is likely to pass. If passed in its present form, this legislation would require that employers with at least 50 employees provide unpaid leaves of absence to employees for up to 12 weeks for family purposes such as:

- The birth or adoption of a child; or
- A serious health condition of the employee or a spouse, child, or parent.

As an employer, you would have to continue health insurance coverage during such a leave and hold the job, or a comparable position, open until the employee returns. Even if this legislation, which has strong backing from organized labor, does not make it through Congress again this year, a number of states — such as California, Hawaii, and New Jersey — have recently enacted similar legislation, and many more are likely to follow suit in the absence of federal legislation on the subject.

Perhaps, then, you can hope that Congress will pass a reasonable bill, and one that preempts all such state laws, so that the law will at least be uniform from state to state.

**Shared Work Programs**

Another program that has been adopted in a number of states and appears to be growing in acceptance is a shared work program under state unemployment insurance laws. Essentially, what the shared work programs do is allow employees to collect full unemployment benefits while still working a minimal number of hours per week. This not only benefits the employee, but can also be very helpful in the case of an employer who, due to the recession or other business difficulties, has to temporarily cut back the hours it can employ workers for a period of time until business conditions improve. In states where there is no such program, it is often necessary to lay a worker off entirely for him or her to collect unemployment benefits.

Under shared work programs, you, the employer, can often retain a good employee during a temporary slow period, while the employee supplements his or her unemployment benefits with a modest amount of wages from working part-time. Together, this may be sufficient to keep the employee in question from taking a permanent position elsewhere. Then, if things improve in a few months, you may be able to restore the cutback employee to full-time status again.

These shared work programs make a lot of sense for everyone, so if your firm is getting to a point where you are considering having to lay off good employees whom you don't want to lose, be sure to contact your local state unemployment office to find out if your state has adopted such a program. If so, you may be able to keep personnel on a part-time basis until business picks up again. Good people are hard to find, and you don't want to lose them.

**Wrongful Termination of Employees**

Wrongful termination of employees is another area of growing importance in terms of employer/employee relations. For a great many years, it was generally the rule that an employer was free to fire employees "at will," without needing any good reason to do so, unless there was some sort of formal contractual arrangement or collective bargaining agreement.

This situation has begun to change in recent years, mainly as a result of a number of revolutionary court decisions in California, which hold employers liable for damages for wrongfully discharging employees. Initially, such cases tended to involve extreme and egregious situations, where employees fired whistle-blowing employees who threatened to report fraudulent activities of their employer.

However, as the legal concept of wrongful termination has become more accepted and spread to courts in states other than California, the scope of what constitutes "wrongful termination" has begun to expand, and at this point, it is difficult to say how far this new right will be extended in the future.

Suffice it to say that in the future, employers are going to have to become increasingly careful about documenting their reasons for firing any employee. The days when you, as an employer, could choose to fire an employee just because you got up on the wrong side of the bed that morning may be coming to an end, soon — at least in a number of states.

## Striker Replacement Law

Another piece of legislation that was introduced in Congress in 1991 but which didn't pass was the Worker Replacement Act. Since it has strong American Federation of Labor & Congress of Industrial Organizations (AFL-CIO) backing, it is by no means dead, and its passage could be extremely damaging to small employers.

This is a hot issue and one you may want to write or call your Congressperson about before it is too late. The legislation, as it was proposed in 1991, would prohibit employers from permanently replacing workers who go on strike. This would fundamentally alter the balance between unions and employers that has been in effect since the New Deal days, tilting the balance strongly in favor of unions.

The law, if passed, would require that you refrain from hiring permanent replacement employees during a strike, and you would have to give the strikers their jobs back when they are ready to return to work after the strike is over.

At present, companies can fire workers who go on strike over economic issues, such as wages, but not if the company refuses to bargain in good faith with the union, or if the walkout stems from other acts of the employer.

The proposed law would extend the firing ban to strikes over economic issues, which are usually the reason for labor walkouts. By extending this protection only to unionized workers — as the House version of the bill, H.R. 55 would do — such a law would give unions tremendous clout in organizing the workers of small companies, since they would be able to offer a major advantage that is not available to nonunion workers.

Finally, the proposed legislation would permit any two workers of a nonunionized small business to walk off a job in protest of working conditions, in effect giving them the benefits of a union without their having to go through the process of a certification election to establish a collective bargaining unit. This provision could also prove to be a major burden on small, nonunion employers.

Although this bill didn't get enacted in 1991, it is almost certain to be on the front burner in 1992, an election year.

## Environmental Legislation

A recent article in the January 1992 issue of *California Lawyer* reported that, despite hard economic times, the demand for lawyers in the field of environmental law is expanding beyond the capacity of many law firms and companies. While this may be wonderful news for the legal profession, at a time when even law firms have been making significant lay-offs, it is decidedly not good news for the typical small business.

The reason for all the new demand for environmental lawyers is that this is an area of the law that is already beginning to have a huge impact on the way many companies do business, and it seems clearly destined to exert an even greater impact in coming years.

The Clean Air Act of 1991, for example, will have a disproportionately large effect on small businesses, particularly because they are small and their economies of scale are not as great; thus, they will tend to be hit much harder by the costs of the new environmental restrictions. All sorts of small firms, such as bakers, dry cleaners, body shops, painters, service stations, and printers, are going to be required to purchase expensive new technology and machinery to reduce emissions of air pollutants, if they wish to remain in business.

For example, gas stations will have to install expensive vapor-recovery devices on each gas pump. This can cost about $30,000 for a typical gas station, plus significant ongoing maintenance costs. Also, businesses operating in extremely smoggy areas — such as parts of California, Houston, and elsewhere — will soon be subject to environmental rules imposed by local government, as well. If those areas are to achieve compliance with federal clean air standards in the next few years, as federal law requires they must, local governments will have to start imposing environmental rules.

While it is beyond the scope of this book to go into great detail on increasing environmental restrictions, you should be aware that almost every business in urban areas of America may need to consult an environmental law specialist at some time in the next few years. Penalties for violations tend to start at levels like $25,000 a day under many of the environmental statutes, so this is an area where you can't afford even a brief slip up.

See Section 9.9 for a general overview of some of the major federal environmental laws your business may be subject to already, in addition to the latest Clean Air Act amendments mentioned here, some of which won't go into effect for up to 20 years.

## State Unitary Taxation of Worldwide Income

If your firm does business overseas as well as in certain states (particularly California), you are undoubtedly already well aware of the worldwide unitary method of taxing your firm's worldwide profits. What you may not be aware of is that legislation is pending in Congress that would ban such worldwide unitary taxation by the states.

If such legislation passes, it may reduce state income and franchise taxes on a number of international companies doing business in the states with such laws. If yours is such a company, keep an eye out for news of any such legislation passing, because it is possible that you may be able to file for refunds of state taxes paid in prior years, if the statutes of limitations for those years have not yet expired. In short, you may need to move quickly to take full benefit of such legislation enacted in the Congress.

## Video Display Terminals

Until recently, white-collar workplaces or offices generally created very little liability exposure for employers, with regard to hazardous working conditions. This, too, is beginning to change.

In recent years, there have been an increasing number of lawsuits filed by employees in connection with hazards of working long hours on computers; and in late 1990, the city of San Francisco adopted an ordinance that provides regulatory safeguards for workers using video display terminals (VDTs) for four or more hours per shift. Apparently, Los Angeles and a number of other city and state governments around the nation are now considering similar laws or ordinances, since use of computers in the workplace is now a universal phenomenon and because a number of threats of employees' health have arisen in connection with the heavy use of computers.

These range from excessive exposure to radiation emitted by VDTs to carpal tunnel syndrome, a now common and debilitating nerve entrapment disorder that can cause severe pain and weakness in the wrist. Carpal tunnel syndrome can a result from too many hours spent typing on a computer keyboard — as well as from many other tasks requiring repetitive flexing and extensions of the wrist.

Laws regulating VDTs are likely to begin appearing all over the country in the near future, and offices that don't pay attention to ergonomics — the study of equipment design to reduce workplace injury — may well become sitting ducks for lawsuits or fines. While most legal claims by employees regarding VDT usage have been imposed on workers' compensation insurers thus far, employers may become directly liable:

- If they participate actively in the design of computer systems or workstations that allegedly caused the injury to an employee, or
- If new state legislation removes such claims from the workers' compensation system and places financial responsibility directly upon employers.

## National Federation of Independent Business

Communicate your thoughts on government policy and pending legislation to groups like the National Federation of Independent Business (NFIB), the U.S. Chamber of Commerce, your local chamber of commerce, or, perhaps even more effectively, to a trade association for your industry. It also wouldn't hurt to call or write your senator, U.S. representative, or the state legislator to voice your strong opinion in favor of or opposition to pending legislation or regulations that will affect your business.

Small business has been hit very hard by the government at all levels in recent years, and the more small business owners join and work together through organizations like the NFIB, the better the chances of shaping the future.

For more information regarding the NFIB, see the letter from the publisher which is located at the back of this book. This letter also contains a handy post card you can cut out, complete, and mail to the NFIB for membership information as well as a complimentary copy of their publication, *Independent Business*.

# Footnotes

1. I.R.C. §168.
2. I.R.C. §168(i).
3. I.R.C. §179(b)(1).
4. I.R.C. §6425.
5. 15 U.S.C. §§1051–1127.
6. I.R.C. §1244(c). The Tax Reform Act of 1984 §481(a).
7. I.R.C. §1211(b).
8. I.R.C. §1244(c)(1)(C).
9. I.R.C. §1244(c)(3).
10. I.R.C. §1244(d)(1)(B).
11. I.R.C. §1244(b).
12. 16 C.F.R. §435.
13. 42 U.S.C.A. §9601 *et seq*.
14. 42 U.S.C.A. §6901 *et seq*.
15. 40 C.F.R. §280.3(a) and (b).
16. 40 C.F.R. §280.20.
17. 40 C.F.R. §280.21.
18. 33 U.S.C.A. §§1251–1376.
19. 33 U.S.C.A. §1344(a).
20. 42 U.S.C.A. §§7401–7626.
21. 15 U.S.C.A. §§2601–2629.
22. 7 U.S.C.A. §135 *et seq*.
23. 42 U.S.C.A. §§4321–4347.
24. 29 C.F.R. §§1910 and 1926.58.
25. 15 U.S.C. §1691.
26. 15 U.S.C. §1601 *et seq*.
27. 12 C.F.R. §226.2(a)(17).
28. 12 C.F.R. §226.4(c)(8).
29. 15 C.F.R. §806.

Chapter 10

# Sources of Help and Information

*If you're going to sin, sin against God, not the bureaucracy.*
*God will forgive you, but the bureaucracy won't.*

— Admiral Hyman G. Rickover

## 10.1  General Considerations

Many government and private organizations provide free or low-cost services and publications to small business. Unfortunately, most small business owners only find out about a few of these sources and then only on a haphazard basis. This chapter summarizes many of the services and publications that you may need to draw on as an owner or operator of a small business.

## 10.2  Professional Services

Select your accountant carefully, for this is the one person outside your business who is most likely to be closely in touch with almost everything going on in your operation. Besides helping to set up your books and to establish systems for handling cash receipts and disbursements, a good accountant can provide a wealth of practical advice on a wide range of subjects that are important to your business, including planning for taxes, managing your money, obtaining financing, and evaluating business opportunities. Attorneys and bankers are often in a good position to recommend accountants whom they know.

**Accountants**

**Attorneys**

Unless you are starting out as a sole proprietor, you will usually need an attorney to prepare a partnership agreement or to set up a corporation. You will probably do well to consult an attorney anyway to make sure you are obtaining necessary licenses and permits or to help you obtain them in some cases. In most parts of the country, local bar associations have lawyer referral services that can put you in touch with attorneys in your area practicing in various fields. In most cases, however, you will do better to ask an accountant or banker to recommend a good business lawyer. If you need highly specialized legal advice or representation, ask an attorney you know to recommend a specialist.

**Bankers**

Establishing a good relationship with officers of the bank branch where you open an account for your business is strongly recommended. While you may find it tough to borrow from your friendly banker when you first go into business, he or she will be interested in keeping an eye on your business to see how it develops. It pays to cultivate the relationship to create a good impression before you want to apply for a business loan from the bank. Ask around before opening an account; find out if there is a bank in your area that is well known for lending to small businesses. Many of the large banks tend to be more interested in larger accounts, although different branch managers of the same bank may have very different ideas about working with small businesses.

Your banker can be a useful source of free financial advice and a good connection when wanting to meeting other business owners in your community.

**Benefit Consultants**

If you intend to establish a corporate pension or profit-sharing plan — or Keogh plan, if you have a number of employees — you may want to seek out a benefit consulting firm and obtain their proposals as to the type of benefit plan you need and how it should be structured. Since many such firms are primarily engaged in selling insurance products, such as life insurance, annuities, and investment contracts, designed for pension plans, the plan those firms design for you will almost invariably involve building in their products. Since an insured retirement plan may not necessarily make sense in your particular situation, you should ask your attorney or accountant to recommend a benefit consulting firm that does not have products to sell other than their consulting and plan administration services.

# 10.3  U.S. Small Business Administration and Other Helpful Agencies

The federal Small Business Administration (SBA) is one government agency that is genuinely helpful to small businesses. The SBA not only guarantees financing for many small businesses (see Section 9.7) but it also provides a number of valuable services.

One service you might find helpful is the Service Corps of Retired Executives (SCORE). SCORE is a program in which retired executives with many years of business experience volunteer their services as consultants to small businesses and charge only for their out-of-pocket expenses.

Other SBA programs designed to provide assistance to small businesses include:

- Small Business Development Centers (SBDCs) — SBDCs are local centers operated by the state or community, with SBA assistance, to provide a wide range of business counseling and training. To see if your state has an SBDC network, refer to Section 11.10.
- Small Business Institutes (SBIs) — SBIs provide in-depth business counseling at hundreds of universities across the country.

In addition, SBA offices perform a variety of seminars and workshops on topics of interest to people who are starting or operating small businesses. Here are some of the seminars recently offered by the SBA.

- *Small Business Seminar with the IRS*
- *Pre-Business Workshop*
- *Starting Your Own Business: A Seminar for Women*
- *Export Workshop*

Contact your local SBA office for more information.

## Telephone Hotlines

The SBA and several other government agencies maintain toll-free telephone hotline information services to assist businesses and taxpayers. Some of the more important ones to know about are listed below.

## SBA Answer Desk

The SBA Answer Desk has a toll-free number of a small business information and referral service offered by the SBA, which you can call from anywhere in the continental United States, except Washington, D.C. In the District of Columbia, call 653-7561. The telephone Answer Desk offers a wide range of prerecorded informational messages, any of which you may access if you have a touch-tone phone.

**SBA Answer Desk**
(800) U-ASK-SBA or 827-5722

## Small Business Hotline

The Small Business Hotline is a specialized free service offered by the Export-Import Bank to small exporters needing general information or problem-solving assistance relating to doing business abroad. It provides information on export credit and on assistance available from other government agencies and the private sector.

**Small Business Hotline**
(800) 424-5201

**Internal Revenue Service**

The IRS has created a new assistance program called Tele-Tax, which went into effect January 1992. The program allows you to call a toll-free number in your state to listen to pre-recorded tax information that will answer many federal tax questions.

About 140 topics are available, including information on the Small Business Tax Education Program (STEP), business income, sole proprietorships, and the self-employment tax.

For more information on Tele-Tax, call the IRS' toll-free number to request *Publication 910, Guide to Free Tax Services*. This publication not only lists the many tax publications you can order, but it also lists the Tele-Tax phone numbers and topic numbers in your state.

**Internal Revenue Service**
(800) 829-3676

**Trade Information Center**

The Trade Information Center has a hotline where you can receive general information on exporting that is provided by various U.S. government agencies.

**Trade Information Center**
(800) USA-TRADE or 872-8723

Or, for information on doing business in the unified European Market after 1992, call for written information and a quarterly newsletter from:

**U.S. Department of Commerce's Single Internal Market – 1992 Information Service**
(202) 377-5276

**European Center – Washington, D.C. Office**
(202) 862-9500

**Ernst & Young**

Ernst & Young, one of the Big Six accounting firms, publishes some helpful guides for anyone interested in expanding their business into the global markets. They are:

- *The Ernst & Young Guide to Expanding in the Global Market* — This guide is for those managers who want to succeed in complex international ventures; book includes step-by-step programs and helpful examples.
- *The Ernst & Young Resource Guide to Global Markets 1991* — This guide is an up-to-date resource to global market trends and regional county data.

For more information, contact:

**John Wiley & Sons, Inc. – Sales Department**
605 Third Avenue
New York, NY 10158-0012
(212) 850-6000

Like certain Scandinavian countries, the Environmental Protection Agency (EPA) now has a small business ombudsman to give easier access to the EPA, help you comply with EPA regulations, and make sure you are treated fairly in any EPA disputes.

**EPA Ombudsman**

**EPA Small Business Ombudsman**
(703) 305-5938
(800) 368-5888

If you want to find out what records the Social Security Administration (SSA) has on your earnings and your projected benefits at retirement age, you can file a simple form requesting a detailed printout of this information.

**Social Security Administration**

This is something everyone should do once every few years because if the SSA has made a serious mistake in your earnings record, you have only a limited number of years in which you can contact them and have your record corrected. To obtain the request form, call the SSA's toll-free number or write the SSA for this form at the Consumer Information Center address below.

**Social Security Administration**
(800) 772-1213

**Consumer Information Center**
Department 72
Pueblo, CO 81009

There are also companies who can assist in the incorporation process, providing a variety of incorporation kits and services. One such company, Corporate Agents, Inc., can help you form your corporation in any state for as little as $99 (plus state fees), depending on the state. Some examples of complete costs for other states are $115 for Delaware, $169 for Florida, $269 for New York, and $1,014 for California.

**Corporate Agents, Inc.**

The fees cover all costs, including all state filing fees and recording costs, preparing and filing articles of incorporation, and registered agents fee service for the first year. Also available for a nominal additional cost are the corporate kits, which include the corporate seal, minute book, stock certificates, and sample forms and bylaws.

For more information on this company, you can send the preaddressed post card located at the back of this book or call Corporate Agents at the toll-free number below:

**Corporate Agents, Inc.**
1013 Centre Road
P.O. Box 1281
Wilmington, DE 19899
(800) 877-4224
FAX (302) 998-7078

# 10.4 Publications Regarding Small Business Operations

**U.S. Small Business Administration**

The U.S. Small Business Administration (SBA) has more than 50 helpful booklets and other publications on subjects of importance to new and existing small businesses. The publications, which sell for a nominal fee — usually about $0.50 (50 cents) to $1.00 each, and never more than $2.00 — can be obtained through your nearest SBA office or by calling the SBA Answer Desk and asking for a list of publications.

**SBA Answer Desk**
(800) U-ASK-SBA or 827-5722

You can also use the preaddressed post card in the back of this book to request lists of SBA publications.

**Small Business Institutes**

Small Business Institutes (SBIs) are located on university campuses throughout the United States. Part of a cooperative program with the SBA, SBIs offer you business assistance while furthering the education of college students. Students, supervised by faculty members, provide your business with:

- Free confidential consulting;
- In-depth analysis of your firm's business situation;
- Alternatives and recommendations to business problems; and
- Written and oral reports.

Headquartered at the University of Central Arkansas, the Small Business Institute Directors' Association (SBIDA) National Center and the Small Business Advancement Network perform research and gather information on small business. The SBIDA National Center is the link between all SBI universities and the government. The SBIDA also:

- Is the center of correspondence for SBI schools;
- Keeps records on all SBI schools;
- Publishes the *SBIDA News*;
- Processes SBIDA membership; and
- Is a center for advocacy.

The Small Business Advancement Network is an electronic bulletin board which provides information on grant opportunities, cooperative ventures between the SBA and SBI, and small business research. The network is available during regular business hours and is updated daily. For information on the SBI nearest you, contact:

**SBIDA National Center**
**University of Central Arkansas**
College of Business
UCA P.O. Box 4983
Conway, AR 72035-5002
(501) 450-5300

For more on the Small Business Advancement Network, contact:

**Small Business Advancement National Center**
**University of Arkansas**
College of Business
UCA P.O. Box 5018
Conway, AR 72035-5002
(501) 450-5377

The publisher of this book, The Oasis Press, also has a number of how-to business guides targeted toward small businesses. A free list of these related resources can be obtained by calling:

**The Oasis Press**
(800) 228-2275

**The Oasis Press**

Here are some magazines that provide continuing information for businesses in general and small businesses in particular. There are also a number of specialized publications you may find helpful. Most of these publications can be located through your local library, or you can contact them at the addresses below.

**Magazines**

***The Wall Street Journal***
84 Second Avenue
Chicopee, MA 01220
(413) 592-7761

***D&B Reports***
299 Park Avenue
New York, NY 10171
(212) 593-6728

***In Business***
419 State Avenue
Emmaus, PA 18049
(215) 967-4135

***Success Magazine***
230 Park Avenue
New York, NY 10169
(800) 234-7324

***Entrepreneur Magazine***
Subscriber Service
2392 Morse Avenue
P.O. Box 19787
Irvine, CA 92713-9441
(800) 421-2300
(800) 352-7449 (in CA)

***Family Business Magazine***
Subscriber Service
One Heritage Way
P.O. Box 420265
Palm Coast, FL 32142-0265
(800) 423-1780
(800) 858-0095 (in FL)

***Business Week***
Subscriber Service
P.O. Box 506
Hightstown, NJ 08520
(800) 635-1200

***Nation's Business***
1615 H. Street, NW
Washington, DC 20062
(202) 463-5650

***INC.***
Subscriber Service
P.O. Box 54129
Boulder, CO 80322-4129
(800) 525-0643

***Small Business Opportunities***
1115 Broadway, 8th Floor
New York, NY 10010
(212) 807-7100

***Small Business Reports***
Subscriber Services
P.O. Box 53140
Boulder, CO 80322-3140
(800) 234-1094

***Independent Business***
National Federation of Independent Business
Membership Development Office
600 Maryland Avenue, SW
Suite 700
Washington, DC 20024
(202) 554-9000

**Statistical Information**

Some of the more important sources of statistical information that you will need if you do your own marketing research are:

| Title | Publisher |
|---|---|
| ***Survey of Buying Power*** <br> ***Sales and Marketing Management Magazine*** <br> Comprehensive data on population, retail sales, and consumer buying income for states, counties, and cities. | **Bill Communications, Inc.** <br> 633 Third Avenue <br> New York, NY 10017-6706 <br> (212) 986-4800 |
| ***Publication Price List*** <br> Titles on corporate relations, human resources, management, economic and business environments, and consumer research. | **Conference Board** <br> 845 Third Avenue <br> New York, NY 10022 <br> (800) 872-6273 |
| ***Survey of Current Business*** <br> U.S. Department of Commerce's monthly survey of business trends and conditions. | **Superintendent of Documents** <br> **U.S. Government Printing Office** <br> Washington, DC  20402 <br> (202) 783-3238 |
| ***The Complete Information Bank for Entrepreneurs*** <br> ***& Small Business Managers, Second Edition*** <br> An excellent sourcebook which lists and describes hundreds of leading business books and other sources of help and information for small businesses. | **Center for Entrepreneurship and** <br> **Small Business Management** <br> Wichita State University <br> Campus Box 147 <br> 1845 Fairmont <br> Wichita, KS 67208 <br> (316) 689-3000 |

# 10.5  Do-It-Yourself Incorporation

If you want to form your own corporation and save several hundred dollars in legal fees, there are books that tell you how to do it and provide the forms you need; however, you should think carefully before you attempt to do this on your own. In some cases, setting up a corporation is not that complicated, and if you follow the instructions in a self-incorporation book precisely — if one is available for your state — you should be able to do it properly. But you will have to spend many hours carefully figuring out and then doing all that is required. Your time might be worth much more than the money you would save in legal fees because you could concentrate more on getting the business off to a good start. Check Section 11.10 to see if there is an incorporation book for your state.

Regardless of whether or not you decide to incorporate your business yourself or work with an attorney, you may find a new publication on incorporation extremely helpful. *The Essential Corporation Handbook,* written by attorney Carl R.J. Sniffen, is an easy-to-read introduction into what you will need to know if you incorporate your business. This handbook could supplement any state do-it-yourself incorporation guide by filling you in on the specifics of bylaws, articles of incorporation, shareholder agreements, required meetings, stocks, and other corporate formalities. If you decide to work with an attorney when incorporating, this book will help you make the best use of your attorney's time because you'll understand the issues and terminology, and you'll know what questions to ask. *The Essential Corporation Handbook* arms you with knowledge so you can avoid common mistakes. To find out more, contact your local book source or contact:

**The Oasis Press**
(800) 228-2275

## 10.6 Information Regarding Payroll Taxes and Withholding

Major offices of the Internal Revenue Service (IRS) frequently put on seminars for new employers regarding payroll tax requirements. Call your local IRS office for information as to when such seminars will be held in your area. In addition, you may want to obtain *Circular E*, *Employer's Tax Guide,* and *Notice 109, Information About Depositing Employment and Excise Taxes*. Both can be obtained from the IRS office nearest you.

In addition, the Matthew Bender publishing company puts out an excellent book called the *Payroll Tax Guide*, which covers almost every aspect of federal payroll tax returns.

## 10.7 Other Useful Tax Publications

The publications below can also be obtained from your local IRS office:

| Publication | Subject |
|---|---|
| Publication 334 | Tax Guide For Small Business Income and other Federal Taxes |
| Publication 349 | Federal Highway Use Taxes on Heavy Vehicles |
| Publication 378 | Fuel Tax Credits and Refunds |
| Publication 463 | Travel, Entertainment, and Gift Expenses |
| Publication 510 | Federal Excise Taxes |
| Publication 541 | Tax Information on Partnerships |
| Publication 542 | Tax Information on Corporations |
| Publication 544 | Sales and Other Dispositions of Assets |
| Publication 552 | Recordkeeping Requirements |
| Publication 583 | Taxpayers Starting a Business |
| Publication 587 | Business Use of Your Home |
| Publication 589 | Tax Information on S Corporations |
| Publication 910 | Guide to Free Tax Services |
| Publication 937 | Business Reporting |

To order these free tax publications or other tax forms, call:

**Internal Revenue Service**
(800) 829-3676

# 10.8  ERISA Compliance

If your business has a pension or profit-sharing plan and you wish to handle your own Employee Retirement Income Security Act (ERISA) filings for the plan, you should obtain a copy of Charles D. Spencer & Associates' publication, *5500 Annual Reports for Employee Benefit Plans.*

This publication will help you prepare the necessary *Form 5500* series through its easy-to-understand, step-by-step instructions. For ordering information, contact:

**Charles D. Spencer & Associates, Inc.**
250 South Wacker Drive, Suite 600
Chicago, IL 60606
(312) 993-7900

# 10.9  Managing Your Own Keogh or IRA Investments

If you want to set up a canned Keogh plan or an individual retirement account (IRA) and have the ability to manage the plan or account's investments for yourself, you can do so through certain stockbrokers. Check with your local bank or stockbroker to compare services and prices. Discount brokers, such as Charles Schwab & Co. and Fidelity Brokerage Services, provide such accounts at competitive rates.

# 10.10  Information on Franchising

| **Title and Author** | **Publisher** |
| --- | --- |
| *Franchise Bible*<br>Erwin J. Keup | **The Oasis Press**<br>300 North Valley Drive<br>Grants Pass, OR 97526 |
| Miscellaneous titles on franchise topics.<br>Write for a catalog. | **International Franchise Association**<br>1350 New York Avenue, NW, Suite 900<br>Washington, DC 20005 |

| Title and Author | Publisher |
|---|---|
| *Business Franchise Guide* | **Commerce Clearing House, Inc.**<br>4025 West Peterson Avenue<br>Chicago, IL 60646 |
| *The Complete Handbook of Franchising*<br>David D. Seltz | **Addison-Wesley**<br>General Books Division<br>Reading, MA 01867 |
| Miscellaneous titles on franchise topics.<br>Write for a catalog. | **Pilot Books**<br>103 Cooper Street<br>Babylon, NY 11702 |
| *Franchise Opportunities Handbook* | **U.S. Department of Commerce**<br>U.S. Government Printing Office<br>Washington, DC 20402 |
| *Franchising in the U.S.*<br>Michael M. Coltman | **Self-Counsel Press Inc.**<br>1704 North State Street<br>Bellingham, WA 98225<br>(800) 663-3007 |
| *Franchisee Rights — A Self-Defense Manual*<br>  *for The Franchisee*<br>Alex Hammond | **Hammond & Morton**<br>1185 Avenue of the Americas<br>New York, NY 10036 |
| *Franchising: Regulation of Buying and Selling*<br>  *A Franchise*<br>Philip F. Zeidman, Perry C. Ausbrook &<br>H. Bret Lowell | **Bureau of National Affairs, Inc.**<br>9435 Key West Avenue<br>Rockville, MD 20850<br>(800) 372-1033 |
| *The Info Franchise Newsletter*<br>*The Franchise Annual* | **Info Press**<br>728 Center Street<br>Lewiston, NY 14092-0550<br>(716) 754-4669 |
| *Survey of Foreign Laws and Regulations*<br>  *Affecting International Franchising*<br>Compiled by the Franchising Committee of the<br>Section of Antitrust Law of the American Bar<br>Association | **Publications Planning and Marketing**<br>**American Bar Association**<br>705 North Lake Shore Drive<br>Chicago, IL 60611 |

# 10.11  Estate Planning

To help you develop a retirement plan, you may want to obtain a copy of *Retirement & Estate Planning Handbook* by Chuck Tellalian and Walter Rosen. This do-it-yourself workbook comes complete with step-by-step instructions, worksheets, samples, and forms. For more information, contact your local book source or:

**The Oasis Fress**
(800) 228-2275

## 10.12  OSHA Publications

If your business will be subject to OSHA laws (see Section 5.6), you should obtain the following free booklet on OSHA requirements from your local office of the U.S. Department of Labor, Occupational Safety and Health Administration:

- *Recordkeeping Requirements for Occupational Injuries and Illnesses*

## 10.13  Mail Order Sales Regulations

If you intend to sell goods by mail order, you need to be familiar with Federal Trade Commission Rule 435.1 (see Section 9.7). For a complete treatment of federal and state laws (all 50 states) affecting mail order businesses, you can obtain the *Mail Order Legal Manual*, by Erwin J. Keup, from:

**The Oasis Press**
(800) 228-2275

## 10.14  "Expert" Software for Small Businesses

As a business owner or prospective owner, you may be interested in a computer software program designed to aid and advise small- to medium-sized businesses with respect to tax, legal, and other business questions. *The Small Business Expert*, developed by Michael D. Jenkins, the principal author of this book, is a "smart" or "expert" program that provides such a capability.

This easy-to-use software is a bit like having a high-powered business, tax, and legal consultant on retainer, available day or night. The program allows you to simply type in a question or a key word or two about various business-related subjects and immediately responds by giving you textual information on that subject. Or you may quickly scan through a lengthy subject index and simply hit one key to view information on any item in the index. The software covers a wide range of subjects applicable to small businesses, with a primary emphasis on tax and legal information relevant to the state you do business in.

The program will first prompt you for numerous details about your business or proposed business. It will then create — and you may print out — detailed checklists of state and federal government regulations and other items your particular business must deal with. The program will also give you specific tax planning suggestions, all tailored specifically to your business. The program does quick calculations of both personal and corporate income taxes — allowing you to do instant "what if" projections — and will also compute federal estate taxes to assist you in income and estate tax planning.

*The Small Business Expert* also provides a number of consulting session topics, where you engage in a question-and-answer sequence with the program, regarding such subjects as whether or not you should incorporate your business, what accounting method can or should your new business adopt, and other topics. After you answer a series of questions, the program will offer you recommendations or advice regarding your specific situation, as well as its reasons for such advice.

Among other useful features, built-in worksheets are also provided for you to simply fill in the blanks on screen and print out a business plan outline, marketing feasibility study, or personnel policies summary for your business. *The Small Business Expert* is available from The Oasis Press which also publishes other economical software to streamline business activities. See the Related Resources section at the back of this book for more information. These and other related resources can be purchased through your book or software source or by calling:

**The Oasis Press**
(800) 228-2275

# State Laws & Related Resources

**Part IV**

# Notes to Tennessee State Section

PSI Research/The Oasis Press is committed to providing the most accurate, up-to-date information possible. Readers of this publication, however, should be aware that constant changes occur in the legislative, organizational, and public affairs activities of government agencies used as reference for this book.

Whenever possible, PSI Research has listed state agencies throughout this state chapter for readers to contact for more information. However, phone numbers and mailing addresses of state offices also change, sometimes, more than the laws and regulations themselves. It is for this reason that we remind readers in this state to contact the following office whenever changes occur that are not covered in this particular revision. This office will be able to answer general inquiries or direct you to the proper state agency.

**Small Business Office**
**Tennessee Department of Economic and Community Development**
Rachel Jackson Building
320 6th Avenue, 7th Floor
Nashville, TN 37219
(615) 741-2626
(800) 872-7201 (in Tennessee)

## About the Author

The co-author of *Starting and Operating a Business in Tennessee*, 1991 state revision, is E. Bishop Leatherbury.

Mr. Leatherbury is a certified public accountant and director of Ernst & Young's Entrepreneurial Services Group in Nashville, Tennessee. He previously served as Director of Advanced Audit Education for the firm and instructs various national audit and entrepreneurial services seminars.

Mr. Leatherbury holds a Bachelor of Science in accounting from Virginia Polytechnic Institute & State University. He is a member of the American Institute of Certified Public Accountants and is Chairman of the Board of Directors of Growth Enterprise Nashville, Inc. — the Nashville Business Incubation Center.

Chapter 11

# State Laws and Taxes

## 11.1 Introduction

Tennessee is characterized by a very favorable business climate for both existing business and new industry, ranking in the top third in a study commissioned by the Conference of State Manufacturing Associations. The state has long enjoyed a stable, well-balanced economy and been recognized as a leading manufacturing center in the Southeast. In recent years, Tennessee has emerged as a growing center for corporate headquarters operations, marketing-oriented regional offices, and specialized research and development.

Evidence of its healthy business environment includes General Motors' decision to locate its new Saturn plant in Spring Hill, Tennessee and the state's success in attracting foreign capital investment, including major Nissan and Bridgestone manufacturing operations. Saturn is the largest one-time industrial investment in U.S. history and the Nissan operation in Smyrna is the single largest Japanese investment in the United States.

A low tax burden and an equitable tax structure, an abundant workforce with a strong work ethic, and the state's central location to major U.S. markets all contribute to Tennessee's advantageous business climate and strong economy.

The state is fiscally conservative with a balanced budget and a low tax burden. Major features of the state's tax structure include:

**Tax Structure**

- State personal income tax on wages and salaries — none. Tennessee does, however, impose a 6% tax on dividends and interest income;

- State property tax — none;
- Corporate excise (income) tax — 6% on net earnings within or apportioned to Tennessee;
- Corporate franchise tax — $0.25 (25 cents) per $100.00 of the corporation's tax base (see Section 11.2 for a discussion of the tax base);
- State sales tax — 5.5% and local sales tax rates varying from 0.75% to 2.75%;
- No sales tax on industrial machinery, farm equipment, and pollution control equipment; and
- Investment tax credit on purchases of certain qualifying machinery of 1%.

Personal taxes in Tennessee are among the lowest in the nation. Tennessee's personal tax burden is the second lowest in the Southeast and fourth lowest in the country based on data compiled by the U.S. Department of Commerce.

## Labor Availability

In addition to having an abundant supply of labor with a strong work ethic, Tennessee is one of several states with a right-to-work law. Under the right-to-work legislation, union membership is optional.

## Central Location

Tennessee's strategic location within 500 miles — one-day delivery — of 76% of the major U.S. markets is a major plus for many businesses. In addition, seven major interstates converge in Tennessee, making the state a significant transportation center.

In 1985, American Airlines selected Nashville as the hub for its service to the Southeast and Central United States. This has substantially increased the volume of air traffic and need for related services in Nashville and has made middle Tennessee more attractive as a headquarters and distribution center.

## Employment Expansion

Employment in Tennessee has grown 27.4% since 1982 to a workforce of approximately 2.37 million in 1989. This employment expansion has led to a decline in Tennessee's unemployment rate from a high of 13.0% in 1982 to 5.1% in 1989. The expansion has been consistently led by the durable goods manufacturing, construction, and service sectors of the economy.

Tennessee's favorable business climate, the state government's commitment to economic development, and its commercial and natural resources combine to offer new businesses exciting opportunities and a fertile environment in which to grow, succeed, and contribute.

## 11.2 Choosing the Legal Form of the Business

In Tennessee, no state approval is needed to start into business as a sole proprietorship. While there are a number of other regulatory requirements which are addressed in Section 11.4, none of these requirements are prerequisites to starting a business in the form of a sole proprietorship.

Except for the Tennessee Stock and Bonds Income Tax — discussed later in Section 11.7 — Tennessee does not impose a personal income tax, and only corporations are subject to the franchise and excise tax. Thus, earnings and capital of a business operated as a sole proprietorship are generally not subject to state taxation. The savings from not being subject to the franchise and excise tax can be substantial. The franchise tax rate is $0.25 (25 cents) for each $100 of a corporation's tax base — the greater of stockholder's equity or depreciated value of real and personal property owned or used in the state — and the excise tax is 6% of Tennessee taxable income.

Since a sole proprietor is not an employee of his or her business, he or she is not subject to state unemployment tax, which is:

- 2.7% of the first $7,000 in wages per employee for a new employer; or
- A maximum of $189 per employee.

After an initial period, an employee's tax rate may be more or less than 2.7% based on an experience rating. A sole proprietor is also not subject to workers' compensation premiums on his or her earnings. For more information, contact the Tennessee Department of Employment Security, Employer's Service Section.

Thus, by operating as a sole proprietorship, rather than as an employee of your own corporation, you will save up to $189 annually in state unemployment tax, in addition to the savings in workers' compensation premiums. Of course, if you hire employees, you will be subject to unemployment tax on their wages. You must also have workers' compensation coverage whether your business is a sole proprietorship, a partnership, or a corporation. For more information on workers' compensation insurance, please refer to Section 11.5.

As a sole proprietor, however, you are exempt from state unemployment taxes on wages paid to your spouse or to your children, if the children are under age 18, and for federal unemployment tax, if the children are under age 21.

As with sole proprietorships, partnerships are not generally subject to state taxation on their capital or income, except for the Tennessee Individual Income Tax. Dividends and interest received by a Tennessee partnership are subject to the Tennessee Stock and Bonds Income Tax.[1]

Like a sole proprietor, a partner usually is not considered an employee of the business and is thus not subject to state unemployment tax or the workers' compensation laws.

There are few special requirements for partnerships in Tennessee, other than those concerning limited partnerships.

## Limited Partnerships

State law governing limited partnerships has recently been revised. The revisions were made to modernize the existing law, to organize the statutes, to clarify ambiguities, and to make operating as a limited partnership more flexible.

A limited partnership may conduct any business except banking or insurance. To form a limited partnership, a *Certificate of Limited Partnership* must be filed with the secretary of state, along with a $50 registration fee, and registered with the register of deeds in the county in which the limited partnership is to have its principal office. At a minimum, the certificate must contain:[2]

- The name of the limited partnership, which must contain the words "Limited Partnership" or the abbreviation "L. P.";
- The address of the limited partnership's initial registered office and the name of its initial registered agent;
- The address of the principal office of the limited partnership; and
- The name and the business, residence, or mailing address of each general partner.

The *Certificate of Limited Partnership* must, at a minimum, be executed by all of the general partners.

Amendments to the *Certificate of Limited Partnership*, including the admission or withdrawal of a general partner, can be made by filing a certificate of amendment with the secretary of state.[3]

## Corporations

To establish a new corporation in Tennessee, the prospective shareholder must apply to the secretary of state by filing a corporate charter and appointing a registered agent. The fee for incorporating is $50.[4]

All filings related to incorporation should be made with the secretary of state and sent to:

**Corporate Division**
**Secretary of State**
James K. Polk Building, Suite 1800
Nashville, TN 37243-0306
(615) 741-2286

The corporate charter for a for-profit corporation must include:[5]

- The name of the corporation, which must include the word "Company," "Corporation," "Incorporated," "Limited," or an abbreviation of one of these titles;

- The number of shares the corporation is authorized to issue;
- The street address, including zip code, of the initial registered office and registered agent;
- The address of the principal office of the corporation;
- The name, address, and zip code of each incorporator; and
- A statement that the corporation is for-profit.

To ensure that a desired corporate name does not resemble an existing corporate or trade name, it can be cleared through the secretary of state's office by letter. A specified corporate name can be reserved for a period of four months by filing an application for reservation of the name and paying a $10 fee.[6]

You must designate a registered agent at the time your corporate charter is filed. The registered agent must either be a Tennessee resident or a corporation authorized to do business in the state. The corporation must maintain a registered agent at all times. You must notify the secretary of state of any changes in your registered agent.

A foreign corporation — one incorporated under the laws of another state — must apply for a certificate of authority with the secretary of state before it can transact intrastate business. A certificate of existence dated no more than one month before the date of application[7] from the state of incorporation must accompany the application, and the corporation must maintain a registered agent within Tennessee upon whom process may be served. The filing fee for a for-profit corporation is $300.

Both domestic and foreign corporations must file an annual report of officers and agents with the secretary of state.[8] The annual report is due the first day of the fourth month following the anniversary date of incorporation or qualification to do business in the state. There is a $10 filing fee for the annual statement.

**Corporate Taxation**

All corporations doing business in Tennessee, including S corporations, are subject to the Tennessee franchise and excise taxes.[9] For Tennessee purposes, S corporations are taxed in the same manner as other corporations. The franchise tax is a tax on the privilege of doing business in the state and is based on capital. The excise tax is an income tax based on federal taxable income adjusted for Tennessee tax purposes.

The franchise tax is generally based on the greater of stockholders' equity or the depreciated cost of real and tangible personal property owned or used in the state. The franchise tax rate is $0.25 (25 cents) per $100 of the corporation's tax base.[10] The minimum franchise tax is $10.

The excise tax is based on federal taxable income with certain adjustments made for Tennessee tax purposes. Section 11.8 addresses the more common differences between federal and Tennessee taxable incomes. The excise tax is 6% of Tennessee taxable income.[11] For more information, contact:

**Franchise, Excise, and Income Tax Division**
**Tennessee Department of Revenue**
Andrew Jackson Building, 8th Floor
Nashville, TN 37242
(615) 741-3133
(800) 342-1003 (in Tennessee)

## State Securities Laws

Due to the complexities of the state's securities laws, it is advisable to use legal counsel in issuing securities — common stock, preferred stock, debentures, etc. — to finance a company.

There are a number of exemptions from the state's securities laws. Generally, securities can be sold to 15 or fewer persons[12] within the state in a given year without being subject to the securities laws. In order to be exempt, the securities cannot be offered for sale by means of publicly disseminated advertisements or sales literature, and the purchase must be made with the intent to hold the securities for investment.

Any securities offering in which the aggregate amount sold in Tennessee does not exceed $250,000 in any 12-month[13] period is exempt regardless of the number of investors.

No state filing or other registration is needed for the sale or issuance of securities, which is exempt from the state's securities laws.

# 11.3  Buying an Existing Business — State Legal Requirements

If you purchase the assets of a business in Tennessee, it is important for you to see to it that someone, preferably your attorney, has taken care of several legal matters. Some of the more important legal matters are discussed below.

## Bulk Sales Law

The Tennessee Uniform Commercial Code – Bulk Transfers Law may apply when the assets of a business are sold. The law is designed to protect creditors and failure to comply with its provisions may make the purchaser of a business' assets liable for obligations incurred by the seller.

The law applies to any transfer or sale of materials, supplies, merchandise, or other inventory in bulk not in the ordinary course of the seller's business by an enterprise whose principal business is the sale of merchandise from stock, including those who manufacture what they sell. If inventory is part of the bulk sale, the law also applies to the sale of machinery, equipment, furniture, and fixtures. It does not apply to purchases of machinery, equipment, furniture, and fixtures if no inventory is included in the purchase.

Transfers and sales not subject to this law include:

- Those occurring under bankruptcy or other judicial or administrative proceedings; and
- Any sale or transfer obligating the buyer to satisfy the debt of the seller. Thus, the law does not apply when a company is acquired by purchasing stock rather than assets.

In a bulk transfer, the seller must provide the buyer with a listing of all existing creditors with their addresses and the amount each is owed (including amounts in dispute) and a schedule of all property being transferred or sold in sufficient detail to identify it. The listing must be signed by the seller or his or her agent and must be maintained by the buyer for six months from the date of the transfer.[14]

Ten days before the buyer takes possession of the assets or pays for them, the buyer must notify the listed creditors of the upcoming transfer either personally or by registered mail.[15] The notice must contain:[16]

- A statement that a bulk transfer is about to be made;
- A list of the names and business addresses of the buyer and seller and all business names and addresses used by the seller in the last three years; and
- A statement regarding whether or not all debts of the seller are to be paid in full as they fall due and the address to which creditors should send bills.

If the debts of the seller are not to be paid in full as they fall due or the buyer is in doubt whether the debts will be paid in full, the notice should further state:

- The location and general description of the property to be transferred and estimated total debt of the seller; and
- The address where the schedule of property and list of creditors may be inspected.

It also must answer:

- Whether the transfer is being made to pay existing debts. If so, it should also state the amount of the debt being paid and each creditor being satisfied.
- If the transfer is being made for reasons other than to satisfy existing debts, the amount of consideration, place of payment, and the time and place where creditors of the seller should file their claims.

The buyer in a bulk transfer is responsible for seeing that listed creditors are repaid from sale proceeds and, if amounts of any debt are in dispute, to withhold enough to provide for satisfaction of the debt when the dispute is resolved.

Tennessee law places responsibility for compliance with the Bulk Transfers Law on the auctioneer if the assets of a business are sold through an auction.[17] Thus, you will not need to comply with the provisions of this law if the business' assets are purchased at auction.

Needless to say, if you are considering purchasing a business through acquiring either its assets or stock, it is advisable to seek professional legal and accounting advice before entering into the transaction.

## Recorded Security Interests

If security interests (liens) are recorded against the business' assets, provisions must be made to assure these claims are satisfied when the purchase transaction closes — if you are not assuming these liabilities. When buying the stock or assets of a business, an attorney should search the country and state records to determine the existence of recorded security interests or liens.

To perfect a security interest, a creditor must file notice of such interest with the county recorder or secretary of state or both. Such filing gives public notice of the creditor's claim against the debtor's assets.

To search the personal property records for liens, one submits *Form UCC-1* with a $5 fee to the county register or secretary of state or both. It is a good idea to check both. They respond in writing, listing any recorded security interests and providing copies of such recordings, if requested. For more information, contact:

**UCC Division**
**Department of State**
(615) 741-3276

If the purchase includes real property, the county's real estate records should be searched for the existence of recorded security and other interests.

Searching these records identifies liens the seller may or may not have disclosed and discovers liens and judgments resulting from nonpayment of property, payroll, or other taxes. The search may also identify past legal actions taken against the business. This is of particular concern if the business is purchased by acquiring stock of the corporation because all liabilities, disclosed or not, will follow the business.

## Obtain Release of Other Liabilities

The buyer of a business who checks for recorded liens and complies with the requirements of the Uniform Commercial Code – Bulk Transfers Law will protect himself or herself from most of a previous owner's liabilities. However, in the case of liabilities for unemployment, sales, and franchise taxes, further steps may be needed.

## Unemployment Tax Release

Unpaid unemployment taxes will not follow a business unless the buyer is related by blood to the seller or there is some other common interest between the buyer and seller. Examples of "common interest" include a sole proprietor selling to a partnership in which he or she is a partner or a sole proprietor selling to a corporation in which a relative is a 10% or greater stockholder.[18]

Each new business in Tennessee is assigned a standard unemployment tax rate of 2.7% (or higher, based on the experience rating of its industrial classification). Businesses that have been subject to the unemployment tax for three calendar years may be entitled to a reduction in rate, based on their experience rating. See Section 11.5. If a business has a low rate, it will be to the buyer's advantage to have the rate transferred to him or her. The Tennessee Department of Employment Security will not transfer the rate unless all prior payroll tax liabilities have been satisfied. A certificate indicating the date through which unemployment tax has been paid can be obtained by writing to the Tennessee Department of Employment Security. This certificate must be requested by the seller of the business.

**Tennessee Department of Employment Security**
Volunteer Plaza, 8th Floor
500 James Robertson Parkway
Nashville, TN 37245-3500
(615) 741-2486

## Sales Tax Release

If a seller of a business is liable for any sales tax and related interest or penalty, he or she must file a final return and make payment within 15 days of selling or quitting the business. The buyer of the business can be held liable for any sales or use taxes not paid by the former owner.[19] The buyer has the right to withhold an amount of the purchase price sufficient to cover any possible tax liability until the seller secures from the Tennessee Department of Revenue an account status statement. This statement can be given only to the seller, except in cases where the seller personally designates, in writing, that the purchaser is the authorized recipient of information from the department pertaining to the seller's account. Requests should be sent to the Sales Tax Division.

**Sales Tax Division**
**Tennessee Department of Revenue**
Andrew Jackson State Office Building
500 Deaderick Street, Room 502
Nashville, TN 37242
(615) 741-3581

## Franchise Tax Certificate

To determine whether a corporation has paid its state franchise and excise taxes, a certificate of existence can be obtained from the secretary of state's office. Unlike other tax releases that must be obtained by the seller of the business, a certificate of existence can be obtained by the purchaser by paying a $10 fee and requesting the certificate from:

**Certifications Division**
**Tennessee Secretary of State**
James K. Polk Building, 18th Floor
Nashville, TN 37219
(615) 741-6488

# 11.4  State Requirements that Apply to Nearly All New Businesses

**State Licenses**

The state of Tennessee requires special licenses for many businesses, occupations, and professions. Requirements for such licenses include certain education and experience or passing state or uniform examinations or both. Since it is illegal to engage in certain types of regulated businesses without being licensed, you should find out whether there is a licensing requirement for the type of business you plan to start and, if so, determine whether and how you will be able to comply with the licensing requirements.

Section 11.6 of this chapter contains a listing of many of the businesses, occupations, and professions that must be licensed under Tennessee law.

**Business and Occupation Tax**

Counties and municipalities are authorized to impose business and occupation taxes by adopting the provisions of the Business Tax Act.[20] Local governments may adopt the tax rates set forth by statute or may impose the tax at a lower rate.[21] A business may be taxed by both the city and county in which it is located.

Exemptions from this tax include:

- Manufacturers who are subject to personal property tax; and
- Services of certain professions, such as:
  - Medical, dental, allied health, and veterinary services
  - Legal, accounting, and bookkeeping services
  - Architects, engineers, and land surveyors
  - Insurance agents

In addition, there are a variety of other exemptions for small or informal businesses. Examples include newspaper peddlers and farmers selling produce directly from the farm, as well as persons not holding themselves out as being in business and making only occasional and isolated sales. Furthermore, businesses that pay tangible personal property tax are allowed to take a credit against the business tax for such property tax paid.

Delinquent payments are assessed with a 5% penalty every month, up to a maximum of 25%, plus the applicable annual interest rate, with a minimum penalty of $15. A 50% fraud penalty may also be levied. For more information on this tax, contact:

**Miscellaneous Tax Division**
**Tennessee Department of Revenue**
808 Andrew Jackson State Office Building
500 Deaderick Street
Nashville, TN 37242
(615) 741-2011
(800) 342-1003 (in Tennessee)

Corporations expecting an excise tax liability of $2,000 or more are required to make estimated tax payments.[22] The estimate is made on *Form 04-020-0139* and payments are sent to:

**Estimated Excise Taxes**

**Franchise, Excise, and Income Tax Division**
**Tennessee Department of Revenue**
Andrew Jackson State Office Building, 8th Floor
500 Deaderick Street
Nashville, TN 37242
(615) 741-3133
(800) 342-1003 (in Tennessee)

There are four estimated tax payments, each one-fourth of the estimate for the year. *Form 04-020-0139* and the first quarterly payment are due on or before the 15th day of the fourth month of the taxable year.[23] The second and third payments are due on or before the 15th day of the seventh and tenth months respectively. The fourth payment is due on the 15th day of the first month of the subsequent tax year.

There is no requirement to make estimated payments of the franchise tax.

The sales and use tax applies to personal property that is consumed in the state, whether manufactured in Tennessee or brought into the state. Usually, the seller is responsible for collecting the tax and remitting it to the state. Businesses must obtain a *Sales and Use Tax Certificate of Registration, Form 13-001-0321*, for each place of business within the state. A sample of *Form 13-001-0321* is provided at the end of this book. Taxable sales include:[24]

**Sales and Use Tax Permits**

- Selling, leasing, or renting tangible personal property in Tennessee, unless specifically exempt from sales tax;
- Furnishing lodging to transient guests by establishments with five or more sleeping rooms;
- Producing or fabricating tangible personal property for consumers who furnish the raw materials;
- Printing and copying;
- Repairing tangible personal property (except for exempt property);
- Installing tangible personal property;
- Washing, waxing, polishing, and painting motor vehicles (except coin-operated auto washes); and
- Providing industrial laundry and linen services.

Generally, sales of industrial machinery and equipment and pollution control equipment are tax-exempt. For your convenience, the Appendix contains a list of sales that are specifically exempt from sales and use tax.

The sales tax rate varies by location in the state. The state levies a 5.5% tax,[25] and counties and cities can levy a local option tax of up to 2.75%. Counties have priority over cities and can levy the entire 2.75%; cities can assess the difference, if any.[26] There is a ceiling on the amount of local tax that can be collected on a single item. The ceiling ranges from $5.00 to $30.25, depending on the locality.

In most cases, the seller/vendor is responsible for collecting sales tax and remitting it to the state. Sales tax is calculated on gross sales, less the following adjustments:

- Cash discounts given at the time of sale;
- Value of a used vehicle traded to a licensed dealer;
- Write-off of bad debts related to sales in which tax has been paid; and
- Returned merchandise.

Out-of-state retailers who mail free catalogs to prospective customers living in Tennessee may be subject to Tennessee use tax on the value of catalogs shipped into Tennessee. Check with your legal adviser or accountant for additional information. Certificates of registration, *Form 13-001-0321*, and a useful publication called *Tennessee Sales and Use Tax Laws* are available from the Sales and Use Tax Division. To request this publication and certificate, contact the division or use the preaddressed post card which is provided for your use at the back of this book.

**Taxpayer Services Division**
**Tennessee Department of Revenue**
Andrew Jackson State Office Building
500 Deaderick Street
Nashville, TN 37242-1399
(615) 741-2481
(800) 342-1003 (in Tennessee)

A certificate of resale must be obtained and retained by the dealer for all goods sold for resale. If a vendor sells to an individual or entity claiming to be exempt from sales tax, the vendor must obtain from the purchaser a certificate of exemption stating the reason for exemption.[27]

Sales tax returns must be filed monthly unless a vendor has an average monthly tax liability of less than $200. Such vendors may file their sales tax returns quarterly.[28] Returns and remittance of taxes are due on the 20th of the month following the month or quarter when the tax is due.

As compensation for collecting sales tax, the vendor is entitled to a credit of 2% of the first $2,500 in taxes collected and 1.15% of the amount over $2,500 each month. This discount is available only if the return is filed on time and all tax due is paid with the return.[29]

Conversely, a penalty of 5% per month — with a maximum of 25% — is levied if the tax return is filed late. A minimum penalty of $5 is charged on all late returns and interest is due on all delinquencies. Extensions may be approved in an emergency, but the extension request must be filed by the due date of the return.

The use tax complements the sales tax and is collected on certain transactions which are not subject to the sales tax. If a Tennessee consumer purchases tangible personal property outside the state for consumption within Tennessee and sales or use tax is not collected by the seller, the consumer is required to pay use tax in Tennessee.

Property taxes applying to real property and tangible and intangible personal property are levied by county and municipal governments. Although the state has the power to levy property taxes, there has been no state property tax since 1949.

**Property Taxes**

Three factors determine the amount of property tax due:

- The value of the property:
- The assessed percentage of fair value; and
- The locally established tax rate.

The value-to-assessment ratio varies by class of property. The ratios for property classes are uniform throughout the state.

Taxpayers who wish to dispute the valuation of their property should file a complaint with their county Board of Equalization. The county board's decision can be appealed to the Assessment Appeals Commission. The final level of appeal for property tax matters is the State Board of Equalization. If taxpayers believe a tax is being collected unjustly or illegally, they must pay the tax under protest and bring an action to recover the tax. An alternative is to bring an action without paying the tax. To do this, the taxpayer must post a bond for 150% of the amount in dispute or pledge collateral in an amount satisfactory to the commissioner.

Industrial and commercial real property is assessed at 40% of fair value.[30] Tax values are determined by county assessor appraisal at least every five years and by monitoring building permits for construction that adds value to the property. Voters of each political subdivision determine the tax rates, which vary by locale.

**Real Property**

Personal property taxes are levied on all tangible property and intangible property, which is not specifically exempted from taxation. Personal belongings, household goods, and farm personal property are the more common exemptions.

**Personal Property**

Tangible industrial and commercial property is assessed at 30% of its value.[31] Inventories of merchandise owned by persons subject to the Business and Occupation Tax — discussed earlier in this section — and unused property are not subject to the property tax. The rates applied to tangible personal property are determined by the voters of the political subdivision and vary by locale.

Intangible personal property includes all personal property not defined as tangible and includes property such as money, stock, receivables, and copyrights. Although state law treats such property as taxable, it has not provided a vehicle for collecting the tax except for the stock of loan, investment, insurance, and cemetery companies. The Tennessee Stock and Bonds Income Tax — see Section 11.7 — in effect takes the place of the property tax on most intangible property, and there is an exemption from this tax for persons paying property taxes on securities.

## Assessment and Payment

No initial or periodic filing is required for real property taxes. The county assessor's office assesses[32] and levies real property taxes, while the county trustee's office is responsible for collecting such taxes.[33]

The personal property tax system is basically a self-assessing system. Every year on January 1, taxpayers file a schedule listing all personal property they own or lease from others, with the estimated market value for each item. The leased property is not taxed; the purpose of reporting it is to locate leased property and ensure that the owner is taxed on it. The county assessor has the responsibility to determine that the property is properly valued and may assess it at a different value than reported by the taxpayer. If the assessor changes the assessment, the taxpayer must be notified.

County taxes on real or personal property are due and payable the first Monday in October. Cities and counties may allow a discount of 1% or 2% for early payment of property taxes. County taxes become delinquent on March 1 of the following year. Delinquent taxes are subject to a penalty of $1/2$% per month and interest of 1% per month[34] beginning the March 1 following the due date. Any unpaid taxes become a lien against the property and may be collected by seizure and sale of the property.[35] Property taxes for municipalities are due at various dates and are payable to the city treasurer.

The local county assessor's office and city treasurer's office can provide the local tax rate and other specific information on local property taxes.

## Fictitious or Assumed Business Name

Assumed names may be registered with the secretary of state, although there is no requirement to do so.[36] Registration of an assumed name prevents registration of the same or similar name by others. To stop another from using your assumed name, you must file suit in a court of law. Registration of an assumed name only gives you a presumption of ownership.

The assumed name must describe the nature of the business and cannot duplicate another registered assumed name or corporate name. The fee for registering an assumed name is $10 and provides registration for five years. Assumed names can be renewed for another five years by filing an application for renewal six months before expiration and paying a $10 fee.[37]

To determine whether an assumed name is available, write or call the secretary of state's office. A specified assumed name can be reserved for a period of four months by filing an application for reservation and paying a $10 fee.

As mentioned earlier in Section 11.2, no special approval is needed to operate as a sole proprietorship. There is no state income tax other than the Tennessee Individual Income Tax at the individual level, and sole proprietorships are not subject to the franchise and excise taxes, which are discussed in sections 11.2 and 11.8.

**Sole Proprietorship Requirements**

Tennessee does not tax partnerships or require partnerships to file any informational return. As with a sole proprietorship, income attributed to a noncorporate partner generally escapes taxation at the state level.

**Partnership Requirements**

If the partnership is a limited partnership, it must file a *Certificate of Limited Partnership* — see Section 11.2 — with the county register of deeds before commencing operation.

Besides those listed in Section 4.12, corporations are subject to several state requirements not applicable to other forms of business organization. These include:

**Corporation Requirements**

- Filing an annual report with the secretary of state with a $10 filing fee. The annual report is due the first day of the fourth month following the anniversary date of incorporation or qualification to do business in the state. Effective July 1, 1990, the due date has been changed to the first day of the fourth month following the close of the company's fiscal year.
- Filing *Form 04-003-0101*, annual franchise and excise tax return.
- Applying for a certificate of authority with the secretary of state — and paying a $300 filing fee — to qualify to do business in Tennessee. This is required only if the corporation was organized under the laws of a state other than Tennessee, such as a Delaware corporation.

In addition to the items listed in Section 4.13, a number of state law requirements apply to most businesses. To comply with these requirements, you should be aware of the state requirements outlined below.

**Checklist of State Requirements**

☐ Determine whether or not a state license is needed to operate your business. If you are in doubt, check with the Tennessee Department of Commerce, Division of Regulatory Boards. See Section 11.6.

☐ Be prepared to make estimated excise tax payments almost immediately after incorporating if you're expecting a tax liability in excess of $2,000 for the year.

☐ Apply for a certificate of registration from the Tennessee Department of Revenue if sales are subject to sales tax. Sales tax returns must be filed monthly or quarterly, depending upon the amount of taxes collected. See Section 11.4.

☐ For a limited partnership, file a *Certificate of Limited Partnership* with the secretary of state and register with the county register of deeds — see Section 11.2.

☐ For a corporation, file its charter with the secretary of state and appoint a registered agent. Foreign corporations must register with the secretary of state to qualify to do business in Tennessee — see Section 11.2.

☐ For both foreign and domestic corporations, file an annual report with the secretary of state.

☐ For a corporation, file an annual franchise and excise tax return — see sections 11.2 and 11.8.

☐ Protect yourself from unintentionally assuming responsibility for prior owners' debts when purchasing a new business, by taking these steps:

- Complying with the requirements of the Tennessee Uniform Commercial Code – Bulk Transfer Law — see Section 11.3;

- Searching for recorded security interests — see Section 11.3; and

- Obtaining the appropriate sales, franchise, and unemployment tax releases — see Section 11.3.

Remember: The preceding state law requirements apply to any business, whether or not it has employees. If you have employees, additional state requirements are covered in the next section. See Section 4.13 for a checklist of federal and other related requirements.

# 11.5  Additional Requirements for Businesses with Employees

**State Unemployment Tax**

In general, businesses with employees are subject to state unemployment tax. The tax is not imposed until total payroll reaches $1,500 or more in any quarter of the year, or when at least one individual is employed for some portion of a day in 20 different weeks in either the current or preceding year.[38] A different criterion exists in situations where the liability is imposed for certain employers, such as agricultural, domestic, government, and nonprofit corporations. A limited number of exemptions from unemployment tax also exist.

The *Report to Determine Status, Application for Employer Number, Form DES 210.1*, is the application you must complete and file in order to determine your unemployment insurance liability and obtain your employer account number.

Generally, wages subject to Federal Unemployment Tax (FUTA) are automatically subject to the state unemployment tax. The Unemployment Tax Program is administered by the Unemployment Insurance Division.

The Tennessee Unemployment Insurance Program is financed solely by employer premiums and federal unemployment taxes. All taxes paid to the state go into a trust fund, which is used solely to pay benefits. Employers in Tennessee pay on wages up to $7,000.[39] Tax rates vary from .15% to 10% depending on the employer's experience rating. Generally, new employers are taxed at a standard rate of 2.7% until an experience rating is established. The employer receives a 5.4% credit against the 6.2% FUTA if all state contributions are paid in full by January 31 following the close of the calendar year.[40] A partial credit is allowed if the state contribution is paid after January 31. Note that the 5.4% credit applies even if the employer's experience rating yields a state rate of less than 5.4%.

An employer's rate is determined by the level of the trust fund and the individual employer's experience rating. Experience ratings are determined by the employer's contribution, benefit payout experience, and taxable payroll. The Tennessee Department of Employment Security maintains a record of contributions paid by and benefits chargeable to each employer.

If you meet the successor-in-interest requirements when acquiring an existing business, you will assume the experience rating of the previous employer. As of January 1, 1985, parties with a direct beneficial interest or relatives by blood or marriage of the predecessor are considered "successors" who automatically retain the experience rating.[41] An acquiring company may also be considered a successor if it acquires substantially all of the assets of a business and requests a transfer of the predecessor's experience rating factors.

Unemployment tax returns — *Form DES 220.5* — are filed quarterly and are due with payment by the end of the month following the close of the calendar quarter. New employers must file *Form DES 210.1* to determine the amount of their liability.

The Tennessee Department of Employment Security has a publication called the *Handbook for Employers*, which is a valuable resource for any Tennessee employer. To request this publication, contact the office listed below or use the preaddressed post card provided at the back of this book.

**Unemployment Insurance Division**
**Tennessee Department of Employment Security**
Volunteer Plaza, 8th Floor
500 James Robertson Parkway
Nashville, TN 37245-1701
(615) 741-1948
(800) 344-8337 (in Tennessee)

## Workers' Compensation Insurance

All employers with five or more employees are required to carry workers' compensation coverage for their employees. Employees include employee–stockholders and corporate officers; however, a corporate officer may elect to be exempt from the workers' compensation law.

Unless they elect to come under provisions of the law, sole proprietors and partners are not considered employers for workers' compensation purposes.

Employers subject to workers' compensation laws should maintain coverage with a private insurer or self-insure, if they meet minimum requirements of financial ability to pay claims arising under the law.[42] The Tennessee Department of Commerce and Insurance determines whether or not a business qualifies for self-insurance. They generally require workers' compensation premiums to be $200,000 or greater before self-insurance is allowed.

Once you have obtained coverage, the insurance carrier must file evidence of your compliance by submitting *Certificate of Insurer, Form LB 0043*,[43] with the Tennessee Department of Labor. This department will then issue a certificate of coverage to you which must be displayed in a conspicuous place.[44] Photocopies may be used for multiple locations.

To self-insure, a business must apply for a certificate of compliance with the Tennessee Department of Commerce and Insurance. If it qualifies and satisfies certain other requirements, the Tennessee Department of Labor will issue a certificate of compliance.

Workers' compensation premium rates are determined by industry and job classification. While the Tennessee Department of Commerce and Insurance determines initial premium rates, employers of sufficient size may qualify for experience ratings.

Employers are required to have workers' compensation claim application forms available for employees. The forms must be filled out by the employer. Forms are available from the Division of Workers' Compensation as well as two publications:

- *Tennessee Workers' Compensation Law – 1990*, which costs $4; and
- *A Guide to Workers' Compensation: Benefits for Work-related Injuries and Diseases* — which is a free brochure.

> **Division of Workers' Compensation**
> **Tennessee Department of Labor**
> 501 Union Building, 2nd Floor
> Nashville, TN 37243-0661
> (615) 741-2395
> (800) 332-2667 (in Tennessee)

## Employee Safety and Health Regulations

The Tennessee Division of Occupational Safety and Health was established in 1977 pursuant to Chapter 111 of the Public Act. The division's charge is to educate employers about the federal Occupational Safety; and Health Act of 1970 (OSHA) standards and regulations.

An employer can request a consultation examination of the workplace from the division to determine compliance with OSHA standards and regulations. For more information, contact the division.

In general, Tennessee has not established employee safety and health regulations separate from OSHA. Section 5.6 addresses OSHA record-keeping and reporting requirements. For more information, contact:

**Division of Occupational Safety and Health**
**Tennessee Department of Labor**
501 Union Building, Suite 300
Nashville, TN 37243-0659
(615) 741-3161

**Labor Laws**

The minimum wage in Tennessee is established by the federal Fair Labor Standards Act. There is no state minimum wage law. Nonexempt workers are entitled to a minimum wage of not less than $4.25 per hour. Overtime is to be paid at not less than one and one-half times the employee's wage rate for hours worked in excess of 40 hours per week.[45]

Employees who are learners or apprentices may, in certain circumstances, be paid less than the minimum wage. The employer is responsible for obtaining the special certificate issued by the Wage and Hour Administration.

If a business employs the aged or mentally or physically disabled, it may obtain a special certificate from the Wage and Hour Division establishing a minimum wage rate lower than the standard $4.25 per hour.

Some employees are exempt from the minimum wage or overtime provisions. Detailed information can be obtained from the U.S. Department of Labor, Wage and Hour Division.

**Child Labor Laws**

The employment of minors age 14 or older is permitted under state law; however, certain conditions must be met. While in school, minors ages 14 and 15 may not be employed.[46]

- During school hours;
- Between 7:00 P.M. and 7:00 A.M., if the next day is a school day;
- Between 9:00 P.M. and 6:00 A.M.;
- More than three hours per day on any school day;
- More than eight hours per day in any day that is not a school day;
- More than 18 hours per week in any week school is in session; or
- More than 40 hours per week in any week that school is not in session.

A minor who is 16 or 17 years of age may be employed in connection with any gainful occupation which does not interfere with the minor's health or well-being or is not a prohibited employment for minors.[47] There are 20 categories of prohibited employment for minors. These generally include dangerous occupations or those involving the operation of heavy machinery.

A minor who is 16 or 17 years of age and enrolled in school may not be employed during those hours when the minor is required to attend classes.[48]

**Anti-Discrimination Laws**

The state's anti-discrimination laws are enforced by the Tennessee Human Rights Commission. The state law applies to all employers that employ eight or more people.[49]

Among the various requirements, employers must post the Fair Employment Practices poster conspicuously in each workplace.

Further information regarding the state's anti-discrimination laws and rules is contained in the booklet, *State of Tennessee Human Rights Commission and Its Jurisdictions: Employment, Handicapped, Housing and Public Accommodations*, which can be obtained from:

**Tennessee Human Rights Commission**
Capitol Boulevard Building, Suite 602
226 Capitol Boulevard
Nashville, TN 37219-5095
(615) 741-5825

# 11.6  State Licenses

As discussed in Section 11.4, many businesses and occupations in Tennessee require special licenses.

Most agencies which issue licenses are part of the Tennessee Department of Commerce and may be contacted through the Division of Regulatory Boards.

**Division of Regulatory Boards**
**Tennessee Department of Commerce and Insurance**
500 James Robertson Parkway
Nashville, TN 37243-0572
(615) 741-3449

The primary functions of these boards are to assess fees, grant licenses, and administer professional examinations. The following is a list of various occupations and businesses that require special licenses through the state, along with the agency to contact for further information.

Some local city and county governments also require licenses for certain businesses. You should contact your local city and county government offices to determine whether special permits or licenses are required for your particular business.

| Business or Occupation | State Licensing Agency | Address and Phone Number |
|---|---|---|
| Accountants | State Board of Accountancy | 500 James Robertson Parkway, 2nd Floor<br>Nashville, TN 37243-1141<br>(615) 741-2550 |
| Architects | Architectural, Engineers and Landscape Examiners | 500 James Robertson Parkway, 3rd Floor<br>Nashville, TN 37243-1142<br>(615) 741-3221 |
| Auctioneers | Auctioneer Commission | 500 James Robertson Parkway, 2nd Floor<br>Nashville, TN 37243-1152<br>(615) 741-3236 |
| Automobile dealers | Motor Vehicle Commission | 500 James Robertson Parkway, 2nd Floor<br>Nashville, TN 37243-1153<br>(615) 741-2711 |
| Automobile race track operations | Boxing and Racing Board | 500 James Robertson Parkway, 2nd Floor<br>Nashville, TN 37243-1157<br>(615) 741-2384 |
| Barbers | Board of Barber Examiners | 500 James Robertson Parkway, Suite 120<br>Nashville, TN 37243-1148<br>(615) 741-2294 |
| Boxing | Boxing and Racing Board | 500 James Robertson Parkway, 2nd Floor<br>Nashviile, TN 37243-1157<br>(615) 741-2384 |
| Building construction | Board for Licensing Contractors | 500 James Robertson Parkway, Suite 110<br>Nashville, TN 37243-1150<br>(615) 741-2121 |
| Cemetery operations | Burial Service Section | 500 James Robertson Parkway, 2nd Floor<br>Nashville, TN 37243-1145<br>(615) 741-5062 |
| Cosmetologists | Board of Cosmetology | 500 James Robertson Parkway, 1st Floor<br>Nashville, TN 37243-1147<br>(615) 741-2515 |
| Debt collection services | Collection Service Board | 500 James Robertson Parkway, 2nd Floor<br>Nashville, TN 37243-1155<br>(615) 741-1741 |
| Private employment agencies | Personnel Recruiting Services Board | 500 James Robertson Parkway, 2nd Floor<br>Nashville, TN 37243-1154<br>(615) 741-4700 |
| Fire fighters | Commission on Firefighting Personnel Standards and Education | 500 James Robertson Parkway, 3rd Floor<br>Nashville, TN 37243-0579<br>(615) 741-6780 |

| Business or Occupation | State Licensing Agency | Address and Phone Number |
| --- | --- | --- |
| Funeral directors and embalmers | Board of Funeral Directors and Embalmers | 500 James Robertson Parkway, 2nd Floor Nashville, TN 37243-1144 (615) 741-2378 |
| Land surveyors | Board of Examiners of Land Surveyors | 500 James Robertson Parkway, 2nd Floor Nashville, TN 37243-1146 (615) 741-3611 |
| Pharmacists | Board of Pharmacy | 500 James Robertson Parkway, 2nd Floor Nashville, TN 37243-1149 (615) 741-2718 |
| Polygraph examiners | Board of Polygraph Examiners | 500 James Robertson Parkway, 2nd Floor Nashville, TN 37243-1156 (615) 741-0697 |
| Real estate brokers | Real Estate Commission | 500 James Robertson Parkway, 1st Floor Nashville, TN 37243-1151 (615) 741-2273 |
| Physicians | Board of Medical Examiners | 283 Plus Park Boulevard Nashville, TN 37243-1010 (615) 367-6231 |
| Nurses | Board of Nursing | 283 Plus Park Boulevard Nashville, TN 37243-1010 (615) 367-6232 |

# 11.7  State Excise Taxes

**Public Utilities/Gross Receipts Privilege Tax**

Utilities are generally taxed on gross receipts from business in Tennessee at a rate of 3%,[50] except manufacturers and distributors of gas and natural gas, which are taxed at 1.5% of gross receipts.[51]

Excluded are the first $10,000 of receipts for telephone and telegraph companies and the first $5,000 for electric current or water companies. An inspection fee is also levied against those utilities. The inspection fee is $3 for each $1,000 in gross receipts of $5,000–$999,999 and $0.75 (75 cents) for each $1,000 in excess of $1,000,000.[52] Utilities operated by governmental entities and certain utilities operated by nonprofit cooperatives are exempt from the taxes.

The annual gross receipts tax return for the year beginning July 1 — based on revenues for the prior year — is due on or before August 1. Payment can be made either with the return or on a quarterly basis.

The utility must also file an annual report with the Tennessee Public Service Commission and pay the annual inspection fee, both due on April 1 based on information from the previous calendar year.

## Gasoline and Special Fuels Taxes

Privilege, use, and excise taxes are imposed on gasoline, gasohol, diesel fuel, and compressed natural gas used as motor vehicle fuel. The privilege tax on gasoline and gasohol — imposed on refiners, dealers, distributors, and importers — ranges from $0.20 (20 cents) to $0.214 (21.4 cents) per gallon. A use tax is imposed on wholesalers of diesel fuel and compressed natural gas if they use it as motor vehicle fuel rather than reselling it.

Exemptions or partial exemptions from these taxes are for fuel used in agriculture, aviation, truck refrigeration, and cement mixing. For more information, contact:

**Petroleum Tax Division**
**Tennessee Department of Revenue**
808 Andrew Jackson Building
Nashville, TN 37242
(615) 741-3501
(800) 342-1003 (in Tennessee)

## Highway User Fuel Tax

This tax is imposed on freight motor vehicles weighing 26,000 pounds or greater, or having three or more axles, that are engaged in interstate commerce in or through the state.[53] The tax is based on total miles traveled in the state. A credit is allowed for taxes paid on purchases of gasoline or diesel fuel in the state.

Operators subject to the tax must obtain permits and file reports quarterly on or before the 25th of January, April, July, and October. Tax payment is remitted when the report is filed.

## Cigarette and Tobacco Products Taxes

This privilege tax is paid by wholesalers of cigarettes at a rate of 6.5 mills per cigarette — $0.13 (13 cents) per pack of 20.[54] The tax is paid by the wholesaler by purchasing stamps from the Tennessee Department of Revenue. In addition, dealers and distributors pay an enforcement and administration fee of $0.0005 (five-hundredths of a cent) per pack. The tax on other tobacco products is 6% of the wholesale price. There may be additional taxes in some counties. Retailers, like consumers, purchase their cigarettes and other tobacco products with tax already paid.

Tobacco dealers, distributors, and manufacturers who distribute directly to retailers must file monthly reports by the 15th of the following month with the Tennessee Department of Revenue's Miscellaneous Tax Division.

**Miscellaneous Tax Division – Tobacco Tax Section**
**Tennessee Department of Revenue**
808 Andrew Jackson Building
Nashville, TN 37242
(615) 741-2011
(800) 342-1003 (in Tennessee)

**Alcoholic Beverage Taxes**

Tennessee levies taxes on alcoholic beverages at three different levels. At the wholesale level, malt beverages containing 5% or less alcohol are subject to a barrel tax on purchases and a distribution tax on sales. For beverages containing more than 5% alcohol, manufacturers and importers pay a brand registration tax and wholesalers pay a distribution tax. The sale of alcoholic beverages at the retail level is subject to a gross receipts tax. Tax rates vary by type of beverage and alcoholic content.

Returns are to be filed monthly and payment of alcoholic beverage taxes is made to the Department of Revenue's Miscellaneous Tax Division.

In addition, licenses are required for manufacturers, distillers, wineries, wholesalers, and retail stores. License fees range from $50 to $1,000. For more information on licensing, contact the Tennessee Alcoholic Beverage Commission:

**Tennessee Alcoholic Beverage Commission**
226 Capitol Boulevard, Suite 300
Nashville, TN 37243-0755
(615) 741-1602

**Natural Resource Severance Taxes**

Three taxes are imposed on the extraction of natural resources in Tennessee. A coal severance tax of $0.20 (20 cents) per ton is imposed on the owners of an interest in coal severed in the state. The oil and gas severance tax is imposed at the rate of 3% of the sale price. Finally, some counties impose a severance tax on sand, gravel, sandstone, chert, and limestone. Due dates for returns and tax payments for the different taxes vary. Return forms and further information can be obtained from the Tennessee Department of Revenue, Petroleum Tax Division.

**Mortgage Tax and Real Estate Transfer Tax**

A tax of $0.115 ($11^1/2$ cents) on each $100 of mortgage indebtedness in excess of $2,000 is imposed at the time the mortgage is recorded.[55] On July 1, 1990, the tax was reduced to $0.10 (10 cents) per $100 of mortgage indebtedness. The real estate transfer tax is $0.33 (33 cents) for each $100 of consideration or property value, whichever is greater, and is due when the property transfer is recorded.

**Stock and Bonds Income Tax**

While Tennessee has no personal income tax, it does tax certain dividends and interest income. This Stock and Bonds Income Tax is also referred to as the Tennessee Individual Income Tax or the Hall Income Tax. The tax should be considered in making investment decisions, because some types of dividends and interest are exempt from it.

All persons, including partnerships, estates, and trusts domiciled in Tennessee more than six months in a given year, unless specifically exempt, must pay the tax on dividends and interest.

The tax is 6% of dividends and interest income that is subject to the tax.[56] The tax does not apply to the first $1,250 of taxable income for individuals filing a single return or to the first $2,500 for joint returns.

More common types of dividends and interest not subject to the tax include:

- Dividends of:
  - National banks (not bank holding companies);
  - State banks in Tennessee;
  - Savings and loan associations in Tennessee;
  - Insurance companies licensed to do business in Tennessee;
  - Loan companies in Tennessee; and
  - Credit unions.

- Interest on:
  - Bonds of the state, counties, and municipalities of Tennessee;
  - Bonds of the U.S. government and its agencies;
  - Certificates of deposit;
  - Commercial paper which matures in six months or less;
  - Passbook savings accounts;
  - Repurchase agreements and other similar instruments; and
  - Loans made to qualified businesses for improvements or operations in an Enterprise Zone and mortgages on real property in an Enterprise Zone.

All taxpayers receiving dividends or interest income of $1,250 or more, or, if filing jointly, $2,500 or more, who are not specifically exempt, must file a return no later than the 15th day of the fourth month after the end of the taxpayer's tax year. A penalty of .5% per month up to 10% is assessed against late payment in addition to interest set at a rate by the commissioner. For more information on the Tennessee Individual Income Tax, contact:

**Franchise, Excise, and Income Tax Division**
**Tennessee Department of Revenue**
807 Andrew Jackson State Office Building
500 Deaderick Street
Nashville, TN 37242
(615) 741-4877
(800) 342-1003 (in Tennessee)

# 11.8 Planning for Tax Savings in a Business — State Tax Laws

As discussed in Section 11.2, since Tennessee has no income tax at the personal level for residents of Tennessee, other than the Tennessee Individual Income Tax on certain interest and dividend income, businesses operating under sole proprietorships and partnerships are generally exempt from income tax.

Tennessee corporate tax laws are generally identical or close to those for federal taxes, and the federal tax planning ideas discussed in Chapter 8 are generally applicable to Tennessee. This section highlights some important differences between federal and state tax laws you should address when tax planning.

## Dividends Received Deduction

Tennessee does not allow any dividends received deduction comparable to the federal dividends received deduction discussed in Section 8.2. Tennessee permits a deduction for dividends received from subsidiaries if the taxpayer owns 80% or more of its stock.[57]

## Tennessee Tax Treatment of DISCs

For purposes of Tennessee taxation, Domestic International Sales Corporations (DISCs) and Foreign Sales Corporations (FSCs) are taxed the same as other corporations without regard to the special provisions of Internal Revenue Code (I.R.C. §§ 991–997 and 921–927).

## Estate Planning

Tennessee's estate tax law is generally similar to the federal system, including use of the federal unlimited marital deduction for state purposes. In addition, both systems set forth a similar means of determining the value of the taxable estate. If the inheritance tax does not exceed the maximum state tax credit allowed for federal purposes, Tennessee imposes an additional tax to bring the total state inheritance tax up to the maximum credit.

Tennessee's estate tax law is similar to the federal system, in terms of how the value of the taxable estate is computed. Prior to 1990, Tennessee law designated two classes of inheritance based upon the relationship of the beneficiary to the deceased. In 1990, the classes were merged into the same tax rates and brackets applying to both classes.[58]

Currently, the top estate tax bracket is 9.5% on net estate values exceeding $440,000 for Class A or Class B beneficiaries. Class A beneficiaries include spouses, children, lineal ancestors and descendants, brothers, sisters, stepchildren, sons-in-law, daughters-in-law, and those related to the decedent by legal adoption. Class B beneficiaries include all other beneficiaries.

As with the federal system, the tax exemption is $600,000.

## State Jobs Tax Credit

There is no state jobs tax credit comparable to the federal targeted jobs tax credit discussed in Section 8.11. However, because the federal salary deduction is reduced by the amount of the jobs credit, federal taxable income is reduced by the amount of the credit to arrive at Tennessee taxable income.

Generally, wages that are subject to federal unemployment taxes will also be subject to Tennessee unemployment tax. As under federal law, when a sole proprietor places a spouse, parent, or child under the age of 18 on the payroll, such wages are exempt from state unemployment tax.[59] This exemption is not available if the family member is employed by a partnership or corporation.

**Hiring a Spouse as an Employee**

Tennessee law does not provide for special treatment of S corporations, but instead taxes them the same as any other corporation.

**S Corporations**

Tennessee does not impose any corporate penalty taxes comparable to the federal accumulated earnings tax or personal holding company tax discussed in Section 8.9.

**No Penalty Taxes on Corporate Earnings**

Tennessee taxpayers may use depreciation methods available under the federal tax law.

**Depreciation**

Tennessee allows net operating losses (NOLs) to be carried forward for seven years. There is no carryback of NOLs.[60] Thus, it will often be more difficult to utilize NOLs for state purposes than for federal purposes — where NOLs can be carried back three years and forward fifteen years.

**Net Operating Losses**

For Tennessee purposes, capital losses are fully deductible in the year they occur[61] and capital gains are taxed at regular tax rates. Gains on the liquidation of a business excluded from federal taxable income under I.R.C. §337 must be included in Tennessee taxable income.

**Capital Gains and Losses**

Charitable contributions are fully deductible for Tennessee tax purposes in the year they are made.[62] Thus, federal contribution carryovers from prior years' gifts are added back to arrive at Tennessee taxable income. Tennessee permits deduction only of the cost of donated property. Thus, Tennessee and federal taxable income differ when the fair value of donated property is deducted for federal purposes.

**Charitable Contributions**

Tennessee allows a credit against the excise tax of 1% of purchases of new industrial machinery and pollution control equipment. Industrial machinery is defined as machinery necessary to fabricate or process tangible personal property for resale.

**Industrial Machinery Tax Credit**

# 11.9  Miscellaneous Business Pointers

**Section 1244 Stock**

The ordinary loss treatment on Section 1244 stock provided under the federal tax law is not relevant in Tennessee, since there is no state tax on capital gains and losses of individuals in Tennessee.

**Federal Business Loan Programs**

The state of Tennessee does not have a business loan program. The Nashville district office of the U.S. Small Business Administration (SBA) oversees the SBA loan program discussed in depth in Section 9.7. The Nashville district office of the SBA can be contacted at:

**U.S. Small Business Administration**
50 Vantage Way, Suite 201
Metro Center
Nashville, TN 37228-1500
(615) 736-5881

**Other Business Loan Programs**

The Energy Division of the Tennessee Department of Economic and Community Development, however, does offer financial assistance to industrial and commercial establishments for the purchase or installation of energy conservation opportunities (ECOs). The financial assistance is used to reduce the cost of interest to zero on loans of five years or less. For more information, contact:

**Energy Division**
**Tennessee Department of Economic and Community Development**
320 6th Avenue, North, 6th Floor
Nashville, TN 37243-0405
(615) 741-6671

Many cities and counties throughout Tennessee have various other loan programs aimed at stimulating business creation and expansion within their jurisdiction. Local chambers of commerce or departments of economic development can provide information about them.

Funding for many local programs comes from the federal government in the form of grants, which allow the local political subdivision a great deal of flexibility in administering the funds.

One such program is the Urban Development Action Grant (UDAG) which is awarded to cities and small communities plagued by economic distress. While private financing of a project is necessary, UDAG funds can supply up to 30% of the project's financing needs.

UDAG applications are considered on a competitive basis by the U.S. Department of Housing and Urban Development. The greater the project's positive impact on the area relative to the amount of UDAG funds being requested, the better the chances are for approval.

Other loans that may be available are:

- EDA Title IX Loan — This program provides funds for up to 50% of a project (maximum $100,000) at rates of one-eighth of a percent over the applicable treasury rate.

- Revolving Loan Fund — This program provides funds for up to 50% of a project (maximum $50,000) at rates as low as two-thirds of the prime rate.

- HUD 108 Program — This program provides 100% financing, up to $20,000, for nonowner occupied real estate at rates one-eighth over the applicable treasury rate. For more information, contact:

**U.S. Department of Housing & Urban Development**
**Attn: Community Planning & Development**
John J. Duncan Federal Building, 3rd Floor
710 Locust Street, SW
Knoxville, TN 37902-2526
(615) 549-9426

- Community Development Block Grants/Loans — These loans provide up to $500,000 (50% of a project) if the project will promote the employment of low income residents. For more information, contact:

**Office of Program Management**
**Tennessee Department of Economic and Community Development**
320 6th Avenue, North
Nashville, TN 37243-0405
(615) 741-6201

- TVA Special Opportunities Counties Program — This program provides up to 50% of project costs for companies located in one of 50 counties in the Tennessee Valley with the lowest per capita income. For more information, contact:

**Tennessee Valley Authority**
400 West Summitt Hill
Knoxville, TN 37902-1499
(615) 632-2101

The key to obtaining funds from any of these programs is job creation. The programs are not intended to be giveaways; they are designed to affect the local economy in a positive way by creating jobs.

## Usury Laws

Usury law deals with the maximum amount of interest that may be charged in a credit transaction, i.e., bond, promissory note, or other instrument requiring the payment of interest.

In general, Tennessee law (TENN. CODE ANN. § 47-14-103) establishes a relatively low maximum rate of interest of 10% per annum; however, there are a number of significant exemptions to this low ceiling, including:

- All transactions in which provisions of other statutes fix a maximum effective rate of interest for particular categories of creditors, lenders, or transactions;

- All written contracts — including obligations issued by the state of Tennessee or certain political subdivisions and agencies — which are signed by the party to be charged may carry an interest rate not to exceed the prime rate published by the Federal Reserve System.

In addition, federal law grants national banks most-favored lender status. Based on this statute, national banks may charge any rate of interest, even interest in excess of the legal state limit.

This discussion highlights the key provisions of the state's usury law; however, not all issues are covered, since complete discussion is beyond the scope of this book.

### Incorporation in Another State

Foreign corporations — those incorporated in a state other than Tennessee — must obtain a certificate of authority from the secretary of state before transacting business in Tennessee.

A certificate of good standing from the state of incorporation dated not more than 30 days before the date of application must be filed with the application.

As with domestic corporations, foreign corporations must appoint a registered agent in Tennessee. The filing fee for an original application for a certificate of authority for a for-profit foreign corporation is $300.

Foreign corporations doing business in the state are subject to the corporate franchise and excise taxes.

## 11.10  State Sources of Help and Information

### Do-It-Yourself Incorporation

The steps you must take to incorporate are outlined in the books *Tennessee Business Corporation Act* and *Tennessee Non-Profit Corporation Act*, which are available from the Corporate Division.

**Corporate Division**
**Tennessee Secretary of State**
James K. Polk Building, Suite 500
Nashville, TN 37219
(615) 741-2286

### State Agency Publications

Several state agencies offer Tennessee business owners a variety of useful publications. They range in topics from tax law to OSHA requirements. Most of the publications are free; however, some charge a nominal fee to cover printing and handling costs. For your convenience, here is a list of the available publications and the state agency addresses and phone numbers where you can learn more about requesting this information.

| Subject | Publication | State Agency |
|---------|-------------|-------------|
| Sales and Use Tax | *Tennessee Sales and Use Tax Law* | **Taxpayer Services Division**<br>**Tennessee Department of Revenue**<br>500 Deaderick Street<br>Nashville, TN 37242<br>(615) 741-3581<br>(800) 342-1003 (in Tennessee) |
| Workers' Compensation | *Tennessee Workers' Compensation Law – 1990* | **Division of Workers' Compensation**<br>**Tennessee Department of Labor**<br>501 Union Building, 2nd Floor<br>Nashville, TN 37243-0661<br>(615) 741-2395<br>(800) 332-2667 (in Tennessee) |
| Employment Security | *Handbook for Employers* | **Department of Employment Security**<br>Volunteer Plaza, 8th Floor<br>500 James Robertson Parkway<br>Nashville, TN 37245-3500<br>(615) 741-1948<br>(800) 344-8337 (in Tennessee) |
| Discrimination Laws and Rules | *State of Tennessee Human Rights Commission and Its Jurisdictions* | **Tennessee Human Rights Commission**<br>Capitol Boulevard Building, Suite 602<br>226 Capital Boulevard<br>Nashville, TN 37219-5095<br>(615) 741-5825 |
| Small Business Information | *A Guide to Doing Business in Tennessee* | **Small Business Office**<br>**Department of Economic and Community Development**<br>Rachel Jackson Building, 7th Floor<br>320 6th Avenue, North<br>Nashville, TN 37243-0405<br>(615) 741-2626<br>(800) 872-7201 (in Tennessee) |
| Business Taxes | *Tennessee Business Act Rules and Regulations* | **Miscellaneous Tax Division**<br>**Tennessee Department of Revenue**<br>808 Andrew Jackson State Office Building<br>500 Deaderick Street<br>Nashville, TN 37242<br>(615) 741-2011<br>(800) 342-1003 (in Tennessee) |
| OSHA | Various pamphlets are available | **Division of Occupational Safety and Health**<br>**Tennessee Department of Labor**<br>501 Union Building, Suite 300<br>Nashville, TN 37243-0659<br>(615) 741-3161 |

**Other State Agency
Assistance**

The Office of Minority Business Enterprise (OMBE) — The OMBE provides help to minority businesses with loan packaging, preparation of business plans, and access to local economic planning data and resources of local governments, including existing and emerging business trends and market conditions within the state. It also prints a business newsletter for minority businesses in Tennessee.

Program details can be secured by writing OMBE at the Tennessee Department of Economic and Community Development or calling (615) 741-2545 or, in Tennessee, (800) 342-8470 or (800) 872-7201.

Industrial Training Service — This office enhances the development of starting and expanding industries by assuring a trained labor force for Tennessee manufacturing facilities. It also helps Tennessee citizens acquire the basic skills and knowledge essential for succeeding in a specific job.

Assistance specifications include initial contact and discussions with industrial prospects, negotiations of specific training requirements, project coordination, developing training content, and monitoring and evaluating ongoing training projects. Further inquiries may be directed to:

**Industrial Training Service
Tennessee Department of Economic and Community Development**
500 James Robertson Parkway, Suite 660
Nashville, TN 37243-0406
(615) 741-1746
(800) 342-8470 (in Tennessee)

**State Business Publications**

Trade and business journals can assist you in keeping up-to-date on business-related activities and events in Tennessee. Daily newspapers are also helpful since they cover current state and local news and information, which may affect your business. For your convenience, several state business and trade journals are listed below should you be interested in learning more about any of these publications.

**Business Journal of Upper East
Tennessee and Southwest Virginia**
23330 Highway 75
Blountville, TN 37617
(615) 323-7111

**Memphis Business Journal**
88 Union, #102
Memphis, TN 38103-5195
(901) 523-0437

**Nashville Business Journal**
One Church Street
P.O. Box 23229
Nashville, TN 37202-3229
(615) 254-9154

**Tennessee Banker**
201 Venture Circle
Nashville, TN 37228-1603
(615) 244-4871

**Tennessee Cattleman and Horseman**
P.O. Box 843
Franklin, TN 37064
(615) 791-1780

**Tennessee Farm Bureau News**
412 E. Highway
P.O. Box 313
Columbia, TN 38402
(615) 388-7862

**Tennessee Farmer**
5844 Scottsville Road
Bowling Green, KY 42101
(502) 781-2249

**Tennessee Home Builder**
P.O. Box 1385
Brentwood, TN 37024-1385
(615) 371-0010

**TVPPA News**
1201 Chestnut Street
Chattanooga, TN 37402-5021
(615) 756-6511

**The Tennessee Magazine**
710 Spence Lane
P.O. Box 100912
Nashville, TN 37210
(615) 367-9284

**Tennessee Public Works**
501 Mulberry Street
P.O. Box 474
Loudon, TN 37774-1445
(615) 458-3560

**Tennessee Realtor**
1910 Adelicia Street
P.O. Box 121980
(615) 321-0515

**Tennessee Restaurateur**
501 Mulberry Street
P.O. Box 474
Loudon, TN 37774-1445
(615) 458-3560

**Tennessee Sportsman**
2250 Newmarket Parkway, #110
P.O. Box 741
Marietta, GA 30061
(404) 953-9222

**Tennessee Teacher**
598 James Robertson Parkway
Nashville, TN 37219-1204
(615) 242-8392

**Memphis Health Care News**
88 Union, #200
Memphis, TN 38105
(901) 526-2007

**Memphis**
460 Tennessee Street
P.O. Box 256
Memphis, TN 38101
(901) 521-9000

**The Memphis Flyer**
460 Tennessee Street
P.O. Box 687
Memphis, TN 38101
(901) 521-9000

**Nashville!**
1801 West End Avenue, #500
P.O. Box 24649
Nashville, TN 37202
(615) 329-1973

**Small Business Development Centers**

Established by the state along with local government and business communities, Small Business Development Centers (SBDCs), usually located throughout the state on college and university campuses, provide start-up information as well as sponsor business-oriented seminars. Please review the addresses listed below for the SBDC office nearest you.

**SBDC: Memphis State University**
330 Fogelman Executive Center
Memphis, TN 38152
(901) 678-2500

**SBDC: Austin Peay State University**
College of Business
Box 4075
Clarksville, TN 37044
(615) 648-7764

**SBDCs** (continued)

**SBDC: Chattanooga State Technical Community College**
100 Cherokee Boulevard
Chattanooga, TN 37405
(615) 752-4308

**SBDC: Cleveland State Community College**
Adkisson Drive
P.O. Box 3570
Cleveland, TN 37320
(615) 478-6247

**SBDC: Dyersburg State Community College**
Office of Extension Services
P.O. Box 648
Dyersburg, TN 38024
(901) 286-3267

**SBDC: East Tennessee State University**
Box 23440A
Johnson City, TN 37614
(615) 929-5630

**SBDC: Jackson State Community College**
2046 North Parkway Street
Jackson, TN 38104
(901) 424-5389

**SBDC: Memphis State University**
320 South Dudley Street
Memphis, TN 38104
(901) 527-1041

**SBDC: Middle Tennessee State University**
School of Business
Box 487
Murfreesboro, TN 37132
(615) 898-2745

**SBDC: Pellissippi State Technical Community College**
P.O. Box 22990
3435 Division Street
Cleveland, TN 37933-0990
(615) 694-6660

**SBDC: Tennessee State University**
School of Business
330 10th Avenue North
Nashville, TN 37203
(615) 251-1178

**SBDC: Tennessee Technological University**
College of Business Administration
P.O. Box 5023
Cookeville, TN 38505
(615) 372-3648

**SBDC: University of Tennessee at Martin**
Pepsi Building
402 Elm Street
Martin, TN 38238
(901) 587-7236

**SBDC: Walters State Community College**
500 S. Davy Crockett Parkway
Morristown, TN 37813
(615) 581-2121

# Footnotes

1. Tenn. Code Ann. § 67-2-102.
2. Tenn. Code Ann. § 61-2-201(a).
3. Tenn. Code Ann. § 61-2-202.
4. Tenn. Code Ann. § 48-11-303(a)(1).
5. Tenn. Code Ann. §§ 48-12-102 and 48-14-101.
6. Tenn. Code Ann. §§ 48-14-102 and 48-11-303(a)(3).
7. Tenn. Code Ann. § 48-25-103(b).
8. Tenn. Code Ann. § 48-26-203.
9. Tenn. Code Ann. § 67-4-903.
10. Tenn. Code Ann. § 67-4-904.
11. Tenn. Code Ann. § 67-4-806.
12. Tenn. Code Ann. § 48-2-103-(b)(4)(A).
13. Tenn. Code Ann. § 48-2-103(b)(6).
14. Tenn. Code Ann. § 47-6-104(1)(c).
15. Tenn. Code Ann. § 47-6-105.
16. Tenn. Code Ann. § 47-6-107.
17. Tenn. Code Ann. § 47-6-108(4).
18. Tenn. Code Ann. § 50-7-206(2).
19. Tenn. Code Ann. § 67-6-513(a).
20. Tenn. Code Ann. § 67-4-704(a).
21. Tenn. Code Ann. § 67-4-710.
22. Tenn. Code Ann. § 67-4-817(c)(1).
23. Tenn. Code Ann. § 67-4-817(c)(1)(B).
24. Tenn. Code Ann. § 67-6-201.
25. Tenn. Code Ann. §§ 67-6-202, 203, 204, 205.
26. Tenn. Code Ann. §§ 67-6-702(a) and 703(a)(1).
27. Tenn. Comp. R. & Regs. 1320-5-1-.78.
28. Tenn. Comp. R. & Regs. 1320-5-1-.74.
29. Tenn. Code Ann. § 67-6-509(a).
30. Tenn. Code Ann. § 67-5-801(a)(2).
31. Tenn. Code Ann. § 67-5-901(a)(2).
32. Tenn. Code Ann. § 67-5-804.
33. Tenn. Code Ann. § 67-5-1801.
34. Tenn. Code Ann. § 67-5-2010(a)(1).
35. Tenn. Code Ann. § 67-5-2101.
36. Tenn. Code Ann. § 47-25-503.
37. Tenn. Code Ann. § 47-25-505.
38. Tenn. Code Ann. § 50-7-206.
39. Tenn. Code Ann. § 50-7-213.
40. I.R.C. § 3302.
41. Tenn. Code Ann. § 50-7-403(b)(5)(B).
42. Tenn. Code Ann. § 50-6-405(a).
43. Tenn. Code Ann. § 50-6-406.
44. Tenn. Code Ann. § 50-6-407.
45. 29 USC § 206(a)(1).
46. Tenn. Code Ann. § 50-5-104(b).
47. Tenn. Code Ann. § 50-5-105(a).
48. Tenn. Code Ann. § 50-5-105(b).
49. Tenn. Code Ann. §§ 4-21-102(4) and 4-21-401.
50. Tenn. Code Ann. § 67-4-406.
51. Tenn. Code Ann. § 67-4-405(a)(2).
52. Tenn. Code Ann. § 65-4-303.
53. Tenn. Code Ann. § 67-3-703.
54. Tenn. Code Ann. § 67-4-1004.
55. Tenn. Code Ann. § 67-4-409.
56. Tenn. Code Ann. § 67-2-102(a).
57. Tenn. Code Ann. § 67-4-805(b)(2)(A).
58. Tenn. Code Ann. § 67-8-314.
59. Tenn. Code Ann. § 50-7-207(c)(5).
60. Tenn. Code Ann. § 67-4-805(b)(2)(C).
61. Tenn. Code Ann. § 67-4-805(b)(2)(D) and (F).
62. Tenn. Code Ann. § 67-4-805(b)(2)(E).

# Index

# Appendix

## Checklist of Tax and Other Major Requirements for Nearly All Small Businesses

| Requirement | Number of Employees of Business | | | | | | | Chapter–Section Reference |
|---|---|---|---|---|---|---|---|---|
| | None | 1–4 | 5–10 | 11–14 | 15–19 | 20–99 | 100+ | |
| Federal estimated taxes | √ | √ | √ | √ | √ | √ | √ | Sec. 4.3, 11.4 |
| Federal income tax returns | √ | √ | √ | √ | √ | √ | √ | Sec. 4.12 |
| Form SS-4, Application for Federal I.D. Number: | | | | | | | | |
|   Sole Proprietorships | | √ | √ | √ | √ | √ | √ | Sec. 5.2 |
|   Partnerships | √ | √ | √ | √ | √ | √ | √ | Sec. 5.2 |
|   Corporations | √ | √ | √ | √ | √ | √ | √ | Sec. 5.2 |
| Form 1099 returns | √ | √ | √ | √ | √ | √ | √ | Sec. 4.7 |
| Federal payroll tax returns | | √ | √ | √ | √ | √ | √ | Sec. 5.2, 5.3 |
| Provide and file W-2's to employees at year-end | | √ | √ | √ | √ | √ | √ | Sec. 5.2 |
| ERISA compliance: | | | | | | | | |
|   For unfunded or insured employees' welfare plan: | | | | | | | | |
|     Provide a Summary Plan Description to employees | | √ | √ | √ | √ | √ | √ | Sec. 5.5 |
|     File a Summary Plan Description | | | | | | | √ | Sec. 5.5 |
|     File Form 5500, Annual Report | | | | | | | √ | Sec. 5.5 |
|     Provide a Summary Annual Report to employees | | | | | | | √ | Sec. 5.5 |
|     File and provide to employees a Summary of Material Plan Modifications | | | | | | | √ | Sec. 5.5 |
|     File a Terminal Report, if plan terminated | | | | | | | √ | Sec. 5.5 |
|   For funded employee welfare plan: | | | | | | | | |
|     File and provide all items described in ERISA list | | √ | √ | √ | √ | √ | √ | Sec. 5.5 |
|   For employees' pension or profit-sharing plan: | | | | | | | | |
|     Provide a Summary Plan Description to employees and file with U.S. Department of Labor | | √ | √ | √ | √ | √ | √ | Sec. 5.5 |
|     File Form 5500, Annual Report | | | | | | | √ | Sec. 5.5 |
|     File Form 5500-C or Form 5500-R | | √ | √ | √ | √ | √ | √ | Sec. 5.5 |
|     Provide to employees and file a Summary of Material Modifications | | √ | √ | √ | √ | √ | √ | Sec. 5.5 |
|     File a Terminal Report, if plan terminated | | √ | √ | √ | √ | √ | √ | Sec. 5.5 |
|     Provide a Summary Annual Report to employees | | √ | √ | √ | √ | √ | √ | Sec. 5.5 |
|     Bonding requirement for plan officials | | √ | √ | √ | √ | √ | √ | Sec. 5.5 |
| Federal Wage and Hour Laws and Regulations — coverage depends on nature of business and employee types not covered | | √ | √ | √ | √ | √ | √ | Sec. 5.7 |
| Federal Fair Employment Laws: | | | | | | | | |
|   Anti-discrimination laws regarding race, color, religion, sex, etc. | | | | | √ | √ | √ | Sec. 5.8 |
|   Equal Pay Act for women | | √ | √ | √ | √ | √ | √ | Sec. 5.8 |
|   Anti-discrimination laws regarding age | | | | | | √ | √ | Sec. 5.8 |
|   Anti-discrimination laws regarding federal contracts | | √ | √ | √ | √ | √ | √ | Sec. 5.8 |

| Requirement | Number of Employees of Business | | | | | | | Chapter–Section Reference |
|---|---|---|---|---|---|---|---|---|
| | None | 1–4 | 5–10 | 11–14 | 15–19 | 20–99 | 100+ | |
| **Federal Fair Employment Laws:** (continued) | | | | | | | | |
| File *Form EEO-1* | | | | | | | √ | Sec. 5.8 |
| Post notice regarding discrimination: racial, sexual, etc. | | | | | √ | √ | √ | Sec. 5.8 |
| Post notice regarding age anti-discrimination laws | | | | | | √ | √ | Sec. 5.8 |
| Post other anti-discrimination notices by certain federal contractors | | √ | √ | √ | √ | √ | √ | Sec. 5.8 |
| **Immigration Laws:** | | | | | | | | |
| Complete INS *Form I-9* for each new hire | | √ | √ | √ | √ | √ | √ | Sec. 5.9 |
| **OSHA Job Safety Regulations:** | | | | | | | | |
| Health and safety | | √ | √ | √ | √ | √ | √ | Sec. 5.6 |
| Post *Job Safety and Health Notice* | | √ | √ | √ | √ | √ | √ | Sec. 5.6 |
| Post *Employee Rights Notice* regarding OSHA | | √ | √ | √ | √ | √ | √ | Sec. 5.6 |
| Record industrial injuries and illnesses | | | | √ | √ | √ | √ | Sec. 5.6 |
| Report job fatalities or multiple injuries to OSHA | | √ | √ | √ | √ | √ | √ | Sec. 5.6 |
| Federal and State Child Labor Laws | | √ | √ | √ | √ | √ | √ | Sec. 5.7, 11.5 |
| Local business licenses | √ | √ | √ | √ | √ | √ | √ | Sec. 4.3, 11.4 |
| Sales and use tax permit and returns, if selling tangible personal property | √ | √ | √ | √ | √ | √ | √ | Sec. 11.4 |
| Tennessee assumed name registration | √ | √ | √ | √ | √ | √ | √ | Sec. 11.4 |
| Tennessee estimated taxes | √ | √ | √ | √ | √ | √ | √ | Sec. 11.4 |
| State Wage and Hour Laws and Regulations — most employees are covered, yet some types are not | | √ | √ | √ | √ | √ | √ | Sec. 11.5 |
| Workers' compensation insurance | | √ | √ | √ | √ | √ | √ | Sec. 11.5 |
| State Fair Employment Laws: General prohibition of discrimination | | √ | √ | √ | √ | √ | √ | Sec. 11.5 |

## Checklist of Official Government Posters and Notices Required to be Displayed by Businesses

| Type of Poster or Notice | When required | Where to obtain |
|---|---|---|
| Local business license | Required of practically all businesses operating in a particular locality | Local city hall or county courthouse |
| Sales tax permit | Must be displayed at each place of business where tangible personal property is sold | Local office |
| OSHA poster regarding Job Safety and Health | Required to be posted by all employers | U.S. Department of Labor Occupational Safety and Health Administration |
| OSHA poster regarding rights of employees under OSHA | Required to be posted by all employers | U.S. Department of Labor Occupational Safety and Health Administration |
| U.S. Fair Labor Standards Act Wage-Hour poster, *Attention Employees,* *(WH Publication 1088)* | Required to be posted by employers with employees whose wages and working conditions are subject to the U.S. Fair Labor Standards Act | U.S. Department of Labor Employment Standards Administration (Wage-Hour Division offices) |
| Federal Equal Employment Opportunity poster | Required to be posted by all employers with 15 or more employees, 20 weeks of the year, or with federal contracts or subcontracts or $10,000 or more | Federal Equal Employment Opportunity Commission offices |
| Federal Age Discrimination poster | Require to be posted by all employers with 20 or more employees 20 weeks a year | U.S. Department of Labor (Wage-Hour Division offices) |
| Federal Rehabilitation Act poster regarding hiring of handicapped persons | Required to be posted by employers with federal contracts or subcontracts of $2,500 or more | Assistant Secretary for Employment Standards, U.W. Department of Labor Washington, D.C. |
| Poster regarding hiring of Vietnam-era veterans | Required to be posted by employers with federal contracts or subcontracts of $10,000 or more | The government contracting officer on the federal contract |

## Sales Exempt from Sales Tax:

As mentioned in Section 11.4, there are several kinds of sales which are exempt from sales tax. These exceptions include:

1. The sale of livestock, nursery stock, poultry, and other farm or nursery products directly by a farmer or nurseryman if 50% or more of such products is grown by the farmer or nurseryman. If less than 50% are grown by the farmer or nurseryman, only the gross proceeds of the sale of the products actually grown by the farmer or nurseryman is exempt;

2. Aircraft parts and supplies used exclusively in servicing and maintaining aircraft used principally in interstate or international commerce;

3. Sale of a motor vehicle to a nonresident member of a uniformed service stationed on a military reservation and located partially within the boundary of Tennessee and another state; or to a nonresident member of a uniformed service stationed at a naval air station located entirely within Tennessee;

4. Sale of human blood, blood plasma, or any part thereof by any institution or organization that has received a determination of exemption;

5. The transfer of demonstration or display property from inventory for 120 days or less. After 120 days, the property must be returned to inventory for sale purposes or the dealer must pay use tax;

6. Transfer of automobile between spouses resulting from a decree of divorce;

7. Energy or resource recovery facilities owned or operated by a municipality complying with certain restrictions;

8. Direct sale or lease of tangible personal property or services to the federal government;

9. Rental of films, transcriptions, and recordings to radio and television stations operating under a certificate from the Federal Communications Commission;

10. Sales at gun shows, displays, or exhibits sponsored by any nonprofit organization of gun collectors;

11. Industrial machinery transferred between parent and subsidiary corporations when applicable tax has already been paid;

12. Sale of insulin and any syringe used to dispense insulin;

13. Tangible personal property imported into the state or manufactured in the state for export, and repair services (including parts and labor) with respect to qualified tangible personal property where these services are performed within Tennessee and where the property is subsequently delivered or shipped outside Tennessee. For this section, "qualified tangible personal property" includes machinery, apparatus, and equipment, with all associated parts and accessories, which may be used in any of the following applications:
    - Extracting or removing any natural resources (including, but not limited to, that which is necessary for mining or logging endeavors);
    - Building or improving roads or highways;
    - Land clearing or excavation, or commercial or residential construction; and
    - Loading and unloading containers or truck trailers on and off rail cars, ships, or barges.

14. Medical equipment and devices for handicapped persons;

15. Motor vehicles, boats, and vessels moved outside the state within three days of purchase;

16. Sales by optometrists, opticians, and opthalmologists of products and appliances to their patients;

17. Sale of oxygen prescribed or recommended for treatment by a licensed practitioner;

18. Sale of pharmaceutical samples outside of the state;

19. Any prescription drug or medicine issued by a licensed pharmacist in accordance with an individual prescription;

20. Transfer of railroad rolling stock or of vessels or barges of 50 tons or more for use in interstate commerce or outside the state of Tennessee;

21. Tangible personal property or taxable services sold, given, or donated to any religious, educational, and charitable institutions;

22. Use, sale, or distribution of religious publications to or by churches or other religious or charitable organizations;

23. Sales of tangible personal property to telephone cooperatives;

24. Sales of tangible personal property to commercial marine vessels for use in deliveries of such property in midstream waterways constituting geographical boundaries of this state;

25. Repairs of vessels and barges of 50 tons or greater, used principally in interstate or international commerce;

26. Sales of tangible personal property to watershed districts;

27. Admission, dues or fees of organizations listed in Major Group 86, imposed by the amusement tax;

28. Admission to an event that an exempt organization produces, controls, and conducts. Prior authorization from the Tennessee Department of Revenue is required;

29. The first $150 of membership dues and fees charged "per member, per annum" to sports or recreation clubs;

30. Transfers by dealers in personal property of motor vehicles used by common carriers;

31. Contributions made to utilities, electric cooperatives, and electric membership corporations as a condition for utility service;

32. Energy for residential use; and

33. Miscellaneous exemptions, including:
    - Newspapers;
    - Seeds, seedlings, plants grown from seed and liners (cuttings) producing food or fiber for human or animal consumption;
    - Fertilizer used to aid in the growth and development of seeds, seedlings, or plants as defined above;
    - Pesticides sold for the purpose of aiding in the production of food or fiber for human or animal consumption;
    - Containers for farm products and plastic or canvas used in the care and raising of plants, seeds or seedlings, as defined above, and plastic or canvas used in covering feed bins, silos, and other similar storage structures;
    - Livestock and poultry feeds, livestock wormers, livestock medication and instruments used for the administration of such medications;
    - Adjuvants and surfactants solutions sold exclusively for the purpose of mixture with insecticides, pesticides, fungicides, or herbicides, or for use as a soil conditioner when such is intended to aid in the growth and development of a food or fiber for human or animal consumption;
    - Shoppers advertisers distributed in Tennessee or within a 25-mile radius thereof and provided without charge to the shopper;
    - Caskets and burial vaults not exceeding five hundred dollars ($500);
    - School books and school lunches;
    - All sales made to the state of Tennessee or any county or municipality within the state;
    - Hearing aids, as defined in TENN. CODE ANN. §63-15-101(2); and
    - Film, including negatives, used in the business of printing.

Source: Tennessee Sales and Use Tax Laws, TENN. CODE ANN. §§67-6-301–67-6-329.

**Notes**

**TENNESSEE DEPARTMENT OF REVENUE**
Andrew Jackson State Office Building
Nashville, Tennessee 37242-1399

*APPLICATION FOR*
**Sales and Use Tax Certificate of Registration**

## WHO MUST REGISTER?

You must register with the Department of Revenue if you sell, or offer for sale, goods and/or services in Tennessee. You must also register if you have out of state suppliers who do not collect Tennessee Sales Tax.

You must complete one application for **each** business location that you own. You will receive a Certificate of Registration for **each** location within a few days after the completion and return of this form(s). This certificate must be publicly displayed at the location for which it was issued.

## HOW TO REGISTER

Fill out page two of this form **(THE BLUE COPY IS A DUPLICATE FOR YOUR RECORDS)** and return it in the envelope provided. — **IMPORTANT** — Each question on the application must be answered fully. Incomplete applications will be returned to you. There are no fees involved in filing this application.

## ABOUT THE APPLICATION

The following information will enable you to fill out this application more accurately. The numbers to the left of each paragraph refer to the specific Item numbers on the application.

Item 1    **YOU MUST PROVIDE THE DATE OF YOUR FIRST SALES IN TENNESSEE.** This is the opening date (or approximate opening date) of your business.

Item 3    **YOU MUST PROVIDE THE EXACT LOCATION OF YOUR BUSINESS.** If your location is a rural route number, also enter the highway number or the road name.

Item 4    **IF A DIFFERENT ADDRESS IS REQUIRED FOR MAILING PURPOSES, ENTER IT AT ITEM 4.** If you have a Post Office Box, enter it here. All correspondence, i.e., Sales/Use Tax Returns and other information will be mailed to the address listed at item 4. If the mailing address is the same **AS #3, WRITE "SAME AS #3" IN THE BLANK.**

Item 6    **YOU MUST PROVIDE US WITH A BUSINESS PHONE NUMBER,** or another number where you can be reached during normal business hours.

Item 7    **YOU MUST HAVE A FEDERAL EMPLOYER'S IDENTIFICATION NUMBER** if your business is a partnership, corporation, or if you pay wages to anyone other than yourself. Information about this number can be obtained from any Federal Internal Revenue Office.

Item 9    **YOU MUST ENTER SOCIAL SECURITY NUMBER(S) HOME ADDRESS AND HOME TELEPHONE NUMBER** for all owners, partners or corporate officers.

Item 17    **THIS APPLICATION MUST BE SIGNED BY THE OWNER, PARTNER, OR A CORPORATE OFFICER OF THE BUSINESS.** Do not print or use a signature stamp. Applications signed by an accountant, bookkeeper or agent for the business will be returned to you. **UNSIGNED** applications will **ALSO BE RETURNED.**

## OTHER INFORMATION

**IMPORTANT — YOU MUST NOTIFY** the Department of Revenue:

1. If the business **OWNERSHIP CHANGES** in any manner, including:
   a. selling or closing of the business
   b. adding or changing partners
   c. any transfer or change in the ownership of the business
   d. any change in corporate structure requiring a new character or certificate of authority

2. **IF THE BUSINESS LOCATION CHANGES**

In either of the above cases, answer the questions on the back of the business's Certificate of Registration and mail it to the Department of Revenue. The new owners or officers (if applicable) must then apply for a new Certificate of Registration.

After completing the registration process, you will begin to receive your Sales/Use Tax Returns on a monthly basis. A return must be filed for each month or portion thereof with the effective date of this application. From that point on, a return must be filed each month with the Department of Revenue even if no sales were made or any tax is due.

## NEED ASSISTANCE?

As a public service, the Tennessee Department of Revenue has installed a toll free telephone number for Tennessee residents. For assistance, call **1-800-342-1003** toll free in Tennessee or, if you are located in the Nashville area or out-of-state, call **615-741-2594**. A Revenue Tax specialist will be available to assist you during normal business hours (8:00 AM to 4:30 PM central time).

TENNESSEE DEPARTMENT OF REVENUE

## APPLICATION FOR SALES AND USE TAX
## CERTIFICATE OF REGISTRATION

FOR DEPARTMENT USE ONLY

---

### ANSWER ALL QUESTIONS COMPLETELY. INCOMPLETE APPLICATIONS WILL BE RETURNED TO YOU.

| **1** OPENING DATE FOR BUSINESS AT THIS LOCATION | **2** WILL YOUR **GROSS SALES** EXCEED $4,800 PER YEAR? | ☐ YES ☐ NO |
|---|---|---|
| | WILL YOUR TAXABLE **SERVICES** EXCEED $1,200 PER **YEAR**? | ☐ YES ☐ NO |
| | DO YOU HAVE SUPPLIERS (IN-STATE OR OUT-OF-STATE) WHO DO NOT COLLECT TENN. SALES TAX? | ☐ YES ☐ NO |
| | **IF ALL THREE OF THE ABOVE ARE "NO", YOU DO NOT NEED A SALES TAX #.** | |

**2a** IF YOU NEED A SALES TAX #, CHECK ONE OF THE FOLLOWING: ☐ NEW BUSINESS?     ☐ CHANGE IN CORPORATE STRUCTURE?

☐ CHANGE IN OWNERSHIP/PURCHASE OF AN EXISTING BUSINESS? ENTER BUSINESS NAME AND ACCOUNT # _____

| **3** BUSINESS NAME AND EXACT LOCATION | **4** BUSINESS MAILING ADDRESS |
|---|---|
| ~~ME~~ (GIVE TRADE NAME AT THIS LOCATION) | NAME (ENTER CORPORATION NAME, IF APPLICABLE) |
| **SAMPLE** ~~EET~~, HIGHWAY, ROUTE (DO NOT USE P.O. BOX #) | P.O. BOX, STREET, ROUTE, OR HIGHWAY |
| CITY          COUNTY          STATE          ZIP | CITY          STATE          ZIP |

| **5** IS THIS BUSINESS LOCATED INSIDE ANY TENNESSEE CITY LIMITS? | **6** BUSINESS TELEPHONE # |
|---|---|
| ☐ YES ☐ NO | (          ) |
| IF YES, WHAT CITY? _____ | AREA CODE |

**7** ENTER YOUR FEDERAL EMPLOYER'S IDENTIFICATION # ☐ — ☐☐☐☐☐☐   ☐ APPLIED FOR   ☐ NOT REQUIRED

**8** TYPE OF OWNERSHIP   ☐ PROPRIETORSHIP ☐ PARTNERSHIP ☐ OTHER _____
☐ CORPORATION - ENTER DATE OF INCORPORATION OR DOMESTICATION IN TENNESSEE _____
☐ NAME OF CORPORATION _____

**9** IDENTIFY OWNERS, OFFICERS, OR PARTNERS (ATTACH ADDITIONAL NAMES AND SOCIAL SECURITY #'S ON SEPARATE SHEET)

| 1) NAME | HOME TELEPHONE # | SOCIAL SECURITY # |
|---|---|---|
| HOME ADDRESS (DO NOT USE P.O. BOX #) | CITY | STATE          ZIP CODE |

| 2) NAME | HOME TELEPHONE # | SOCIAL SECURITY # |
|---|---|---|
| HOME ADDRESS (DO NOT USE P.O. BOX #) | CITY | STATE          ZIP CODE |

| 3) NAME | HOME TELEPHONE # | SOCIAL SECURITY # |
|---|---|---|
| HOME ADDRESS (DO NOT USE P.O. BOX #) | CITY | STATE          ZIP CODE |

**10** DESCRIBE THE MAJOR PRODUCTS AND/OR SERVICES AT THIS LOCATION

IS THE BUSINESS ☐ RETAIL ☐ WHOLESALE ☐ BOTH? ☐ MANUFACTURER ☐ AMUSEMENT ☐ CONTRACTOR?

| **11** USING THE BUSINESS ACTIVITY CODE LISTING ON THE PREVIOUS PAGE ENTER THE CODE THAT BEST DESCRIBES YOUR BUSINESS. | **12** DO YOU OPERATE MORE THAN ONE BUSINESS LOCATION IN TENNESSEE? |
|---|---|
| | ☐ YES ☐ NO |
| | IF YES, HOW MANY ADDITIONAL LOCATIONS? |

| **13** DO YOU INSTALL EVERYTHING YOU SELL? ☐ YES ☐ NO | **14** IF APPLICATION IS FOR A BUSINESS LOCATED **OUTSIDE THE STATE OF** |
|---|---|
| ARE YOU REGISTERING TO PAY USE TAX ONLY? ☐ YES ☐ NO | **TENNESSEE**, ANSWER THE FOLLOWING                     YES   NO |
| **15** WILL YOU BE COLLECTING OVER $200 PER MONTH IN SALES TAX? ☐ YES ☐ NO | a  SELL FROM A MOTOR VEHICLE IN TENN?   ☐ ☐ |
| | DO YOU { b  HAVE A PLACE OF BUSINESS IN TENN?   ☐ ☐ |
| **16** HOW MANY MONTHS OF THE YEAR WILL YOU HAVE SALES AND/OR USE TAX TO REPORT? _____ | c  HAVE REPRESENTATIVES SOLICITING BUSINESS IN TENN?   ☐ ☐ |
| | d  LEASE MOTOR VEHICLES OR OTHER TANGIBLE PERSONAL PROPERTY IN TENN?   ☐ ☐ |

| **17** THE STATEMENTS MADE ON THIS APPLICATION ARE TRUE TO THE BEST OF MY KNOWLEDGE AND BELIEF (THIS **APPLICATION MUST BE SIGNED BY THE INDIVIDUAL OWNER, A PARTNER, OR AN OFFICER OF THE CORPORATION.**) | FOR DEPARTMENT USE ONLY |
|---|---|
| **SIGN HERE ▶** _____ OWNER, PARTNER, OR OFFICER (DO NOT PRINT OR USE STAMP) | |
| TITLE          DATE | |

13 001 0321          RV - 0462 (REV 4-90)

# CODES FOR BUSINESS ACTIVITY AND PRINCIPAL PRODUCT OR SERVICE

Using the list below (1) Find the underlined industry group that best describes your principal business activity area. The code that you enter should be for that product or service from which the greatest percentage of your total gross receipts is derived. (2) Find your principal product or service under that industry group. (3) Enter the correct 4-digit code in Item 11. For example, if your principal business is a retail gasoline service station, your code would be 5541. For assistance, call **1-800-342-1003** toll free in Tennessee or, if you are located in the Nashville area or out-of-state, call **615-741-2594.**

## AGRICULTURE, FORESTRY AND FISHING FARMS

| | |
|---|---|
| 0100 | Crop Production |
| 0120 | Field Crop |
| 0150 | Fruit, Tree Nut and Vegetable |
| 0180 | Horticultural Society |
| 0200 | Livestock Production |
| 0230 | Livestock |
| 0270 | Animal Specialty |

## AGRICULTURAL SERVICES AND FORESTRY

| | |
|---|---|
| 0740 | Veterinary Services |
| 0750 | Animal Services, Except Veterinary - |
| 0780 | Landscape and Horticultural Services |
| 0790 | Other Agricultural Services |
| 0800 | Forestry |

## FISHING, HUNTING AND TRAPPING

| | |
|---|---|
| 0900 | Commercial Fishing |
| 0930 | Commercial Fishing, Hatcheries & Preserves |
| 0970 | Hunting, Trapping and Game Propagation |

## MINING

| | |
|---|---|
| 1000 | Metal Mining |
| 1150 | Coal Mining |
| 1300 | Oil and Gas Extraction |
| 1400 | Nonmetallic Minerals Except Fuel |

## CONSTRUCTION
## GENERAL BUILDING CONTRACTORS AND OPERATIVE BUILDERS

| | |
|---|---|
| 1510 | General Building Contractors |
| 1531 | Operative Builders |

## HEAVY CONSTRUCTION CONTRACTORS

| | |
|---|---|
| 1611 | Highway and Street Construction |
| 1620 | Heavy Construction, Except Highway |

## SPECIAL TRADE CONTRACTORS

| | |
|---|---|
| 1711 | Plumbing, Heating and Air Conditioning |
| 1721 | Painting, Paper Hanging and Decorating |
| 1731 | Electrical Contractors |
| 1740 | Masonry, Stonework and Plastering |
| 1750 | Carpentering and Flooring |
| 1761 | Roofing and Sheet Metal Work |
| 1771 | Concrete Work |
| 1781 | Water Well Drilling |
| 1790 | Miscellaneous Special Trade Contractors |

## MANUFACTURING

| | |
|---|---|
| 2000 | Food and Kindred Products |
| 2086 | Bottling Companies |
| 2100 | Tobacco Manufacturers |
| 2200 | Textile Mill Products |
| 2300 | Apparel and Other Textile Products |
| 2400 | Lumber and Wood Products, Except Furniture |
| 2500 | Furniture and Fixtures |
| 2600 | Paper and Allied Products |
| 2700 | Printing, Publishing and Allied Industries |
| 2800 | Chemicals and Allied Products |
| 2900 | Petroleum Refining and Related Industries |
| 3000 | Rubber and Misc. Plastics Products |
| 3100 | Leather and Leather Products |
| 3200 | Stone, Clay, Glass and Concrete Products |
| 3300 | Primary Metal Industries |
| 3400 | Fabricated Metal Products |
| 3500 | Machinery, Except Electrical |
| 3600 | Electrical and Electronic Equipment |
| 3700 | Transportation Equipment |
| 3800 | Measuring, Analyzing & Controlling Instruments |
| 3970 | Other Manufacturing Industries |

## TRANSPORTATION, COMMUNICATION, ELECTRIC, GAS AND SANITARY SERVICES
## LOCAL AND INTERURBAN PASSENGER TRANSIT

| | |
|---|---|
| 4010 | Railroads |
| 4121 | Taxicabs |
| 4189 | Other Passenger Transportation |

## TRUCKING AND WAREHOUSING

| | |
|---|---|
| 4210 | Trucking, Local and Long Distance |
| 4211 | Common Carrier Trucking Companies |
| 4289 | Public Warehousing and Trucking Terminals |

## OTHER TRANSPORTATION INCLUDING TRANSPORTATION SERVICES

| | |
|---|---|
| 4400 | Water Transportation |
| 4440 | Barge Companies |
| 4510 | Airlines |
| 4600 | Pipe Lines, Except Natural Gas |
| 4722 | Passenger Transportation Arrangement |
| 4723 | Freight Transportation Arrangement |
| 4799 | Other Transportation Services |
| 4810 | Telephone Communication |
| 4820 | Telegraph Communication |
| 4830 | Radio and Television Broadcasting |
| 4899 | Other Communication Services |
| 4910 | Electric, Services |
| 4920 | Gas Production and Distribution |
| 4930 | Combination Electric and Gas |
| 4999 | Water, Sanitary, Steam and Other |

## WHOLESALE TRADE
## DURABLE

| | |
|---|---|
| 5010 | Motor Vehicles and Automotive Equipment |
| 5020 | Furniture and Home Furnishing |
| 5030 | Lumber and Construction Materials |
| 5040 | Sporting, Recreational, Photo, Hobby and Toys |
| 5050 | Metals and Minerals, Except Petroleum |
| 5060 | Electrical Goods |
| 5070 | Hardware, Plumbing and Heating Equipment |
| 5081 | Commercial Machines and Equipment |
| 5082 | Construction and Mining Machinery and Equipment |
| 5083 | Farm Machinery and Equipment |
| 5084 | Industrial Machinery and Equipment |
| 5089 | Other Machinery, Equipment and Supplies |
| 5095 | Other Durable Goods |

## NONDURABLE

| | |
|---|---|
| 5110 | Paper and Paper Products |
| 5120 | Drugs, Drug Proprietaries & Druggists' Sundries |
| 5130 | Apparel, Piece Goods and Notions |
| 5140 | Groceries and Related Products |
| 5150 | Farm-Product Raw Materials |
| 5160 | Chemicals and Allied Products |
| 5170 | Petroleum and Petroleum Products |
| 5181 | Beer and Ale |
| 5182 | Wines and Distilled Alcoholic Beverages |
| 5191 | Farm Supplies |
| 5194 | Tobacco and Tobacco Products |
| 5195 | Other Nondurable Goods |

## RETAIL-TRADE
## BUILDING MATERIALS, HARDWARE, GARDEN SUPPLY & MOBILE HOME DEALERS

| | |
|---|---|
| 5210 | Paint, Glass and Wallpaper Stores |
| 5220 | Building Materials Dealers |
| 5251 | Hardware Stores |
| 5261 | Retail Nurseries and Garden Stores |
| 5271 | Mobile Home Dealers |

## GENERAL MERCHANDISE AND DEPARTMENT STORES

| | |
|---|---|
| 5311 | Department Stores |
| 5331 | Variety Stores |
| 5398 | Other General Merchandise Stores |

## FOOD STORES

| | |
|---|---|
| 5411 | Grocery Stores |
| 5420 | Meat and Fish Markets and Freezer Provisioners |
| 5431 | Fruit Stores and Vegetable Markets |
| 5441 | Candy, Nut and Confectionary Stores |
| 5460 | Retail Bakeries |
| 5480 | Other Food Stores |

## AUTOMOTIVE DEALERS AND SERVICE STATIONS

| | |
|---|---|
| 5511 | New and Used Car Dealers |
| 5521 | Used Car Dealers |
| 5531 | Auto and Home Supply Stores |
| 5541 | Gasoline Service Stations |
| 5580 | Boat, Aircraft and Other Automotive Dealers |

## APPAREL AND ACCESSORY STORES

| | |
|---|---|
| 5611 | Men's and Boy's Clothing and Furnishings |
| 5621 | Women's Ready to Wear Stores |
| 5631 | Women's Accessory and Specialty Stores |
| 5641 | Childrens and Infant Wear Stores |
| 5651 | Family Clothing Stores |
| 5661 | Shoe Stores |
| 5681 | Furriers and Fur Shops |
| 5698 | Other Apparel and Accessory Stores |

## FURNITURE, HOME FURNISHING AND EQUIPMENT STORES

| | |
|---|---|
| 5712 | Furniture Stores |
| 5713 | Floor Covering Stores |
| 5718 | Miscellaneous Home Furnishing Stores |
| 5722 | Household Appliance Stores |
| 5732 | Radio and Television Stores |
| 5733 | Music Stores |

## EATING AND DRINKING PLACES

| | |
|---|---|
| 5812 | Eating Places |
| 5813 | Drinking Places |

## MISCELLANEOUS RETAIL STORES

| | |
|---|---|
| 5912 | Drug Stores and Proprietary Store |
| 5921 | Liquor Stores |
| 5931 | Used Merchandise Stores |
| 5941 | Sporting Goods Stores and Bicycle Shops |
| 5942 | Book Stores |
| 5943 | Stationary Stores |
| 5944 | Jewelry Stores |
| 5945 | Hobby, Toy and Game Shops |
| 5946 | Camera and Photographic Supply Stores |
| 5947 | Gift, Novelty and Souvenir Shops |
| 5948 | Luggage and Leather Good Stores |
| 5949 | Sewing, Needlework and Piece Goods Stores |
| 5961 | Mail Order Houses |
| 5962 | Merchandising Machine Operators |
| 5963 | Direct Selling Organizations |
| 5980 | Fuel and Ice Dealers |
| 5984 | Liquified Petroleum Gas (Bottled Gas) |
| 5992 | Florists |
| 5993 | Cigar Stores and Stands |
| 5996 | Other Miscellaneous Retail Stores |

## FINANCE, INSURANCE AND REAL ESTATE

| | |
|---|---|
| 6000 | Banking |
| 6100 | Credit Agencies Other Than Banks |

**CONTINUED ON REVERSE SIDE**

## SECURITY, COMMODITY BROKERS, DEALERS, EXCHANGES AND SERVICES

| | |
|---|---|
| 6200 | Security and Commodity Brokers |
| 6212 | Security Underwriting Syndicates |
| 6218 | Security Brokers and Dealers, Except Underwriting Syndicate |
| 6299 | Commodity Contracts Brokers and Dealers, Security and Commodity Exchanges and Allied Services |
| 6300 | Insurance Carriers |
| 6411 | Insurance Agents, Brokers and Services |

## REAL ESTATE

| | |
|---|---|
| 6500 | Real Estate |
| 6511 | Real Estate Operators (Except Developers) and Lessors of Buildings |
| 6520 | Lessors of Real Property Other Than Buildings |
| 6531 | Real Estate Agents, Brokers and Managers |
| 6541 | Title Abstract Offices |
| 6552 | Subdividers and Developers Except Cemeteries |
| 6553 | Cemetery Subdividers and Developers |
| 6611 | Combined Real Estate, Insurance, Loans and Law Offices |

## HOLDING AND OTHER INVESTMENT COMPANIES

| | |
|---|---|
| 6746 | Investment Clubs |
| 6747 | Common Trust Funds |
| 6748 | Other Holding and Investment Companies |

## SERVICES
## HOTELS AND OTHER LODGING PLACES

| | |
|---|---|
| 7011 | Hotels, Motels and Tourist Courts |
| 7032 | Sporting and Recreational Camps |
| 7033 | Trailer Parks and Campsites |
| 7089 | Other Lodging Places |

## PERSONAL SERVICES

| | |
|---|---|
| 7215 | Coin-Operated Laundries and Dry Cleaning |
| 7219 | Other Laundry, Cleaning and Garment Services |
| 7221 | Photographic Studios, Portrait |
| 7231 | Beauty Shops |
| 7241 | Barber Shops |
| 7251 | Shoe Repair and Hat Cleaning Shops |
| 7261 | Funeral Services and Crematories |
| 7299 | Miscellaneous Personal Services |

## BUSINESS SERVICES

| | |
|---|---|
| 7310 | Advertising |
| 7320 | Consumer Credit Reporting Agencies |
| 7332 | Blue Printing and Photo Copying Services |
| 7333 | Commercial Photography, Art and Graphics |
| 7340 | Services To Buildings |
| 7360 | Personnel Supply Services |
| 7370 | Computer and Data Processing Services |
| 7392 | Management, Consulting & Public Relations Services |
| 7394 | Equipment Rental and Leasing |
| 7395 | Photo Finishing Laboratories |
| 7398 | Other Business Services |

## AUTOMOTIVE REPAIR AND SERVICES

| | |
|---|---|
| 7510 | Automotive Rentals and Leasing, Without Drivers |
| 7520 | Automobile Parking |
| 7531 | Automobile Top and Body Repair Shops |
| 7538 | General Automotive Repair Shops |
| 7539 | Other Automotive Repair Shop |
| 7540 | Automotive Services, Except Repair |

## MISCELLANEOUS REPAIR SERVICES

| | |
|---|---|
| 7622 | Radio and TV Repair Shops |
| 7628 | Electrical Repair Shops, Except Radio and TV |
| 7631 | Watch, Clock and Jewelry Repair |
| 7641 | Reupholstery and Furniture Repair |
| 7692 | Welding Repair |
| 7699 | Other Miscellaneous Repair Shops |

| | |
|---|---|
| 7812 | Motion Picture Production, Distribution & Services |
| 7830 | Motion Picture Theaters |

| | |
|---|---|
| 7920 | Producers, Orchestras and Entertainers |
| 7932 | Billiard and Pool Establishments |
| 7933 | Bowling Alleys |
| 7999 | Other Amusement and Recreational Services |

| | |
|---|---|
| 8011 | Offices of Physicians |
| 8021 | Offices of Dentists |
| 8031 | Offices of Osteopathic Physicians |
| 8041 | Offices of Chiropractors |
| 8042 | Offices of Optometrists |
| 8048 | Other Health Practitioners |
| 8050 | Nursing and Personal Care Facilities |
| 8060 | Hospitals |
| 8071 | Medical Laboratories |
| 8072 | Dental Laboratories |
| 8098 | Other Medical and Health Services |

## OTHER SERVICES

| | |
|---|---|
| 8111 | Legal Services |
| 8200 | Educational Services |
| 8211 | Elementary and Secondary Schools |
| 8300 | Social Services |
| 8400 | Museums and Art Galleries |
| 8600 | Membership Organizations |
| 8911 | Engineering and Architectural Services |
| 8930 | Accounting, Auditing and Bookkeeping Services |
| 8932 | Certified Public Accountants |
| 8933 | Other Accounting, Auditing and Bookkeeping Services |
| 8999 | Other Services, Not Elsewhere Classified |

DES 210 1
ES-0265
(Rev. 8 89)

**SAMPLE**

**EMPLOYER STATUS**
**TN DEPT. OF EMPLOYMENT SEC.**
**NASHVILLE, TN 37245-3555**
615-741-2486

**REPORT TO DETERMINE STATUS**
**APPLICATION FOR EMPLOYER NUMBER**

**1.** Enter Federal Number, Business Name & Address

Federal No.

Name

Address

| OFFICIAL USE ONLY | | | | |
|---|---|---|---|---|
| Tenn. I.D. No. | M. No. | S.I.C. | County | Area |
| Liab. Org. | Date Liab. | First Emp | | |
| Rate | Q/Y | Comp. T/L | Memo Date | R.O.C. |
| Previous No. | FAC | | | Verified By |

**2.** **A. PHYSICAL ADDRESS** in Tennessee if different from above:

_____ COMPANY PHONE _____

**3.** **A.** Circle type of Organization   Corporation   Individual   Partnership   Other, Explain_____

**NOTE:** If your organization is exempt from Federal Income Taxes under Section 50 1(C) (3) of IRS Code, attach copy of letter of exemption.

**B.** Name of Owner, Partners or Corporate Officers   Title   Social Security Number   Residential Address & Phone

**C.** Name of person responsible for payroll records _____ Phone _____
Address If different from above _____

**D.** If an out of state corporation, give name and address of Agent for Process in Tennessee.
NAME_____ ADDRESS_____ PHONE _____

**4.** **A.** Number of workers in Tennessee_____
**B.** Date you first employed a worker in Tennessee._____
**C.** Date you first paid a worker in Tennessee. _____

**D.** Are you presently reporting for U. I. purposes in another state?
Yes_____ No_____ If yes, which state _____
Which years _____
**E.** If a Corporation, give Date and State of Incorporation.
DATE_____ STATE_____

**5.** Have you previously had an account with this department? Yes____ No____ Account Number _____

NOTE: If the organization, trade or business of another employer was acquired, Section 10, on the reverse side of this form must be completed.

**FAILURE TO COMPLETE SECTION 10 COULD RESULT IN SUBSTANTIAL PENALTY CHARGES.**

**6.** **REGULAR BUSINESS EMPLOYMENT**

**A.** Have you employed or do you expect to employ at least ONE worker in twenty different calendar weeks during a calendar year? _____ Yes ____ No
If yes, give earliest month and year the twentieth week occurred (will occur).   MONTH _____ YEAR _____

**B.** Have you had or do you expect to have a quarterly payroll of $1,500 or more? _____Yes _____No
If yes, give earliest quarter and year this occurred (will occur).   QUARTER _____ YEAR _____

**7.** **HOUSEHOLD EMPLOYMENT:**   Have you had or do you expect to have a $1,000 quarterly payroll for domestic services? _____Yes ____ No
If yes, give earliest quarter and year this occurred (will occur).   QUARTER _____ YEAR _____

**8.** **AGRICULTURAL EMPLOYMENT:**

**A.** Have you employed or do you expect to employ at least ten or more agricultural workers in some part of a day in twenty different weeks during a calendar year?____Yes ____No   If yes, give earliest quarter and year this occurred (will occur)   QUARTER _____ YEAR _____

**B.** Have you had or do you expect to have a quarterly payroll of $20,000 or more?___Yes ____No
If yes, give earliest quarter and year this occurred (will occur)   QUARTER _____ YEAR _____

**9.** Enter below amount of total payroll for each quarter in which you have had employment or if you have not yet had a complete quarterly payroll, indicate the amount you expect it to be.

| YEAR | JAN-MARCH | APRIL-JUNE | JULY-SEPT | OCT-DEC | YEAR | JAN-MARCH | APRIL-JUNE | JULY-SEPT | OCT-DEC |
|---|---|---|---|---|---|---|---|---|---|
| 19___ | | | | | 19___ | | | | |

If you answered yes in any one of the questions 4(d), 6, 7, or 8, you are liable for unemployment insurance premiums based on the first $7,000 ($6,000 for years prior to 1983) paid each employee per year.

SIGNATURE _____ TITLE _____ DATE _____

Must be owner, partner, or officer of the corporation.

**PLEASE COMPLETE REVERSE SIDE**

10. TCA 50-7-403 (b)(5) states that any successor, controlled either directly or indirectly by any individual, type of organization, or employing unit having a commonality of beneficial interests as those of the predecessor will be considered the same party of interest as the predecessor and will acquire the experience rating factors and liabilities of the predecessor employer. Otherwise, if you wish to succeed to the experience rating record of the predecessor account, form DES 226.13 must be submitted no later than the end of the quarter following the quarter in which the acquisition occurred. ( This provision becomes effective 1-1-85. )

(A) Name and address of predecessor employer _____

(B) Account Number of predecessor employer _____

(C) Date of acquisition _____

(D) Did you acquire all of your predecessor's business in Tennessee? Yes _____ No _____     If No, what percentage did you acquire?     _____ %

(E) Did your predecessor continue in business in Tennessee? Yes _____ No _____

(F) Did you previously have an interest in the business acquired or are you related to a previous owner by blood or marriage?     Yes _____ No _____
If yes, please explain.

_____

_____

## FAILURE TO COMPLETE THIS SECTION COULD RESULT IN A HIGHER PREMIUM RATE.

This section will be used to insure proper industrial classification of your establishment(s). Please provide detailed information in the appropriate spaces below. Failure to fully complete this section will greatly delay the processing of your records.

List below the trade name, Tennessee County and nature of business of each establishment to be reported under the Account Number being requested in Item Number 1 on the front of this form.

| Trade Name | County | Nature of Business | Average Number of Employees |
|---|---|---|---|
| | | | |
| | | | |

Check the block which describes the nature of your business in Tennessee and state the principal product produced or activity (sales or service) performed. If you are engaged in more than one activity, specify which is the primary activity, product sold or service rendered.

MINING & QUARRYING type
(Examples: sand & gravel, crushed limestone, metals)

CONSTRUCTION type _____
(Examples: residential buildings, commercial bldgs., highways, bridges, electrical, plumbing, installations, paving)

MANUFACTURING product produced _____

Note:
If primarily engaged in manufacturing, indicate in order of importance the principal product produced, materials used, and the estimated percentage of the total value of each product produced. Was material used produced in this establishment?

YES _____     NO ☐

| Products | Materials or Process Used | % of Value |
|---|---|---|
| | | |
| | | |
| | | |

[ ] TRANSPORTATION, COMMUNICATION & PUBLIC UTILITIES Type _____

[ ] WHOLESALE TRADE - principal product to be resold _____

[ ] RETAIL TRADE principal product sold _____

[ ] FINANCE, INSURANCE, REAL ESTATE - Type of establishment _____
(Examples: bank, savings and loan, personal loan, life insurance carrier, insurance agency, real estate broker, holding company, investments)

[ ] SERVICES service performed _____
(Examples: motel, laundry, beauty shop, auto repair, appliance repair, doctor, attorney, school, hospital)

[ ] PUBLIC ADMINISTRATION
(Examples: government, administration of human resource, environmental, economic programs, national security)

Other - Specify _____

_____

Most of your products sold or service rendered to [ ] General Public [ ] Business: Specify type [ ] Other: specify _____

# You'll get at least 5 new ideas the day you start this book

We were impressed! In our world of business publishing, we sometimes see the unusual. A book so well conceived and well written, that it gives you, the reader, value in ways you would never expect.

*The Successful Business Plan* by Rhonda M. Abrams is a great example.

Here's why we think this new book is a "must-get" for your business. First, it's a very readable book about raising your payoff chances, whether you are *already in business, just starting, or looking for financing*. Ms. Abrams is a working specialist in these areas, and her clients *know* planning pays off.

Second, by actively planning, you are giving your dream every reason to work. In fact, research shows that new venture success rates and focused planning are very closely connected.

Third, *The Successful Business Plan* will give you the same planning advantage enjoyed by over 20,000 entrepreneurs already using it. (The first printing has completely sold out.)

See for yourself. It's your business, and we want you to succeed. You might say our success depends on it.

**– The Editors at Oasis Press, PSI Research**

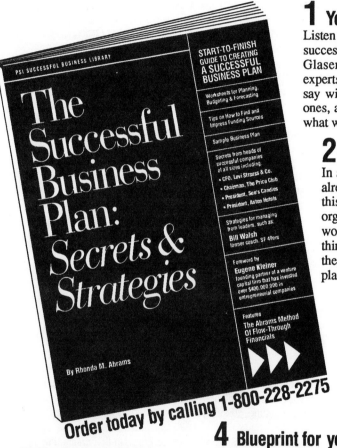

Order today by calling 1-800-228-2275

## 1 You get expert help
Listen in, as Rhonda M. Abrams interviews some of today's most successful business owners and managers. Bill Walsh, Nancy E. Glaser, Eugene Kleiner, and a dozen more. 159 tips from 15 experts reveal tested ideas and business secrets. What they have to say will help you get new customers, do more with your present ones, and run your operation with more profit. Straight talk about what works in a business today. These ideas will work for you too.

## 2 Worksheets make it easy
In a business, two of your most important assets are what you already know, and what you can find out. The 72 worksheets in this book are packed with questions designed to draw out and organize your ideas. This lets you bring them out and get them working. What's more, the sheets are great at helping you find things you *need* to know. It's easy. The questions are worded so they show you what to look for. You're not just reading about planning. You are right there, working to make it happen.

## 3 You get the whole picture
Every chapter of *The Successful Business Plan* is rich in detailed help. Marketing. Sales. Operations. Competition. Financials. Plus retail, service, manufacturing and more. All of it laid out so the author and the experts work right with you, to plan each step. The effect on your competitive edge will make you glad you got this book. Buy yourself an extra highlighter for the first time you read it.

## 4 Blueprint for your success
Planning and business success go together. No question. Why not start today? Link results-oriented planning to *your* business, using the secrets and strategies revealed here. No dry theory to wade through. Just 327 pages of the ideas and planning help you need to start, and stay successful in business. Year after year.

### About Rhonda M. Abrams
Educated at both UCLA and Harvard, Ms. Abrams heads a west coast management consulting firm. Her common sense approach to problem solving has made *The Successful Business Plan* as readable as it is powerful. Over 11 months of writing, two hundred hours of interviews, and Ms. Abrams' years of experience make this new book the best for business planning today.

Her comment? *"No other work propels you as far forward in your enterprise as building your plan of action."* © 1992 Publishing Services Inc.

---

**YES! Send me *The Successful Business Plan: Secrets & Strategies*  Paperbound $21.95**

Name _____  Title _____

Company _____  Phone _____

Street Address _____

City/State/Zip _____

☐ Check payable to PSI Research (With a check, UPS ground shipping is free within the Continental U.S.A.)

☐ Charge to my: ☐ VISA ☐ MASTERCARD ☐ AMEX ☐ DISCOVER  SO1

Card Number: _____ Expires: _____

Name on card: _____ Signature: _____

**PSI Research  300 N. Valley Drive, Grants Pass, OR 97526  800-228 2275  FAX: 503-476-1479**

# Gain the power of increased knowledge — Oasis is your source.

## Acquiring Outside Capital

**Financing Your Small Business**

 *Book*

Essential techniques to successfully identify, approach, attract, and manage sources of financing. Shows how to gain the full benefits of debt financing while minimizing its risks. Outlines all types of financing and walks you step by step through the process, from evaluating short-term credit options, through negotiating a long-term loan, to deciding whether to go public.

**The Loan Package**

 *Book*

Preparatory package for a business loan proposal. Worksheets help analyze cash needs and articulate business focus. Includes sample forms for balance sheets, income statements, projections, and budget reports. Screening sheets rank potential lenders to shorten the time involved in getting the loan.

**Venture Capital Proposal Package**
*Book*

Structures a proposal to secure venture capital. Checklists gather material for required sections: market analyses, income projections, financial statements, management team, strategic marketing plan, etc. Gives tips on understanding, finding, and screening potential investors.

**Financial Templates**
*Software for IBM-PC & Macintosh*

Software speeds business calculations including those in PSI's workbooks, *The Loan Package, Venture Capital Proposal Package, Negotiating the Purchase or Sale of a Business, The Successful Business Plan: Secrets & Strategies*. Includes 40 financial templates including various projections, statements, ratios, histories, amortizations, and cash flows. *Requires Lotus 1-2-3, Microsoft Excel 2.0 or higher, Supercalc 5, or Lotus compatible spreadsheet and 512 RAM plus hard disk or two floppy drives.*

## Managing Employees

**A Company Policy and Personnel Workbook**

 *Book*

Saves costly consultant or staff hours in creating company personnel policies. Provides model policies on topics such as employee safety, leave of absence, flextime, smoking, substance abuse, sexual harassment, performance improvement, grievance procedure. For each subject, practical and legal ramifications are explained, then a choice of alternate policies presented.

**A Company Policy and Personnel Workbook**
*Software for IBM-PC & Macintosh*

The policies in *A Company Policy and Personnel Workbook* are on disk so the company's name, specific information, and any desired changes or rewrites can be incorporated using your own word processor to tailor the model policies to suit your company's specific needs before printing out a complete manual for distribution to employees. *Requires a word processor and hard disk and floppy drive.*

**People Investment: How to Make Your Hiring Decisions Pay Off for Everyone**
*Book — available September 1992*

Makes the hiring process easier for small business owners. Clarifies the processes of determining personnel needs; establishing job descriptions that satisfy legal requirements; and advertising for, selecting, and keeping good people. Over 40 worksheets help forecast staffing needs, define each job, recruit employees, and train staff.

**Managing People: A Practical Guide**

 *Book*

Focuses on developing the art of working with people to maximize the productivity and satisfaction of both manager and employees. Discussions, exercises, and self-tests boost skills in communicating, delegating, motivating, developing teams, goal-setting, adapting to change, and coping with stress.

**Safety Law Compliance Manual for California Businesses**

 *Book plus optional binder for your company's safety program*

Now every California employer must have an Injury and Illness Prevention Program that meets the specific requirements of Senate Bill 198. Already thousands of citations have been issued to companies who did not comply with all seven components of the complicated new law. Avoid fines by using this guide to set up a program that will meet Cal/OSHA standards. Includes forms.

***Also available — Company Illness and Injury Prevention Program Binder*** — Pre-organized and ready-to-use with forms, tabs, logs and sample documents. Saves your company time, work, and worry.

## Mail Order

**Mail Order Legal Manual**

 *Book*

For companies that use the mail to market their products or services, as well as for mail order businesses, this book clarifies complex regulations so penalties can be avoided. Gives state-by-state legal requirements, plus information on Federal Trade Commission guidelines and rules covering delivery dates, advertising, sales taxes, unfair trade practices, and consumer protection.

**Why hesitate?** If any product you order doesn't meet your needs, just return it for full refund or credit. 800-228-2275.

# Proven tools and ideas to expand your business.

## Marketing & Public Relations

**EXECARDS®**
*Business Communication Tools*

EXECARDS, the original business-to-business message cards, help build and maintain personal business relationships with customers and prospects. Distinctive in size and quality, EXECARDS get through even when other mail is tossed. An effective alternative to telephone tag. Time-saving EXECARDS come in a variety of handsome styles and messages. Excellent for thanking clients, following up between orders, prospecting, and announcing new products, services, or special offers. *Please call for complete catalog.*

**How To Develop & Market Creative Business Ideas**

 *Book*

Step-by-step manual guides the inventor through all stages of new product development. Discusses patenting your invention, trademarks, copyrights, and how to construct your prototype. Gives information on financing, distribution, test marketing, and finding licensees. Plus, lists many useful sources for prototype resources, trade shows, funding, and more.

**Marketing Your Products and Services Successfully**

 *Book*

Helps small businesses understand marketing concepts, then plan and follow through with the actions that will result in increased sales. Covers all aspects from identifying the target market, through market research, establishing pricing, creating a marketing plan, evaluating media alternatives, to launching a campaign. Discusses customer maintenance techniques and international marketing.

**Customer Profile and Retrieval (CPR)**
*Software for IBM-PC & compatibles*

Stores details of past activities plus future reminders on customers, clients, contacts, vendors, and employees, then gives instant access to that information when needed. "Tickler" fields keep reminders of dates for recontacts. "Type" fields categorize names for sorting as the user defines. "Other data" fields store information such as purchase and credit history, telephone call records, or interests.

Has massive storage capabilities. Holds up to 255 lines of comments for each name, plus unlimited time and date stamped notes. Features perpetual calendar, and automatic telephone dialing. Built-in word processing and merge gives the ability to pull in the information already keyed into the fields into form or individual letters. Prints mail labels, rotary file cards, and phone directories. *Requires a hard disk, 640K RAM and 80 column display. (Autodial feature requires modem.)*

**Publicity and Public Relations Guide for Businesses**

 *Book*

Overview of how to promote a business by using advertising, publicity, and public relations. Especially for business owners and managers who choose to have promotional activities carried out by in-house staff rather than outside specialists. Includes worksheets for a public relations plan, news releases, editorial article, and a communications schedule.

**Cost-Effective Market Analysis**

 *Book*

Workbook explains how a small business can conduct its own market research. Shows how to set objectives, determine which techniques to use, create a schedule, and then monitor expenses. Encompasses primary research (trade shows, telephone interviews, mail surveys), plus secondary research (using available information in print).

## International Business

**Export Now**

 *Book*

Prepares a business to enter the export market. Clearly explains the basics, then articulates specific requirements for export licensing, preparation of documents, payment methods, packaging, and shipping. Includes advice on evaluating foreign representatives, planning international marketing strategies, and discovering official U.S. policy for various countries and regions. Lists sources.

**EXECARDS®**
*International Communication Cards*

EXECARDS offer unique cards you can send to businesspeople of many nationalities to help build and maintain lasting relationships. One distinguished EXECARD choice is a richly textured and embossed white card of substantial quality that expresses thank you in thirteen languages; Japanese, Russian, French, Chinese, Arabic, German, Swahili, Italian, Polish, Spanish, Hebrew, and Swedish, as well as English. Another handsome option is an ivory card with thank you embossed in Russian and English. To each, you can add a personal note or order a custom printed message. *Please call for more information.*

**Give yourself & your business every chance to succeed. Order the business tools you need today. Call 800-228-2275.**

# Unique cards get you noticed. Books & software save you time.

## Business Communications

**Proposal Development: How to Respond and Win the Bid**

 Book

Orchestrates a successful proposal from preliminary planning to clinching the deal. Shows by explanation and example how to: determine what to include; create text, illustrations, tables, exhibits, and appendices; how to format (using either traditional methods or desktop publishing); meet the special requirements of government proposals; set up and follow a schedule.

**Write Your Own Business Contracts**

 Book

Explains the "do's"and "don'ts" of contract writing so any person in business can do the preparatory work in drafting contracts before hiring an attorney for final review. Gives a working knowledge of the various types of business agreements, plus tips on how to prepare for the unexpected.

**Complete Book of Business Forms**

 Book

Over 200 reproducible forms for all types of business needs: personnel, employment, finance, production flow, operations, sales, marketing, order entry, and general administration. Time-saving, uniform, coordinated way to record and locate important business information.

**EXECARDS®**
Communication Tools

EXECARDS, business-to-business message cards, are an effective vehicle for maintaining personal contacts in this era of rushed, highly-technical communications. A card takes only seconds and a few cents to send, but can memorably tell customers, clients, prospects, or co-workers that their relationship is valued. Many styles and messages to choose from for thanking, acknowledging, inviting, reminding, prospecting, following up, etc. *Please call for complete catalog.*

**PlanningTools™**
Paper pads, 3-hole punched

Handsome PlanningTools help organize thoughts and record notes, actions, plans, and deadlines, so important information and responsibilities do not get lost or forgotten. Specific PlanningTools organize different needs, such as Calendar Notes, Progress/Activity Record, Project Plan/Record, Week's Priority Planner, Make-A-Month Calendar, and Milestone Chart. *Please call for catalog.*

**Customer Profile & Retrieval (CPR)**
Software for IBM-PC & compatibles

Easy computer database management program streamlines the process of communicating with clients, customers, vendors, contacts, and employees. While talking to your contact on the phone (or at any time), all notes of past activities and conversations can be viewed instantly, and new notes can be added at that time. *Please see description under "Marketing & Public Relations" section on previous page.*

## Business Relocation

**Company Relocation Handbook: Making the Right Move**

 Book

Comprehensive guide to moving a business. Begins with defining objectives for moving and evaluating whether relocating will actually solve more problems than it creates. Worksheets compare prospective locations, using rating scales for physical plant, equipment, personnel, and geographic considerations. Sets up a schedule for dealing with logistics.

## Retirement Planning

**Retirement & Estate Planning Handbook**

 Book

Do-it-yourself workbook for setting up a retirement plan that can easily be maintained and followed. Covers establishing net worth, retirement goals, budgets, and a plan for asset acquisition, preservation, and growth. Discusses realistic expectations for Social Security, Medicare, and health care alternatives. Features special sections for business owners.

## Career Recordkeeping

**Career Builder**

 Book

This workbook collects all of an individual's career-related data in one place for quick access. From educational details, through work history, health records, reference lists, correspondence awards, passports, etc., to personal insurance policies, real estate, securities and bank accounts, this manual keeps it all organized. Gives tips on successful resumés.

**Need it tomorrow? In most cases that's possible if you order before noon, PST. Just give us a call at 800-228-2275.**

# Step-by-step techniques for generating more profit.

## Financial Management

**Financial Management Techniques for Small Business**

*Book*

Clearly reveals the essential ingredients of sound financial management in detail. By monitoring trends in your financial activities, you will be able to uncover potential problems before they become crises. You'll understand why you can be making a profit and still not have the cash to meet expenses, and you'll learn the steps to change your business' cash behavior to get more return for your effort.

**Risk Analysis: How to Reduce Insurance Costs**

*Book*

Straightforward advice on shopping for insurance, understanding types of coverage, comparing proposals and premium rates. Worksheets help identify and weigh the risks a particular business is likely to face, then determine if any of those might be safely self-insured or eliminated. Request for proposal form helps businesses avoid over-paying for protection.

**Debt Collection: Strategies for the Small Business**

*Book*

Practical tips on how to turn receivables into cash. Worksheets and checklists help businesses establish credit policies, track accounts, and flag when it is necessary to bring in a collection agency, attorney, or go to court. This book advises how to deal with disputes, negotiate settlements, win in small claims court, and collect on judgments. Gives examples of telephone collection techniques and collection letters.

**Negotiating the Purchase or Sale of a Business**

*Book*

Prepares a business buyer or seller for negotiations that will achieve win-win results. Shows how to determine the real worth of a business, including intangible assets such as "goodwill." Over 36 checklists and worksheets on topics such as tax impact on buyers and sellers, escrow checklist, cash flow projections, evaluating potential buyers, financing options, and many others.

**Financial Accounting Guide for Small Business**

*Book*

Makes understanding the economics of business simple. Explains the basic accounting principles that relate to any business. Step-by-step instructions for generating accounting statements and interpreting them, spotting errors, and recognizing warning signs. Discusses how banks and other creditors view financial statements.

**Controlling Your Company's Freight Costs**

*Book*

Shows how to increase company profits by trimming freight costs. Provides tips for comparing alternative methods and shippers, then negotiating contracts to receive the most favorable discounts. Tells how to package shipments for safe transport. Discusses freight insurance and dealing with claims for loss or damage. Appendices include directory of U.S. ports, shipper's guide, and sample bill of lading.

**Accounting Software Analysis**

*Book*

Presents successful step-by-step procedure for choosing the most appropriate software to handle the accounting for your business. Evaluation forms and worksheets create a custom software "shopping list" to match against features of various products, so facts, not sales hype, can determine the best fit for your company.

**Financial Templates**
*Software for IBM-PC & Macintosh*

Calculates and graphs many business "what-if" scenarios and financial reports. Forty financial templates such as income statements, cash flow, and balance sheet comparisons, break-even analyses, product contribution comparisons, market share, net present value, sales model, *pro formas*, loan payment projections, etc. *Requires 512K RAM hard disk or two floppy drives, plus Lotus 1-2-3 or compatible spreadsheet program.*

---

**Yes, we accept credit cards — VISA, MasterCard, American Express, Discover, or your personal or business check.**

# Get business tips from over 157 seasoned experts.

## Business Formation and Planning

### The Successful Business Plan: Secrets & Strategies

*Book*

Start-to-finish guide to creating a successful business plan. Includes tips from venture capitalists, bankers, and successful CEOs. Features worksheets for ease in planning and budgeting with the Abrams Method of Flow-Through Financials. Gives a sample business plan, plus specialized help for retailers, service companies, manufacturers, and in-house corporate plans. Also tells how to find funding sources.

### Starting and Operating a Business In... series
*Book available for each state in the United States, plus District of Columbia*

One-stop resource to current federal and state laws and regulations that affect businesses. Clear "human language" explanations of complex issues, plus samples of government forms, and sources for additional help or information. Helps seasoned business owners keep up with changing legislation, and guides new entrepreneurs step-by-step to start and run the business. Includes many checklists and worksheets to organize ideas, create action plans, and project financial scenarios.

### Starting and Operating a Business: U.S. Edition
*Set of eleven binders*

The complete encyclopedia of how to do business in the U.S. Describes laws and regulations for each state, plus Washington, D.C., as well as the federal government. Includes lists of sources of help, plus post cards for requesting materials from government agencies. This set is valuable for businesses with locations or marketing activities in several states, plus franchisors, attorneys, and other consultants.

### The Essential Corporation Handbook

*Book*

This comprehensive reference for small business corporations in all 50 states and Washington, D.C. explains the legal requirements for maintaining a corporation in good standing. Features many sample corporate documents which are annotated by the author to show what to look for and what to look out for. Tells how to avoid personal liability as an officer, director, or shareholder.

### Surviving and Prospering in a Business Partnership

*Book*

From evaluation of potential partners, through the drafting of agreements, to day-to-day management of working relationships, this book helps avoid classic partnership catastrophes. Discusses how to set up the partnership to reduce the financial and emotional consequences of unanticipated disputes, dishonesty, divorce, disability, or death of a partner.

### California Corporation Formation Package and Minute Book *Book and software*

  *for IBM & Mac*

Provides forms required for incorporating and maintaining closely held corporations, including: articles of incorporation; bylaws; stock certificates, stock transfer record sheets, bill of sale agreement; minutes form; plus many others. Addresses questions on fees, timing, notices, regulations, election of directors and other critical factors. Software has minutes, bylaws, and articles of incorporation already for you to edit and customize (using your own word processor).

### Franchise Bible: A Comprehensive Guide

*Book*

Complete guide to franchising for prospective franchisees or for business owners considering franchising their business. Includes actual sample documents, such as a complete offering circular, plus worksheets for evaluating franchise companies, locations, and organizing information before seeing an attorney. This book is helpful for lawyers as well as their clients.

### How To Develop & Market Creative Business Ideas

*Book*

Step-by-step manual guides the inventor through all stages of new product development. Discusses patenting your invention, trademarks, copyrights, and how to construct your prototype. Gives information on financing, distribution, test marketing, and finding licensees. Plus, lists many useful sources for prototype resources, trade shows, funding, and more.

### The Small Business Expert
*Software for IBM-PC & compatibles*

Generates comprehensive custom checklist of the state and federal laws and regulations based on your type and size of business. Allows comparison of doing business in each of the 50 states. Built-in worksheets create outlines for personnel policies, marketing feasibility studies, and a business plan draft. *Requires 256K RAM and hard disk.*

---

**To order these business tools, use the enclosed order form, FAX 503-476-1479 or call us toll-free at 800-228-2275**

## PSI Successful Business Library / Tools for Business Success Order Form (Please fill out other side also)

### BOOKS FROM THE OASIS PRESS® Please check the edition (binder or paperback) of your choice

| TITLE | BINDER | PAPERBACK | QUANTITY | COST |
|---|---|---|---|---|
| **Accounting Software Analysis** | ☐ $ 39.95 | | | |
| **California Corporation Formation Package and Minute Book** | ☐ $ 39.95 | ☐ $ 29.95 | | |
| **Career Builder** | ☐ $ 34.95 | ☐ $ 12.95 | | |
| **A Company Policy and Personnel Workbook** | ☐ $ 49.95 | ☐ $ 29.95 | | |
| **Company Relocation Handbook** | ☐ $ 49.95 | ☐ $ 19.95 | | |
| **Complete Book of Business Forms** | ☐ $ 49.95 | ☐ $ 19.95 | | |
| **Controlling Your Company's Freight Costs** | ☐ $ 39.95 | | | |
| **Cost-Effective Market Analysis** | ☐ $ 39.95 | | | |
| **Debt Collection: Strategies for the Small Business** | ☐ $ 39.95 | ☐ $ 17.95 | | |
| **The Essential Corporation Handbook** | | ☐ $ 19.95 | | |
| **Export Now** | ☐ $ 39.95 | ☐ $ 19.95 | | |
| **Financial Accounting Guide For Small Business** | ☐ $ 39.95 | | | |
| **Financial Management Techniques For Small Business** | ☐ $ 39.95 | ☐ $ 19.95 | | |
| **Financing Your Small Business** | | ☐ $ 19.95 | | |
| **Franchise Bible: A Comprehensive Guide** | ☐ $ 49.95 | ☐ $ 19.95 | | |
| **How to Develop & Market Creative Business Ideas** | | ☐ $ 14.95 | | |
| **The Loan Package** | ☐ $ 39.95 | | | |
| **Mail Order Legal Manual** | ☐ $ 45.00 | | | |
| **Managing People: A Practical Guide** | ☐ $ 49.95 | ☐ $ 19.95 | | |
| **Marketing Your Products and Services Successfully** | ☐ $ 39.95 | ☐ $ 18.95 | | |
| **Negotiating the Purchase or Sale of a Business** | ☐ $ 39.95 | ☐ $ 18.95 | | |
| **People Investment: How to Make Your Hiring Decisions Pay Off for Everyone** | ☐ $ 49.95 | ☐ $ 19.95 | | |
| **Proposal Development: How to Respond and Win the Bid** (HARDBACK BOOK) | ☐ $ 39.95 | | | |
| **Publicity & Public Relations Guide For Businesses** | ☐ $ 39.95 | | | |
| **Retirement & Estate Planning Handbook** | ☐ $ 49.95 | ☐ $ 19.95 | | |
| **Risk Analysis: How To Reduce Insurance Costs** | ☐ $ 39.95 | ☐ $ 18.95 | | |
| **Safety Law Compliance Manual for California Businesses** | | ☐ $ 24.95 | | |
| **Company Illness & Injury Prevention Program Binder** (OR GET **KIT** WITH BOOK AND BINDER $49.95) | ☐ $ 34.95 | ☐ $ 49.95 BOOK & BINDER KIT | | |
| **Starting and Operating A Business in...** BOOK INCLUDES FEDERAL SECTION PLUS ONE STATE SECTION → | ☐ $ 29.95 | ☐ $ 21.95 | | |
| PLEASE SPECIFY WHICH STATE(S) YOU WANT: | | | | |
| STATE SECTION ONLY (BINDER NOT INCLUDED) → SPECIFY STATES: | ☐ $ 8.95 | | | |
| U.S. EDITION (FEDERAL SECTION → 50 STATES AND WASHINGTON, D.C. IN 11-BINDER SET) | ☐ $295.00 | | | |
| **Successful Business Plan: Secrets & Strategies** (GET THE BINDER...IT'S A BUSINESS PLAN KIT) | ☐ $ 49.95 | ☐ $ 21.95 | | |
| **Surviving and Prospering in a Business Partnership** | ☐ $ 39.95 | ☐ $ 19.95 | | |
| **Venture Capital Proposal Package** | ☐ $ 39.95 | | | |
| **Write Your Own Business Contracts** (HARDBACK BOOK) | ☐ $ 39.95 | ☐ $ 19.95 | | |

**BOOK TOTAL (Please enter on other side also for grand total)**

### SOFTWARE Please check whether you use Macintosh or 5-1/4" or 3-1/2" Disk for IBM-PC & Compatibles

| TITLE | 5-1/4" IBM Disk | 3-1/2" IBM Disk | MAC | PRICE | QUANTITY | COST |
|---|---|---|---|---|---|---|
| **California Corporation Formation Package Software** | ☐ | ☐ | ☐ | ☐ $ 69.95 | | |
| ★ **California Corporation Formation Binderbook & Software** | ☐ | ☐ | ☐ | ☐ $ 89.95 | | |
| **Company Policy & Personnel Software** | ☐ | ☐ | ☐ | ☐ $ 99.95 | | |
| ★ **Company Policy Binderbook & Software** | ☐ | ☐ | ☐ | ☐ $129.95 | | |
| **Customer Profile & Retrieval: Professional** | ☐ | ☐ | | ☐ $149.95 | | |
| **Financial Templates** | ☐ | ☐ | ☐ | ☐ $ 69.95 | | |
| **The Small Business Expert** | ☐ | ☐ | | ☐ $ 59.95 | | |

**SOFTWARE TOTAL (Please enter on other side also for grand total)**

Please add above totals on other side to complete your order.

SO 4/15/92

## PSI Successful Business Library / Tools for Business Success Order Form (please see other side also)
**Call, Mail or Fax to: PSI Research, 300 North Valley Drive, Grants Pass, OR 97526 USA**
**Order Phone USA (800) 228-2275   Inquiries and International Orders (503) 479-9464   FAX (503) 476-1479**

**Sold to:   PLEASE GIVE STREET ADDRESS NOT P.O. BOX FOR SHIPPING**

Name _____

Title _____

Company _____

Street Address _____

City/State/Zip _____

Daytime Telephone _____

**Ship to:** (if different)   **PLEASE GIVE STREET ADDRESS NOT P.O. BOX FOR SHIPPING**

Name _____

Title _____

Company _____

Street Address _____

City/State/Zip _____

Daytime Telephone _____

**Payment Information:**

☐ Check enclosed payable to PSI Research (When you enclose a check, UPS ground shipping is free within the Continental U.S.A.)

Charge - ☐ VISA  ☐ MASTERCARD  ☐ AMEX  ☐ DISCOVER  Card Number: _____ Expires ____

Signature: _____     Name on card: _____

### EXECARDS — The Proven & Chosen Method of Personal Business Communications

| ITEM | PRICE EACH | QUANTITY | COST |
|------|-----------|----------|------|
| **EXECARDS Thank You Assortment** (12 assorted thank you cards) | $ 12.95 | _____ | _____ |
| **EXECARDS Recognition Assortment** (12 assorted appreciation cards) | $ 12.95 | _____ | _____ |
| **EXECARDS Marketing Assortment** (12 assorted marketing cards) | $ 12.95 | _____ | _____ |
| **EXECARDS TOTAL (Please enter below also for grand total)** | | | **$** |

Many additional options available, including custom imprinting of your company's name, logo or message. Please request a complete catalog.

### PLANNING TOOLS — Action Tracking Note Pads

| ITEM | | NUMBER OF PADS |
|------|---|---------------|
| **Calendar Note Pad** | ☐ 1992 | _____ |
| | ☐ 92/93 | _____ |
| | ☐ 1993 | _____ |
| ☐ **Progress/Activity** | | _____ |
| ☐ **Make-A-Month** | | _____ |
| ☐ **Milestone Chart** | | _____ |
| ☐ **Project Plan/Record** | | _____ |
| ☐ **Week's Priority Planner** | | _____ |
| **Total number of pads** | | _____ |
| **Multiply by unit price:** | x | _____ |
| **PLANNING TOOLS TOTAL** | **$** | _____ |

**UNIT PRICE FOR ANY COMBINATION OF PLANNING TOOLS**

1-9 pads        $3.95 each
10-49 pads     $3.49 each
50 or more pads  $2.98 each

### YOUR GRAND TOTAL

| | |
|---|---|
| **BOOK TOTAL (from other side)** | **$** _____ |
| **SOFTWARE TOTAL (from other side)** | **$** _____ |
| **EXECARDS TOTAL** | **$** _____ |
| **PLANNING TOOLS TOTAL** | **$** _____ |
| **TOTAL ORDER** | **$** _____ |

*Rush service is available. Please call us for details.*

**Please send me:**

_____ **EXECARDS Catalog**

_____ **Oasis Press Software Information**

_____ **Oasis Press Book Information**

SO 4/15/92

# Use this form to register for advance notification of updates, new books and software releases, plus special customer discounts!

Please answer these questions to let us know how our products are working for you, and what we could do to serve you better.

**Title of book or software purchased from us:**_____

**It is a:**
- ☐ Binder book
- ☐ Paperback book
- ☐ Book/software combination
- ☐ Software only

**Rate this product's overall quality of information:**
- ☐ Excellent
- ☐ Good
- ☐ Fair
- ☐ Poor

**Rate the quality of printed materials:**
- ☐ Excellent
- ☐ Good
- ☐ Fair
- ☐ Poor

**Rate the format:**
- ☐ Excellent
- ☐ Good
- ☐ Fair
- ☐ Poor

**Did the product provide what you needed?**
- ☐ Yes ☐ No

**If not, what should be added?**_____
_____
_____
_____
_____

**This product is:**
- ☐ Clear and easy to follow
- ☐ Too complicated
- ☐ Too elementary

**Were the worksheets (if any) easy to use?**
- ☐ Yes ☐ No ☐ N/A

**Should we include:**
- ☐ More worksheets
- ☐ Fewer worksheets
- ☐ No worksheets

**How do you feel about the price?**
- ☐ Lower than expected
- ☐ About right
- ☐ Too expensive

**How many employees are in your company?**
- ☐ Under 10 employees
- ☐ 10 – 50 employees
- ☐ 51 – 99 employees
- ☐ 100 – 250 employees
- ☐ Over 250 employees

**How many people in the city your company is in?**
- ☐ 50,000 – 100,000
- ☐ 100,000 – 500,000
- ☐ 500,000 – 1,000,000
- ☐ Over 1,000,000
- ☐ Rural (under 50,000)

**What is your type of business?**
- ☐ Retail
- ☐ Service
- ☐ Government
- ☐ Manufacturing
- ☐ Distributor
- ☐ Education

**What types of products or services do you sell?**
_____
_____
_____
_____

**What is your position in the company?**
(please check one)
- ☐ Owner
- ☐ Administration
- ☐ Sales/marketing
- ☐ Finance
- ☐ Human resources
- ☐ Production
- ☐ Operations
- ☐ Computer/MIS

**How did you learn about this product?**
- ☐ Recommended by a friend
- ☐ Used in a seminar or class
- ☐ Have used other PSI products
- ☐ Received a mailing
- ☐ Saw in bookstore
- ☐ Saw in library
- ☐ Saw review in:
  - ☐ Newspaper
  - ☐ Magazine
  - ☐ TV/Radio

**Where did you buy this product?**
- ☐ Catalog
- ☐ Bookstore
- ☐ Office supply
- ☐ Consultant
- ☐ Other_____

**Would you purchase other business tools from us?**
- ☐ Yes ☐ No

**If so, which products interest you?**
- ☐ EXECARDS® Communication Tools
- ☐ Books for business
- ☐ Software

**Would you recommend this product to a friend?**
- ☐ Yes ☐ No

**If you'd like us to send associates or friends a catalog, just list names and addresses on back.**

**Do you use a personal computer for business?**
- ☐ Yes ☐ No

**If yes, which?**
- ☐ IBM/compatible
- ☐ Macintosh

**Check all the ways you use computers:**
- ☐ Word processing
- ☐ Accounting
- ☐ Spreadsheet
- ☐ Inventory
- ☐ Order processing
- ☐ Design/graphics
- ☐ General data base
- ☐ Customer information
- ☐ Scheduling

**May we call you to follow up on your comments?**
- ☐ Yes ☐ No

**May we add your name to our mailing list?**
- ☐ Yes ☐ No

**If there is anything you think we should do to improve this product, please describe:**_____
_____
_____
_____

**Thank you for your patience in answering the above questions.**
**Just fill in your name and address here, fold (see back) and mail.**

Name_____
Title_____
Company_____
Phone_____
Address_____
City/State/Zip_____

**PSI Research creates this family of fine products to help you more easily and effectively manage your business activities:**

The Oasis Press®                          PSI Successful Business Software
PSI Successful Business Library      EXECARDS® Communication Tools

**If you have friends or associates who might appreciate receiving our catalogs, please list here.  Thanks!**

Name_____          Name_____

Title_____          Title_____

Company_____          Company_____

Phone_____          Phone_____

Address_____          Address_____

City/State/Zip_____          City/State/Zip_____

**FOLD HERE FIRST**

---

# BUSINESS REPLY MAIL

FIRST CLASS MAIL PERMIT NO. 002 MERLIN, OREGON

POSTAGE WILL BE PAID BY ADDRESSEE

**PSI Research**
*PO BOX 1414*
*Merlin OR 97532-9900*

NO POSTAGE
NECESSARY
IF MAILED
IN THE
UNITED STATES

**FOLD HERE SECOND, THEN TAPE TOGETHER**

✂
Please cut
along this
vertical line,
fold twice,
tape together
and mail.
Thanks!

Cut out these post cards along the dashed lines. Just write in the information on reverse side, add your return address, then apply the proper postage and drop in the mail.

---

Affix
Stamp
Here

Name
Title
Company
Address
City
State & Zip

**Division of Workers' Compensation**
**Tennessee Department of Labor**
501 Union Building, 2nd Floor
Nashville, TN 37243-0661

---

Affix
Stamp
Here

Name
Title
Company
Address
City
State & Zip

**Tennessee Department of Employment Security**
Volunteer Plaza, 8th Floor
500 James Robertson Parkway
Nashville, TN 37245-3500

---

Affix
Stamp
Here

Name
Title
Company
Address
City
State & Zip

**Small Business Office**
**Department of Economic & Community Development**
Rachel Jackson Building
320 6th Avenue, North, 7th Floor
Nashville, TN 37243-0405

---

Affix
Stamp
Here

Name
Title
Company
Address
City
State & Zip

**Sales and Use Tax Division**
**Tennessee Department of Revenue**
Andrew Jackson State Office Building
500 Deaderick Street
Nashville, TN 37242

## Attn: Division of Workers' Compensation

**Please send me:**

☐ *State of Tennessee Workers' Compensation Law*, booklet [Enclosed is a check for $4 payable to State of Tennessee Treasurer.]

☐ *A Guide to Workers' Compensation*, brochure

Name _____

Title _____

Company _____

Address _____

City _____ State _____ Zip _____

Post card provided by The Oasis Press, 300 North Valley Drive, Grants Pass, OR 97526  5/91

---

## Attn: Tennessee Department of Employment Security

**Please send me:**

☐ *Handbook for Employers*, booklet

☐ *Report to Determine Status, Application for Employer Number*, Form DES 210.1

Name _____

Title _____

Company _____

Address _____

City _____ State _____ Zip _____

Post card provided by The Oasis Press, 300 North Valley Drive, Grants Pass, OR 97526  5/91

---

## Attn: Small Business Office

**Please send me:**

☐ *A Guide to Doing Business in Tennessee*, booklet

☐ *Business Start-Up Package*

Name _____

Title _____

Company _____

Address _____

City _____ State _____ Zip _____

Post card provided by The Oasis Press, 300 North Valley Drive, Grants Pass, OR 97526  5/91

---

## Attn: Sales and Use Tax Division

**Please send me:**

☐ *Tennessee Sales and Use Tax Laws*, booklet

☐ *Sales and Use Tax Certificate of Registration*, Form 13-001-0321

☐ *Tax Facts*, brochure

Name _____

Title _____

Company _____

Address _____

City _____ State _____ Zip _____

Post card provided by The Oasis Press, 300 North Valley Drive, Grants Pass, OR 97526  5/91

✂ Cut out these post cards along the dashed lines. Just write in the information on reverse side, add your return address, then apply the proper postage and drop in the mail.

---

Affix
Stamp
Here

Name
Title
Company
Address
City
State & Zip

**Attn: Communications Dept. — CWS4**
**Pacific Bell Directory**
101 Spear Street, Room 429
San Francisco, CA 94105

---

Affix
Stamp
Here

Name
Title
Company
Address
City
State & Zip

**U.S. Small Business Administration**
**Office of Business Development**
Sixth Floor
409 3rd Street, SW
Washington, DC 20416

---

Affix
Stamp
Here

Name
Title
Company
Address
City
State & Zip

**U.S. Department of Labor**
**ESA/OMAP Support Service Division**
Room S3013C
200 Constitution Avenue, NW
Washington, DC 20210

---

Affix
Stamp
Here

Name
Title
Company
Address
City
State & Zip

**U.S. Department of Labor**
**OSHA Publications Distribution**
200 Constitution Avenue, NW
Washington, DC 20210

## Attn: Communications Dept. – CWS4

**Please send me a complimentary copy of** *Small Business Success.*

Name _____

Title _____

Company _____

Address _____

City _____ State _____ Zip _____

Post card provided by The Oasis Press, 300 North Valley Drive, Grants Pass, OR  97526    4/92

---

## Attn: U.S. Small Business Administration

**Please send me a list of the Business Development publications you offer (SBA 115A).**

Name _____

Title _____

Company _____

Address _____

City _____ State _____ Zip _____

Post card provided by The Oasis Press, 300 North Valley Drive, Grants Pass, OR  97526    4/92

---

## Attn: U.S. Department of Labor – ESA/OMAP Division

**Please send me your most current version of** *Your Rights Under the Fair Labor Standards Act* **(WH Publication 1088).**

Name _____

Title _____

Company _____

Address _____

City _____ State _____ Zip _____

Post card provided by The Oasis Press, 300 North Valley Drive, Grants Pass, OR  97526    4/92

---

## Attn: U.S. Department of Labor – OSHA

**Please send me:**

☐ *OSHA Handbook for Small Businesses* (OSHA 2209)

☐ *On-site Consultation for the Employer* (OSHA 3047)

☐ Booklet on OSHA's free consultation service for small businesses

☐ *Job Safety and Health Protection* (OSHA 2203)

☐ Other publications for my type of business, which is _____

Name _____

Title _____

Company _____

Address _____

City _____ State _____ Zip _____

Post card provided by The Oasis Press, 300 North Valley Drive, Grants Pass, OR  97526    4/92

✂ Cut out these post cards along the dashed lines. Just write in the information on reverse side, add your return address, then apply the proper postage and drop in the mail.

Affix
Stamp
Here

Name
Title
Company
Address
City
State & Zip

**Corporate Agents, Inc.**
1013 Centre Road
P.O. Box 1281
Wilmington, DE 19899

Affix
Stamp
Here

Name
Title
Company
Address
City
State & Zip

**The Oasis Press**
300 North Valley Drive
Grants Pass, OR 97526

Affix
Stamp
Here

Name
Title
Company
Address
City
State & Zip

**Equal Employment Opportunity Commission**
2401 E Street
Washington, DC 20507

Affix
Stamp
Here

Name
Title
Company
Address
City
State & Zip

**PSI Research**
300 North Valley Drive
Grants Pass, OR 97526

## Attn: Corporate Agents, Inc.

Please send me *How To Form Your Own Corporation.*

Name _____

Title _____

Company _____

Address _____

City _____ State _____ Zip _____

Post card provided by The Oasis Press, 300 North Valley Drive, Grants Pass, OR 97526   4/92

---

## Attn: The Oasis Press

**Please send information on the Successful Business Library to these friends and associates:**

Name _____

Title _____ Phone _____

Company _____

Address _____

City _____ State _____ Zip _____

Name _____

Title _____ Phone _____

Company _____

Address _____

City _____ State _____ Zip _____

Post card provided by The Oasis Press, 300 North Valley Drive, Grants Pass, OR 97526   4/92

---

## Attn: Equal Employment Opportunity Commission

Please send me your free poster, *Equal Employment Opportunity is the Law* (GPO 192 0 383798).

Name _____

Title _____

Company _____

Address _____

City _____ State _____ Zip _____

Post card provided by The Oasis Press, 300 North Valley Drive, Grants Pass, OR 97526   4/92

---

## Attn: PSI Research

**Please send me information on:**

☐ The next edition of *Starting and Operating a Business in* (list states) _____

☐ PSI Successful Business Software

☐ *EXECARDS*® Business-to-Business Communication Tools

Name _____

Title _____ Phone _____

Company _____

Address _____

City _____ State _____ Zip _____

Post card provided by The Oasis Press, 300 North Valley Drive, Grants Pass, OR 97526   4/92

# A Letter from the Publisher

Dear *Starting and Operating a Business* Reader,

During the past 10 years as we have published our guides for starting and operating a business in each of the states, we have seen a tendency of state and federal government to demand that businesses bear an ever greater responsibility for achieving the goals defined by government. These changes affect every business person in his or her daily business operation.

While it is not my objective to advise you how you should feel about this trend, I want to make you aware that there is a way you can voice your opinion about legislation that affects you.

If owners of small- and medium-sized businesses do not make their opinions known to their elected representatives, they will find that demands are made of them that they may feel are unfair or may adversely affect their businesses.

If you would like to have a better voice in government, please use the card below to obtain information about NFIB and obtain a free copy of their very fine publication, *Independent Business (IB)* magazine.

Yours truly,

Emmett Ramey
President, PSI Research / The Oasis Press®

---

✂
Cut out this postcard along the dashed lines. Just write in the information on reverse side, add your return address, then apply postcard postage and drop in the mail.

Affix
Stamp
Here

**Membership Development Department**
**National Federation of Independent Business**
Suite 700
600 Maryland Avenue, S.W.
Washington, DC  20024

## About the National Federation of Independent Business

The National Federation of Independent Business (NFIB) is the nation's largest small business organization, with more than half a million member business owners. NFIB has been America's small business advocate since 1943 and is dedicated to preserving free enterprise.

As the guardian of small business, NFIB has 70 lobbyists at work across the country. One lobbyist is located in each state capital with the remainder representing small business owners in Washington, D.C.

NFIB members vote on state and national ballots to set the organization's lobbying position on the issues affecting business owners.

NFIB's dues are flexible to ensure that membership is affordable to even the smallest business.

## Attn: Membership Development Department

Please send me information about NFIB and a free copy of *Independent Business (IB)* magazine.

Name _____

Title _____ Phone ( _____ ) _____

Company Name _____

Street Address _____

City _____ State _____ Zip _____

Mailing Address (if different) _____

City _____ State _____ Zip _____

Post card provided by The Oasis Press  300 North Valley Drive, Grants Pass, OR  97526